Dressage *from* *A* *to* X

THE DEFINITIVE GUIDE
TO RIDING AND COMPETING

Dressage *from* A *to* X

THE DEFINITIVE GUIDE
TO RIDING AND COMPETING

Barbara Burkhardt

Trafalgar Square Publishing
North Pomfret, Vermont

First published in 1999 by
Trafalgar Square Publishing
North Pomfret, Vermont 05053

The author has made every effort to obtain a release from all person appearing in the photographs used in this book. In some cases, however, the persons may not have been known and therefore could not be contacted.

Library of Congress Cataloging-in-Publication Data
Burkhardt, Barbara
Dressage from A to X : the definitive guide to riding and competing /
Barbara Burkhardt.
p. cm
Includes bibliographical references and index.
ISBN 1-57076-100-0 (hc)
1. Dressage—Competitions. 2. Dressage. I. Title.
SF309.6.B86 1999
798.2'4—dc21 99-17915
CIP

Cover and book design by Edith Crocker
Typeface: Garamond 11/14

Printed in Canada

10 9 8 7 6 5 4 3 2 1

Front cover: Cheryl Dixon-Mullen riding Trafalgar Square Farm's Mystery Lady. Photo by Reflections of Killington.

Back cover: Photo by Charlene Strickland.

Dedication

This book is dedicated to all those seeking to experience the world of competitive dressage. To those who want fun, excellence, truth, and results in their equine partnerships — and to the horse.

Acknowledgments

Of all the pages in this book this one was the hardest to write, because I didn't want to leave anyone out. I would like to thank the following, who have profoundly influenced my thinking.

First of all to the late Colonel Bengt Ljungquist, who so inspired me to take up dressage. His dedication to the art of dressage and the beauty of the partnership between horse and rider convinced me that, "This is what I want to do."

To all my mentors for their skill and knowledge. To the United States Dressage Federation "L" ("Learner Judge") Program instructors, of which my favorite will always be Elizabeth Searle. To Sally Swift, who at the 1985 National Instructors Seminar so intrigued me with her images of how our bodies function. To Jane Savoie, who through her books, articles, and motivational talks so inspired this timid rider to "take charge." To my trainer and coach, Jose Luis Perez-Soto, for his endless patience and expertise while working with several less than ideal horses and a rider of somewhat limited aptitude.

To Charlene Strickland, who guided me through the intricacies of becoming "published." Charlene also contributed many of the photographs, somehow interpreting the concepts that existed only in my head. To Patricia Johnston, who so very generously donated her time to edit and critique parts of this manuscript, simply because she believed in this project. I would also like to thank my editor, Martha Cook, and publisher, Caroline Robbins, who took a chance with a first-time author. I have tremendous admiration for their scrupulous attention to detail as well as enormous patience deciphering my sometimes unclear, wordy anecdotes.

To my dear friends, Kathryn "Kat" Kyle, Dick Johnson, Dian and Steve More, Harold Kern, and Marybeth McAdoo, for their unconditional support and encouragement throughout this and all my other endeavors.

To all my students, too numerous to mention, whose quest for knowledge motivated me to write such a book in the first place. And lastly, to my horses, who have taught me more than any human could.

Table of Contents

	Acknowledgments	*vii*
	Introduction: Why Compete?	*xi*
Chapter 1	An Introduction to Competitive Dressage	1
Chapter 2	Here Comes the Judge	11
Chapter 3	Know the Score	17
Chapter 4	Dressage, Combined Training, or Pony Club —What's Your Choice?	28
Chapter 5	Where to Start	37
Chapter 6	The Horse	47
Chapter 7	Equipment	60
Chapter 8	Dress Code	75
Chapter 9	Making a Good Impression —Rider Position and Posture	84
Chapter 10	Rider Fitness and Diet	96
Chapter 11	All the Horse Needs to Know	108
Chapter 12	What are Working Gaits?	119
Chapter 13	At What Level Should You Compete?	129
Chapter 14	Memorizing and Visualizing Tests	140
Chapter 15	Practice Makes Perfect (Almost)	147
Chapter 16	Developing a Warm-Up	160

Chapter 17	More Practice	168
Chapter 18	Grooming the Horse	179
Chapter 19	A Rider's First Show	190
Chapter 20	Dealing with Nerves	201
Chapter 21	The Horse's First Show	210
Chapter 22	Ride Your Best Test	222
Chapter 23	Evaluating Your Test	230
Chapter 24	Musical Freestyle	250
Chapter 25	Quadrille	259
Chapter 26	Onward and Upward	270
	Appendix	*287*
	Bibliography	*288*
	Index	*290*
	About the Author	*296*

Introduction

Why Compete?

It is human nature to compete — to see where we stand compared to our peers. Improving on past performances is a typically human compulsion. It is programmed into our genes.

On the purely practical side, horses might well be an endangered species, or at best relegated to being "curiosities," perhaps in zoos, if equestrian sports had not been "invented." There are very few utilitarian niches left for the horse today.

Then there is the emotional attraction. Many of us are attracted to horses because of their size, beauty, and nobility combined with a cooperative nature. It is amazing that such a large, powerful animal would submit to our will without complaint or reservation.

But what is in it for the horse? We take away the horse's freedom, but we give something back. Correct training and correct handling develop the horses' character. They become perkier and more confident in themselves. They tend to stop shying because they feel confident in their world. Their bodies become more beautiful through correct riding and they live longer and healthier lives. We develop the horse's mind and body; we give him food, comfort and security.

So why dressage over the other equine sports? In the past 20 years, dressage as a competitive sport has grown tremendously in the number of shows, number of entries, and the emerging award programs, especially at local and regional levels.

You probably know that dressage is the French word for training, but it is more than that. Dressage is a method of riding and schooling the horse so as to bring out the best in both partners. Dressage is an artistic expression, a sport, and an equestrian discipline. Dressage challenges our intellect while it satisfies our compassion for the horse.

Dressage can be showy — top hat and tails and braided manes — or it can be an intimate experience of companionship and learning shared by one horse and one rider.

Riders are attracted to dressage over other equestrian pursuits for many reasons:

- Riders can pursue dressage either competitively or for backyard pleasure.
- Dressage is a sport that is available to almost every horse owner. It doesn't require the daredevil courage of jumping or eventing. It doesn't require the distance training needed for endurance, the space needed for western riding, or the trappings of driving. All it needs is a horse and an insightful rider who is suited to making a commitment to learning.
- Dressage training and competition, with its structured levels, attracts goal-oriented people who like to work with a plan. When competing, you ride a graded test that gives you a score against which you measure all your previous performances. A ribbon becomes secondary.
- Dressage is something you can continue into and beyond middle age. It is an endeavor where age and maturity can in fact be bonuses, not limitations. Riders can be overweight or thin, athletic or not, brave or timid — it's their choice and they can still find satisfaction.
- With dressage you proceed at your own pace, and if you already own a horse, it doesn't take much additional financial outlay to be successful.
- The nature of dressage allows its most diligent participants to enjoy its offerings over the course of a lifetime. The elegance and intelligence inherent in dressage hold appeal for riders of all ages who are drawn to its ranks at various stages of their lives. Once hooked on the idea that training can be fun and rewarding, the dressage rider is born. As soon as she progresses through the very basics, the self-challenge is on and the neverending quest for perfection begins. A rider never stops learning and a horse never stops improving — it's a continuous process.

And if you're looking for a challenge — dressage has that too. For something that looks so beautiful and so effortless, it takes a tremendous amount of concentration, especially at the higher levels. It's supposed to be beautiful. It's supposed to look effortless. You look at a dressage movement and you say, "That looks nice, I can learn to do that," but it's astonishing how much work goes into that six to nine minutes in the arena. It is often this hard work that attracts so many people to dressage — how the time required for proper training and conditioning of a horse makes a more complete athlete of it and enhances the horse's beauty, character, and longevity.

The very basic concept — that results are obtained through cooperation and guidance rather than force or coercion — has much appeal to the true dressage enthusiast and may well be the main reason for involvement in the first place.

Dressage is never wasted time. Even if you decide not to compete, you and your horse will be better for the experience of dressage riding. And as another advantage, there is always a market for reliable, happy, well-trained riding horses, which is exactly what a "dressage horse" is.

So much for all the reasons for *training* dressage, but why compete? Aside from the phenomenon that we crave the approval of our peers, dressage competition does in fact build character and confidence. It teaches responsibility, patience, and self-discipline. The sport of dressage is satisfying, challenging, and rewarding.

By learning to train our horses we also learn about ourselves, our emotional stability, and our self-worth. We learn discipline and the importance of cooperation with another living being.

By competing we learn even more about ourselves, about our horses, and about our fellow humans. Dressage competitors learn early on that winning is not the name of the game. It's nice to win the prizes — but the biggest enjoyment is the daily riding, the horses, working out training problems, and working with people whom you enjoy.

Although not totally devoid of politics, fads, and changing trends, dressage shows have less of these factors than some other forms of equine competition.

With dressage competitions, one does not get "lost in the crowd." Everyone has her turn in the spotlight. Many competitors like having the undivided attention of the judge or judges, which they cannot get in group classes.

Additionally, competitive riding can add a certain focus and efficiency to your training at home. We tend to practice the things we are already good at and avoid the tougher issues. Perhaps show riding is most beneficial to overly passive riders — those of us who tend to avoid the more difficult areas of training.

Riding a dressage test can encourage a more complete approach because we know we will be marked on each part as well as the total performance. Because movements are required in a specific order, they also tend to expose faults that we may otherwise be able to keep well-hidden in our daily schooling.

Riding tests at home is also a good way to chart progress in training. Riding tests at shows can be used for the same purpose. To be able to demonstrate the horse's training on strange ground is the true "test."

Any trainer worth her salt knows it is easy to ask the horse to do something it is about to offer by himself. It is "proof" of training when you ask for a transition or a movement at a marker, according to a pre-chosen plan.

For junior riders, dressage can be an important tool in stimulating attention to detail and planning. The more carefully they plan where and how they will ask for a transition or exactly how to ride the lines of the test, the more successful they will be in the show ring — and in life.

And lastly, dressage competition can and should be some fun, particularly in the lower levels. You are perfectly entitled to smile at the mishaps of your competitors, but only if you can just as easily laugh at yourself and your own misfortunes.

Put in perspective, all you have to do is induce your horse to show his best side for five to ten minutes in front of the judge. For all the feed, grooming, tidbits, and care provided, this appears to be a small favor to ask of your four-legged friend.

A person never stops learning and appreciating dressage, whether as a trainer, a competitor, a coach, or spectator. (Yes, it can be enjoyable to watch, especially if you know what you're looking at!)

Dressage has had such a wide-range appeal because it eventually becomes a philosophy — not just of training horses but also as a way of living — an approach to life.

Author's Note

When I started this text, I very much wanted to be "politically correct" and use he/she whenever referring to the human participants. I soon realized this was very cumbersome and was consequently persuaded to use "she" as the rider, and "he" for the horse. I certainly do not want to imply that all riders, judges, trainers, etc., are female, nor that only male horses are suitable for riding; it is for convenience only. I therefore beg the reader's indulgence (whatever his/her sex) for this treatment and hope that the clarity gained justifies the imprecision.

Chapter 1

An Introduction to Competitive Dressage

What's the major difference between the experienced competitor and the typical beginner in the dressage arena? The main difference is the seasoned competitor leaves nothing to chance. She is prepared for every eventuality; she has made every preparation ahead of time. She rides every step of the test, practically carrying her horse, like a mother holding the hand of a small child. She tries never to put the horse in a situation that the horse is not prepared to handle confidently.

On the other hand, the beginner often has a confused idea of what is actually expected of her. She tends to put the horse in difficult situations, expecting the horse to somehow "know" what to do. With this scenario, the outcome of the placings is obvious to everyone else, yet the rider usually has no clue.

I believe that if you really understand the requirements of the sport — what is expected of you and your mount and what you are supposed to do in the ring (protocol of the arena) — and know what is actually being judged, you can experience success and satisfaction your first time out.

The primary purpose of this book is to guide those who are interested in what is called "competition dressage." That is, preparing themselves and their horses to perform the American Horse Shows Association (AHSA) dressage tests at dressage shows. A second purpose is to dispel some of the mystery and misconceptions inherent to the sport.

You will find step-by-step preparations, a discussion of the rules, as well as guidelines, suggestions, and insights into preparing for, and riding in, your first (or fiftieth) dressage competition. You will discover how you can learn from each test and each competition. This should reduce the "trial and error" period and put you on a par with "the professionals."

Dressage competition should be some fun. Dressage competitors probably cause themselves unnecessary mental stress by calling the competitions "tests." "Riding a test" can evoke visions of high school history class where the end-of-semester "test" caused great anxiety and apprehension. You might instead think of competing in a dressage show as similar to a music recital: You know what you need to do, you are prepared, you perform for your five to ten minutes and when you're done, people always politely applaud.

What IS Dressage?

Have you ever had your friends or acquaintances ask you, "What is it you do?" or "What is 'dressage'?" Although most people these days do know how to pronounce it (pronounced "dra'sazh": the "sazh" pronounced like the "s" in "pleasure") there still seems to be difficulty in coming up with a one-sentence definition of "dressage."

It is of course the French word for "training," but this may confuse it with many other styles of training, such as training a racehorse. Therefore, we say it is a "system" of training, distinctly different from training racehorses or gaited horses, for instance. Sometimes comparing a dressage test to an "obedience test," as done by dogs, seems to evoke an understanding nod. Whether the listeners really understand or whether they just want to go on to another subject is open for debate.

The *American Horse Shows Association Rule Book* describes it thus:

"The object of Dressage is the harmonious development of the physique and ability of the horse. As a result, it makes the horse calm, supple, loose and flexible but also confident, attentive and keen, thus achieving perfect understanding with his rider.

"These qualities are revealed by:

"a) The freedom and regularity of the paces;

"b) The harmony, lightness and ease of the movements;

"c) The lightness of the forehand and the engagement of the hind quarters, originating in a lively impulsion...

"The horse gives the impression of doing of his own accord what is required of him. Confident and attentive he submits generously to the control of his rider...free from the paralyzing effects of resistance the horse...responds to the various aids calmly and with precision, displaying natural and harmonious balance both physically and mentally." (Art 1901. "Object and General Principles")

The American Horse Shows Association (AHSA) is the national federation for dressage competition in the United States. Every would-be competitor should become familiar with its rules and guidelines. Unlike other show divisions where the placings are sometimes a total mystery to spectators, the Dressage Division outlines not only rules for eligibility, but guidelines for all the movements and arena protocol. The pertinent AHSA rules and some explanations are included in each chapter. As rules change from time to time, be sure to scan the latest rule book for any changes.

The Bare Necessities

You will need a reasonably trained horse with the three basic gaits: walk, trot, and canter on both leads. You also need an English type saddle and a bridle with a plain snaffle bit.

You will need a pair of tall English boots and light-colored breeches or jodhpurs and jodhpur boots. In most schooling shows, you will not need a coat, whereas in competitions recognized by the AHSA you will need a hunt-style coat, a hunt cap or derby, a white short or long-sleeved shirt, and a tie. There is more on tack and attire in Chapters 7 and 8.

The Horse

You do not have to have an expensive horse to be "competitive." Dressage is one of the few sports where the harder you work, the more knowledgeable you are, and the better you can interpret the training exercises. The better you are in tune with your horse, the higher your scores are apt to be.

Any horse can "do" dressage. It is very likely the horse you already have is capable of competition, at least at the lower levels — which are where everybody starts out.

For one thing, many newcomers are still experimenting, still pondering whether this is "the thing" for them. They may decide that they would rather trail ride, or event, or just occasionally go in a dressage competition to test their skills. Or maybe find they have no inclination to compete at all.

It is also perfectly feasible to use a horse that has been ridden in another discipline, although you may have to do some retraining. The good news is that the horse is usually more adaptive than the rider! While it may be easier to start a young horse using the dressage methods from the beginning (because they are so natural), with hard work and study, any horse with the three basic gaits can be converted to dressage.

The Rider

Even if you, the rider, come from another riding discipline, this is seldom a hindrance. Previous experiences can in fact enhance your dressage capability. Take what experiences you can use and modify the rest! For example, from a background in western riding the rider's position is essentially the same (figure 1.1). You already have the straighter leg, a longer stirrup, and your upper body position is perpendicular to the horse. A big part of western equitation is sitting properly. The transition is quite easy. The concepts of more power, bigger gaits, and a different kind of contact on the bridle may

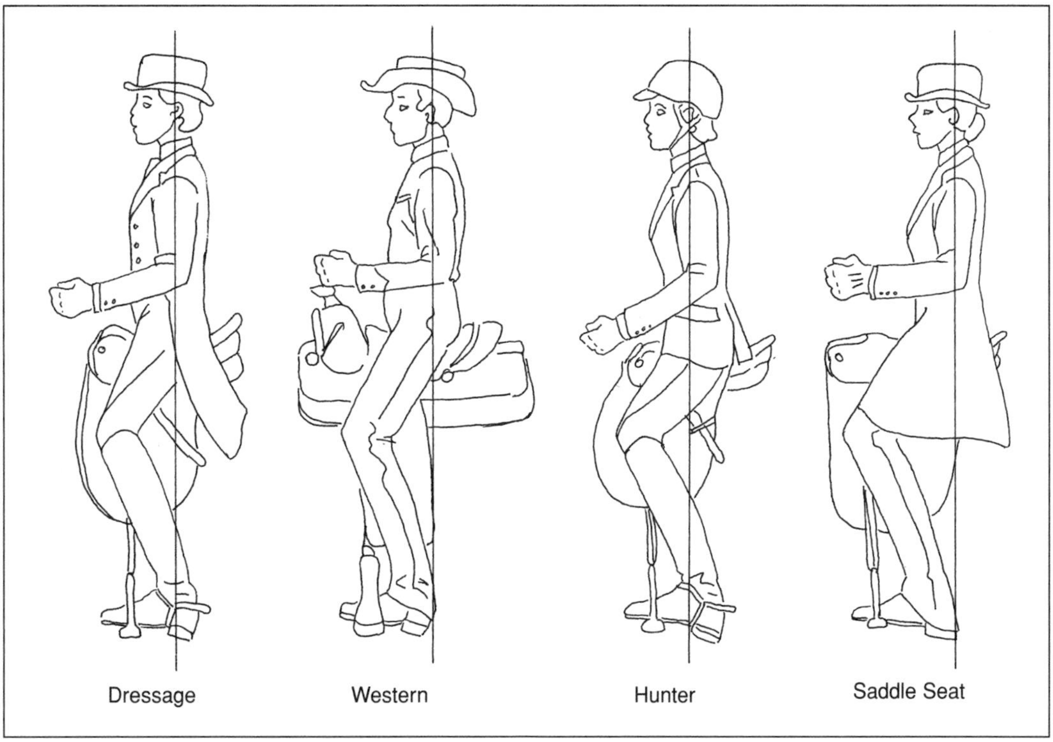

Figure 1.1 Comparison of different "seats."

be difficult at first but will be easily overcome.

Those who come from a hunter or jumper background are just as adaptable. The jumping is good for confidence as well as balance because you develop confidence in going forward and you learn to trust the horse as well as yourself. You have to think and react, and you have to be able to do those things when you are riding dressage, also.

Nor is saddle seat riding a hindrance. These riders already have the upright, elegant position and knowledge of how to handle four reins, but will have to learn to refine their leg aids and adapt to a single rein snaffle bit.

The Right Attitude

It should be appreciated that, except at the major competitions, dressage tests can generally be considered as less a competition against other horses and riders and more as a competition against individual circumstances. It is not so much a case of "Can I beat so and so?" as of "Can we do better than last time?" or, "How well can I get this horse to perform today?"

Although it is certainly pleasant to win, the key issue is not so much the actual placing but rather the assessment of progress, either of an established horse and rider partnership or of a rider's ability to produce a good performance on any given day.

Join Your Local Group Member Organization

If you are considering competing in dressage, or even if your only fascination is in the training, join your local dressage club. Here you will find friends with a common goal. You can compare experiences, practice together, and participate in educational projects. Most local dressage clubs are "Group Member Organizations" (GMOs) of the United States Dressage Federation (USDF), a national organization devoted to education. USDF sponsors Adult Education Camps, an "L" (Learner Judge) Program for the education of prospective judges, and Rider and Performance Awards based solely on the achievement of a number of qualifying scores (usually the magical 60 percent, which is obtainable for even "average" horses and riders).

There is also a "Horse of the Year" competition where scores from all over the nation qualify the top 20 or 25 horses in each level, Training through Grand Prix.

If you plan to compete in shows recognized by The American Horse Shows Association you should become a member. This will get you a *Rule Book*, by which all "Recognized" dressage competitions (and most schooling shows) must abide.

What's Your Level of Expertise?

There are as many levels of dressage competitions as classes of riders: from informal schooling shows, staged in a grassy pasture with classes for Walk-Trot, Beginning Rider and Novice Horse, to multi-ring "Recognized" shows with divisions for Juniors, Young Riders, Adult Amateur, Open classes, etc., all the way up to the world class competitions: the Concours Dressage International (CDI), the World Cup, and, of course, the Olympics.

There is a never-ending challenge for the rider. A rider just never stops learning and a horse never stops improving; it's a continuous process.

The "Mechanics" of a Dressage Competition

Dressage competition is regulated worldwide by the Fédération Equestre Internationale (FEI). Each country has its own national federation — in the United States, it is the American Horse Shows Association (AHSA) (figure 1.2). The AHSA Dressage rules closely follow those of the FEI, modified for the lower level tests. The AHSA publishes the tests for six levels of dressage competition: Training

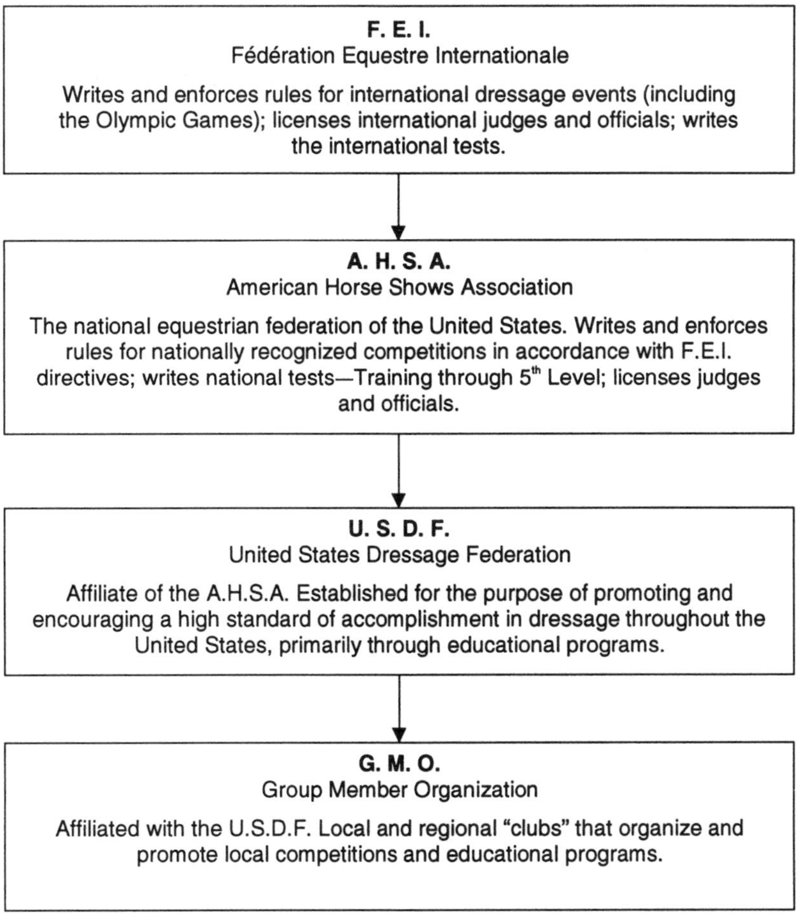

Figure 1.2 The various levels of dressage organizations.

Level and then First through Fifth Level. Training Level is the simplest and each succeeding level is progressively more difficult. The three or four tests within each level are also graduated in difficulty. The tests are designed to follow the training regime that would lead from novice horse to advanced (figure 1.3).

While each nation has its own lower level tests ("national" tests), there are three "international" levels or tests, called respectively: Prix St. Georges, Intermediare I and II and Grand Prix. These four tests are the same all over the world and are written and sanctioned by the FEI. The AHSA's Fifth Level has four tests that correspond to the four FEI tests. Below the AHSA levels are two USDF Introductory tests, that are walk and trot only. The tests follow a definite plan of ever-increasing requirements of balance, suppleness, collection, and extension.

A competitor is usually allowed to enter in two consecutive levels at the same show. In other words, at the lower levels the competitor has six to eight tests from which to choose (figure 1.4).

Competitors must enter their test(s) of choice weeks in advance. The show secretary will assign each entry a "ride time" and this schedule is usually mailed out to all exhibitors a week or so in advance of the competition. Because each competitor knows her ride time(s), the horse can be prepared so as to give an optimum performance.

The dressage test is, of course, ridden one horse at a time in a specifically sized, marked-off

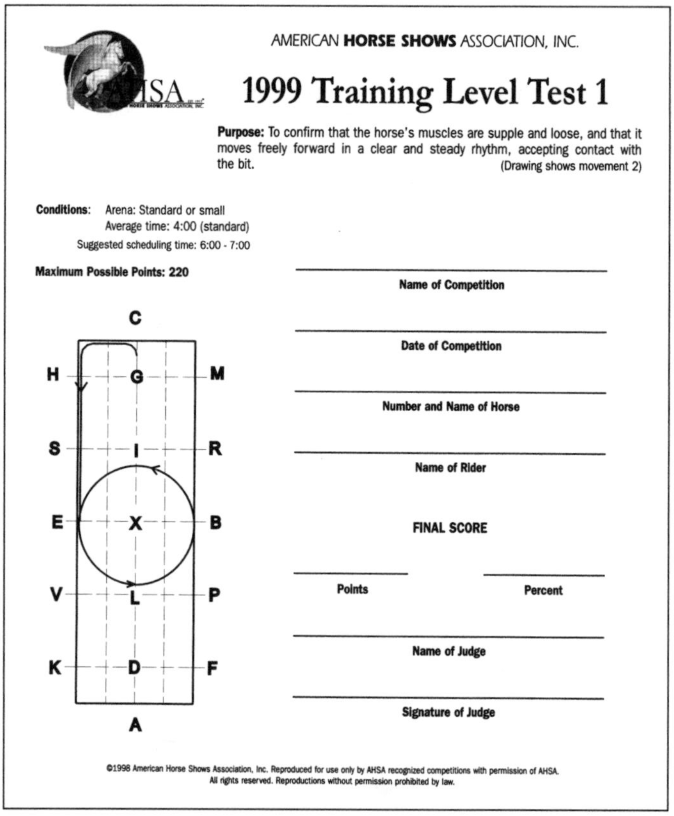

AMERICAN **HORSE SHOWS** ASSOCIATION, INC.

1999 Training Level Test 1

Purpose: To confirm that the horse's muscles are supple and loose, and that it moves freely forward in a clear and steady rhythm, accepting contact with the bit. (Drawing shows movement 2)

Conditions: Arena: Standard or small
Average time: 4:00 (standard)
Suggested scheduling time: 6:00 - 7:00

Maximum Possible Points: 220

Name of Competition

Date of Competition

Number and Name of Horse

Name of Rider

FINAL SCORE

Points Percent

Name of Judge

Signature of Judge

Figure 1.3 A sample cover of an AHSA dressage test score sheet. Reprinted by permission of the American Horse Shows Association

Tr							
1st	**1st**						
	2nd	**2nd**					
		3rd^	**3rd^**				
			4th*+	**4th*+**			
				PSG*/ 5th 1	**PSG*/ 5th 1**		
					Int I/ 5th 2	**Int I/ 5th 2**	
						Int II/ 5th 3	**Int II/ 5th 3**
							GP/5th 4

^ The FEI Junior Preliminary test is equivalent to Third Level.
+ The FEI Junior Team and Individual Tests are equivalent to Fourth Level.
* FEI Young Riders' Tests vary in difficulty between Fourth Level & Prix St. Georges; therefore, at each individual competition, young riders must decide whether they are riding the Young Rider Tests as equivalent to Fourth Level, or as equivalent to Prix St. Georges.

Figure 1.4 According to Article 1919.2 of the AHSA Rule Book, *horses may enter no more than two consecutive levels at any one competition. Reprinted by permission of the American Horse Shows Association.*

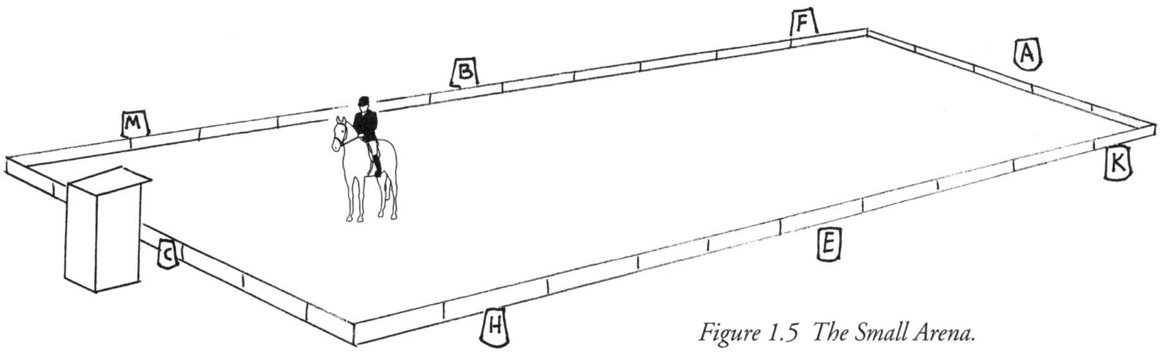

Figure 1.5 The Small Arena.

arena. The "Standard" or large arena is 20 by 60 meters [66 x 198 feet]. The "Small" arena is 20 meters by 40 meters [66 x 132 feet] (figure 1.5). The arena is bordered by a low fence to mark its perimeter and letters are placed at specific locations to designate where to perform "transitions" — changes of gait — or place "figures" — circles, figure eights, etc. — or "movements" — such as a leg yield. See Chapter 15 for a more detailed description of the arena.

At first glance, dressage tests probably look like nothing more than a pattern of circles and straight lines, interrupted here and there by an interesting movement, such as a medium or extended trot or canter, a half pass, or a flying change of lead. In reality, each movement "tests" some aspect of training.

For example, a simple 20 meter (66 foot diameter) circle tests the rider's ability to make it round; it tests the ability to make it the correct size; it tests the ability to place it between (or at) the correct markers; and it tests the ability to maintain the optimum rhythm, speed, and balance. It tests the obedience of the horse to hand and leg cues and the rider's understanding of how intensely, or how lightly, to apply the aids (signals with the rider's hands, legs, and, weight).

The national (AHSA) tests are usually rewritten every four years. This allows competitors and judges to become familiar with the tests. Tests can be ridden from memory, or the rider may have a "caller" (see Chapter 5). Except in championships, combined training, and freestyles, the tests must be ridden from memory.

Each test is divided into "movements" that are numbered on the left margin. For instance, the first movement in virtually every test is: "A – Enter (trot or canter); X – Halt, salute, proceed (whatever gait)" (figure 1.6).

Each movement is given a numerical score, from 0 (not executed) to 10 (excellent).

Scoring System

The scale of marks is as follows:

0 Not executed

1 Very Bad	**6** Satisfactory
2 Bad	**7** Fairly Good
3 Fairly Bad	**8** Good
4 Insufficient	**9** Very Good
5 Sufficient	**10** Excellent

"Not executed" means that practically nothing of the required movement has been performed. (AHSA, Art. 1922.6.7)

Also note that "10" means "excellent" NOT "perfect."

Some movements have coefficients (multiplied by 2 or more) that give them more weight. The "Collective Marks" at the bottom of the test sheet emphasize the major training requisites of the overall test. The scores are totaled and a percentage score awarded. Scores

NO.

Conditions:
Arena: Standard or small
Average time: 4:00
Maximum Possible Points: 220

	TEST	DIRECTIVE IDEAS	POINTS	COEFFICIENT	TOTAL	REMARKS
1. A X	Enter working trot Halt, Salute proceed working trot	Straightness on centerline, transitions, quality of halt and trot	7		7	almost str & □
2. C E	Track left Circle left 20m	Quality of turn at C quality of trot, roundness of circle	5		5	needs rounder & more fwd.
3. Between K&A	Working canter left lead	Calmness and smoothness of depart	6		6	prompt, sl. labored
4. A	Circle left 20m	Quality of canter, roundness of circle	6		6	needs more fwd impulse
5. Between B&M	Working trot	Balance during transition	7		7	fluid trans fwd better
6. C	Medium walk	Transition, quality of walk	6		6	smooth
7. HXF F	Free walk Medium walk	Straightness, quality of walk	6	2	12	needs better stretch
8. A	Working trot	Smoothness of transition	6		6	fwd improving
9. E	Circle right 20m	Quality of trot, roundness of circle	5		5	not totally round
10. Between H&C	Working canter right lead	Calmness and smoothness of depart	6		6	prompt, could be more fwd
11. C	Circle right 20m	Quality of canter, roundness of circle	6		6	O small, needs more impulse
12. Between B&F	Working trot	Balance during transition	6		6	fluid trans need more imp.
13. A X	Down centerline Halt, Salute	Straightness on centerline, quality of trot and halt	7		7	almost str □ halt

Leave arena at walk at A.

85

COLLECTIVE MARKS:

	POINTS	COEFFICIENT	TOTAL	
Gaits (freedom and regularity)	7	2	14	
Impusion (desire to move forward, elasticity of the steps, relaxation of the back)	5	2	10	
Submission (attention and confidence; harmony, lightness and ease of movements; acceptance of the bit)	6	2	12	
Rider's position and seat; correctness and effect of the aids	6	2	12	

48

FURTHER REMARKS:

needs better forward from behind to get rounder outline

SUBTOTAL 133
ERRORS (-________)
TOTAL POINTS 133
60.045%

Figure 1.6 A sample AHSA test sheet with scores and judges comments.
Reprinted by permission of the American Horse Shows Association.

in the 60th percentile are excellent; some scores reach into the 70th percentile, indicating magnificent performances.

It is perfectly respectable in dressage to advance to the next level if you get scores in the range of 50 to 60 percent, even if your horse never wins a blue ribbon. It is also permissible to stay in the lower levels as long as you want. Dressage accomplishment is measured in the scores, not on beating anyone or being first place in a class. If you get a 60 percent and place 20th in the class, it can be just as fulfilling as if you get that 60 percent and place first.

The tests are designed to give the judge at "C" the preferred view; thus shoulder-in, half-passes, movements on the centerline, and some other exercises are best viewed from "C", while the extended trots and canters and some other movements are more spectacular viewed from the side. Prestigious events often have two, three, or five judges, with each judge stationed at a specific point around the arena.

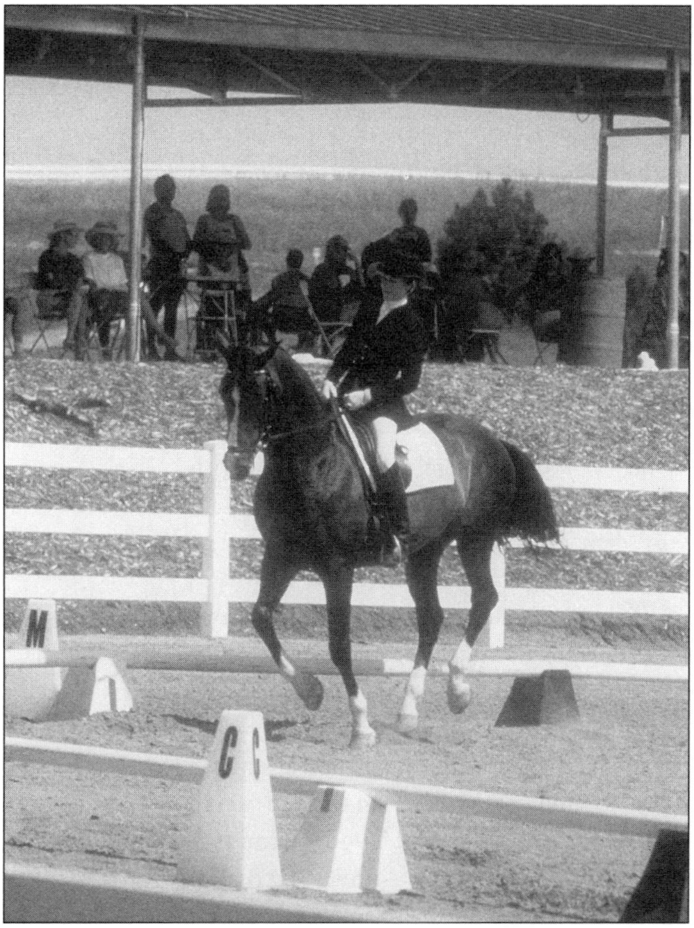

Figure 1.7 Dressage can be enjoyable to watch, especially if you know what you are looking at. Photo by Charlene Strickland.

Each movement is judged as to the regularity (purity) of the gait (a "pure" four-beat walk, two-beat trot, and three-beat canter); the impulsion (the amount of thrust or carrying power of the horse's hindquarters); and the submission (the cooperation of the horse, the lightness and ease of the movements, and the general harmony of the pair).

All of the movements have guidelines for their form and presentation that are published in the *American Horse Shows Association Rule Book* and the *Fédération Equestre Internationale Rules and Regulations.*

Becoming a Better Spectator

Watching dressage competitions, especially at the lower levels, cannot be rated as a exciting spectator sport. It has in fact been compared with watching grass grow.

Like Little League baseball, friends, relatives, and other competitors most commonly observe dressage. Still, much can be learned by watching at least a few rides at each level at even the most basic of competitions, the schooling show. At Recognized shows, one can often watch and admire the upper level classes and dream of being there someday (figure 1.7).

Spectators are required to stay several yards away from the actual dressage ring. This area will usually be roped off, or marked off, and no one is to enter this area while a horse is performing except the rider's caller or show employees.

Absolute quiet is expected while a horse is performing, but after the final salute, it is appropriate to politely applaud. By watching dressage tests you can sharpen your skills of observation. You can "practice judge." Assign each movement a number and add it up — then see how close you come to the judge's final score (posted on the Result Board).

If you observe others having problems similar to yours — watch how they deal with it. If a ride is really impressive, try to figure out why, then see if you can imitate it.

You can compare your horse to others of somewhat equal ability. What you may have thought of as an insurmountable problem may be common in other horses or riders in your area.

Observe how the rider's position affects the horse's training or presentation and the overall look of quality or lack of it. If you are competing at the show, assess the footing and possible distractions near the arena so you can optimize your test. If you are acting as groom or coach to someone else, think up helpful showmanship tips to boost their self-esteem.

Dressage (which is training the horse while you ride) is a matter of having a good understanding of what is expected of you and your horse. Having a friendly rapport with your own individual horse and being able to concentrate and react to the situation at hand. This is what levels the field between the fancy horses and the plainer horses — the rider makes all the difference. You can be as successful or as casual as you want and your scores will reflect the amount of work, attention to detail, and thought you are willing to put into it. Now let's get to work!

Chapter Two

Here Comes the Judge

It isn't easy being a judge. While the competitor need only be at her best for five to ten minutes in the arena, with perhaps a 45 minute warm-up and preparation for her horse, the judge must sit and adjudicate for six, eight, sometimes ten hours (*"judges... cannot be required to be on the show grounds longer than 10 hours."* AHSA, Art. 1926.2).

It is common to hear criticism about the quality of judging, but there is also little awareness of the enormous responsibility and dedication of the judges.

Sitting in the judge's box (most often a cleaned out — you hope — two-horse trailer parked at "C"), the judge and scribe must endure heat, cold, wind, and sometimes damp, all the while keeping focused on the job at hand (figure 2.1).

And, as any judge can tell you, she can only perform as well as show management allows. Scheduling too many rides too close together, creating conflicts between rings, providing an incompatible scribe, and not having a gate person to assure competitors are on time are some of the easiest ways to irritate a judge. Of course the judge also has a large measure of responsibility in making this a pleasant experience, as well.

While we cannot expect any judge to be perfect, most judges try very hard to be as good as they can possibly be. The dressage scores you receive are the solid product of a judge's educated, experienced opinion, anchored in pages of carefully thought out Fédération Equestre Internationale (FEI) and American Horse Shows Association (AHSA) rules, standards, and regulations.

The judge must know every movement of every test by heart. She must know exactly at which letter each movement begins and ends, so that the comment and score are in the correct box. The judge must keep those comments brief and to the point, so that the scribe or secretary has time to hand write them.

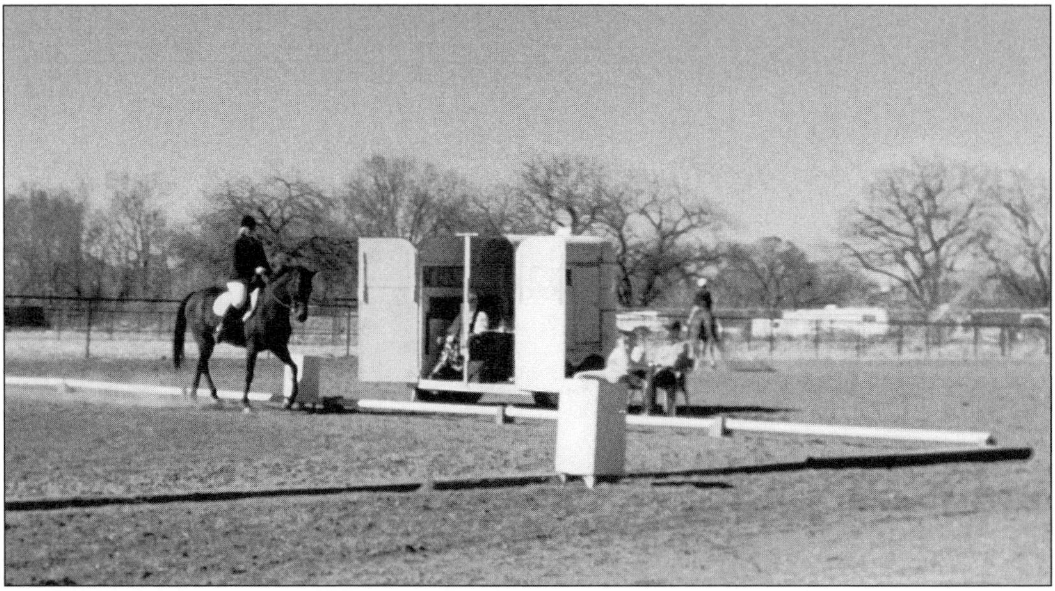

Figure 2.1 Very often the "judge's box" is a horse trailer parked at "C".

The judge can't teach but must guide. Exhibitors will quickly adapt to what they perceive the judge wants to see. What the judge "wants to see" is many beautiful rides with the horse and rider performing as one. To this end, the judge must encourage riders but be honest. The judge tries to tell the rider what is right or wrong, but is not required to tell them how to fix it. That is the realm of the instructor or coach.

The schooling show judge has even greater responsibility of guidance and encouragement, often dealing with very green horses that may be ridden by inexperienced riders.

It is more difficult to judge the lower levels because there are more problems with basics. At higher levels most of the problems have either been worked out, or they have become so bad that it's easy for anyone to see them.

Also, at the lower levels there are many "average" horses that will get "average" scores (5,6,7). Judges are cautioned not to use a different scale for schooling and recognized shows or for amateur or novice classes. When novices and amateurs have their own classes, the scores should still fit the standard. Amateurs have the advantage that they do not compete for placings with the professional trainers.

Nor should judges "adjust" their standard for the region of the country. Doing so does not help the exhibitor. Everyone should be judged against the same standard, especially in areas that don't have exposure to many high-quality riders. Otherwise the scores will be misleading. Exhibitors need to know where they fit in the standard.

Judges must be fair and unbiased. They must forget what they might have heard or know about the horse and rider and judge what they see at that moment. They must judge each ride as if they have never seen that horse and rider combination before.

The judge also has the responsibility to excuse a misbehaving horse from the arena (*"sustained resistance for more than 20 seconds,"* Art. 1922.6.12) or to excuse a horse that appears unsound or ill. There is no appeal to the judge's decision in these cases.

The judge is responsible for all those rules which apply to the performance of the test, including saddlery and dress. For instance,

Classifications of Judges

"Only licensed judges in good standing may officiate at Recognized competitions in those divisions covered by the rules and specifications of the current Rule Book." (AHSA, Art. 1004.2)

"L" — The USDF developed the Learner Judge's Program to educate and screen potential judges as they begin their way up through the ranks. One must graduate the "L" Program with a score of 85% or better to be eligible to apply for an AHSA judge's license.

AHSA

"r" — "Recorded" judges may officiate at Training, First and Second Levels, Suitability and Equitation. An "r" combined training judge may officiate below the level of intermediate horse trials, but not at a two- or three-day event.

"R" — "Registered" judges may officiate in classes through Fourth Level.

"S" — "Senior" judges may officiate in all AHSA and FEI Levels (through Grand Prix) classes at AHSA recognized shows.

FEI

After demonstrating ability at the national levels, an American judge may appeal to the AHSA for promotion to the FEI "C" category: "International Candidate Judge."

"I" – "International" judge can judge all levels through Grand Prix, but cannot judge at the Olympics.

"O" – Can judge any competition at any level anywhere in the world. Are qualified to judge the Olympics. There are fewer than 25 "O" judges in the world, two of whom reside in the United States.

Figure 2.2 Classifications of judges

if the judge sees the horse enter the arena wearing leg wraps, or the rider is carrying a whip in a class that forbids it (in championships or combined training, for instance), the judge must enforce the rule. Any rule infringement in the arena is the judge's responsibility; any rule infraction outside the arena is show management's responsibility (for example, coats required or not; illegal equipment in the warm-up area; eligibility of entries). But if the judge sees someone warming up in illegal equipment, for instance, she should inform the technical delegate or management. At schooling shows there is no technical delegate, so if at all possible, the judge should try to head off disputes before they occur. Infractions should not go unheeded. Part of the judge's job is to educate about the rules so everyone has a fair and equal chance.

Who Can Judge?

Only AHSA or FEI licensed judges in good standing can officiate at AHSA recognized competitions.

"Recognition" means that the show or competition has applied for, and was granted, "recognition" from the AHSA and/or FEI. This means that the competition must abide by all the rules of the recognizing organization. In addition, exhibitors are eligible for zone and national prizes.

Many times at schooling shows (competitions not recognized by the AHSA or FEI), a knowledgeable trainer, instructor, or USDF "L Program graduate" (see figure 2.2) will officiate. These people are often very conscientious and even more careful of the rules and details, probably because they are in the learning process and it is very fresh in their memory.

Becoming a Judge

It may surprise you that it is more difficult to become licensed as a dressage judge than it is in most other horse show divisions. Only dressage, combined training, and combined driving require the applicant to complete a training program approved by the AHSA Licensed Officials Committee.

For dressage, the applicant must first enroll in (and pass) the United States Dressage Federation's "L" Program. For admission to the "L" Program, the applicant must have ridden Second Level (or higher) successfully.

While the "L" program was initially created to train dressage schooling show judges, the AHSA Licensed Official Committee saw a wider application of the "L" Program: prescreening for potential AHSA "r" (recorded or licensed) judge candidates. Passing the USDF "L" Education Program "with distinction" (a minimum written score of 80% and a practical score of 70%) is now a prerequisite to entering the AHSA Dressage Learner Judge program.

The USDF "L" Program has an educational format and most of the sessions are open to auditors. It is well worth the nominal fee to audit if you are a serious competitor. Guidelines for candidates and organizers are available from the USDF office.

The next step to becoming a licensed (recorded or "r") judge is to apply to take part in the AHSA Learner Judge Program.

The learner system isn't meant to teach a novice how to judge; its purpose is to take experienced horsemen and women, sharpen their skills through exposure to seasoned judges, and help them create a system that works for them.

Application must be made to the AHSA on the appropriate official enrollment form and accompanied by the required fee. Applicants must be senior members (21 years of age or older) of the AHSA who have completed all of the requirements of the United States Dressage Federation "L" Program with a passing score and can document knowledge and experience at Fourth Level or above.

The applicant also must submit 15 references who are members of the Association, eight of whom must be licensed dressage judges, technical delegates, or members of the AHSA Dressage Committee.

If approved, the applicant may enter a "Learner Judge" training program approved by the AHSA Dressage Committee. Candidates are allowed two years to complete the structured training program. As in the USDF "L" Program, the participants must pay for their own enrollment.

A day and a half of formal examination follows the training program. The examiners send their report and evaluations directly to the AHSA Licensed Officials Committee. The Committee again reviews the applicant and a decision regarding licensing of the individual will be made. If licensed, the judge can officiate through Second Level ("recorded" judge).

To upgrade to "R", then "S" status, an applicant must meet ever-increasing criteria for application to the next higher rate. Candidates must also learner judge with higher rated judges and pass an examination for each upgrade.

Expectations

Judges come to a competition with expectations. They want to see those "ideal" rides. Exhibitors come to a competition with their own set of expectations, usually with the opinion that since they are doing the very best they can (at that moment, anyway), they should win — or score highly — if for no better reason than "an 'A' for effort"!

Spectators have, perhaps, the highest expectations. When you see a famous rider who seems to be out of position, he or she may indeed be having a bad moment. But even in the Olympics, there are no perfect horses or riders. There is only a constant *striving for perfection.* So when you hear someone criticize a top rider — "Did you see that? His horse was behind the bit!" or "His hands are moving all the time." — remember that even top riders are not perfect all the time. Even a "10" is not "perfect", it's "excellent". A top rider can usually get a horse back in balance or back on the bit in a heartbeat, but no one is "perfect."

A Matter of Luck Or Politics?

It's easy to try to second-guess a judge, particularly if you don't think too much of her skill or you have not placed where you thought you should. It's human nature. Other times, you may get a good ribbon simply because you were the only one who didn't make a major mistake. If you are really honest about your ability, you will find that most of your scores will be "right on", while your placing depends on how the other competitors did.

Then there is sometimes the perception that judges rank the big, fancy moving horses over the smaller, plainer horses that may be putting in a very correct, obedient test. That is not exactly how dressage tests are scored. While there is a Collective Mark for obedience (submission) in the test itself, the quality of the gaits and obedience are scored in every movement, with resistance or evasion lowering the score — depending on what is happening. Severe disobedience can result in error points or elimination.

As disobedience comes and goes, a good mover can sometimes make enough high scores when obedient to cancel out the lows when resisting and get a better overall score than a consistently obedient, yet mediocre, mover.

In other words, an "average" mover who is consistently obedient will tend to get "average" scores. A "brilliant" horse who is also obedient will usually get above average scores. Brilliance is rewarded in dressage. After all, the object of dressage is "the harmonious development of the physique and ability of the horse." If the horse is already a beautiful mover, this is not to be penalized.

Judgment of dressage is an opinion. It is not like judging stadium jumping or cross country where certain actions incur a certain number of "penalty points." The judge can only act in accordance with her impression (and judgment) of the moment.

Judges, despite many horse owners' opinions to the contrary, are human. The AHSA Rule Book should govern their preferences. But still, there is a lot of room to bring personal preferences to those by-the-book evaluations. It's the rare judge who isn't captivated by a dropdead gorgeous horse with wonderful movement. Whether or not that's fair often depends on whether you own that horse or not!

At times, a judge may hesitate, say between a 6 and a 7. In that, there may be an element of luck, or bad luck, between one horse and another. Another element of "luck" may be the very good performer who follows an indifferent or poor one, or perhaps a succession of indifferent ones. The more attractive horse will generally profit a little. Conversely, the average, so-so performer who follows upon the heels of an outstanding one will sometimes be "unlucky." The better the judge, the less these elements will be an influence, but some there will always be. That's one reason the large, multiday, rated shows strive to bring in highly respected judges.

To be sure, judges are under enormous pressure to pin the best horse. Expensive "high potential" horses need good riders to achieve their expected potential, which is why the best horses are often ridden by the top trainers. Who knows, you may be that owner or trainer some day!

One thing for sure, you're making a big mistake if a horse with a superfancy trot goes into the ring ahead of you and you say, "Oh, he's got it made. I don't have a chance."

Most judges would rather see an all-over nice mover who is consistent and honest in all three gaits than a horse who may be brilliant but unsteady, or fabulous in one gait and a little (or a lot) weak in two. Or a young or green horse with a fancy trot or overpowering canter that is so hard to control that he falls on his forehand and "runs" or gets irregular and unbalanced in his turns and on his circles.

Remember, each movement gets a score, adding up to the final result. A mistake here, a brilliant movement there can give an unexpected final score. Straight 6's almost always do better than a combination of 7's and 4's. The bottom line is, it's more important for you to know how your own test is being scored than to worry about luck or politics. In Chapter 3 you will learn more about how a test is scored.

Should You Talk to the Judge?

During a test, *never* speak to the judge unless spoken to (other than a "good morning" or "good afternoon," before your test, or a "thank you" afterward). If you get off course and the judge does not notice, stop, ride to the judge and explain you are off course, would she tell you where to begin again?

Sometimes at a schooling show, the judges will talk to the exhibitors before they exit the ring. Always let the judge initiate the conversation, do not offer excuses, and do not expect a lengthy narrative.

After a test, if you do not understand the comments or remarks on your test sheet, you might want to speak to the judge. At a recognized show it is a violation of the rules to approach the judge without permission of the technical delegate or show management. If you are granted permission, it will probably be after you have completed all your rides. At most schooling or informal shows, it's fairly easy to get permission to speak to the judge — it's an expected part of the job at those shows. At a recognized show, however, it's much harder to talk to the judge. The theory here is that by the time you reach this level, you should already have enough experience to figure out for yourself why you finished where you did.

When you approach the judge, be courteous and respectful. Ask if she has any suggestions for improving your ride or what was meant by a particular comment. Be prepared to describe your horse's color or some distinctive description of your ride. It is rare for the judge to have kept notes, so it is usually necessary to refresh their memory with some visual description. The judge may be able to give you some clear, concise explanation for why the test was scored the way it was, and maybe offer at least one suggestion on what you can do to come closer to the ideal.

Riding a dressage test is not a confrontation — it's not your ride against the judge. The judge is not trying to trip you up or planning to eat you after your final salute. You are paying him or her to watch you ride, and in all likelihood she is sitting there rooting for you. Every judge I know wants to see you do your best.

Chapter Three

Know the Score

In order to plan a ride and later understand the comments, suggestions, and scores of the judge, the rider must have a basic understanding of the criteria by which the performance will be evaluated. Only when you understand exactly what is being judged in each movement and ride each movement to the best of your ability will you have the best opportunity to receive a good score.

The tests test training. A fancy mover only has the advantage *if* he is better trained. An average mover can enhance his natural gaits with a test that's consistent, accurate, and flowing. You can always pick up points doing what you're supposed to do in the right shape at the right place.

The actual purpose of the scores and comments is to allow the judge to rank those horses in that class, on that day. Keep in mind that the judge must mark down what she sees at the moment, not what she thinks the horse may be capable of doing in different circumstances; nor can the judge give concessions because the horse or the rider might be having a bad day. Also, the judge is not expected to comment on *why* she thinks the problems are there or what caused them; the judge is supposed to confine his or her comments to the fact that there is a problem or a deficiency or on what in his or her estimation would constitute a higher score for that movement. There will always be differences in scores from judge to judge (some score high, some score low), but the final placings should be very close from judge to judge.

When tests are dual-judged (more than one judge), don't be surprised if scores between judges are different. Different positions around the arena will give a different perspective. For instance, the judge at "C" can see if the entrance is straight but cannot see if the hind legs are "square." A judge at "B" or "E" cannot see straightness, but may note a hind leg "left behind" or "leaning onto the forehand" in the halt.

Throughout this text, patterns and movements typical of Training and First Level tests will be used to illustrate various points. They are not from any current test. AHSA rules will be quoted as appropriate.

Protocol

"A test begins with the entry at A and ends after the final salute, as soon as the horse moves forward. (Except in Free Style, where the test begins in the first stride after the salute and ends at the final salute.) Anything before the beginning or after the end of the test has no effect on the marks." (AHSA Art. 1922.6)

"A competitor who does not enter the arena within 60 seconds after the entry bell is rung for his ride shall be eliminated. No competitor can be required to ride prior to his scheduled time." (Art. 1922.6.11)

"If during the test (between the time of entry and the time of exit at A), the horse leaves the arena (all four feet outside the fence or the line marking the arena perimeter) the competitor is eliminated." (Art. 1922.6.7)

"The judge may stop a test and/or allow a competitor to restart from the beginning or from any appropriate point in the test if, in his discretion, some unusual circumstance has occurred to interrupt a test." (Art. 1922.6.10)

"The competitor should leave the arena in the way prescribed in the test." (Art. 1922.6.8)

The test contains the Movements and the Collective Marks on which you are scored. The way your horse performs each movement shows up in your movement scores. Errors show up as minus points. The judge's overall impression of each of the "basics" exhibited by you and your horse shows up in the Collective Marks (figure 3.1).

Let's take a closer look at all three sections of a test.

Scoring the Movements

Each test movement has a numbered box on the test sheet. As you ride, the judge gives each box a score on a scale of 0 to 10.

Meaning of the Marks

The United States Dressage Federation published this "Meaning of the Marks" for the "L Judge's Program":

0-3	= something is basically wrong
4	= "not enough", but basically not wrong (for instance: breaking gait, once only)
5	= marginal
6-7	= satisfactory to fairly good
8	= good
9-10	= technically correct with brilliance and harmony

Many times a movement will have several parts. For example, Movement #2 (figure 3.1) has: two turns; a trot section; a 20-meter circle; another trot section, and finally two corners. The movement is complete at "K" (the start of the next movement). The judge must prioritize the movement so the most important aspect (in this example, probably the circle; then the trot overall) gets the most credit.

NO.

Conditions:
Arena: Standard or small
Average time: 4:00
Maximum Possible Points: 220

		TEST	DIRECTIVE IDEAS	POINTS	COEFFICIENT	TOTAL	REMARKS
1.	A X	Enter working trot Halt, Salute proceed working trot	Straightness on centerline, transitions, quality of halt and trot	6		6	sl. crooked
2.	C E	Track left Circle left 20m	Quality of turn at C quality of trot, roundness of circle	7		7	attractive trot
3.	Between K&A	Working canter left lead	Calmness and smoothness of depart	6		6	a bit sluggish
4.	A	Circle left 20m	Quality of canter, roundness of circle	5		5	inconsistent bend
5.	Between B&M	Working trot	Balance during transition	5		5	on forehand into trot
6.	C	Medium walk	Transition, quality of walk	6		6	
7.	HXF F	Free walk Medium walk	Straightness, quality of walk (-2)	7	2	14	ERROR WENT H-E-F fairly good str.
8.	A	Working trot	Smoothness of transition	7		7	
9.	E	Circle right 20m	Quality of trot, roundness of circle	7		7	
10.	Between H&C	Working canter right lead	Calmness and smoothness of depart	~~8~~ 6		6	smooth VOICE
11.	C	Circle right 20m	Quality of canter, roundness of circle	7		7	fair bend & bal
12.	Between B&F	Working trot	Balance during transition	5		5	not enough fwd.
13.	A X	Down centerline Halt, Salute	Straightness on centerline, quality of trot and halt	6		6	haunches right of C.L.

Leave arena at walk at A. 87

COLLECTIVE MARKS:

	POINTS	COEFFICIENT	TOTAL	REMARKS
Gaits (freedom and regularity)	8	2	16	
Impulsion (desire to move forward, elasticity of the steps, relaxation of the back)	6	2	12	
Submission (attention and confidence; harmony, lightness and ease of movements; acceptance of the bit)	5	2	10	loses balance in down trans.
Rider's position and seat; correctness and effect of the aids	7	2	14	

FURTHER REMARKS: lovely horse!

SUBTOTAL 139
ERRORS (- -2)
TOTAL POINTS 137
62.272 %

Figure 3.1 A test sheet with a judge's scores and comments. Note a two-point deduction for an error in section 7, the Free walk; also a two-point deduction for use of voice in section 10, Working canter right lead.

Basic, Major, and Minor Faults

Every judge must have a very clear idea of the weight to apply to various faults, whether basic, main, or minor:

> **Basic Faults:**
> (Must be severely penalized.)
>
> - Impure gaits (pacing, irregular trot, 4-beat canter — a momentary irregularity is not a basic fault)
> - Incorrect basics (not stretching into the bit; back not swinging, not accepting bridle)
> - Incorrect head position (tilting, behind vertical)
> - Insufficient impulsion (or desire to move forward for the level)
> - Disobedience, resistance, or evasions
> - Incorrect seat of rider
>
> **Main Faults:** (Not quite as bad.)
>
> - Unsteady head position (constantly moving)
> - Poor transitions
> - Insufficient or wrong bend
> - Not in self-carriage (relative to the level)
> - Lack of straightness (hind legs not following in hoofprints of front legs on straight lines; wide behind)
>
> **Minor Faults:** (Treated lightly unless they keep occurring.)
>
> - Any of the above if it happens momentarily
> - Things that can happen to anyone (shying, stumbling)
>
> *Reprinted with permission from the United States Dressage Federation, "L" Program.*

Basic Faults will usually receive 3's or 4's (sometimes lower); Main Faults will usually receive 4's or 5's; and Minor Faults will usually receive 5's, or, if the movement warrants it, may even receive higher than a 5.

Modifiers

Each movement has a start, a middle, and an end — if the basic movement is good but one or two "bobbles" occur, the judge will modify the score up or down. Modifiers that decrease the difficulty of the movement will decrease the score: for example, a circle too large; the canter depart in the corner (when called for at the letter); not enough rein back steps; not collected after medium or lengthened gait (letting the corner slow the horse). Modifiers that *increase* the difficulty of the movement are seldom scored higher; in fact, if a circle is smaller because the horse "cut in" or "lost balance," it may receive a *lower* score.

Accuracy

Significant inaccuracies will be marked down. For example, a circle with straight sides — this evades the difficulty and purpose of the movement, which is to show bending. Minor inaccuracies, such as a transition a little early, or a diagonal not quite on the letter, are usually treated quite lightly in Training and First level, but will gain importance as you move up the levels.

Penalty Points

Errors of Course or Errors of Test

Taking a wrong turn, leaving out a movement, posting when you're supposed to be sitting, and other similar errors are penalized by deducting penalty points: two points for the first error; four points for the second error; eight points for the third error; and elimination for the fourth — although the judge may allow you to finish the test. When a competitor goes "off course," the judge will ring the bell; the competitor should stop and wait for the judge's instructions.

"When the competitor makes an "error of test" (for instance trots rising instead of sitting, or at the salute does not take the reins in one hand,

etc.) he must be penalized as for an "error of the course," but the bell may not be rung, as it would interrupt the flow of the test." (AHSA, Art. 1922.4.3)

"In principle, a competitor is not allowed to repeat a movement of the test unless the President of the jury (the judge at C) has instructed him to do so. If a competitor does repeat a movement, the judges must consider the first movement shown only and at the same time deduct penalties for an error of course." (Art. 1922.4.3)

"If the bell is not sounded (for instance the competitor makes a transition at D instead of at L) and ringing the bell would interrupt the test), if the same error is repeated (as from the other direction) only one error is recorded." (Art. 1922.4.1)

"If the jury has not noted an error, the competitor has the benefit of the doubt." (Art. 1922.4.4)

Penalty points are written in the "Remarks" section of the movement during which they occur and are later deducted from the total score.

Voice Penalties

The use of the voice is not an "error." *"The use of the voice in any way whatsoever or clicking of the tongue once or repeatedly is a serious fault involving the deduction of at least two marks from those that would otherwise have been awarded for (each) movement where this occurred."* (Art. 1922.3)

Judges will usually indicate voice deductions by putting down the score for the movement in its box, drawing a line through it, and then putting beside it the new score reflecting the deduction. In the "Remarks" section may be the note "voice" with a circle around it. In this way there is no confusion between errors of test or course and voice penalties.

When more than one judge officiates, all judges do not have to agree on a voice penalty. Only the judges who hear the voice will mark it down.

Fall of Horse or Rider

It may surprise you that *"In the case of a fall of horse and/or rider the competitor will not be eliminated. He will be penalized by the effect of the fall on the execution of the movement being performed and also in the Collective Marks."* (Art. 1922.6.6)

Lameness

The AHSA Rule Book is quite specific about lameness: *"all animals except stallions and mares in Breeding classes must be serviceably sound for competition purpose, i.e. such animal must not show evidence of lameness..."* (Art. 303)

"In the case of marked lameness the president of the jury (judge at C) informs the competitor that he is eliminated. There is no appeal against his decision." (Art. 1922.5)

The judge does not need to know the cause of an apparent lameness. If the horse looks lame the judge is required to eliminate the horse from that test. When the judge eliminates a horse for lameness, it means the horse was lame in front of her, *at that moment.* It does not matter if a veterinarian certifies the horse sound before or after a class.

The judge will usually observe a horse several minutes before excusing them and may make comments such as: "irregular in rhythm or tempo," "unlevel," or "uneven." Sometimes a rider doesn't know that there is anything wrong — maybe the horse moves like this all the time. Maybe the horse walked across a gravel lane on the way to the ring. Something as simple as removing a rock from the horse's shoe could enable the horse to go sound. If you feel the horse is okay, you may go in your next scheduled class.

Elimination

"Horses can only be eliminated for the following reasons:

- *misrepresentation of entry or inappropriate entry* (Arts. 1501 & 1919)
- *use of illegal equipment* (Art. 1921)
- *unauthorized assistance* (including caller "ad-libbing" test, or someone adjusting a competitor's equipment after the test has started) (Art. 1922)
- *four errors of course* (Art. 1922)
- *horse's tongue tied down* (Art. 1922)
- *late entry into the arena* (longer than 60 seconds after the bell) (Art. 1922)
- *all four feet of the horse leave the arena* (during the test or exiting other than at "A" after the final salute.) (Art. 1922)
- *cruelty* (Art. 302)
- *Marked lameness* (Art. 1922)
- *Resistance longer than 20 seconds* (Art. 1922)
- *In FEI Freestyle classes, performing movements that are not allowed* (Art. 1928)
- *Any situation where a direct rule violation can be cited. Where a violation cannot be cited, a competitor is not eliminated."*

"Only the officiating jury (panel of judges) may eliminate a competitor for a rule violation; only from the test in question and (except for late entry into the arena) only after the competitor has entered the arena. Members of the ground jury have no authority to eliminate under any other circumstances. Authority for rule enforcement outside the competition ring rests solely with the show committee." (Art. 1924.2)

The Collective Marks

The body of the test critiques the movements as performed by the horse. The Collective Marks show the strengths and weaknesses of the basics of training. Here the judge can distinguish where the root causes of any problems with the movements lie.

Unless — or until — you score well in the Collectives, don't expect to receive good scores on the movements. For instance, if you get a low score on your canter transitions, you may try to raise your performance expectations by repeatedly practicing the transition itself. However, without the ingredients of regularity, impulsion, suppleness, and submission, chances are your scores will not be improved (figure 3.2).

The Collective Marks read the same at Training and First Level. At Second Level and above, "lightness of the forehand," is added to "Submission."

In the Collective Marks the judge may underline or circle the problem(s) demonstrated in the test. This technique doesn't work in the body of the test because the Directives are not specific enough.

Gaits (Freedom and Regularity)

The Collective Mark for "Gaits" should not be confused with the beauty of the horse's movement. The quality of the gaits (elasticity, suppleness, scope, range of motion, and so forth) was judged in the body of the test. Here in the Collective Marks only the freedom and regularity are scored.

"Freedom" is the "amplitude of range of motion of the fore and hind limbs." (USDF Glossary of Judge's Terms)

Freedom is also a lack of restraint. The horse should take long steps and swing his shoulders and hips "freely." If the horse looks restrained, the neck is contracted and this will impede the mobility of the shoulders. In this case the score may be lowered under Gaits *and* Impulsion.

Lack of suspension in the trot or canter is not necessarily a lack of freedom; it belongs with Impulsion.

If the horse is stiff or tense he is not moving freely, and this is often reflected in a shortness of steps. "Stiff" and "tense" could go

Training & First Level: **COLLECTIVE MARKS:**				
Gaits (freedom and regularity)		2		
Impulsion (desire to move forward, elasticity of the steps, suppleness of the back,engagement of the hindquarters)		2		
Submission (attention and confidence; harmony, lightness and ease of movements; acceptance of the bridle)		2		
Rider's position and seat; correctness and effect of the aids		2		
Second Level & Above: **COLLECTIVE MARKS:**				
Gaits (freedom and regularity)		2		
Impulsion (desire to move forward, elasticity of the steps, suppleness of the back, engagement of the hindquarters)		2		
Submission (attention and confidence; harmony, lightness and ease of movements; acceptance of the bridle and lightness of the forehand)		2		
Rider's position and seat; correctness and effect of the aids		2		

Figure 3.2 The Collective Marks, scored at the bottom of every dressage score sheet, grade the strengths and weaknesses of a horse and rider's basic training. Reprinted by permission of the American Horse Shows Association

under Freedom or Submission (resistant) — or both.

"Regularity" is the correctness (purity) of the gait, evenness and regularity of the rhythm. It is synonymous with "rhythm," but not with "tempo." The difference between rhythm and tempo is that rhythm is constant "correctness" of the beat: a four-beat walk, two-beat trot, and three-beat canter. "Tempo" is the rate of the beat, fast or slow. Elizabeth Searle, an "S" judge and instructor in the USDF "L" Program, says, "Tempo (of the rhythm) goes under 'Submission.' A lack of even tempo (speed ups or slow downs) is a resistance."

"Regularity" is where the judge can address purity of gait, for instance a lateral walk or four-beat canter. A momentary irregularity (for instance, an unlevelness that appeared in extended trot once only), is not a basic fault of gait. A sustained irregularity *is* a major fault.

"Uneven" means "unequal in length of steps." "Unlevel" means "unequal height of steps or bearing of weight on both sides." (USDF Glossary)

Both are major faults because both indicate that instead of the pairs of feet taking even weight as they come to the ground, one may be taking more weight than the other, or one leg is coming further forward than the other, implying that one of the hind legs may be stronger or weaker than the other. Both can give the appearance of slight lameness, when that may or may not be the cause.

Faulty gaits are most often the product of faulty training or riding techniques. Negative, defensive tension in the horse's back is often the cause of irregularities in the gaits. A horse trained with mechanical aids (tie downs, draw-reins, etc.) very often has his gaits ruined. Mechanical aids cause the horse to "freeze" in a defensive position, sometimes termed producing a "head set." Sometimes these horses can be retrained with a lot of hard work and dedication to detail.

Very often if the horse exhibits one bad or faulty gait, even if the other two are good, it will bring the Collective Mark for Gaits down. Actually, there are different philosophies about scoring the gaits. At one time one bad or faulty gait caused a horse to be given a "4" for *all* gaits. Some judges score each gait and divide by three to get the Gait score. For instance: if the walk was a "5", the trot was a "7", and the canter was a "6", then the score is a "6" for Gaits.

Impulsion (desire to move forward; elasticity of the steps; suppleness of the back; engagement of the hindquarters)

"Impulsion" is "Forward/upward thrust; releasing the energy stored by engagement." (USDF Glossary)

Impulsion refers to the propulsive efforts of the hind legs. The rider should not confuse impulsion with speed. In dressage terms it translates to how the horse carries himself in a forward manner. Impulsion is lift, springiness, and suspension.

"Desire to move forward" means just what it says. Is the horse always ready to move on, in a good tempo? Was the whole test forward enough, plus enough to lengthen or extend the gait — if required? If a horse doesn't have much overstep (see Chapter 6 "The Horse") but looks diligent, judges usually won't penalize.

Here it is hard to separate impulsion and submission. Is the horse doing all it can or does it just not want to do more? If the horse looks either resistant or lazy, he will probably score low under Impulsion and Submission.

A four-beat canter can be a judgment call: if due to a loss of connection, it is scored under Submission; if due to a loss of energy, it is scored under Impulsion.

The definition of "elasticity" is "The ability or tendency to stretch and contract the musculature smoothly, giving the impression of 'stretchiness' or 'springiness'." (USDF) When the joints of the hind leg bend and spring off the ground at each stride of working trot, you've got elasticity.

"Suppleness of the Back" is reflected in the horse's outline. We say the horse should have a "rounded" outline. There should be a slight arching of the neck, which would indicate a reciprocal arching of the loin. If the neck looks stiff, immobile, or shortened, chances are the back is stiff (contracted) and immobile. If the back is stiff, the legs move in short, restricted steps. If the neck is sagging, or too relaxed, the back is probably not working. Too much relaxation will look like laziness. The toes may drag or the strides lack length.

"Suppleness" is "pliability; ability to smoothly adjust the carriage (longitudinally) and the position or bend (laterally), without impairment of the flow of movement, or of the balance." (USDF)

In other words, suppleness is the easy bending of the horse and the horse's ability to shift his center of gravity forward, backward, or from side to side. A horse who leans in or throws his haunches out on circles or corners lacks suppleness.

The USDF definition of "Engagement" is: "Increased flexion of the joints of the hind legs and the lumbosacral joint (the spinal joint immediately in front of the peak of the croup) during the moment of support, causing a relative lowering of the croup/raising of the forehand, with the hind legs supporting a relatively greater proportion of the load." If the horse lacks suppleness, he will also lack engagement. From Second Level up you can't have impulsion without engagement (figure 3.3).

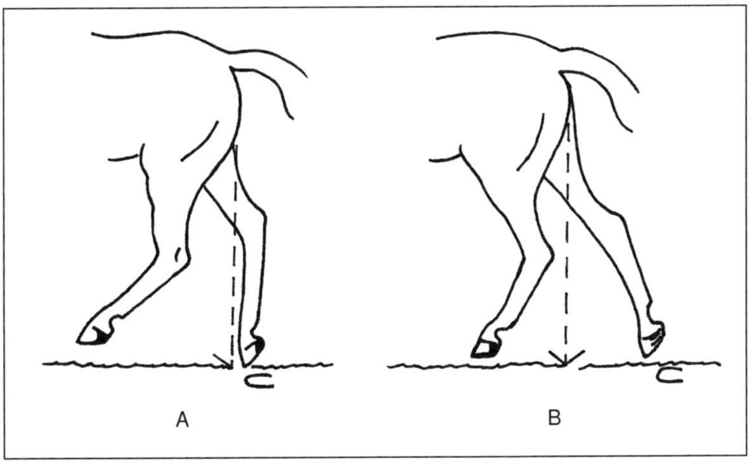

Figure 3.3 Engagement is not judged by how far forward the horse moves the hind legs, but rather how little the hind leg "trails" behind a vertical line dropped from the buttock. Horse A is showing better engagement than Horse B.

Submission (attention and confidence; harmony, lightness and ease of movements; acceptance of the bridle)

Submission is the opposite of resistance, irritation, and unwillingness. In Training Level, simple obedience is expected. For example, if the horse is asked to halt, it does so, or if asked to move off does so. Transitions (between gaits) demonstrate submission (or lack of it), as well as "lightness and ease of movements." Submission is not mechanical obedience, however. Mechanical obedience shows as labored movements or a sullen attitude.

Submission is "revealed by a constant attention, willingness, and confidence in the attitude of the horse, as well as by the harmony and ease displayed in the correct execution of the movements, including correct bend, acceptance of and obedience to the rider's aids (including the bridle), and a balance appropriate to the task at hand." (USDF)

If the horse is attentive to the rider, he will respond promptly to the aids and is not easily distracted by extraneous sights and sounds. His ears will be cocked toward his rider. If the horse has confidence in his rider, he will look calm and happy. Everything he does should look simple and natural, that is, harmonious, light, and easy.

The judge often has a difficult task here. Most resistance displayed by a young horse is due to nervousness in strange surroundings and not willful resistance. While inexperience may be the cause of inattention or resistance, it should not be skipped over lightly. The rider must understand that obtaining his horse's acceptance of the show atmosphere must be obtained before the horse can be expected to receive good scores. Lack of attention and confidence results in looking around, whinnying, and shying.

Disobediences if shown once only affect the score in the movement only. For instance, judges only tend to deduct points for shying as it affects the particular movement. But if a horse shows the same disobedience several times, this will significantly affect the score.

Other occurrences that might be considered under Submission are:

- Mouth open — if it is just ajar all the time it is probably all right. However, an open mouth with a tight jaw or tongue out for a length of time will usually get marked down.
- Grinding teeth — some horses grind their teeth when they are concentrating, but if the horse is tense, tight, and grinding the teeth, it is penalized severely.
- Wringing tail — the horse may be tense, may have lost balance, or the rider may be overusing spurs.

- Varying tempo — usually goes under Submission because the horse is not accepting the aids to stay even.

"Lightness and ease of movements" refers to the horse's lightness on its feet and lightness in the reins — components of self-carriage. A horse that is tired, bored, or resistant will land heavily.

A horse that is "running" — moving with a tempo that is too quick — will be heavy on the forehand and resistant to the reins. "On the forehand" usually implies that the horse's balance is toppling forward. The Training Level horse should be in "horizontal balance."

"Acceptance of the bridle" is "lack of evasion, resistance, or protest; acquiescence." (USDF) Here it is used in reference to the horse's unresisting willingness to allow the maintenance of a steady contact and the application of the aids.

At Second Level and above, *"Lightness of the forehand"* is called for. This is carrying power and requires a degree of "collection". Most judges will say that the collection is sufficient for the level if the horse can perform the movements without losing his balance: forward, backward, or sideways.

Rider's Position and Seat, Correctness and Effect of the Aids

In a test, it is the horse that is evaluated. The judge must score the movements only on their quality — how the horse performs them. To what extent the rider affects the movements, for better or worse, is evaluated in the Collectives — once only.

While judges always like an elegant rider, most will choose effectiveness over elegance. If the rider's seat and aids are ineffective, it will be reflected in the horse's performance. If the rider sits crooked, the horse can't be straight or move correctly. If the horse speeds up or slows down when going around corners and circles, this is often the rider's problem. Judges do the rider a favor if they comment on some position fault that is consistently affecting the horse's performance. For example, wrong leads, if not corrected promptly, are the rider's fault. Or an abusive rider who "throws" the horse around is an almost automatic "4" or "insufficient."

In cases of poor geometry (failing to ride accurate figures), bad transitions, or not accepting the bit, the judge must decide if it is the rider or the horse. If it's the horse, it goes under Submission. If the judge decides it's the rider, the test loses double or triple points: under the Movement(s), under Submission, *and* under the Rider.

What about the horse that is spooking or inattentive? This will be scored under Submission, but is the horse being "allowed" to misbehave or is the rider effectively dealing with a bad situation? One thing for certain, the rider will not get a higher score simply because she managed to "ride out" a spook or buck.

The rider should never make a show of punishing the horse. If the horse is scared, punishment will only do harm; the best option for the rider is to "finesse" the horse through the test and be a good sport.

And the Winner Is...

After each performance and after each judge has given her marks, the judges' sheets pass into the hands of the scorers. The marks are multiplied by the corresponding coefficients where applicable and then totaled. Penalty points incurred for errors in the execution of the test are then deducted where applicable. Usually a percentage score is awarded. With one judge, the sum total is used for placings. If there are two or more judges, the points awarded by each judge will be published separately in addition to the total score.

In all competitions, the winner is the competitor having the highest total points, the second the one with the next highest total points, and so on. In case of equality of points (ties), the competitor with the highest marks received under the Collective Marks shall be declared the winner. When the scores for the Collectives tie, the judge may be required to decide on the winner after review of both score sheets, or the horses may remain tied.

"Videotape may not be used to dispute a judge's decision." (AHSA, Art. 1923.4)

"After awards for a class have been presented, the judge's score sheet should be given to the exhibitor. Tests must be handed directly to the competitor or his representative. Privacy must be maintained." (Art. 1926.4)

"If a mathematical error on the score sheet is discovered, it must be brought to the attention of show management within one hour of the official posting of the scores from the last class of that show day. Show management must announce said posting, and must make test sheets available to competitors immediately." (Art. 1923.7)

Chapter Four

Dressage, Combined Training, or Pony Club — What's Your Choice?

Dressage schooling shows, recognized shows, combined training events, and Pony Club all feature dressage. Many of the same tests are used, and the method of scoring the tests is the same (except that in combined training the score is converted to "penalty points" — the higher the percentage score, the lower the penalties). The rules they operate by and the divisions within each are where the differences lie. There are only minor differences in tack, attire, and protocol.

Dressage Shows

A "dressage division" may be held in conjunction with breed or specialty shows. More commonly, a dressage show will be strictly limited to dressage classes. Dressage shows are further divided into either schooling or recognized categories. By definition, a schooling show is any horse show that has not acquired American Horse Shows Association (AHSA) recognition.

Recognition means that, in addition to paying fees to the AHSA, exhibitors, show management, and all officials must adhere to AHSA rules and regulations. Those rules are for the protection of the exhibitors, the horses, the officials, and show management. This is not to say that schooling shows are not run by rules. Many use the AHSA rules verbatim (or by reference), but do not, usually, have a way of enforcing them.

Additionally, schooling shows are not required to hire licensed judges and a technical delegate (T.D.), or adhere to lighting, stabling, or security regulations. This allows schooling shows to operate on a much smaller budget; thus, the entry fees are much lower.

Since almost all schooling shows operate by AHSA rules, the exhibitor should be familiar with those rules.

Dressage Schooling Shows

If you have never competed in dressage (or any other form of equestrian competition), probably the easiest place to start would be a schooling show. Schooling shows are not just for beginners or Training Level horses however. They can be used every step of the way: to learn, to experiment, and to test.

You can learn much at a schooling show by watching others and sharing their comments. Even though the judge is not there to give you a riding lesson, at a schooling show the judges are much more likely to add informative tips or comments on what you might do to improve your performance. At recognized shows, judges are discouraged from making such comments. By the time you get to a recognized show you should know the premise for the comments and scores you receive.

Schooling shows are great shows for a green horse or a beginner rider just starting out. You or your horse can learn about competing in a real but casual setting because there is not so much pressure, and it doesn't make as much difference if the rider makes a mistake. It's a place where both horse and rider get showing experience. At recognized shows, on the other hand, you can get intimidated pretty fast if you don't understand the process.

Although schooling shows are not a replacement for competent instruction, they are a very valuable supplement to instruction or coaching and can cost less than a clinic on a time-per-dollar basis. What is more, it is written down for you to refer to later!

You can use schooling shows to experiment. Try different warm-up routines to see which works best for your horse. You can see if the methods you are using are indeed getting the proper result.

For instance, you can use schooling shows to see if your horse performs better if you ride aggressively or if you need to give him more "free space." Don't waste expensive entry fees at a recognized show if you're still in the experimentation stage.

You can, of course, use schooling shows to test your horse's training under the pressure of competition. You can find the holes — weaknesses that only show up under pressure — in your performance and training.

Schooling shows give trainers a place to bring young horses where they can get some experience before they take them to recognized shows. You have to train a horse at home and then take it away from home to see what kind of problems you're going to run into. Many is the horse (and rider) who can "do it perfectly" at home, but fall apart when out of familiar territory and in the midst of distraction, or just in front of an audience. This is not necessarily because you aren't doing it right, or your horse is a basket case; it is a natural phenomenon. Everyone reacts differently under pressure, away from home. Schooling shows are the perfect answer to working out your stage fright blues before the real pressure of higher level competition is on.

Schooling shows often offer special divisions or classes, including the USDF Introductory Level (walk-trot tests); classes for "New Riders" (usually for riders who have never won a blue ribbon); "Green Horses" (horses that have not shown above, say, First Level), and other unique classes.

WHO PUTS ON SCHOOLING SHOWS?

Generally, local dressage clubs, the management of training barns, or the staff of equestrian academies initiates schooling shows. However, private individuals or boarders at training or boarding barns can also get together to undertake and put on shows (with the permission and cooperation of the barn owners, of course).

You can probably find prize lists by talking to local trainers and instructors or by belonging to a club. Show organizers are always looking for volunteers to fill in at the shows and this is an excellent way to learn about the accepted practices and protocol of showing.

Who's invited? This depends on whether the show is open to in-house students only or to the public. Usually, in-house schooling shows are far more casual than are public shows and don't require as much preparation or notice. Entry fees are usually modest; often no dress code is required; and there may be no outside judges, stewards, and so forth. Notice of an in-house schooling show may be no more than a flyer tacked up on the barn bulletin board. In-house schooling shows offer the rider the least amount of competitive pressure: they're showing in a familiar barn among familiar students.

Open schooling shows, on the other hand, are typically run more formally and require more advance notice, depending on how many outside exhibitors are being sought (how many arenas and parked trailers can be accommodated). Show prize lists are usually sent to mailing lists of the area clubs and perhaps posted in feed or tack stores. A dress code is more likely; entry fees cost a bit more, and overall, a more serious atmosphere pervades with the presence of judges, secretaries, assigned riding times, and so forth. Competitors include riders outside the barn who trailer in, and the competitive atmosphere is heightened.

CASUAL OR FORMAL

Casual or formal depends on the class of riders the show is trying to attract. Some shows prefer to keep the show atmosphere casual. These shows usually don't have a very strict dress code. The looseness invites relaxation, reduces pressure, and is especially helpful for riders who are easily intimidated or who lack confidence.

Many shows opt to present a more formal ambiance, akin to that at rated (recognized) shows. The more you can make a schooling show look like the real thing, the less intimidating the rated shows are when you get to them. Many organizations believe in presenting it as the real thing, allowing students to come and learn what is going to be expected so far as dress, equipment, eligibility of entries, protocol, and so forth. It is an introduction to what is expected next.

As a forerunner to rated shows, a formal schooling show mimics much of the bustle, format, and rules of a rated show. Often, appropriate dress is strongly encouraged, judges and ring officials are treated with the same respect and formality as those in rated shows, and competition can be more earnest. A formal schooling show is a good venue for learning to deal with horse or rider show ring jitters and an excellent preview of how a rated show is structured.

League competitions are local competitions that are recognized by the USDF but not the AHSA. Scores from league competitions do not count toward Qualified Rider Awards (USDF), nor AHSA Awards. League competitions are "formal" schooling shows that go by all the AHSA rules but without the AHSA fees and expenses.

THE SHOW PRIZE LIST

Some organizations produce a prize list that covers show ring and barn rules; how or if to approach judges; committee rights concerning splitting, combining or canceling classes, and so forth. Other schooling shows leave an exhibitor wondering about rules.

At a schooling show, **unless you know otherwise, assume AHSA rules of dress, equipment and protocol** and you shouldn't get in any trouble.

SCHEDULING

Advance planning of schooling shows varies considerably from area to area. A casual, in-house show without outside judges and personnel (or outside entries) doesn't require nearly the amount of preparation that a formal, open to the public schooling show needs. Still, the norm for a dressage show is that entries should be postmarked or received 10 days before the show date. If the organization puts on a series of shows, the prize list may also have an "opening date," a date before which you must not send entries. This is to prevent confusion as to which show you are entering.

JUDGES

Often local trainers or instructors are invited to judge schooling shows. The show may or may not allow competitors to ride in front of their own trainers or instructors. In dressage tests, the practice of instructors judging their own students is more accepted than with equitation classes, because in dressage the horse is being judged and not so much the rider. Students (of the judge) are actually sometimes at a disadvantage. Many instructors penalize their own students' test rides because they know their weaknesses.

This is not to say trainers or instructors make poor judges, because they are often excellent. But it is recommended that judges be brought from outside the area so that they are less likely to be judging their own students. Nonetheless, as in rated shows, it is the competitor's responsibility to avoid conflicts of interest when it comes to entering classes that would be judged by their instructors or trainers.

So far as the judge talking to the exhibitors at schooling shows, sometimes the organizers leave extra time in between the rides and tell the judge specifically that they may talk to each exhibitor after their ride. In these cases, the judge initiates the conversation. If the judge does not motion you to come forward after your final salute, do not initiate a conversation.

It is not always possible for the show to allow time for interaction between judges and competitors. Schooling shows can have three or more arenas going at once, and organizers like to accommodate as many exhibitors as they can, according to space and time. Entry fees finance the show. A judge is usually paid on an eight-hour basis, whether he or she judges 60 rides or 16. The maximum number of rides that can be fitted into a single ring in a full day is about 60. This does not allow any time for discussion between rides.

Combined Training

Most of the directives that apply to dressage schooling versus recognized shows also apply to combined training competitions. The AHSA and the United States Combined Training Association (USCTA) sanction recognized combined training competitions.

To the uninitiated, there seems to be a number of terms for the sports that fall under the umbrella of combined training: combined training, horse trials, and eventing are all related to each other.

On a basic level, all of these terms refer to the sport of combined training, which asks horse and rider to compete in dressage, cross-country, and show jumping. The horse and rider team that garner the best (actually the lowest, since it is scored on a penalty basis) overall score are the winners of the competition.

Horse trials, which in the United States are usually held over a weekend, include dressage, cross-country, and show jumping. When steeplechase and road-and-track phases are added to the cross-country portion, it is called the endurance segment and a horse trial becomes an event.

Events, or three-day events, are held only at the more experienced Intermediate, Preliminary, and Advanced levels, and they traditionally last for three days (hence the name "three-day event"), with dressage held on the first day, endurance on the second day, and show jumping on the third day. They may last four days, the dressage portion lasting two days to accommodate all competitors.

The Levels

The terms used to label the various levels of dressage and combined training are confusing because the same words denote different things. The AHSA writes tests for six dressage levels: Training, and First through Fifth, with three or four graduated tests at each level. Above these are the four international (FEI) levels: Prix St. Georges, Intermediare I and II, and Grand Prix, which is the Olympic-level test. (The AHSA's "Fifth" level has four tests that correspond to the four FEI levels.)

The AHSA offers five levels of combined training: Novice, Training, Preliminary, Intermediate, and Advanced. Three-day events are held at Preliminary and above. Advanced level is equivalent to the Olympics. An introductory "pre-novice" level may be offered at schooling shows under several different names. Other countries do not use the same terms: in England, for instance, their Novice level is the equivalent of our Preliminary level.

The confusion increases with the dressage tests that are assigned to each combined training level, determined yearly by the United States Combined Training Association (USCTA). Event organizers choose the specific test they want to use. In 1995 the tests were:

- Novice – AHSA Training Level, tests 1 or 2.
- Training – AHSA Training Level, tests 3 or 4.
- Preliminary – AHSA First Level, tests 1 or 3; or FEI 1992 One-Star Three-Day test (available from USCTA).
- Intermediate – British Horse Society (BHS) 1984 test G; or FEI 1992 Two-Star Three-Day test; or AHSA 1995 Intermediate Horse Trials test (a modified Second Level, test 1, removing coefficients and separate transition scores).
- Advanced – BHS 1984 test P, 1985 test R, or 1992 test S; FEI 1995 Three- and Four-Star Three-Day test, which is roughly equivalent to between the AHSA's Second and Third Levels.

Is Combined Training Dressage Judged Differently?

Talk to a dozen different judges and a dozen different competitors and you will get two dozen opinions! The dressage ring is set up the same way. There is some variance in the rules for dress, equipment, tack, and protocol. The only significant differences are: combined training tests must be ridden from memory; a whip cannot be carried in any combined training test; rowel spurs are permitted in regular dressage but are not allowed in combined training, and bit restrictions are a little more lax in combined training warm-up (figure 4.1).

In theory, there should be no difference between combined training dressage and straight dressage. Dressage means "training", and the standards and goals of correct training are the same for any discipline.

In the United States and Canada, all the combined training judges are also dressage judges. That's unusual in the rest of the world, where the two communities have little to do with each other.

There is not a double standard in the judging of the horse. They all have their jobs to do. You see every bit as bad and as good dressage in both disciplines. The difference is in the perception of both judging and riding by those who know dressage well but not combined training, and vice versa.

International three-day horses need to be exceptional cross-country athletes but can be merely good on the flat, whereas in this country the dressage needs to be very, very good to get in the top placings. This is because the cross-country courses here aren't so challenging, so the dressage score has a greater effect on the placings. At the really tough three-day events, if you're not in the top third after dressage, you're not going to get a ribbon.

At the lower levels of both disciplines (below Second Level dressage and Intermediate combined training), there is very little

Figure 4.1 **A Comparison of Dressage Rules**

	AHSA Dressage:	AHSA Combined Training:	FEI Dressage Events:
1. Dress	1. Training to 4th Level. **Required:** Short conservative color coat w/tie, choker or stock tie, breeches or jodhpurs, boots or jodhpur boots, hunt cap or riding hat w/ hard shell, derby or top hat. Protective headgear may be worn at any level. Warm-up: Boots/shoes must have a distinguishable heel. FEI Levels: Dark tailcoat w/top hat, or dark jacket w/bowler, hunt cap or protective headgear. White or light-colored breeches, hunting stock, gloves, black riding boots and spurs.	1. Same as AHSA or hunting dress or uniform with regulation headgear. Recommended: Gloves; white, fawn or cream breeches; black boots with or without brown tops. Inappropriate: Shadbelly & top hat in horse trials below Advanced Level. Warm-up: Upon arrival, wearing a hard hat or appropriate dressage headgear is compulsory for anyone riding on the flat. Boots/shoes must have a distinguishable heel.	1. CDIOs*, Championships, Regional & Olympic Games: Black or dark blue tail coat, with top hat, white or offwhite breeches, hunting stock, gloves, black riding boots and spurs. Military, police: same as civilian or service dress. CDIs*: Same or black or dark blue jacket w/ bowler hat. * CDIO & CDIs (Concourse Dressage International) Competitions open to foreign competitors. Each category has different requirements as to judges, passports & levels of competition.
2. Saddlery	2. At all levels: English saddle w/stirrups. Training to 3rd Level: Snaffle bridle w/ cavesson, dropped, flash, crescent or crossed noseband. 4th to 5th Level: Same as above or simple double bridle w/ cavesson noseband. FEI: simple double bridle w/cavesson noseband. Warm-up: snaffle or regulation bridle.	2. Same as AHSA for test. Warm-up: English saddle and any bridle, including double, snaffle, gag or hackamore.	2. English saddle. Double bridle with cavesson noseband. Warm-up: same or may use snaffle with cavesson, dropped, crossed or flash noseband.
3. Bits	3. As pictured in AHSA Rule Book. All bits must be smooth and solid. Warm-up: same restrictions.	3. Same as AHSA for test. Warm-up: No restrictions on bits.	3. Same as AHSA FEI dressage except S-curved curb permitted.
4. Equipment	4. FORBIDDEN: martingales, bit guards, gadgets (such as bearing, side, running or balancing reins, tongue tied down, etc.) boots (including Easy Boots®), bandages (incl. tail bandages), blinkers, ear muffs or plugs, nose and seat covers & hoods. Breastplate and/or crupper allowed. Decoration of horse forbidden except braiding of mane and tail. Warm-up: Same except nose covers, running martingales, boots, bandages are permitted.	4. Same as AHSA for test. Fly shields prohibited but may be allowed by Ground Jury. Decoration of horse & braiding not addressed. Warm-up: Running and Irish martingales, bit guards, boots, bandages, fly shields, nose and seat covers permitted. Forbidden: Other martingales, gadgets (such as bearing, running or balancing reins, and blinkers.	4. Same as AHSA dressage.
5. Whip	5. One whip no longer than four feet permitted except in AHSA/USDF Championships. Competitors riding sidesaddle may carry whip in any class. Warm-up: Two whips not over six feet permitted.	5. Forbidden in test, except competitors riding sidesaddle. Warm-up: dressage whip may be used on flat before the dressage test.	5. Test: forbidden. Warm-up: permitted.
6. Spurs	6. Training to 5th Level: Optional. Spurs must be metal, w/shank pointing directly back from center of spur. Arms must be smooth. If rowels are used, they must be free to rotate. Warm-up: same.	6. Optional below Intermediate, required at Intermediate and Advanced Levels. Forbidden if capable of wounding horse. Must be smooth metal w/shank pointing only to rear. Shank must be no more than 3.5 cm. long (13/8 in.), without rowels and with blunt end. If shank is curved, it must direct down.	6. Required. Must be metal w/shank pointing directly back from center of spur. Arms must be smooth. If w/rowels, must be free to rotate.
7. Inspection	7. Ring stewards appointed by show management may spot check saddlery.	7. A steward must check each horse before it enters the arena. If a competitor requests,the bridle & bit may be checked immediately after completion of test, if bridle or bit are illegal the competitor will be eliminated.	7. Steward must check saddlery of each horse immediately as he leaves the arena. Any discrepancy will entail immediate elimination. Horses must be under supervision of stewards and officials at all times upon arrival at the event.

– continues next page

Figure 4.1 **A Comparison of Dressage Rules**

	AHSA Dressage:	AHSA Combined Training:	FEI Dressage Events:
8. Start Order	8. Organizers should prepare a time schedule including all rides, to be available by noon the day before the competition.	8. Determined by drawing conducted by the Organizing Committee.	8. There is a separate drawing for each competition, made in the presence of the President or a member of the Ground Jury, the T.D. and the Chefs d'Equipe. If a team competition, a drawing is conducted for the starting order of teams, and next for the order of competitors within each team. For Grand Prix Special and freestyles, the organizer may determine starting order by reverse order of placing or by a drawing.
9. Weather	9. In extreme heat and/or humidity, management can waive jackets. Riders must wear regulation hat and solid white or very pale colored short or long sleeve shirt, without neckwear. Inclement weather: may wear hat cover & transparent or conservative color raincoat.	9. In extreme heat and/or humidity, the Ground Jury has option to allow riders to compete without jackets. Riders must wear either a long or short sleeved shirt of conservative color without neckwear.	9. Waiving coats is not addressed; therefore is not permitted by rules.
10. Caller	10. Permitted except in Finals, Championships, Freestyle and FEI levels.	10. Prohibited.	10. Prohibited.
11. Enter Before Bell	11. No rule, therefore no penalty.	11. A competitor who enters the ring before the starting signal will be eliminated, at the discretion of the Ground Jury.	11. A competitor who enters the arena at A, before the starting signal has been given, will be eliminated.
12. Lameness	12. In the case of marked lameness the judge or President of the Jury informs the competitor that he is eliminated.	12. In the case of marked lameness, the judge at C, after consultation with the other judge(s) if appropriate, will inform the competitor that he is eliminated.	12. Same as AHSA dressage.
13. Unauthorized Assistance	13. Unauthorized assistance is forbidden under penalty of elimination. Unauthorized assistance includes, but is not limited to: calling other than the written test, a bystander adjusting the horse's or rider's equipment, outside intervention by voice, signs, etc.	13. A competitor receiving unauthorized assistance will be eliminated at the discretion of the Ground Jury.	13. Same as AHSA dressage.
14. Score	14. Points are posted as a positive score. Total final results must be published in marks as well as percentage.	14. Scores are posted as penalty marks; the average good marks for all judges is obtained and subtracted from the maximum good marks, then the final score is determined by multiplying the total by .6 and the result is posted as a penalty score.	14. Same as AHSA dressage.
15. Ties	15. The judge may be required to decide on a winner, after review of both score sheets, if the Collective Marks score is tied.	15. Ties in dressage scores are not broken.	15. In the case of equality of points (except for the Grand Prix Special, Grand Prix Freestyle at CDIOs & Championships & the World Cup Freestyle test) the competitors are given the same placing.

Figure 4.1 A comparison of dressage rules among three dressage-sanctioning organizations: the AHSA Dressage Division, AHSA Combined Training Division, and FEI Dressage. Reprinted with permission from the United States Dressage Federation. Compiled by Janine Malone 12/95. Updated 1999.

difference in the expected performance of each. Many horses compete in both disciplines successfully at the lower levels. Some of the differences that may be noticeable are that the Training Level dressage horse in its first year of showing often is very green, while a horse doing a Training Level dressage test at an event is often more experienced because of its preparation for jumping. As a result, one often sees better tests at combined training events than at dressage shows, although the quality swings wider at the lower end of the scale as well.

However, event horses sometimes show a mechanical obedience — absolutely accurate from point A to point B, "straight as an arrow and stiff as a board" — with a determination to get there the quickest way possible. This means that event horses tend to be more "forward" but are sometimes stiff because of lack of suppleness in the jaw or topline. In other words, event horses may go forward but not always the right way.

On the other hand, dressage specialists often produce boring, less forward tests. At dressage shows, the horses are sometimes too pulled together, ridden too conservatively. Judges know that many of these differences are influenced by the different mentality required of the two disciplines.

The dressage horse is taught to wait for every command and must give himself completely to his rider. The combined training horse can't give up his independence totally because jumping cross-country requires a certain amount of self-motivation and self-protection.

At the higher levels of both disciplines (Second Level and Intermediate combined training and above), the temperaments, the physiques and the fitness levels of the horses vary to a significant degree. A three-day horse can't be expected to perform exactly like a Grand Prix dressage horse any more than the upper level dressage horse can be expected to handle a cross-country course exactly like the event horse.

At higher levels of eventing another difference is the breeding of the horses. The hotter Thoroughbreds typically found in eventing have to be handled differently than the typical warmblood found in upper level dressage. The higher level three-day horse loses the round, compact, collecting muscles. The dressage training takes a back seat to fitness work. Also, speed work requires a different level of concentration.

Still, the dressage test is very, very important. Eventers have a saying, "You can only *win* the event in dressage, but you can *lose* it in cross-country or stadium."

What is meant by that is the dressage score is the only place you can hope to *gain points;* after that, penalty points are deducted from your score. The only way to better your placing beyond the dressage phase is for competitors above you to make mistakes and drop back.

All this seems to point out the fact that good dressage training is just as important to the combined training horse as to the "straight" dressage horse. And don't worry, the judges will know it when they see it.

Pony Club

This organization of dedicated volunteers began in England in 1929 as the junior branch of the Institute of the Horse. The Pony Club name refers to the age of the members, not the size of the animal. Children may join at a young age and be active members until their twenty-first birthday. Parents are encouraged to be active in club activities, although responsibility for the horse is in the hands of the "Pony Clubber."

Pony Club, which has expanded to many parts of the world (the United States joined in 1953), encourages young people to ride and enjoy all kinds of sport connected with horses. It provides instruction in the English style of riding and in the proper care of horses. It promotes the highest ideals of sportsmanship, citizenship, and loyalty, thus teaching strength of character and self-discipline.

The United States Pony Club welcomes children at all riding levels. Like an ascending alphabet, the horsemanship ratings begin at "D 1" (safe horsemanship at a walk or trot), to "D 2" (walk, trot, and canter with preliminary jumping) up through "C" and "B" to "A." Very few reach the "A" rating, for it represents outstanding achievement and dedication.

Instructors stress stable management at all levels to insure that horses are comfortable and safe, well-fed, watered, groomed, and their feet kept properly shod. They also teach basic principles of first aid for horses and humans and care and correct use of saddlery.

Pony Club Rallies

The competitions staged by Pony Clubs are called rallies. They are meant to be an opportunity for the children to exhibit their progress in the requirements of their various Pony Club ratings. A rated dressage judge usually judges the dressage portion. The standards of the tests are somewhat different from the AHSA dressage tests. The Pony Club "D1" and "D2" tests are similar to the USDF Introductory tests.

The A, B, C, and D standards of performance for the dressage ring are outlined below.

D LEVEL

The Pony Clubber is judged on her ability to control the horse at an elementary level. She learns to ride independently, maintaining a secure position at the walk, trot, and canter. She must be able to direct the horse through the required movements and not merely be carted around the ring. She is encouraged to ride quietly and the horse should be basically obedient and consistent.

C LEVEL

The Pony Clubber learns to ride with confidence and control. She develops an independent seat with coordinated use of the aids. She learns to initiate and maintain free, rhythmic, forward movement, and to make smooth transitions. The horse is relaxed and obedient, stretching into and accepting the bit in a calm, receptive manner.

B LEVEL

The Pony Clubber should be able to demonstrate a secure seat with effective and tactful use of the aids. She should be able to ride the horse forward with relaxation and rhythm, while establishing soft response to the aids. Examples of this are: softening of the lower jaw, some flexion at the poll, lateral bending, and quiet transitions.

A LEVEL

The Pony Clubber should demonstrate competence and sympathy for the horse's capabilities. She should be able to maintain suppleness, lightness, rhythm, and balance while engaging the horse in school figures and accurate dressage movements. She must be able to put the horse to the aids; in other words, put the horse on the bit and keep it there without evasion or a fight and without shortening the strides. (Equivalent to AHSA First Level.)

In Pony Club it is highly recommended that dressage judges give a brief, constructive critique to each rider immediately following her test. Organizers should allow time in the schedule for this purpose. This is in keeping with the Pony Club concept that a rally has not been successful if it has not been educational. Pony Club sincerely appreciates the judges who give of their time and talents for the benefit of these youngsters.

Chapter Five

Where to Start

Most novice and amateur dressage riders opt for a do-it-yourself approach to dressage competition — and are very successful. They like caring for and training their horses at home, with occasional, or at most once-a-week lessons. Part-time lessons comfortably fit their horse budgets, and they get an "I did it myself!" buzz from hands-on training and showing. The last contributes to a critical element of show ring success — confidence.

Can it work for you? Of course it can — if you have the commitment necessary to study and practice and consistently put what you've learned to work at home and at the shows.

Are You a Good Enough Rider?

It is desirable to achieve a basic competence before your first dressage competition. Ask yourself if you can sit still and keep a steady contact with the reins while applying the aids. You must be able to sit the walk and canter and post the trot without becoming unbalanced. (No need to sit down to the trot until Training Level test 3.)

Many people do not realize how much they move their bodies and how unsteady their hands and legs are. They lean forward when they want to go faster and lean backward when they slow down; they kick with the heels, and their arms unintentionally react by jerking; they lose their balance slightly and save themselves from being left behind by hanging onto the reins. They think they have a steady contact with the horse's mouth, but frequently the reins sag for a moment or two, showing that the contact has been broken. Some do not hold the reins firmly, so that the reins are always slipping through the fingers, causing the rider to readjust them constantly. Other people do not sit straight —

one hip may be higher than the other, or one shoulder ahead of the other.

A good equitation teacher can usually correct these and other faults so that the rider is relaxed, yet can control her movements and not give unintentional signals to the horse with legs, reins, or weight. The rider must be able to keep a consistent contact with the horse's mouth at the walk and canter and to keep the hands steady while trotting.

You don't need to be a perfect rider, however. In Chapter 9 are corrections for minor posture and position problems that you can correct on your own.

Can You School a Horse?

After all, dressage is training, and there is a difference between equitation and training. Equitation is the *ability to adapt to the movement* of the horse, to insure security and harmony. Training is being able to *gain influence* over the horse's movements.

This is not to say equitation is not important, because without equitation, training (from the horse's back) is impossible! But there is a big difference between the two.

A person is not ready to undertake dressage (which is training the horse while you ride) until her seat and aids are so well-developed that it takes virtually no thought to apply them. In other words, in order to train, the rider's reactions must be both secure and automatic. The good news is, since dressage competition starts with Training Level, which is simple walk, trot, canter, and easy transitions, if you can ride those basics, you can ride, train, compete, and improve right along with your horse.

In the United States, nearly every aspiring dressage rider schools her own horse. Some have previously schooled other types of horses and know how to go about it, but most have only ridden horses for pleasure. So the instructor has to teach the rider how to do something new and how to teach the horse as well. It is surprising how well it works. Almost any reasonably adept rider seems to manage, provided she is determined, patient, hard working and thoughtful, and provided she has confidence in her horse, instructor, and herself.

You Need to Learn to Concentrate

It takes a tremendous amount of concentration to train dressage. After all, this dressage is *your* idea, not your horse's. If you want him to perform to the best of his ability, it is up to you to make it happen, because he would much rather lounge around the pasture! If you want your horse to concentrate, you need to concentrate.

But you can't make yourself concentrate by telling yourself "I have to concentrate now." Instead, you must assign yourself tasks. If you concentrate on the task, you will concentrate on how your horse and you are performing.

How do you achieve this happy state of concentration while riding? For some, the path is more difficult than others. The stirrups may feel wrong, a dog starts barking, your horse sees a gremlin behind a tree, a gust of wind comes along. The way to deal with these intrusions is to accept them as facts and immediately disregard them without further consideration. Simply tell yourself, "That is a dog, it means no harm," and go on with your riding. Do not dwell on the negative. The stirrups really are okay, the dog is friendly, the gremlin disappears, and the wind actually feels good. Your riding awareness and concentration have hardly been disrupted after all. Having dismissed it all from your mind, you can get back to the business of riding — and your horse will take his cue from you.

Throughout this business of dressage training, the physical demands will increase for the horse, but the mental demands will increase for the rider.

How Much Time? How Often?

How much time do you need to devote to riding and training? At a *minimum*, three riding sessions a week for the rider on a schooled horse. This is usually enough practice time for a rider that is still learning position and aids. For the purpose of schooling the young or inexperienced horse, at least four days a week. Five or six sessions may be better.

Short work sessions are best. Twenty or 30 minutes per training session is generally plenty for a young or unfit horse, 40 to 45 minutes for the mature animal. Also with the mature animal, vary the time from day to day. Thirty minutes one day, 40 to 45 the next, then back to 30, maybe an hour on some days. This way your horse doesn't say, "Ah, 30 minutes is up, I quit!"

If you need more work on fitness, then work the horse twice a day (at least on weekends). This way you will get the horse fit (muscled) without boring him to death or teaching him to conserve energy. You will have a hard time achieving "brilliance" if your horse believes he is being trained for endurance!

A COUPLE OF TRAINING TIPS:

Don't bore your dressage horse or overstress his legs by only working in the ring. Most trainers agree that at least part of your riding time should be outside the arena. Furthermore, you shouldn't follow the same routine day after day. A businesslike (no dawdling) hack through the woods or a group ride with other horses will do your horse as much good as a lesson in the ring — and more mental good because he won't realize he's working!

Do not drill. The tedium of pointless drilling is at the root of many horses' resistance and problem behaviors. If the horse can already perform a skill perfectly, why repeat it without variation? If the horse *can't* perform the skill perfectly, why hammer at it incessantly, as though a hundred unceasingly frustrated wrong executions suddenly are going to produce a right? If you hit a snag in your training, get some expert advice, do some research or do some experimenting on your own.

Another training aid can be to periodically longe your horse so you can see what he is doing and how he is moving. Trainers recommend longeing at almost every stage of training because it can be used to improve as well as monitor the horse.

In addition, there are many books (see listing in the Appendix), magazines, and videos on riding, training, and showing in dressage. Make use of every opportunity to learn more about this fascinating subject.

Science or Art?

Dressage is never tricks. Each movement or exercise has a purpose and a reason for being performed. When performed properly, the movements make a horse move more beautifully than he did before. But dressage must be practiced as a science before it becomes an art. Just like you must practice the scales before you can play a Mozart concerto, you must practice the basics before you can ride a Grand Prix test. The good news is you are probably familiar with at least some of the basics already. Dressage is training by natural methods.

A Plan

Training and showing with minimal professional help will require you to be proactive, investigative, and sometimes innovative. You must learn to set goals, keep appointed lesson and show times, ask questions, and consistently follow through with what you've learned. What shouldn't you do? Whine, make excuses, and give up your program if your first show experience doesn't net you an expected score or ribbon. The following steps will help you prepare for a "show-alone" program.

Finding the Right Competition

Interested in attending a dressage competition but unsure how to find a prize list? In addition to keeping an ear out for the local equestrian word of mouth, check out these sources of information:

- Ask your trainer or instructor to keep you informed of shows appropriate to your riding level.
- Review tack store bulletin boards and flyers for event announcements.
- Check the advertisements and events calendars in equestrian publications and local and regional newsletters. Advertising flyers, available for free in some tack stores, also provide good listings of upcoming events.
- Contact the United States Dressage Federation listing of Group Member Organizations.
- At local horse shows, talk to riders participating in your discipline about upcoming events.
- Contact your state horse council for events, dates, and schedules.
- Post a query on a horse-related Internet bulletin board, and do some browsing on the World Wide Web for listings of the events that interest you.

1. FIND A COACH, TRAINER, OR GROUND PERSON

No one can train in a vacuum. Even the top international-caliber competitors have a coach or ground person to be their "eyes on the ground", to watch and verify that the horse is progressing as he should. A ground person is an experienced horse person who watches you work and tells you what she sees. If you are just starting in dressage, it is a definite advantage to have a knowledgeable instructor or trainer who is familiar with the objects of dressage.

If you don't already have a dressage instructor or trainer, check around. Most trainers will accept "haul in" students; check with the trainer of your choice, to be sure she will. If your candidate won't accept part-time students, ask her to recommend a reputable trainer in your area who will.

If you already have a trainer, discuss with her your interest in competition and ask her if she would be able to help you outline your goals and establish a plan for you to attain those goals. It is important that you be able to work with her to set a specific, attainable objective for each lesson — one that will build toward your success in the show arena.

If you don't have a trainer, or even if you do, it is an advantage to occasionally have a knowledgeable "ground person" watch you. This person can be a spouse, relative, or friend you trust to give moral support when you need it, observe how your horse responds to new experiences, perhaps groom for you at the show, and call your tests if you need it.

You can't see your horse's suspension or his stride, and you can't always be sure whether he's truly relaxed, for instance, or being lazy. You can't see if he's tracking straight, or if you're sitting straight. Something that feels good, or that you've grown used to, may in fact be incorrect. The ground person is interpreter between what the rider *thinks* is happening and what is *actually* happening.

If you don't have an experienced person to watch you, you can train a ground person to observe and relate what she sees. In dressage, generally speaking, when it's right, it looks right. Find photos of horses that move like yours and have similar conformation (so abilities will be similar) and show them to your helper with the instruction, "When we look like that, tell me." Your helper can see the horse's position, tell you what's happening, and help you avoid ingraining bad habits.

Figure 5.1
Although you should know your test thoroughly, it is comforting to have a caller.

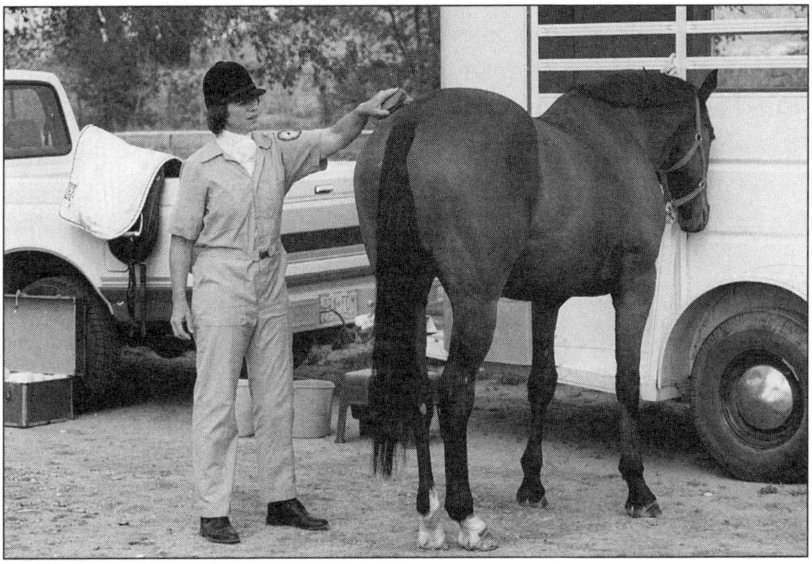

Figure 5.2
At most schooling shows plan on working out of your horse trailer. Photo by Charlene Strickland.

2. BRING HELP OR GREAT ORGANIZATION TO A SHOW

At dressage shows, you don't need a trainer with you as much as you need someone to help get you and your horse ready and perhaps call your tests. This person is traditionally called a groom, although the position calls for much more than grooming the horse. It is very helpful, for example, to have someone hold the horse while you get your hat and stock tie on straight, to carry your coat to the warm-up arena if it's a hot day, or to be your caller during the test (figure 5.1).

About ten minutes before the test, put on your coat and ask your groom to wipe the dust off your boots and the slobber off the horse's mouth. After the test the groom can take the horse when you dismount. White gloves, breeches, and black coats do not look good after a slobbery horse has rubbed his head on you!

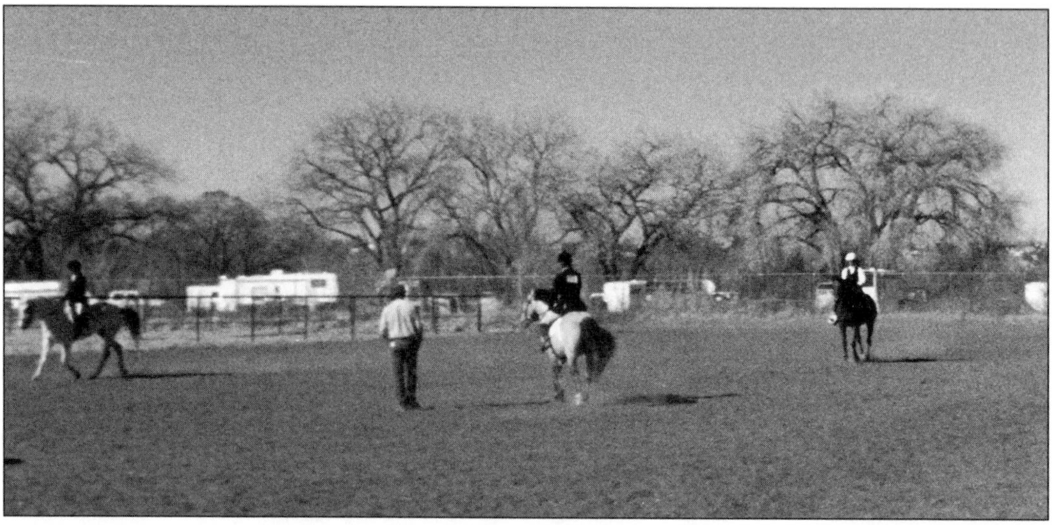

Figure 5.3 Many times the warm-up "arena" is merely an open area.

It is possible to go to shows by yourself. You just have to have everything planned. Wear coveralls until you are ready to mount. If it's really hot, turn your coat inside out and hang it on the fence near the warm-up area. It is probably not a good idea to try this until you are very experienced at showing, however (figure 5.2).

3. DO NOT BITE OFF MORE THAN YOU CAN CHEW

When sending in entries to a competition, enter at the level and the tests you are presently comfortable with. Don't enter a test with the idea that, "We will learn to leg yield (or whatever) by the time the show comes around." Most likely, in your scramble to learn to leg yield, you will compromise your other qualities (an even bend, forward impulse, for example). You can still use a leg yield in schooling, which will probably improve your other qualities in the meantime.

Know what level and test you are aiming for and the exercises and movements that are required. Plan the order of accomplishments you are aiming for and don't over-face yourself or your horse.

4. LEARN TO PROBLEM-SOLVE

Even if your trainer is at the show, she can't coach you *during* a test. You must learn how to work through specific dilemmas independently. For example, if your horse tends to speed up his canter on the straightaway, don't just wait for your trainer to tell you what to do. Ask how to fix it when she's not there. If you can learn to solve problems in a lesson, you can do so at home. And if you can do it at home, you can do it at a show. If you don't have someone to rely on all the time, you eventually get the problems figured out and the solutions stick with you.

5. DO YOUR HOMEWORK

After each lesson, ask for assignments or exercises that will help you reinforce achievement of the prior lesson's objective. Then, in your next lesson, your trainer can grade your progress. She then may choose to spend more time on that objective, or to move on to another.

6. DEVELOP A WARM-UP STRATEGY

Work with your trainer to develop a consistent warm-up routine. By using that warm-up sequence every time you school your horse, you'll have a comfortable, familiar routine to use when you're on your own at shows (figure 5.3). This not only will work to focus both your own and your horse's attention on the task at hand, it will also help you both battle horse-show jitters. See Chapter 16 for a sample warm-up routine.

7. STAY AWAY FROM GADGETS

Knowledgeable trainers train with a plain snaffle (or a simple double bridle when the horse is ready). Martingales, draw reins, chambons, gag reins — forget them. They are crutches and when you take them away the problem is still there, perhaps even worse. If a horse is stiff, resistant, lazy, or strong, these are training issues, not bitting or gadget issues. Gadgets may conceal a problem for a while, but they cure nothing, and they eventually create attitude problems. When you find yourself asking, "What bit do I need to put in his mouth?" change the question to "What do I need to teach him?"

8. HAVE YOUR CLASSES AND TESTS VIDEOTAPED

This can be one of the best tools for a rider to see the "picture" she is presenting. Regardless of how it may feel to you, whoever said "a picture is worth a thousand words," probably rode dressage.

A videotape gives you and your trainer or ground person a rail-side view of your performance under pressure. If the person making the video stands at "A" or "C", it helps you to see how your performance looks to a judge.

9. DO NOT ALWAYS BLAME YOURSELF

Of course, check yourself out first. If you think you rode correctly, then figure out why the horse is not responding. Is he being lazy? Is he tired or sore? Is he scared or uncertain of what you want? Or is he just testing to see if he can get his own way? You need to take in all the data available to you and figure out the solution.

10. DO NOT SWEAT THE MISTAKES

You rode off course? Missed a lead? Let it go, regain your composure, and concentrate on performing well for the rest of the test. Keep in mind that even professionals make such mistakes. However, they've learned, as you will, that persevering in spite of problems can salvage more than your pride — it could net you a ribbon, or even a really good score.

Always Remember:

- Enjoy your horse.
- Establish a firm and warm friendship with him right from the beginning.
- Love and discipline him as a parent would.
- Lots of brushing and cleaning makes a horse feel good.
- Remember, your horse will be able to sense your feelings and emotions from the moment you enter his presence, and will act accordingly.

Competing on a Budget

Another often asked question is "What is dressage competition going to cost me?" Dressage competition doesn't cost any more than any other form of equestrian competition and a good deal less than some. This assumes that you already have a horse, English saddle, bridle, and riding boots. You must come up with the ways and means to cover show attire (for both horse and rider), transportation, hotel, food, supplies, and show fees.

The good news is clothing styles (or colors) don't change from year to year, nor does horse equipment. Once you have a good, well-fitting coat, hat, boots, saddle, and bridle, they will give you many years of service.

Maximizing your assets simply requires knowing and choosing the best options for you and your horse while on the road. Here is a sampling of cost-cutting suggestions designed to do just that. Keep in mind that the prices quoted were averaged from different regions around the country. Call your local supplier for specific information.

Transportation

Obviously you must be able to get yourself and your horse to the competition. If you intend to show often, buying your own trailer (and a vehicle to tow it with) will probably be the most economical route, rather than paying for transportation to every show. Although you'll be faced with insurance, upkeep, and the cost of gas for a trailer laden with horses and tack, there are ways to help sideline some of the expense. For example, since it costs virtually the same to haul one horse as it does two, charging your trailerless friends to take their horse to the show can help.

Of course it's important for the trailer owner to consider the ramifications of friends hauling friends in the case of an accident. Check that your auto insurance covers hauling livestock. If you already have a mortality policy on your horse, check to see if the transportation clause is active and who is included. And be sure to include the cost in your show budget.

If you are hauling others, you should know that you'll need a commercial hauling license if your rig is over 26,000 pounds (a semi-trailer). A normal two-horse trailer weighs 1800 to 2400 pounds when it's empty. Add the weight of each horse and 300 pounds of equipment and feed per horse.

If you do not have your own trailer you might be able to find someone else going to the same show that has a trailer. If you board at a large facility, word of mouth and advertising on the bulletin board in advance may get you a ride. The barter system, or working off trailering, is a viable option — braiding, body clipping, boot and tack cleaning, mane pulling, show trimming, and other specialized grooming projects are valuable commodities to the time-pressed horse owner. Put up signs offering braiding in exchange for trailering, with the fees and skill you have to offer.

If you do haul your horse with someone else, do her and yourself a favor: teach your horse to load and travel *before* the show day. The trailer owner will probably be experienced enough to help you teach your horse to load and travel.

But suppose you don't know anyone with a trailer? What if you live miles from civilization? If you only frequent two or three shows per year, using a professional shipper may be the answer. Or perhaps you can rent a two-horse trailer and a truck with a trailer hitch. Consult the yellow pages. And be sure to practice driving it before the day of the show.

Transportation companies, which can often be found in regional horse publications, haul horses by distance. Their prices usually range from $0.90 to $1 per mile with a minimum dollar amount. Therefore, traveling to a one-day show 30 miles away could cost $54 to $60, depending on the average rates. One way to cut the expense is to double up; a second horse often goes for half price and more than three horses may merit a group discount.

If you use a commercial hauler, you will probably take your tack, clothes, and equipment in your private car. Here again, you may be able to carpool.

Lodging

When you are going to one day shows, you may opt to leave early enough to arrive in sufficient time for your scheduled ride times, then pack up and leave after your last ride. Therefore, you will not need lodging.

You may be able to stay with friends or relatives in the area for multi-day shows. Sometimes show management can suggest homes of local exhibitors who will put you up for a night or two, or suggest user-friendly hotel or motel accommodations near the showgrounds. Sometimes the show will contract with a local hotel for group rates.

Contacting the show organizers is the best way to locate receptive lodging in the area, saving you valuable time on phone calls. Before that, scan your prize list for the advertising motels since these are the most likely to be close to the show grounds.

If you know of other competitors, ask about suites designed for four people. If you have a large group, contacting the manager of the motel you intend to stay in is the best bet for reserving a block of discount rooms.

For hardier individuals, camping represents a viable and frugal alternative, if weather permits. Many competitors travel to competitions in recreational vehicles, saving money on lodging and meals and allowing them to stay close to or on the show grounds.

Adventurous types find that the most economical alternative involves sleeping in a stall, 4-H style. At shows that aren't heavily attended, a spare stall and cot may be an abode for a night or two. Tough do-it-yourselfers have been known to stretch out on air mattresses in the back of pickups or conversion vans. Of course, bringing bug repellent and even mosquito netting is advisable, depending on the season. If you do plan to sleep on the show grounds, let management and security personnel know.

Food on the Go

While fast food restaurants are priced right, no one wants to eat hamburgers and fries three times a day (nor is it nutritionally sound to do so — see Chapter 10). Grocery store and delicatessen fare is economically feasible, and requires only a little advanced planning. Potato salad from the deli, plus sandwiches and fruit, make a fast lunch with almost no preparation. Keeping quantities of lemonade or fruit juices and iced tea in a cooler saves money over expensive concession stand drinks. In a well-insulated cooler, simple dishes, sandwiches, and drinks can be made in large quantities ready to be nibbled at all day long.

Stabling

You will probably need stabling for your horse if you go to a multi-day show. Some shows require you to keep your horse on the grounds; at others you may be able to stable in the area.

Overnight stabling averages $25-40 per night for a stall with bedding. Sometimes bedding (either straw or wood shavings) are included, sometimes you must bring or buy them separately.

THE SHOW TACK ROOM

If you don't have a trailer, but need to store tack at the show, consider renting a tack stall. This will give you a place to store your tack for a multi-day show and can double as a resting spot either between classes or even for overnight. If you are leaving tack in a stall overnight, be sure to padlock the entrance. Fellow exhibitors are very unlikely to touch your equipment, but there may be others who are not so conscientious. This goes for locking your car and trailer and keeping your purse out of sight at all times. At overnight shows where you must leave your trailer unhitched, put an inexpensive locking device on the hitch to prevent theft.

Show Fees

One unavoidable expense is the price of entry fees. Entry fees at recognized shows or events can run $20 to $40 per test, plus drug fees, stabling fees, office fees, and sometimes membership fees. Schooling show fees generally run considerably less than $20 per class.

If you plan to show more than once at AHSA-recognized shows, it's prudent to buy an annual membership, because otherwise you are subject to a $20 non-member fee at every show. You will also receive the current AHSA Rule Book with your membership.

At recognized shows (and sometimes at schooling shows) you may need a couple of medical documents on hand when you travel. This is especially important if you'll be crossing state lines en route to your destination. While the documentation requirements vary from state to state, at the very least you'll need to have the results of a recent Coggins test for Equine Infectious Anemia (EIA). Many states require that you also have a certificate of veterinary inspection (CVI). To avoid confusion, you may want to check with the state veterinarian for the requirements of each state you plan to travel through.

Figure 5.4 Dressage shows should be fun. Remember to smile! Photo by Charlene Strickland.

Chapter Six

The Horse

Almost any sound, free-moving horse of fair conformation is capable of attaining at least "sufficient" scores in Training and First Level — which is where nearly everybody starts out. If a rider feels comfortable on a particular horse, the rider can learn to help the horse beat minor structural and even temperamental disadvantages with correct riding. It is only for advanced work that a horse with special talents or conformation is needed.

Of course you can buy a horse that is already well schooled and has successfully competed in dressage competitions, but a horse with a lot of training or a successful show record is going to be expensive. Training adds value to any horse.

If you are contemplating buying or borrowing a "school master" (see Sidebar 6-A) with the intention of competing, be certain that the horse is serviceably sound. Judges are quite strict about dismissing a horse that so much as appears lame, and only certain mild medications are allowed.

In addition, if you choose to buy a proven competitive horse, do not underestimate the amount of training you will require in order to ride the horse effectively. There is a saying: "You can't *buy* a dressage horse." Dressage is not a matter of "learning where the buttons are" or mounting a horse after the trainer has "tuned it up." Dressage (remember it means training the horse *while* you ride), is a matter of having good balance and "feel" for the horse. If a rider is not in good balance, does not have a good grounding in the dressage method of riding, and does not have an understanding of the mind and body of the horse, she cannot give an aid the way it should be given, and the horse will perform poorly or not at all. *This is what levels the field* between the fancy horses and the plainer horses — the rider makes all the difference. It's the rider who is the "brains" of the partnership. Your scores will reflect the amount of work,

The Care of Feeding of Older Horses

Many new to dressage riders opt to buy an already dressage trained and campaigned horse. These well-trained horses are called "school masters." Typically, these horses are in their teens or even 20's. Also, many riders take up dressage riding later in life, and often continue to use the horse they already own.

The good news is, dressage horses commonly stay healthier and in work longer than horses in many other "professions." Of course it takes a little more care, time, and attention to keep an older horse going, but the rewards often outweigh the disadvantages. The key to keeping an older horse in work is keeping him fit. The way to keep him fit is with moderate but consistent exercise. Exactly how much and what kind of work to do depends on the individual, but a few guiding principles apply overall:

Take it easy. "Little and often" is the key. Plan work that keeps your horse in good shape without pounding joints. Use various exercises to work different sets of muscles. Older horses also tend to lose aerobic capacity — the heart and lungs become less efficient at delivering oxygen to muscles. Use easy cross-country hacks and three- to five-minute trot and canter intervals, walking in between to let his breathing and heart rate recover.

Be consistent. Keep the work level as consistent as you can. Ideally, ride lightly every day or every other day. If you save your horse for the weekends, he'll get stiff and out of shape over the week and be more prone to injury when you do ride. Before a clinic or show, build up over a period of weeks to the level of work he'll do there. Have a plan, whether it's fifteen or forty-five minutes of work a day — whatever suits the horse.

Warm up, cool down. Your horse's muscles and joints may be stiff when he starts work, making his strides short and his back tight. An older horse will take at *least twice* as long to warm up and cool down. Walk him for at least ten minutes, then trot on a long rein or until you feel him moving forward freely. If the weather's cold, warm his hindquarter muscles with a quarter sheet. Finish sessions with an equally long cool down walk (until he's totally dry). If the cool down is too short the horse will be stiff the next day.

In cool weather immediately put a woolen cooler over his shoulders, back, and loins. In hot weather wash his back with lukewarm water and keep him moving until he's cool.

Work on good footing. Old muscles, tendons, and ligaments aren't as resilient as young ones. Don't take chances asking your horse to work on hard, slick, or too-deep surfaces. If it rains the night before an outdoor show and the arenas are deep or slippery, ask yourself: "Is the price of the entry fee worth possibly crippling my horse?"

Team up. Your veterinarian and your farrier are your partners in seeing that your horse gets what he needs before minor problems snowball. Rare is the older horse that doesn't show some signs of stiffness and soreness. Yours may need the support of a bar shoe or wedge pads, or an occasional dose of aspirin or phenylbutazone ("bute") to stay comfortable, or he may need his hocks injected with hyaluronic acid or supporting treatment with dietary joint-health supplements your veterinary recommends. He may need more turnout time to keep him moving around and staying limber or an extra long grooming session to massage his muscles.

Be alert for signs that it's time to reduce his work level. Even with the most caring maintenance, athletic abilities gradually decline, usually beginning in the late teens. One of the first symptoms is a decrease in stride length. He's just not covering the amount of ground he was a year ago, or you're having to push harder to get the same stride length. You're not getting that extended trot anymore — it has degraded to a Second Level "medium." When that becomes a pattern, and you can't manage it with your usual veterinary care, drop down to a lower level or perhaps it's time to pass the horse on to a pleasure rider. Dressage horses are used to people and the attention, so don't just dump your old campaigner in a back pasture and forget about him. He'll still be a useful, happy horse for several more years if he gets the attention he deserves.

attention and thought you are willing to put into it.

When looking at a horse for a novice rider, focus on steadiness and suitability to the rider. Novice riders will do best if they begin their dressage competition career on quiet, reasonably trained horses — what we Westerners call "well broke": capable of a steady walk, trot, and canter on both leads and able to stop and turn with little effort. The horse must be controllable in a plain snaffle bit (more on this later); and be compatible with the rider in size and temperament.

The horse must be able to perform calmly in a strange place. (The rider will probably want to take lessons, which may be away from home, even if they don't actually compete.) The rider who feels comfortable on her horse can put all her energy into performing a good test, rather than into worrying about her horse's behavior. This cooperation between horse and rider is necessary if you are going to earn good scores.

Always work with a horse compatible with your ability at the time. The older, already trained horse for the novice rider and the young horse in the hands of the experienced rider are training rules that also apply to competition. For one thing, an older horse is more set in his patterns of behavior, which gives a novice rider more time to think about what she needs to do to alter or improve a particular performance.

It is usually not a good idea for beginning riders who are still in the basic learning process to buy expensive young horses with "lots of potential." A horse that moves well is actually much more difficult to ride because its stride is quite different (much bigger) than that of the horses that are ideal to learn on.

Also consider how much work is going to be on *you*, the rider. If you need to do a lot of repetition work (correcting position habits and perfecting aids, for example), you need a horse that has a lot of patience. Bright, intelligent horses will get bored quickly. If you need a lot of work on your position, or you are a bit awkward, the calmer, quiet horse is less likely to resent the repetition.

Even horses with less than ideal conformation can still "do" the dressage movements — although they may not be impressive enough to get top scores. Do not let that be an obstacle to learning, however.

The bottom line is if you already have a horse that suits you, he's what you should use for learning dressage. If he isn't ideal but you can't go out and buy yourself a fancier or better-trained horse — and most of us can't — use what you have.

Here are the AHSA rules pertaining to the horse:

"Dressage competitions are open to...horses or ponies. Stallions are permitted in all classes. Horses showing evidence of broken wind or complete loss of sight in either eye are permitted to compete. No horse may compete in any under saddle class if it is under thirty-six months of age at the time of competition." (AHSA, Art. 1919.1)

As you can see there are no restrictions to size, breed, or sex. Mules are not permitted in AHSA recognized competitions, but are permitted in USDF sanctioned competition. (This would be league competitions and schooling shows, which are not AHSA recognized.) One other requirement of the horse, pony, or mule is a true walk, trot, and canter.

Gaits

Every movement of every test is based on a gait. Circles are done at trot or canter, leg yield is done at the trot, shoulder-in at the trot, flying lead changes at the canter, and so on. Therefore, the dressage horse (for any level) must have three pure gaits. This does not mean gorgeous gaits, although that is a definite advantage in the competition arena; the requirement is that the gaits be pure and regular.

The definition of "Gait" is: "Any of the various foot movements of a horse, as a walk,

	TEST	DIRECTIVE IDEAS	PT	coefficient	TOTAL	REMARKS
1. A X	Enter working trot Halt, Salute Proceed working trot	Straightness on centerline transitions, quality of halt and trot				
2. C M-B-F	Track right Straight ahead	Quality of turn at C, quality of trot, straightness				
3. A	Circle right 20m	Quality of trot, roundness of circle				
4. K-X-M	Change rein	Quality of trot, straightness				
5. C	Circle left 20m	Quality of trot, roundness of circle				
6. H-X-F	Change rein	Quality of trot, straightness				
7. A	Medium walk	Transition, quality of walk				
8. K-B B-M	Free walk Medium walk	Straightness, quality of walks, transitions		2		
9. M	Working trot	Balance during transition				
10. between C & H	Working canter left lead	Calmness and smoothness of depart				
11. E	Circle left 20m	Quality of canter, roundness of circle				
12. between E & K	Working trot	Smoothness of transition				
13. B E	Turn left Turn right	Quality of trot, quality of turns at B and E, straightness between turns				
14. between C & M	Working trot	Calmness and smoothness of depart				
15. B	Circle right 20m	Quality of canter, roundness of circle				
16. between B & F	Working trot	Smoothness of transition				
17. A X	Down centerline Halt, Salute	Straightness on centerline, quality of trot and halt				
Leave arena at walk at A						

Figure 6.1 Every test has a column of "directive ideas" listing the essential qualities a judge is looking for in each movement. Reprinted by permission of the American Horse Shows Association.

trot, pace, canter or gallop. For dressage purposes, there are three (required) gaits — walk, trot, and canter." (USDF Glossary)

The "pace" as defined above is a gait in which the lateral pairs of legs move in unison — not a correct gait for dressage! For the purposes of this book "pace" will be used interchangeable with "gait" to mean a walk, trot, or canter.

The "*quality*" of a gait (as listed under "directives ideas" of the test) is defined as elasticity, suppleness, suspension, and overtrack, and is judged in virtually every movement. Therefore the dressage rider must be able to demonstrate her horse's very best gaits in a test (figure 6.1).

The movements (circles, leg yield, shoulder-in, lengthenings, and flying changes, to name a few) are not really the important aspects of the tests. They are the training tools that allow you to enhance and show off your horse's good gaits and give the judge a method

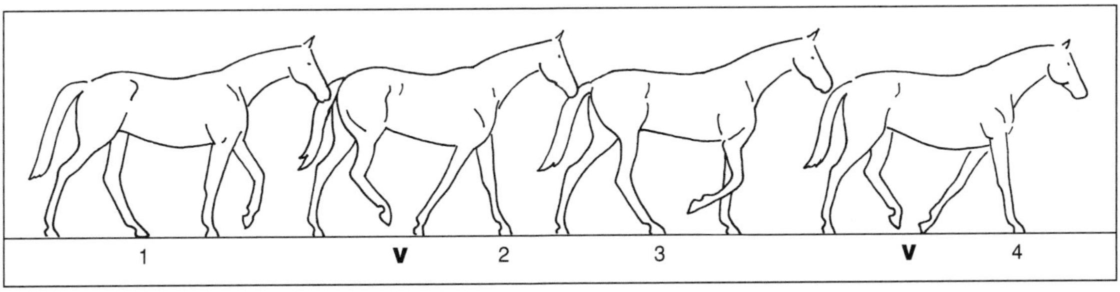

Figure 6.2 A correct walk shows a "V" twice in every stride.

Figure 6.3 A lateral walk, where a horse moves both legs on one side forward simultaneously, is a bad fault.

to compare the different horses. This is why the gaits must be pure, as discussed under judging the Collective Marks in Chapter 3, and the gaits must be shown to that horse's best ability.

Any properly trained horse with a pure four-beat walk, an even two-beat trot, and a three-beat canter on both leads is capable of at least 6's on all movements involving a gait. These scores can, of course, be raised by demonstrating excellent transitions and figures, or lowered by demonstrating the opposite. Granted, a horse with "brilliant" gaits may get 7's and 8's on the very same movements, but 6's are not to be scoffed at.

Now let's look at the gaits individually.

The Walk

The ideal walk shows the qualities stated in the AHSA Rule Book:

"The walk is a marching pace in which the footfalls of the horse's feet follow one another in "four time", well marked and maintained in all work at the walk.

When the four beats cease to be distinctly marked, even and regular, the walk is disunited or broken." (AHSA, Art. 1903)

In the walk the horse should move his legs one after the other so that four hoof beats may be heard. There should be a characteristic "V" apparent in the configuration of the legs (see figure 6.2) in every stride. It is a fault when the legs are not put forward in the same rhythm and the same length of stride. It is a very bad fault if the horse moves forward with both legs of one side at the same time, called a "lateral walk" (figure 6.3).

Irregularities or a lateral walk are usually caused by tension in the horse's back. This can be caused by the rider restricting the horse's movement with the reins or by natural tension in the horse. It is the rider's responsibility to school the horse so it is relaxed and confident in the competition arena.

Sometimes a lateral walk is caused by conformation (too long or too much bend in the hind legs). The rider may be able to minimize it at the lower levels but the horse is not a good candidate for the upper levels. There are suggestions for correcting a lateral walk in Chapter 12.

A good medium walk (required in Training Level) will show the horse stepping into or slightly past the hoof prints of the front feet. The head carriage will look fairly still but the rider can feel the neck lengthen and shorten at each stride. In the AHSA tests most walk movements have a coefficient that emphasizes its importance.

The Trot

"The trot is a pace of 'two time' on alternate diagonal legs (near left fore and right hind leg and vice versa) separated by a moment of suspension.

"The trot, always with free, active and regular steps, should be moved into without hesitation." (AHSA, Art. 1904)

In the trot, the diagonal legs must be raised from the ground simultaneously and be replaced on the ground together, making two hoof beats. In other words, the forearms and the hind cannon bones must be at the same angle at any point in the stride. There needs to be at least a slight moment of suspension (all four feet off the ground), without which the horse may be described as "earth bound" and will definitely lack impulsion, thrust, or lift (figure 6.4).

Tracking up (stepping the hind hoof into the track left by the fore), or over stride (hind feet stepping beyond the tracks left by the forefeet) is often mentioned by breeders or trainers when assessing the suitability of a horse for dressage. Actually, judges do not look at over stride (or tracking up) so much as whether the horse is putting in an honest effort.

On the other hand, irregularities at the trot are heavily penalized. One of the most common faults in the trot is hurried steps of the forelegs, in which they reach the ground before the diagonal hind legs, so that the front and back diagonal legs make two separate hoof beats instead of one. These horses carry a greater proportion of their weight on their shoulders ("on the forehand"). This is often caused by conformation, but can usually be corrected with diligent riding.

Conformation can also cause an unequal length of stride between front and hind legs. For instance, the horse may make a longer stride with his forelegs, which causes the hind legs to quicken to "keep up."

This type of unequal stride problem

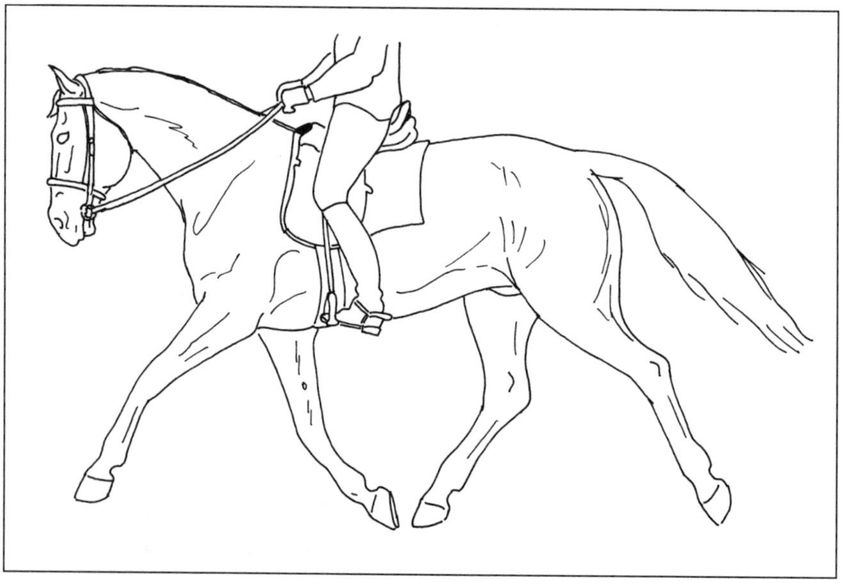

Figure 6.4
In the trot, the diagonal legs must move in unison, and there should be at least a slight moment of suspension.

usually does not become apparent until a lengthened or medium trot is asked for, at First and Second Level. This is because at the low levels the horse will often be able to adjust his strides to match.

A more serious fault is when one hind leg steps more under the body than the other, thus making the strides on one side unequal to those on the other side. If the muscles on one side are stronger or weaker than those on the other side, the horse will find it easier to push off with the strong hind leg. The weaker leg may lag behind, which will make the horse uneven or unlevel.

If you get back a test that says "uneven," "irregular," or "unlevel" (and not just a stride or two in a lengthened trot), but you were not eliminated (for lameness), those words are indicators to you that you need to consider reevaluating your horse's movement. It might be that you did not realize that you had a problem. You may have thought the horse was resisting out of obstinacy.

"Rein lame" and "bridle lame" are terms that some judges use to indicate an unevenness in the horse's gait, presumably caused by a blockage or restriction in the strides on one side. This blockage is thought to be caused by the rider being too restrictive with the reins.

If you get comments like these on a test, go to your trainer and see what she has to say about them. Check that all your tack fits and that you are sitting evenly. You may also need to check for unbalanced shoeing. If angles of the pastern and coffin bone of opposite limbs don't match, the stride can be uneven.

A mechanical deformity such as a clubfoot or the aftermath of a healed injury such as a stretched or contracted tendon that fails to return to its original length when it has mended can certainly cause unevenness. "Loose stifles" (where the joint slips in and out) are often caused by the conformation of hind legs that are too straight (very little angle at stifle and hock), which allows the stifle joint to "slip" during the stride. Loose stifles can sometimes be alleviated by appropriate exercise.

Club feet and mechanical differences can go unnoticed in low or moderate performance, but might be a disadvantage in higher levels where lengthened, medium, or extended trots are more likely to become uneven.

It's also possible you need a veterinary

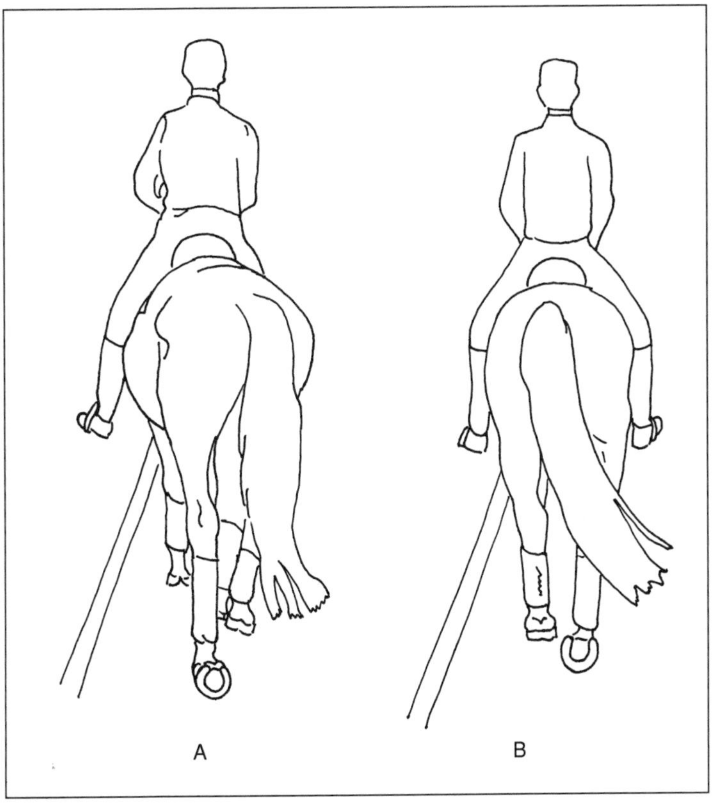

Figure 6.5 Most horses have a slight unevenness at the trot due to natural crookedness. (A) Traveling sideways or "crooked." (B) The same horse traveling straight.

check with stress tests on the limbs. Many horses are sound with no saddle, no rider, and no stress but become lame when one or more of these factors are added. Perhaps the horse's hocks are bothering him (a common problem with older dressage horses). If he is pushing unevenly behind, it may be because he is crooked, or because he just doesn't push with the same intensity with each leg. He may be weak or lazy on one side. These things need to be explored. It may then be possible to correct the unevenness with schooling, training, and maintenance of the horse.

The most common cause of slight unevenness at the trot is the horse's natural crookedness. The crooked horse travels slightly sideways, often on three tracks (figure 6.5).

Most horses have a dominant side (much like humans who are right or left handed). In horses, the dominant side is called "stiff" and the weak side is called "hollow." During the normal process of training, the rider has to try to even up the two sides of the horse.

Crooked horses move with a shortened stride on one side and may favor one canter lead over the other. Minor crookedness or unevenness can often be corrected with appropriate work and exercises; indeed, it is rare to find a horse that is perfectly even on both sides. That is why it is important to work and periodically observe the horse on straight lines as well as circles to check the evenness of development. (Methods for straightening the horse are covered in Chapter 11.)

The Canter

"The canter is a pace of 'three time', where at canter to the right, for instance, the footfalls follow one another as follows: left hind, left diagonal (simultaneously left fore and right hind), right fore, followed by a movement of suspension with all four feet in the air before the next stride begins.

"The canter is always with light, cadenced and regular strides, should be moved into without hesitation." (AHSA Art. 1905)

The canter is incorrect if four hoof beats can be heard (or seen), which happens when the hind leg is put down separately from the corresponding diagonal foreleg. Most four-beat canters can be corrected with proper training (figure 6.6).

Correct leads are a major concern. (On the right lead the horse is bent or curved to the right; on the left lead, bent to the left.) Very often the horse has a "good" lead (takes it easily, stays balanced), and a "poor" lead (difficult to get, and usually or often awkward when the horse does take it). One side of the body being more developed than the other usually causes this discrepancy. Unless the horse is hopelessly "one sided," this can usually be corrected, or at least lessened, with correct training (see Chapter 12).

To Assess Your Horse's Gaits

Many people believe that nothing can be done about the way a horse moves. This simply is not true. Many people have poor posture or walking habits, and it has nothing to do with their conformation. We can change our own "muscle habits" (see Chapter 9), so why can't a horse alter his gait? Barring really bad conformation, a poor mover can be made acceptable, and a good mover made better, as we will see in Chapter 12.

How can you recognize, create, and keep the qualities of good gaits? One way is to put your horse on the longe line. Very often horses do not exhibit their best gaits under saddle. By working a horse on a longe line without the rider, you can observe, adjust, and more importantly, discover your horse's best gaits. Once you know what your horse is capable of, then you can work under saddle to achieve those same qualities (figure 6.7).

At the walk, the horse should over stride at least five or six inches. Some horses are capable of twelve inches or more. The walk

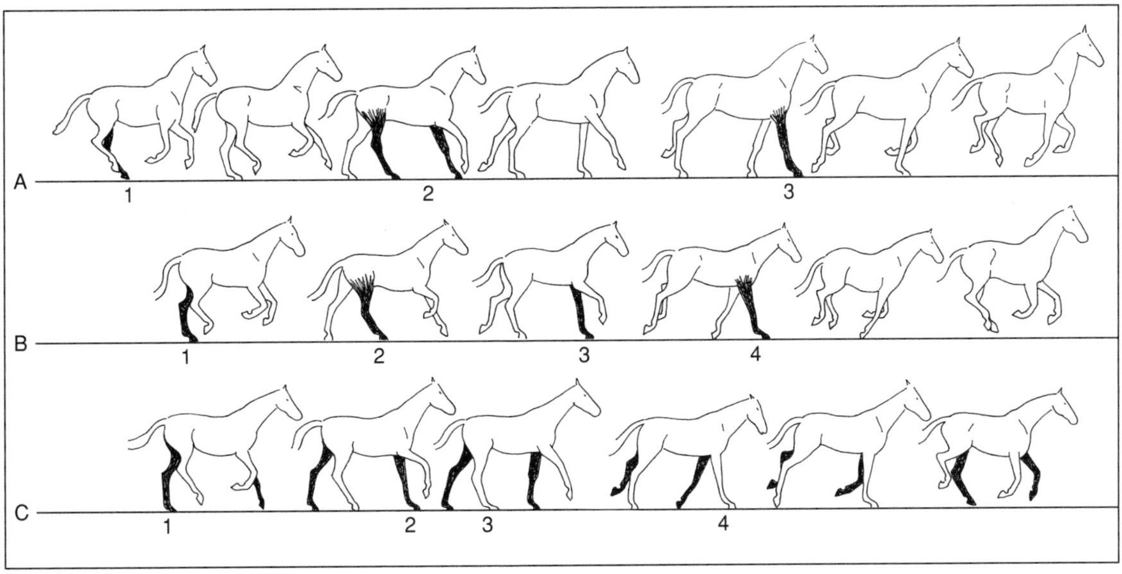

Figure 6.6 (A) A correct three-beat canter, (B) a four-beat or "slow-motion gallop," (C) a lateral canter (also four-beat).

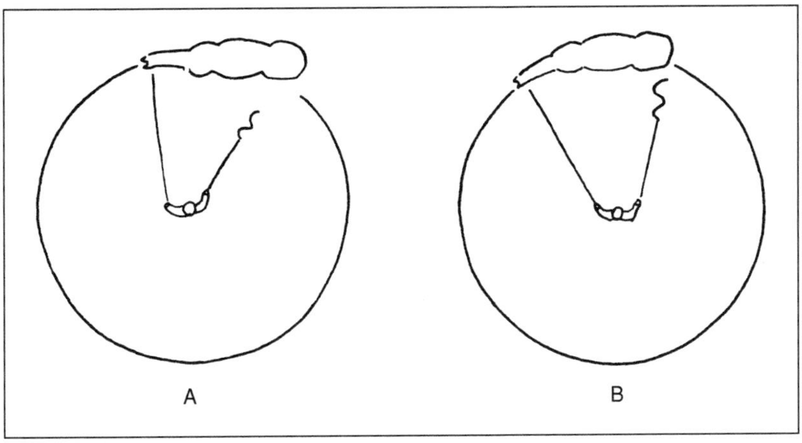

Figure 6.7
A common fault is to try to "pull" the horse with the line, as in (A), which causes the haunches to "fall out." Instead, one should face into the middle of the horse, or a little toward the haunches, and drive the horse into the line, as shown in (B).

should have four definite beats, be long strided, and be energetic without hurrying.

To encourage a longer stride, tap the horse's haunch each time the *inside hind foot* steps forward. If the horse tends to get into two beats — two legs on the same side start striding together — you are probably rushing the horse too much. Experiment until you get your horse's best walk, maintain it for one or two minutes, and then move on to the trot or canter.

At the trot, you want as long a stride as possible with as slow a rhythm as possible. A dressage horse should be able to step in the tracks of his front feet (track up) with energy but without rushing or straining. Drive your horse forward with the whip, "clucking" to accentuate his best rhythm, or slow and calm him with your voice until you find the best trot your horse is capable of. Very often a horse's best trot occurs right after a canter. If this is the case, do a lot of transitions between canter and trot. The cantering loosens their back muscles, and if you don't let them get lazy at the trot you will be amazed at the improvement.

At the canter you are looking for a "rocking" motion. The horse will be very un-balanced on a circle if he "gallops" — no matter how slowly — with a long, flat stride.

You can encourage the rocking motion by flipping the line up at each stride while driving the horse's haunches under with flicks of the whip (figure 6.7). Again, balance driving and calming to find your horse's best canter. The canter must be three-beat, with the hind feet overstriding the front tracks by at least 12 to 18 (or more) inches. If the canter looks "pacey" (legs on the same side are moving together), the horse is either too straight in his body or looking to the outside of the circle. Step a little more to his rear and drive him into a taut line to encourage him to bend his body on the circle. It's like pulling on a bowstring — the more tension you can generate, the more "bow" (bend) you will get.

At all three gaits the horse's hind feet should follow the front on the path of the circle. Bending (the spine) on the circle causes the horse to use his back muscles, which will be visible as the muscles flex over his loins. A horse who uses his back has less bounce, is capable of freer, more powerful motion, and saves his legs from a lot of pounding and strain.

When his steps are springy, when his back is moving and he seems relaxed and free yet energetic, listen to his footfalls and count along with them. Memorize the tempo of each gait until his best working gaits are fixed in your mind. Note how fast the scenery is going past him. Do this at all three gaits and memorize the rate of the beats as well as the rate of progression (relative speed).

When you get on your horse after making these observations, you'll have a good chance of reproducing the tempo and the speed (watch the rate at which the scenery went by). If you have a trainer or ground person, have them tell you when the gait is "good," "better" "not so good," and so forth, so you can memorize the "feel." You will know you have a good working gait when it feels "big" but "springy." If it is strained, jolting, or quick, that is not the horse's best gait.

Making Do with What You've Got

The vast majority of horses below Second Level (and a fair number in Second and Third) are average horses ridden by average riders. They are the same sort of horse that makes a great pleasure horse: horses that are quiet, consistent, attentive, and cooperative.

If you want to compete at the higher levels, however, most trainers concede that you will probably have to work harder with a "non-traditional" horse than with one bred for the performance. Still, most judging bias is in the competitor's mind, not the judges'.

The confident judges are looking more at the critical aspects of the tests than at the conformation of your horse. You can get really good scores at the lower levels with super accuracy and correctness: transitions performed fluently when and where they're supposed to be and having the horse genuinely "on the aids." That is, obedient, forward, straight, and with rhythmic gaits.

At the lower levels, any horse is capable of 5's and 6's (which should result in acceptable scores). Most horses are capable of 6's and 7's — which are usually winning scores.

The horses that are naturally good movers may get higher scores than yours — if they're equally correct, straight, forward, quiet, supple, and rhythmic. But there are a lot of horse-rider relationships out there that are not performing up to their potential. Every horse can be improved with good training and good riding.

In the final analysis, it often boils down to how good the rider is at bringing out the horse's talent and utilizing it. The point is, don't use your "ordinary" horse as an excuse for low scores.

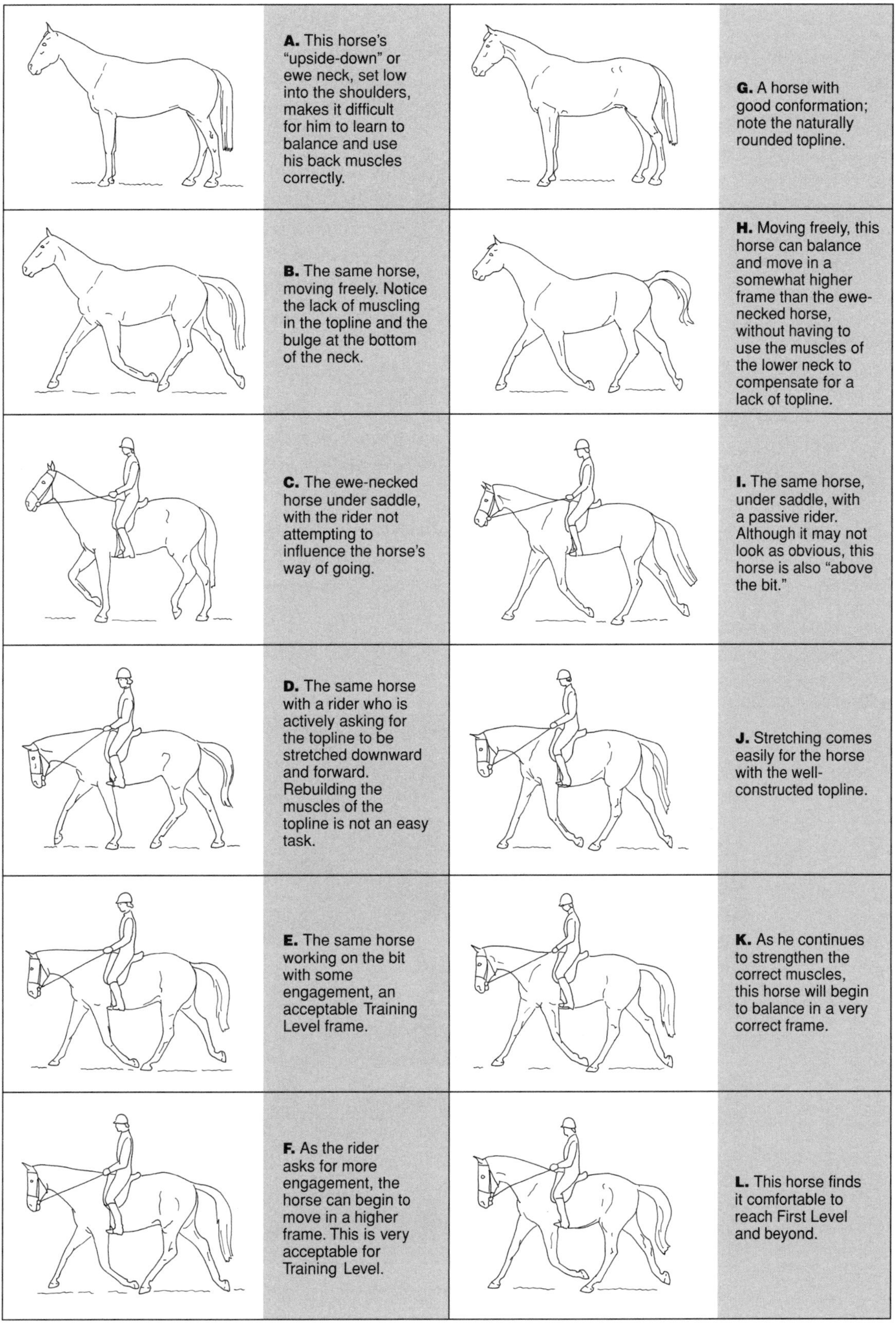
A. This horse's "upside-down" or ewe neck, set low into the shoulders, makes it difficult for him to learn to balance and use his back muscles correctly.
G. A horse with good conformation; note the naturally rounded topline.
B. The same horse, moving freely. Notice the lack of muscling in the topline and the bulge at the bottom of the neck.
H. Moving freely, this horse can balance and move in a somewhat higher frame than the ewe-necked horse, without having to use the muscles of the lower neck to compensate for a lack of topline.
C. The ewe-necked horse under saddle, with the rider not attempting to influence the horse's way of going.
I. The same horse, under saddle, with a passive rider. Although it may not look as obvious, this horse is also "above the bit."
D. The same horse with a rider who is actively asking for the topline to be stretched downward and forward. Rebuilding the muscles of the topline is not an easy task.
J. Stretching comes easily for the horse with the well-constructed topline.
E. The same horse working on the bit with some engagement, an acceptable Training Level frame.
K. As he continues to strengthen the correct muscles, this horse will begin to balance in a very correct frame.
F. As the rider asks for more engagement, the horse can begin to move in a higher frame. This is very acceptable for Training Level.
L. This horse finds it comfortable to reach First Level and beyond.

Figure 6.8 Working with downhill conformation.

The Downhill Horse

Probably the most common conformation problem that lower level riders have to contend with is the horse built slightly "downhill." This means a horse that may be lower at the withers than the croup, but almost always has a low point of shoulder and a neck that is attached at a low point. This is conformation typical of many racehorses — either Thoroughbred or Quarter Horse — because this conformation produces speed.

This does not condemn all racehorses as unsuitable for dressage competition. Thoroughbreds and Quarter Horses have many redeeming traits and you must always consider the individual animal and never condemn a whole breed. In fact, in the 1970's and 1980's, Thoroughbreds in dressage were very popular — competition organizers even contemplated putting them in separate classes. Then the warmbloods started arriving on the scene and were an instant success. Still, the Thoroughbreds and Quarter Horses outnumber other breeds at low levels because they are less expensive than warmbloods. At the lower levels their conformation is not an insurmountable obstacle, after all — that's why we call it training!! (figure 6.8)

To counteract the downhill balance, first encourage a little lateral (sideways) flexion behind the poll, called "positioning." This will prevent the horse from "freezing" his neck and leaning on your hands. Now you should be able to encourage the horse to bring his hind legs more forward to "leverage up" his forehand. Keep the tempo as slow as possible with as powerful a stride as possible. Use lots of trot-walk-trot transitions and trot-halt-trot transitions to enforce prompt response to your leg aids and cause the horse to use his hindquarters and back. Multiple figure eights or well-bent serpentines should also encourage the horse to reach forward with alternating inside hind legs to carry more weight and "engage."

Figure 6.9 Very likely the horse you have right now will be just fine for competition. Photo by Charlene Strickland.

Do not let the horse lean on circles or curves; insist that he bring the hind legs forward to take the weight. Exercises of shoulder-fore and shoulder-in, along with lots of half-halts, will help balance the horse more on his hind legs. Cavalletti and hill work are also good to teach the horse to bend and lift with his hind legs.

Conformation Isn't Everything

While "suitable" conformation may improve the scores and make a horse easier to train, (because he can execute the movements more easily), the horse's mental attitude, temperament, and training have as much, if not more, to do with the outcome of the scores. **The most perfect specimen in the world is of no use if the human cannot command him to perform.** There are many, many less-than-ideal horses that perform adequately or better, because they cooperate with their riders. When judging "suitability" for dressage competition, mental attitude should hold equal weight with conformation (figure 6.9). See Chapter 26 for additional suggestions on working with less than ideal conformation or temperaments and suggestions on choosing a horse for upper level competition.

Chapter Seven

Equipment

The tack and equipment required for dressage competition are fairly simple: an English type saddle, a well-fitting leather bridle with a snaffle bit, a conservative (black or white) saddle pad (actually optional), and a whip (also optional) are all that is required.

The Saddle

"An English type saddle with stirrups is compulsory at all levels." (AHSA Art. 1921.1)

A park saddle (the flat English saddle used in saddle seat riding) is not properly balanced for dressage training or riding, nor is an extreme forward seat (jumping) saddle. Almost any other English type saddle will do as long as it fits both you and your horse.

An ill-fitting saddle — whether inappropriate for you or your horse — will put you out of balance and will contribute adversely to your sense of security. When you are out of balance, your horse has to compensate and usually does so by stiffening through his shoulders and back. This affects his gaits, as well as being very jolting to the rider. A bouncing rider causes the horse to become even stiffer, and so goes a vicious cycle. A saddle that doesn't fit the horse causes uneven distribution of rider weight, resulting in sore spots on the horse's back as well as confusing aids.

With a well-fitting saddle, you don't need a very thick pad — 1/2 inch thick should be sufficient. The purpose of the pad is to protect the underside of the saddle from sweat. The reason for the popular square "dressage pads" is that they also protect the tails of the shadbelly coat from sweat and dirt. It is best to use cotton or wool next to the horse. Synthetic pads retain heat and can cause a heat rash, or worse. Sometimes a "riser pad" — 1/2 to 3/4 inch of firm material — is

Fit the Saddle to the Horse

If you are considering buying a saddle, or if you want to make sure the one you are using fits, consider these points:

1. Every horse has a unique conformation to his back that determines tree angle and length, gullet width, panel thickness, and girth type. First run your hand over the back of the horse's shoulder blade. You may have to press rather hard to find the location. The saddle should not sit directly on the shoulder blade, which would cramp your horse's movement.

Now place the saddle on the horse's back, preferably over a thin white sheet or towel. Start with the saddle two or three inches forward of where you think it should set, then slide it back until it seems to drop into place. Saddle makers call this spot the "lock-in point" (figure 7.1A). A well-fitting saddle will sit firmly in this location without a girth. When a saddle doesn't fit a horse's back well, it tends to slide past the lock-in point, to rock, or to shift around.

2. The panels are the two pads running the length of the saddle. They should rest on the muscles of the back and prevent the saddle from resting on the horse's spine.

The tree is the frame that holds the panels at an appropriate angle (figure 7.1B). If the tree is too wide, the saddle will sit on the spine; if too narrow, it will pinch the muscles or rub the spine.

Off-the-rack English saddles come in three more or less standard widths (measured across the points of the tree). The categories are usually listed as: wide, (for Arabians, Quarter Horses, and some Morgans), medium (most warmbloods), and narrow (most Thoroughbreds).

No part of the saddle should touch the spine. You should be able to fit at least one finger (preferably two), between the saddle and the withers when the rider is mounted.

3. Look at the balance of the saddle from the side. If the saddle is out of balance it will throw the rider either forward or back, rocking the saddle and either pinching the horse's back or disturbing his balance.

The lowest point of the seat should fall in the approximate center of the saddle (figure 7.1C middle). If the saddle is too high at the pommel (front) of the saddle, there will be three fingers or more height above the withers and the rider's weight is placed too far back (figure 7.1C top). The problem is usually that the tree is too narrow. If the front of the saddle sits too low (figure 7.1C bottom), it is usually too wide for the horse's withers. (Note: sometimes an additional "riser" pad can compensate for a saddle that is slightly out of balance.)

Figure 7.1 A

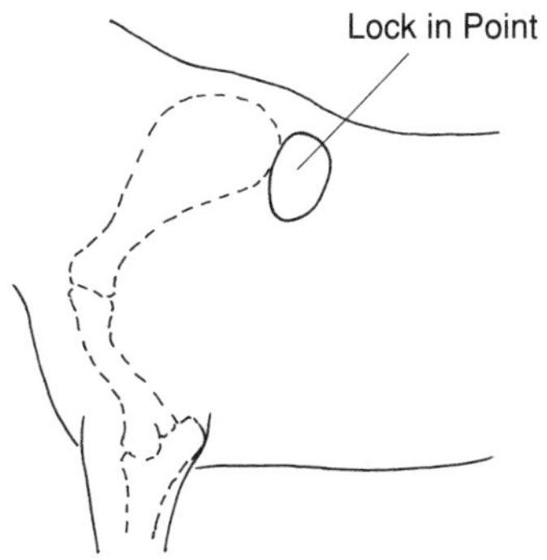

Figure 7.1 B

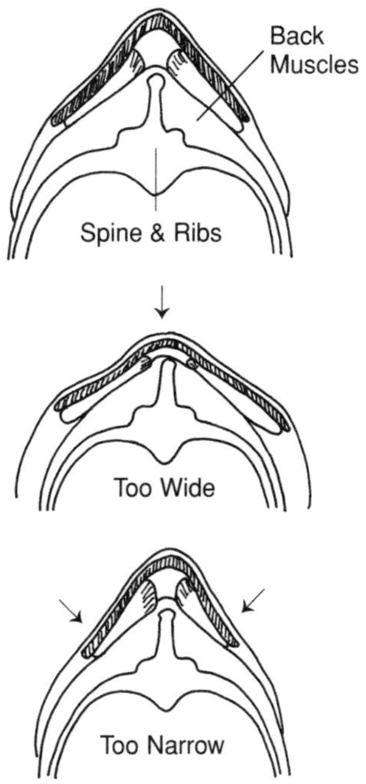

—Continues next page

Figure 7.1 C

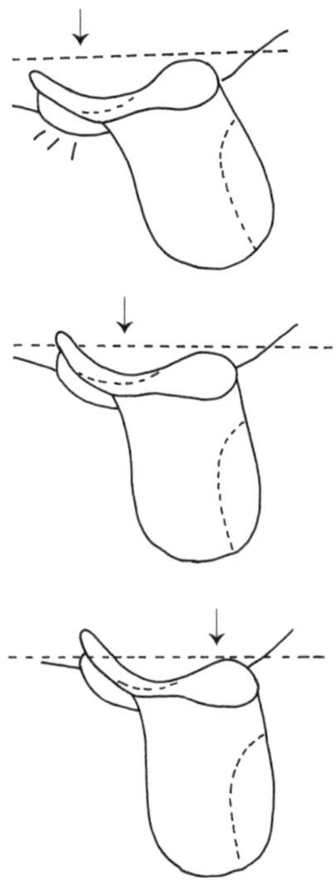

Top Incorrect

- Cantle lower than pommel.
- Deepest point of seat too far back.
- Too much clearance under pommel.

Wider tree indicated

Middle Correct

- Cantle sligtly higher than pommel.
- Deepest point of seat in center of saddle.
- Two fingers clearance under pommel.

Bottom Incorrect

- Although the pommel/cantle relationship is correct, there is inadequate clearance under the pommel.

Narrower tree indicated

Next, check the following points:

1. Do the panels distribute the weight evenly along the length of the saddle onto the long back muscles? If your saddle pad is more soiled in certain places than others, it does not. Do both sides of the saddle fit equally well?

2. When the horse moves, the saddle should remain in place, shifting neither forward, backward, nor sideways.

3. When you view the saddle from behind, it should appear to sit straight along the midline of the horse's back.

4. Does the girth alignment suit the horse? The girth can be fitted to the two front billets or the two back billets, but this does not change the alignment by more than half an inch.

When you find a saddle that fits your horse properly, it will seem to drop onto his back with no effort and even when you fiddle with the saddle, it won't shift. Your horse will move freely and willingly. A wringing tail, pinned ears, and tightening of the back are signs that the saddle doesn't fit.

Fit the Saddle to the Rider

Just as important that the saddle fit the horse perfectly, it must also fit the rider. The best way to determine if a saddle fits is to sit on it, preferably while on the horse.

Width and length of the seat determines comfort. The twist (also called the "throat" or "waist") refers to the area of the saddle between the pommel and cantle, under the rider's crotch. The twist creates a narrower space that allows the rider's legs to fall naturally in a correct position. If the saddle causes discomfort in the crotch, you will take a defensive posture to avoid the pain. Having a twist that is too narrow for you will make you feel quite precarious when you are riding.

A. Seat size is measured from the nail to the center of the cantle. Measure from the point of your hip to your kneecap: this is your approximate seat size. However, this rough estimate doesn't work well for all saddles because some are flatter and some are deeper than others. A better gauge is: you should be able to place one hand's width in front of and one hand's width behind the rider's seat. This is also inexact. The one constant is that the longer your thigh, the larger the saddle seat you'll need. If you are sliding around a lot, the seat is probably too big. If your crotch is pinched against the front of the saddle, it's too small (figure 7.2A).

B. Stirrup bars should be located so that the stirrups hang straight down when your body alignment of shoulder, hip and heel are correct. For almost all riders this means the distance between the stirrup bar and the deepest point of the saddle seat should be the same distance as from your heel to the ball of your foot (figure 7.2B). If the distance is too long or too short, you'll be forced into an awkward position, constantly trying to compensate for the difference.

Another consideration is that the flap of the saddle needs to be long enough to extend below the top of the your boot but not so long that it blocks the use of the calf on the horse's sides. A standard flap length fits most riders between 5'4" and 5'11"; a short flap is approximately 2" shorter; the long flap is approximately

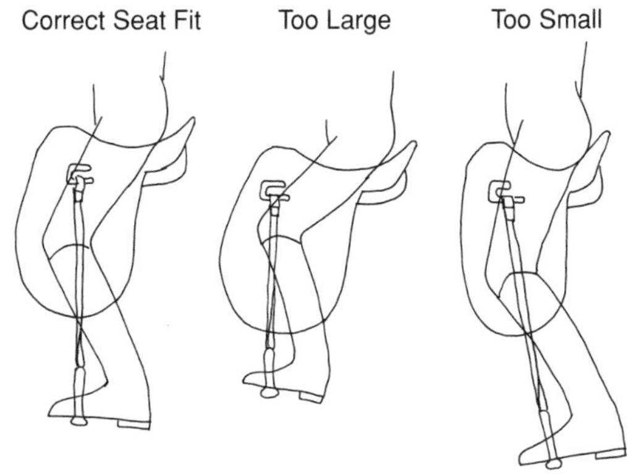

Figure 7.2 A

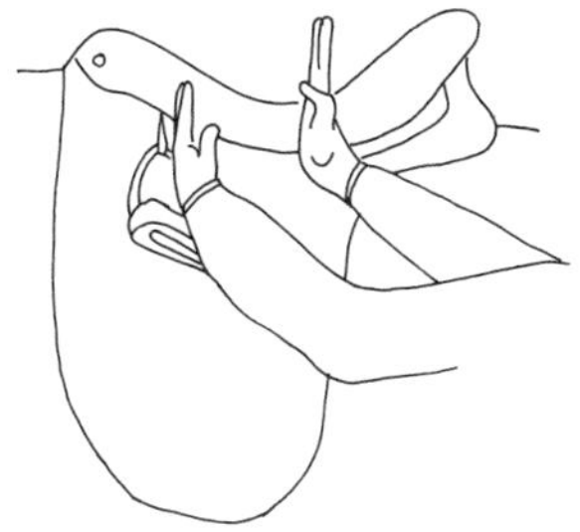

Figure 7.2 B

2" longer than the standard flap. There should be the same amount of leather before and behind the leg.

Try the saddle while putting your horse through its usual paces, while asking yourself the following questions:

1. Do you feel instantly comfortable, or are you and your horse fidgeting?

2. Does the seat let you sit fully in the saddle without being thrown forward, backward or off to one side?

3. Can you move around freely, or are you being forced into a position? If you're comfortable in the fixed position and your horse is performing well, this may be your choice. But if you're not absolutely in balance with the horse, you may feel that the saddle is holding you hostage.

4. Does your leg remain comfortably underneath you?

5. Can you sit without effort, with your seat bones pointing straight down or does the saddle tip your pelvis forward onto your pubic arch or rock you back onto your tailbone?

Generally, it takes only a few minutes to determine whether a saddle fits well. If, instead, you find yourself fussing and fidgeting trying to make it work, you have the wrong saddle for you or your horse.

needed with a low-backed, high-withered horse, but be careful not to unbalance a saddle by stuffing too much padding under it.

The Bit

The bit of choice for dressage training is a simple snaffle. A snaffle is any bit that works directly on the bars of the horse's mouth, *without leverage.* A snaffle can be single-jointed, double-jointed, or non-jointed (bar bit). Any bit that works on leverage is *not* a snaffle, even if it has a jointed mouthpiece.

Figure 7.3 shows the bits allowed by the AHSA. A snaffle is required through Third Level competition. At Fourth Level and above, a simple double bridle (a snaffle and a curb) is allowed. It is always best to train with the same bit that you compete with.

Any of the pictured bits may be covered with rubber or leather. Bits with mouthpieces made of synthetic material are permitted, provided that the contours of the bit conform to the bits pictured. Note that while most bits take their name from the shape of the cheekpieces, it is the *mouthpiece* that determines if it is legal or not.

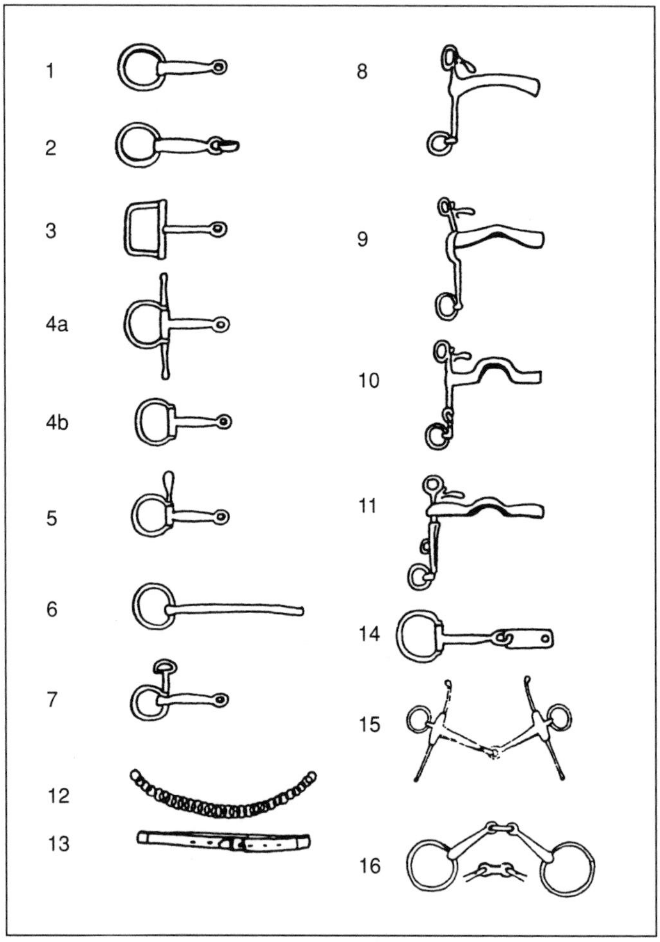

Figure 7.3 A sampling of the legal bits for dressage and combined training competitions sanctioned by the AHSA. Pay particular attention to the mouthpiece, because the brand name usually indicates the shape of the side rings and has little relevance to whether the mouthpiece is legal or illegal. As always, consult the latest Rule Book *for current regulations. Reprinted by permission of the American Horse Shows Association.*

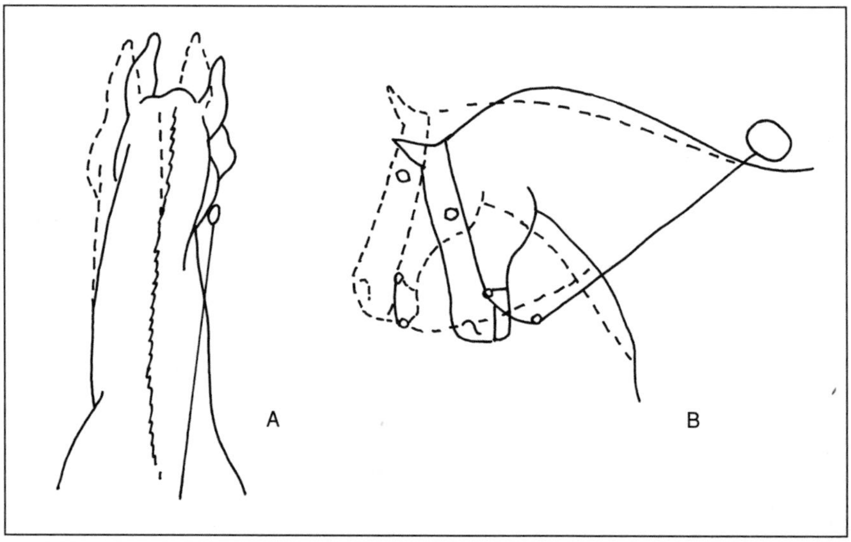

Figure 7.4 Snaffle and curb bits work according to different principles. A snaffle works upon the bars of the mouth allowing for lateral flexion (A), and a curb works via leverage causing longitudinal flexion at the poll (B).

All the bits must be smooth. Twisted, wire, and roller bits are prohibited. All parts of a bit that are in the horse's mouth, (including curb and bridoon bits of a double bridle) must be made entirely of the same metal. The lever arm of the curb must not exceed ten centimeters (3.9 inches) and must be straight. The ring of the bridoon of a double bridle must not exceed eight centimeters (3.12 inches) in diameter. All the restrictions on bridles and bits also apply to the warm-up areas at dressage competitions.

Why a Snaffle?

The reason for a snaffle in the beginning stages of training is that it functions in the manner that makes dressage training possible. To understand this, let's look at how the two basic types of bits work.

The snaffle works directly on the bars (the toothless part of the gums) of the horse's mouth. It can press on each side either separately or equally. This allows the rider to influence one side of the horse at a time (for instance to bend or position him). A leverage bit (curb or Weymouth) works on both sides of the mouth simultaneously, so that a pull on one rein causes the whole bit to pivot and put pressure on the mouth and chin.

The amount of pressure on the snaffle bit is in direct relation to the strength of the rider. A pull straight backwards may not be enough to stop an uneducated horse. But with the snaffle we can *bend* the horse (cause the horse to turn his head to the side). This allows us to position the horse precisely where we want him for the various movements or gaits, while it gives us tremendous power to control him. This is because he is relatively powerless to ignore us from a bent position: he can not brace his neck and pull against us if he is flexed to the side (figure 7.4A).

The curb bit, on the other hand, works on leverage to magnify the pull of the rider's hand (figure 7.4B). Thus the rider can force the horse to flex longitudinally at the poll (arch his neck), and by the very power of the bit, the horse will seldom pull against the hands. The shortcoming of the curb bit is that it is very difficult (but not impossible) to get the horse to bend in the exact position that we want. Thus, the snaffle is the most versatile *single* bit we can use.

The snaffle is often labeled a mild bit, but this is totally dependent on the rider's hands. Sawing, pulling, and banging a snaffle in the horse's mouth will deaden the mouth more quickly than a leverage bit. Once a horse chooses to ignore a bit, you no longer have any control (or influence) over the horse's action, and it is very difficult to regain sensitivity, even with a stronger (and possibly illegal) bit. Therefore, it takes more education *on the rider's part* to use a snaffle properly.

Before you ride a horse with a snaffle bit (if you have never used one), read Chapter 11, "All the Horse Needs to Know." Because the snaffle is a comparatively mild bit, you must know how to use it in order to get its full benefits.

To Fit a Snaffle

The bit must be comfortable, so the horse will not be constantly fussing and worrying about it, yet it must be strong enough to get the job done.

When choosing a bit, you must consider the shape of the horse's mouth and his natural sensitivity. The rings on the sides of the bit need to be large enough or of a shape to prevent the bit from pulling through the horse's mouth.

While the rings of a snaffle often give it its name, such as "D-ring," "loose ring," "egg-butt," and so forth, they have very little to do with the fit or workings of the bit. The important consideration is the part that is in the horse's mouth.

The **width** of the mouthpiece should allow the bit to lie comfortably across the horse's tongue without pinching his lips or protruding too much at the sides. If the snaffle is too wide there is a likelihood of it being pulled too far to one side, with the result that the joint in the mouthpiece is no longer in the center of the mouth and may even be poking the horse in the roof of the mouth. If the bit is too narrow it will rub and pinch the horse's lips. The mouthpiece should be approximately 1/4 inch wider that the mouth.

The correct **shape** of the mouthpiece will depend on the shape of the horse's tongue and palate (roof of the mouth). A horse with a thin tongue and a high palate can accept a big, fat, single-jointed bit with no fuss, but a horse with a thick tongue or a low palate does not have much room for a bit. These horses may go well in a double-jointed (French) snaffle or a "bar bit" (no joint), as these bits are less likely to poke them in the roof of the mouth.

The **thickness** of the mouthpiece determines its severity. A thin mouthpiece is sharper in its action than a thick one. A horse with a thick tongue needs a thinner mouthpiece, to allow enough room for the bit and the tongue inside the mouth, even though he might not need the extra control the thinner mouthpiece provides. Unfortunately, a thin snaffle will often make a horse snatch and jerk at it in an attempt to avoid its sharp, painful action. This is especially true with Thoroughbred-type horses. You may find that a thicker snaffle will cause your horse to "lighten" on the bit! You may have to experiment to find the best bit for your individual horse. Generally speaking, the more sensitive the horse, the thicker the mouthpiece, but don't fall in the trap of putting too mild a bit in his mouth. You need a bit that is strong enough to get your message across: **As strong as you need, as mild as you can handle.** If you have to pull and nag to get a response, the bit is too mild for that particular horse.

When adjusting the snaffle, you should have one and a half wrinkles on each corner of the horse's mouth. If the bridle is too tight, it will rub sores on the lips, if too low, the bit may bang on the horse's teeth or the horse may get his tongue over the bit.

The Bridle

"For Training, First, Second and Third Level tests a plain snaffle bridle and a regular cavesson, a dropped noseband, a flash noseband (a combination of a cavesson noseband and a dropped noseband attachment), crescent noseband or a crossed noseband. Except for the crescent noseband, buckles and a small disk of sheepskin, which may be used in the intersection of the two leather straps of a crossed noseband, the noseband must be made entirely of leather or leather-like material. A padded noseband is allowed." (AHSA Art. 1921.2)

"For AHSA Fourth and Fifth Level tests same as above, or a simple double bridle (bridoon (snaffle) and bit (curb) and curb chain, lip strap and rubber or leather cover for curb chain optional, cavesson noseband only.)" (Art. 1921.3)

The bridle needs to be in good repair, clean, and of course fit the horse (figure 7.5). You may want to have a "work bridle" for everyday use and a "show bridle" for competition. If you have a separate bridle for showing, always try it on the horse the day before a competition. Arriving at the competition with the bit in backward or a piece of leather missing is very embarrassing.

Cavesson or Drop Noseband?

A noseband (or cavesson) is necessary when using a snaffle (figure 7.6). The purpose of a noseband is to prevent the bit from sliding or moving around too much in the mouth and to prevent the horse from learning to open his mouth to evade the bit. If the bit doesn't fit, or the noseband is too tight or uncomfortable, the horse will open his mouth anyway.

The purpose of the drop noseband or "flash" (a regular cavesson with a "drop" attachment) and the crossed noseband is to prevent the bit from sliding through the horse's mouth,

Figure 7.5 *Good bridle fit is important. The snaffle should cause one wrinkle at the corner of the mouth, no more, no less (A); three fingers should fit between the jaw and the throatlatch (B); the cavesson must be snug, but not uncomfortable. You should be able to fit a finger between the cavesson and jaw (C). Photos by Charlene Strickland.*

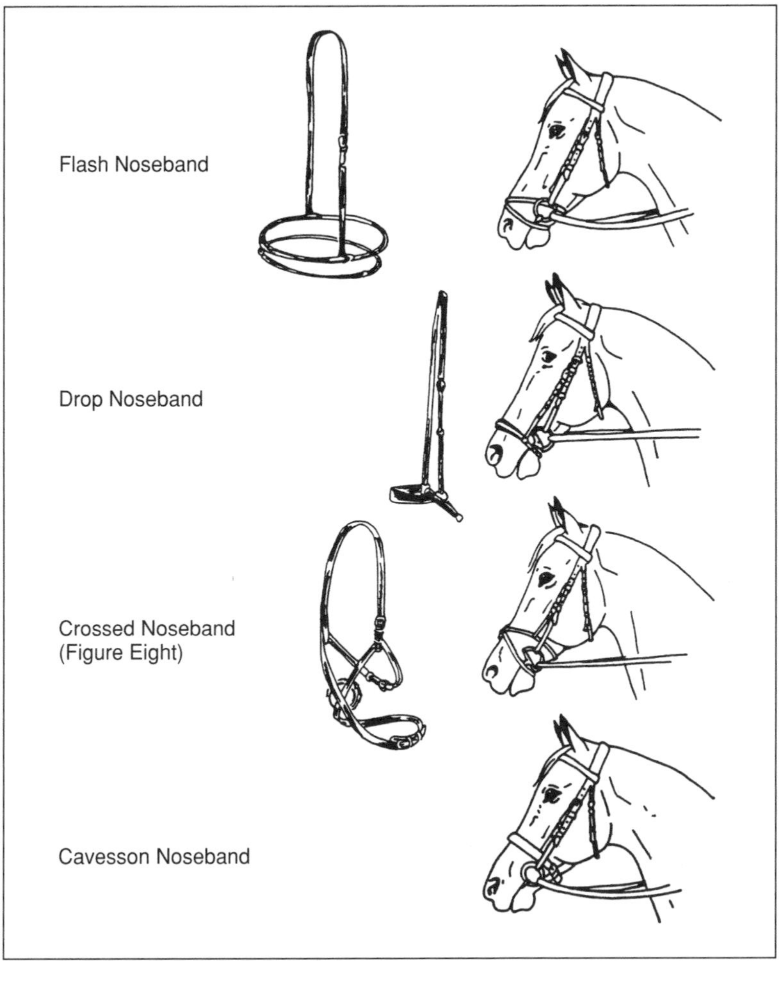

Figure 7.6
Permitted nosebands for dressage and combined training. Reprinted by permission of the American Horse Shows Association.

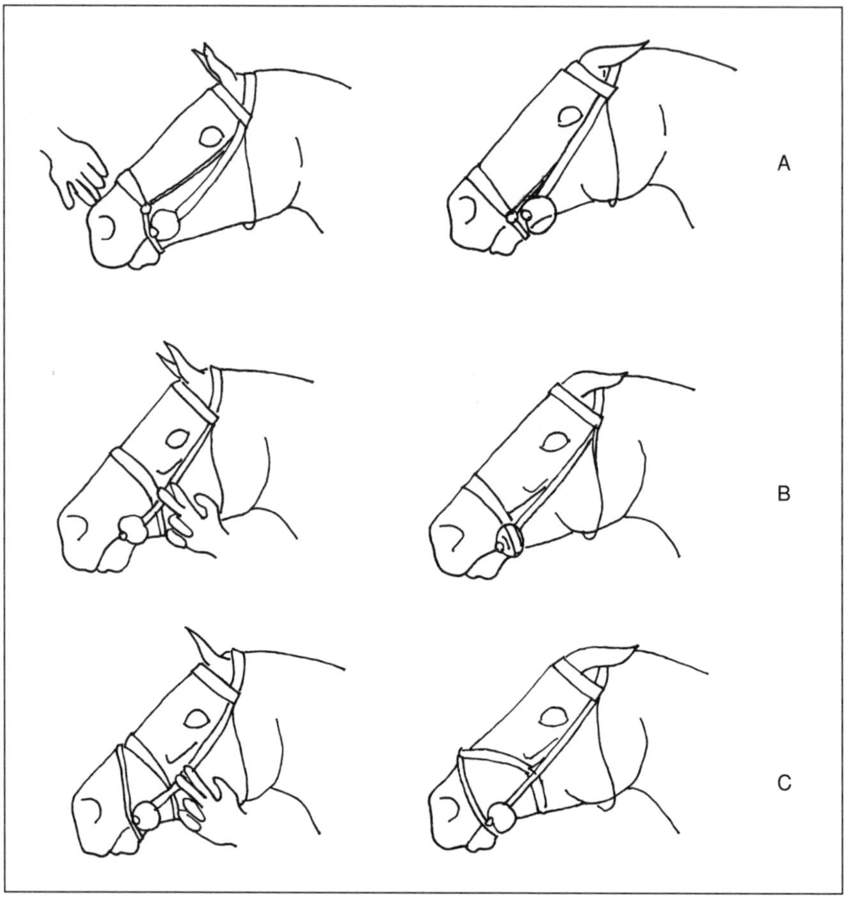

Figure 7.7 On the left, correct fit of noseband or cavesson. On the right, incorrect. Note use of fingers to judge accurate placement

as well as to keep the mouth closed around the bit.

The drop noseband is the hardest to fit. A small leather strap or a spike ring keeps the nosepiece in a horizontal position. This is important because a slipping nosepiece can interfere with the horse's breathing. The chinstrap is adjusted below the bit. The drop noseband is correctly adjusted when it lies about four fingers above the nostrils. The side rings of the noseband must lie in front of the bit, otherwise the nosepiece is too long. The buckle of the chinstrap, when fastened, must lie on the left side of the lower jawbone; otherwise it can pinch the back of the lower jawbones (figure 7.7A).

The standard cavesson with its slightly wider, sometimes padded nosepiece, is adjusted higher than the drop noseband; it should lie two fingers below the protruding cheekbone. Its chinstrap is adjusted above the bit and underneath the cheekpiece of the bridle. It may be adjusted tightly enough to allow one finger to fit between the noseband and the jaw (figures 7.5C & 7.7B).

The flash noseband is adjusted like the standard cavesson but the thin chinstrap is threaded through a little loop below the nosepiece of the cavesson and is adjusted below the bit. It should be buckled on the left side of the lower jawbone. A flash noseband that is adjusted too tightly distorts the cavesson it is attached to and causes it to pull down on the horse's face (figure 7.7C).

Care of Leather Goods

Your saddle and bridle are major investments. If you take care of them, they can give you years of service.

Most judges say that while they never let fancy tack sway their judgment, dirty or ill-fitting tack does affect their decisions, because it indicates carelessness and disrespect.

You may not be able to afford the most expensive tack in the latest styles. Everyone, however, can afford elbow grease. Cleaning, conditioning, and attention to little details, like always wiping the sweat off your leather girth and the crown of your bridle, will add years of life to your equipment.

Leg Protection

Although leg protection for the horse (bandages or boots) is not allowed in the competition arena, it is allowed in the warm-up area. With some horses it is a very good idea to school with leg protection.

Of course, many riders use boots and wraps purely for decoration, as evidenced by the choice of colors and patterns available. Wraps attract attention to the horse's legs and

Tack Care and Cleaning Tips

Always remember that leather was once living tissue. When leather was a living substance in the form of skin, its pliability was preserved by natural oils secreted by the glands of the animal. As leather, some external application must be made from time to time to preserve the "life" of the skin. By the same token, it should not have to sustain prolonged periods of exposure to cold, water, or direct sunlight. Most commercial brands of leather treatment are adequate for periodic oiling, although Neatsfoot Oil and Lexol® are the old and trusted standbys. Always use an animal oil — never a vegetable oil. And don't over-oil leather either. Soggy leather is weak and excess oil will rot the stitching.

To clean and condition leather, the first thing to do is to remove dirt and hair by use of a Castile soap, using a sponge and very little water to work up a good, stiff lather. When the leather is clean, do not rinse it off with water. Instead, remove all the soap you can from the sponge by wrapping it in a dry rag and squeezing it firmly. Then, without rewetting, use the sponge to remove the remaining soap film. Don't scrub so hard that you scuff the leather. For black leather equipment, apply black leather dye to any scuffed areas after cleaning them. Don't use shoe polish because it will easily rub off on your clothes and saddle pad.

Castile soap does a good job of cleaning the leather, but it doesn't preserve or soften it. For this use a glycerine soap, saddle soap, or Lexol®. Some people believe that saddle soap cleans leather. Most saddle soaps contain glycerine or oils, so won't get really built-up dirt off the leather. Its purpose is to preserve, so it is important that the leather be clean before the saddle soap is put on. Excess soap or conditioner is again wiped off with a barely damp cloth. After drying, the leather can be rubbed with a soft cloth (preferably flannel) and buffed to a mellow shine or glow.

If a saddle is really clean it will show its stitches clearly and will not soil a clean white towel that is rubbed on it. Some saddle soaps, owing to an amount of beeswax in their composition, easily produce a gloss on the leather when applied, but also cause smudges and grease marks on the clothes of the rider. Glycerine also tends to build up on tack, becoming greasy and trapping dirt.

Bits and stirrups should be cleaned regularly. Stirrups and bits can be put in the dishwasher or scrubbed with warm water or toothpaste. The toothpaste gets into the joints of the bit to remove all the dried food particles. And because toothpaste isn't poisonous like conventional metal polish, you don't have to worry about leaving traces on the bit. Toothpaste also tastes better and leaves bits really clean.

To clean and refluff fleece saddle pads, take a hose vacuum cleaner to them after they've been washed (or before). The vacuum removes any horsehair left on the pad and makes it look new for the next show.

emphasize his movement. For a parade, a quadrille, clinic or exhibition performances, bandages add a wonderful final polish.

While schooling, leg protection should be used if your horse shows any tendency to hit his legs, for instance when beginning lateral work or in difficult footing to protect against blows from the opposite hoof when a horse is learning lateral work. Splint boots or any of the various sports boots will provide the same (sometimes better) protection and are much safer to use than bandages.

In deep going, bandages are more likely to hinder the tendons' needed circulation than be of help. In fact, a constrictive bandage can "bow" a tendon in short order. On the other hand, if the wrap comes loose while the horse is working, he can trip or get tangled in it with disastrous results. About the only time bandages are better than boots is on slippery going, where bandages can help stabilize the fetlock joint to a small degree.

Most trainers (and veterinarians) agree that boots are good, safe, time-saving, and even

Bandaging for Exercise

The wrap itself must be stretchy (either elasticized or a stretchy-weave polo bandage) so that it will conform to the leg and won't start to sag and slip when the horse works. Because stretchy bandages give, they don't need padding and can be put on with more pressure than flannel wraps (figure 7.8).

Start about midcannon (1) and wrap down, making absolutely certain the bandage is smooth and flat. (Place the start of the bandage in the groove of the tendons.) This first layer must be about the tightness of your own stretch stockings. Overlap one or two inches on each turn.

When you get to the fetlock joint, if your intention is to stabilize the joint, take one snug turn under the back of the joint and then start back up (2). This is the only place where the support comes in. If your only aim is to present a nice, neat appearance or if your horse does not have a predisposition to hit his ankles, you can go right back up the cannon (4) without going under the fetlock.

On your way up the cannon you want the wrap to be quite snug. It's hard to describe how snug but if your bandage is stretchy enough you probably won't get it too tight. If the bandage slips during work, you didn't have it snug enough. You must be extremely careful to keep the pressure absolutely even and not have any wrinkles in the bandage. If the bandage is too tight, it will cut off circulation to the lower leg. Most trainers recommend not leaving the bandages on longer than two hours.

Horses that wear exercise bandages can develop sores where the wraps chafe or where sand gets under the bandage. (This can happen with leather or rubber boots also.) But there's another risk with any exercise bandage: if the wrap comes loose while the horse is working, he can trip or get tangled in it with disastrous results. Sports boots are a much safer and less time-consuming way to protect the legs.

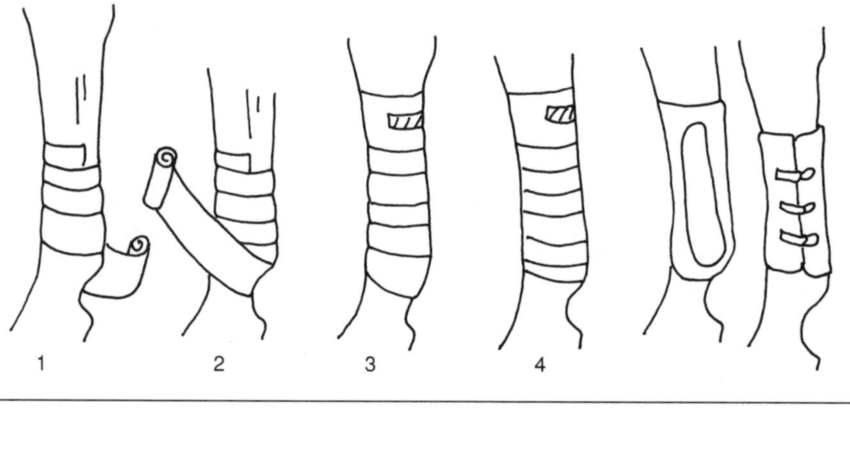

Figure 7.8

better protection than bandages. There are boots made for nearly any situation or anatomical part you can think of, from knee and hock to coronary band. Properly fitted, they're unlikely to slip or bind and even less likely to get the horse in trouble if they do. Two minutes to put these precautions in place may save weeks nursing a cut or bruised leg. They are also nearly impossible to put on too tight (which can be a problem with bandages), and they're easy to clean.

If you ever do use bandages, get someone to show you how to wrap them so they are not too tight or too loose.

Other Equipment

"Martingales, bit guards, any kind of gadgets (such as bearing, side, running, balancing reins, tongue tied down, etc.) any kind of boots (including 'Easy boots') or bandages (including tail bandages) and any form of blinkers, earmuffs or plugs, nose covers, seat covers, hoods are, under penalty of elimination, strictly forbidden. However, leg bandages are allowed in Pas de Deux and Quadrille classes. A breastplate and/or crupper may be used. A side rein is defined as an auxiliary rein affixed to the bit and to the girth, saddle or surcingle on the side of the horse (not between the legs). Any decoration of the horse with unnatural things, such as ribbons or flowers, etc. in the tail, etc., is strictly forbidden. Braiding of the horse's mane and tail, however, is permitted." (AHSA Art. 1921.6) (Black or white tape on the braids is permitted.)

"The above restrictions (including saddle, bridle, and bit) also apply to warm-up areas and other training areas; however, nose covers, running martingales (with snaffle only), boots and bandages are permitted. Single direct side reins are permitted only when longeing (mounted or unmounted) only with one lunge line. Horses competing at 4th Level and above may be warmed up in a snaffle if the rider so chooses." (AHSA Art. 1921.7) A horse warming up for a Third Level test or below may not do so in a double bridle.

A running martingale consists of a divided strap attached to the girth or breastplate at the front of the horse's chest; the extension of each strap must be connected from the point of division only to the rein on the same side and must be free to slide.

"Ring stewards appointed by show management must spot check saddlery at the direction of the technical delegate. Inspection of saddlery should be done immediately as the horse leaves the arena. ...The responsibility for the correct attire and equipment, however, still rests with the competitor." (AHSA Art. 1921.8)

The bit is commonly inspected by the ring steward inserting a finger into the horse's mouth — it is greatly appreciated if the horse accepts this without fuss!

Whips

"The following whips are permitted for schooling only: A standard longeing whip and 2 whips no longer than 6' including lash." (AHSA Art. 1921)

"One whip, no longer than 4' including lash may be carried in all classes except AHSA/USDF Championships (or qualifying classes or combined training tests). Exceptions: competitors riding sidesaddle may carry a whip in any class." (AHSA Art. 1921.9)

Introducing the Whip to the Horse

A whip is commonly carried during any and all training sessions. It is not carried to punish the horse, but only to reinforce the driving aids. If it is not used when it is needed — such as when a horse ignores the leg or seat — the horse will learn that he really doesn't have to pay attention to the rider.

The whip is indispensable to the training of the horse because the animal catches on to its meaning very quickly. The whip has a very different action than the spurs (see Chapter 8). Horses seem to instinctively move away from the action of the whip and can very quickly

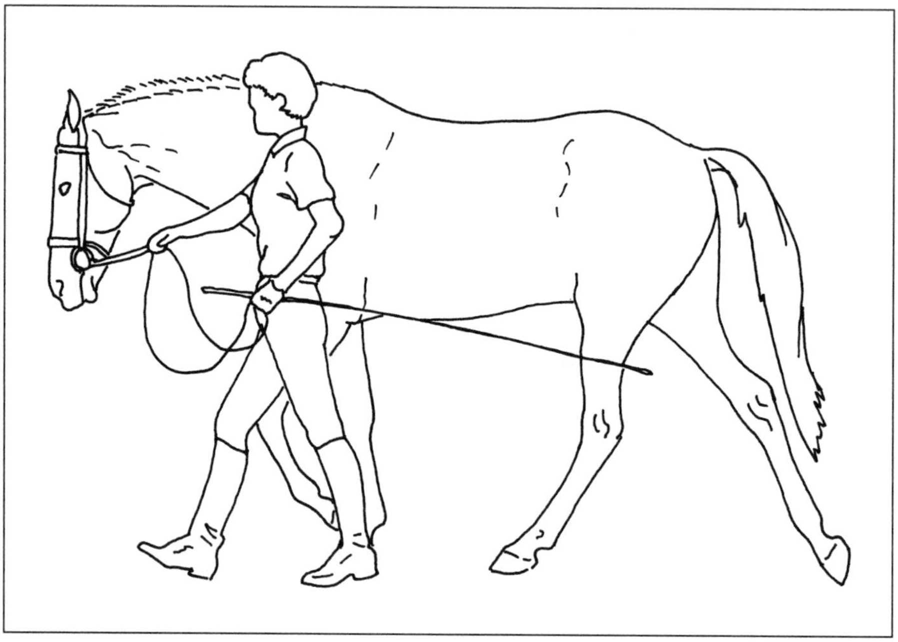

Figure 7.9 To teach the horse to move forward in response to the whip, stand by the horse's shoulder, facing forward, with the reins or lead shank in the hand toward the horse. Carry the whip in the outside hand, pointed backward so you can tap the horse in the approximate place a rider's leg would touch. Say "walk" and tap the horse on the side.

learn that if they move before it touches them, they will be spared discomfort.

The whip is not for punishment except in those instances when the horse is ignoring the leg.

Sometimes horses train riders not to carry whips: they threaten the rider by acting hysterical any time a rider dares to mount with a whip in hand. This is a situation that can be reversed by the following procedure:

The horse's education should begin on the ground, where we can insure the horse's understanding and obedience to our aids. The horse does not instinctively know that it should move away from pressure on his side (our leg). In fact, his natural reaction will be to press against it! Leading from the ground or longeing, we can use the whip to teach the horse that pressure on the sides means to move away from that pressure (figure 7.9).

Just like any other piece of equipment we use on or around the horse, we must introduce the whip in such a manner that the horse does not fear it, but rather understands it. To do this, we gently, methodically, stroke the whip over the horse's entire body, both sides, over the back and under the belly, thereby showing him that there is no reason to fear it.

This understood, the trainer now stands by the horse's shoulder, facing forward, with the reins or lead shank in the hand toward the horse, the whip in the outside hand pointed backward, so she can tap the horse in the approximate place a rider's leg will touch. Say "walk" and tap the horse on the side. Do not step forward until the horse moves — the response you want is movement. If you don't tap hard enough, the horse will not move; if you hit too hard, the horse may be so startled as to bolt or kick at the whip in response. Find your horse's "response zone." Find out how much tap you must use to get the horse to respectfully step away.

Do this from both sides. Your goal is to

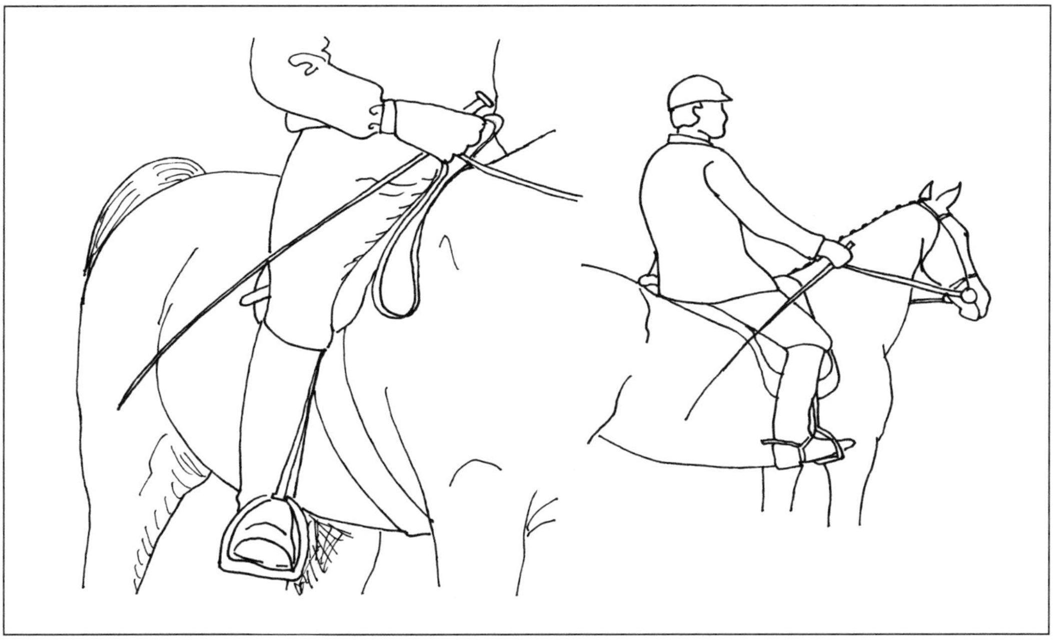

Figure 7.10 Carry the whip across your thigh. When you want to touch the horse with it, move your hand to the side without disturbing the contact with the horse's mouth.

have the horse understand that a tap of the whip is not cause for excitement; it is simply the signal to move! As long as the horse understands this, there is no cause to punish with the whip.

The whip cannot replace the leg, however. Many riders complain that their horse only works correctly in the ring with a whip. If the horse only performs under duress with a whip in the warm-up area, and fails to perform in the ring without one, there is something fundamentally wrong with the horse's training.

The whip is meant to teach the horse to understand and respond to the rider's leg. Do not let it become a crutch that you must have in order to perform. Use of the whip will be further explained in Chapter 11.

Carry the Whip

Carrying a whip (in a test) is allowed in most national levels and some international tests. A whip is not *required* in any test, but if a rider wants to carry a whip, she should certainly do so correctly. Judges get upset with riders who simply sit there carrying a whip and let problems happen without even trying to correct them. Just as bad is carrying the whip on the wrong side of the horse, opposite from where he has problems.

The whip is usually carried in the inside hand (for schooling purposes) and should cross the thigh just above the knee. The snaffle rein passes between the ring finger and the little finger; the little finger is around the whip handle. The dressage whip with a heavy mushroom butt is desirable because it is very nicely balanced and you are less likely to drop it by getting your hand too far out on the handle. A thin flexible whip will sting more than a heavier, less flexible one. A stiffer whip is probably desirable with a sensitive horse.

When you wish to use the whip, you move your hand to the side — without disturbing the contact of the bit with the horse's mouth — and then twist the wrist, still without disturbing the contact any more than can be helped, so that the whip taps the horse just behind the calf of the leg (figure 7.10). The whip should be 36 to 48 inches long (including lash). Do not use a short crop — which can only be used behind the leg if you put both reins in one hand, thereby disturbing the contact.

Whenever the horse and rider "change the rein" (change direction in the ring), the whip should be passed to the new inside hand. Some judges do not want the rider to change the whip hand because it sometimes disturbs the horse. To overcome this, decide which hand you will carry it in during the test and practice your tests that way. Do not carry the whip in your saluting hand, however, because it is impolite to salute the judge with your whip. (You are allowed to salute with either hand.)

Shoeing

With dressage horses, no attempt is made to enhance their foot action other than to assure that it is as efficient as possible for that horse. The most important thing you can do for your horse is to make sure his feet are in balance.

Incorrect shoeing or infrequent hoof care are two ways to cause uneven gaits. Sometimes one hoof will grow faster than the others, and owners may not realize that uneven growth throws the spine out of alignment, which throws the foot pattern out of alignment.

Dressage judges heavily penalize horses that "forge" — knock a shoe of the hind foot against that of the front. It can result when horses are driven at a faster rhythm than their abilities allow. It can also be a sign of lack of balance (on the forehand), lack of swing (suppleness of the back), tiredness, or weakness. It can be a major problem with a horse that is extremely short in the back. If that is the case, consult your farrier and see if the horse's footwear can be adjusted.

Chapter Eight

Dress Code

Dressage riding is a sport steeped in tradition, and riders should take their cue from that. Fads come and go in the other equestrian sports, but dressage has always exhibited elegant simplicity.

You want tack and clothing that is workmanlike, well-fitted, and clean. Clothing that is too tight or too loose and sloppy (or is too revealing) is distracting and does not present a pleasing picture in the show ring.

Why is good fit essential? If you are not comfortable and confident in the way you look, you can not concentrate on the test. If you are worried that your hat is going to come off any minute or your coat is going to pop a button, then you can't concentrate on riding.

Judges caution riders to avoid flamboyance and to spend any extra money on lessons rather than fancy equipment or flashy clothes.

It is the competitor's responsibility to know what apparel is required by the rules and to present an appropriate appearance (figure 8.1).

The AHSA rule reads:

"The dress code for Training through Fourth Levels is a short riding coat of conservative color, with tie, choker or stock tie, breeches or jodhpurs, boots or jodhpur boots, a hunt cap or riding hat with a hard shell, derby or top hat.

"For all tests above Fourth Level, the dress code is: a dark tailcoat with top hat, or a dark jacket with bowler hat or hunt cap, and white or light-colored breeches, stock or tie, gloves, and black riding boots. Members of the Armed Services and police units may ride in the uniform of their service at any level. Spurs are mandatory for FEI tests and optional at (AHSA) Fifth Level." (AHSA Art. 1920.1, 2)

Paddock shoes are not legal with or without halfchaps or leggings. *"Boots and shoes worn while riding anywhere on the competition grounds must have a*

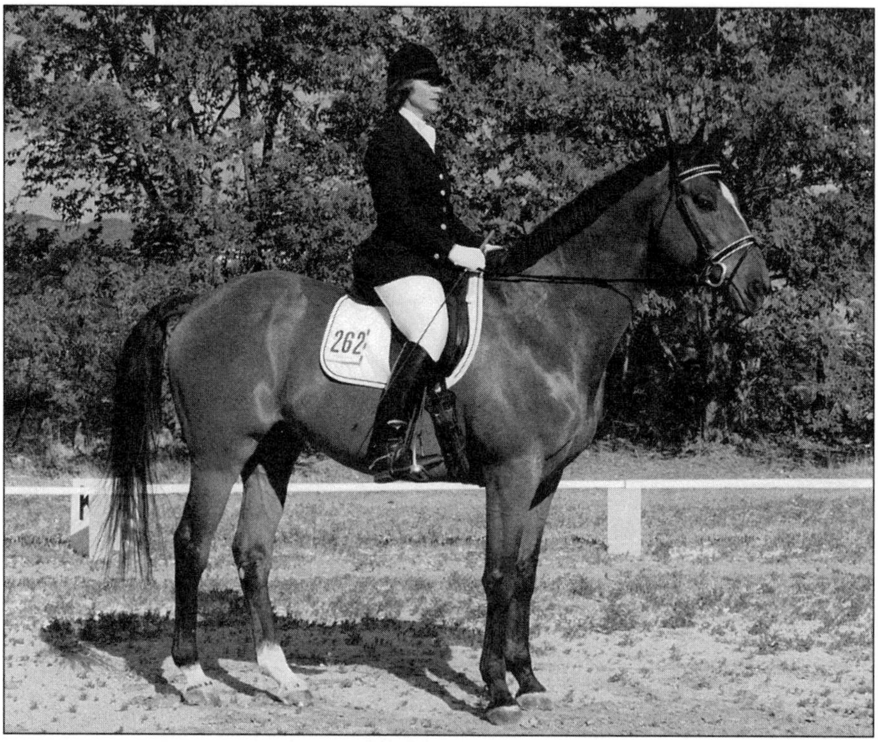

Figure 8.1 A rider properly attired for the lower levels. Photo by Charlene Strickland.

distinguishable heel." (AHSA, Art. 318.7)

"Riders at all levels of competition must wear one of the following: A hunt cap or riding hat with a hard shell, derby or top hat, military/police cap or hat, or protective headgear. Any exhibitor may wear protective headgear at any level of competition without penalty from the judge. Exhibitors choosing to wear protective headgear must wear a short, dark jacket, dark hat covers (where applicable) and must otherwise conform to Art 1920." (AHSA Art. 1920.3)

"In extreme heat and/or humidity, management (at AHSA shows) can allow competitors to show without jackets. However, competitors must wear a regulation hat and solid white or very pale-colored long or short sleeved shirt, without neckwear." (AHSA Art. 1920.5)

Sleeveless shirts and T-shirts are not permitted. Members of the Armed Services or police units may wear summer uniforms.

"Competitors will be allowed to wear a hat cover and a transparent or conservative color rain coat in inclement weather." (AHSA Art. 1920.6)

At schooling shows dress is fairly optional. Hunt-style coats, light-colored breeches, and hunt-type boots and hats are the norm. In fact, many schooling shows only designate: "hunt cap or derby, breeches (any color), boots (any color), coat optional."

Basic hunt attire is perfectly acceptable up through Fourth Level. However, show management or the judge may bar an entry or person from entering the ring if they are not suitably presented to appear before an audience. (AHSA Art. 1920)

Coat

Coats or jackets are usually optional at schooling shows, but you'll find most exhibitors wear one.

Most coats worn for dressage are black, although for lower levels any conservative color (usually dark) is acceptable. Shadbellies (tailcoats) are either black or midnight blue (very dark navy). The hunt vest or vest points worn with shadbellies are canary (pale yellow).

The term "hunt coat" is generally used for riding jackets that are worn in hunter and jumper competitions. The coat has notched lapels, front welt pockets, three buttons in the front, and side vents in the back. A "dressage" short coat is a tiny bit longer at the hips, a little more tapered at the waist, and has three or four buttons.

Many coats worn in the show ring are tailored. A tailored coat means it has a lapel, a rolled collar, two-part sleeves, and a lining. Interfacing and some special techniques give the tailored coat a crisp look and provide extra durability. Hip-length coats are usually vented — that is, split to the waist in the back or side back.

The coat should fit well, but should have enough ease for needed movement. Women's coats should taper in a little at the waist. The coat should be wide enough at the hips in back so that the vents do not gape open. The coat length should be at or slightly below crotch level, depending upon what looks best for your build (while sitting on the horse).

On foot, the coat should come to the top of your leg; in the saddle, it just covers your fanny but isn't so long that you sit on it. The bottom button should be slightly above your waist. The coat should be wide enough across the shoulders so that it doesn't pull when you bring your arms forward. (You also need room to raise your arms above your head to mount.) The correct sleeve length allows a small amount of cuff to show when your arms are in the riding position. The sleeves should also be wide enough to give you enough room for movement, but should look trim.

Wool and wool-blend gabardines are excellent fabrics for coats because they are comparatively lightweight, breathable, and durable. Gabardine is a twill fabric, with a fine, diagonal weave. You can use wool-blend or synthetic gabardines if your budget is tight, but buy the best quality you can afford. Synthetic fabrics do not shape as nicely as wool and do not breathe.

The usual choices for color (other than black) are dark navy (the most conservative choice), charcoal with subtle pinstripes, and dark green. The color of the lining fabric should match that of the coat fabric. Short coats run $150 to $300 but should last for years.

Shadbellies are formal coats with tails and are worn for higher level dressage and for some formal hunt classes. They have double-breasted bodices fitted to the waist in front, with notched wing lapels. The coat is worn over a hunt vest or often has fake vest points attached to the inside of the lower front of the bodice to give the appearance of a vest being worn beneath it. The tails are split at center back and have side-back pleats.

Shadbellies are usually made of wool. The tails are lined with leather or water-resistant nylon to protect them from the horse's sweat. The tails are also weighted (usually with drapery weights), so that they hang correctly. Just as with dressage coats, shadbellies are always black or very dark navy blue. The collar can be faced with satin or velvet. Buttons can be the same color as the coat, or silver or gold. The vest points are always canary yellow.

The shadbelly bodice should be form-fitting, but should allow enough ease through the back and shoulders for a smooth fit. The sleeves should be long enough so that they hit the wrist bone when the rider's arms are in the riding position. The tails should lie neatly behind the rider, with their hems hanging at the same level as the rider's knee. When the rider is standing, the hem length of the tails will be at or slightly above the back of the knees.

Care and Cleaning

Horses always seem to rub their runny noses on you when you're wearing your riding coat, so it's a challenge to keep your coat clean. At the show you may have someone hand you your coat just before you enter the arena, putting it on as someone holds your horse. Advise the groom to carry the coat turned inside out. This will keep it away from dust and flying horsehair. After each show, brush off as much dirt and hair as possible. Remove spots with a barely damp sponge, and gently lift stubborn hairs with cellophane or masking tape. Press the coat if you need to, but do not press dirt spots.

When necessary, have your coat dry-cleaned. The less frequently you dry-clean your coat, the longer it will last. Don't store a coat in plastic. Use a fabric garment bag so that the coat fabric can breathe, and hang it on a padded hanger so that it retains its shape.

Breeches

Riding pants, which include breeches and jodhpurs, differ from regular pants in that they are designed to fit correctly while you're riding. There are several fitting considerations that must be considered while you're shopping.

In recent years, manufacturers have come out with a wide range of breech styles. The most common style seen in the show ring is the stretch breech. This very close-fitting style has a front or side zipper. Most have no inseam and the side seam curves to the front of the leg for riding comfort. Breeches have knee or leg reinforcement patches, and the legs end above the ankles. Hunt jodhpurs are similar, but are full length with cuffed bottoms and are worn with jodhpur boots. Full-seat breeches, popular with dressage riders, have a leather insert along the inside of the legs to the seat.

Styles range from semi-fitted pants with pleated fronts to the old cavalry-type flared breeches made from non-stretch fabrics. Show riders usually wear fitted stretch breeches.

White breeches are commonly worn with a black coat, although light beige or light gray are sometimes worn. With white be sure your underwear doesn't show through. Breeches usually need a belt — plain brown or black, with a thin buckle that doesn't make the jacket bulge.

The best fabrics for stretch breeches and jodhpurs are heavyweight knits with a spandex content of two to ten percent. (Spandex is the generic name for Lycra® and similar fibers.) Heavyweight polyester and nylon double knits also make inexpensive, durable pants. Look for double knits without shiny or slippery surfaces.

All stretch breech fabrics should have four-way stretch, that is, both crosswise and lengthwise stretch. A crosswise stretch of at least 30 percent is recommended (this means that ten inches of fabric will stretch to thirteen inches).

The classic choice for non-stretch breeches and jodhpurs is a cotton twill, but consider other cottons and cotton-blends, corduroy, wools, and wool blends. Cotton is the choice for hot weather and corduroy or wool pants for cold weather.

Riding pants have knee and leg reinforcements for added protection at these friction points and to minimize slipping. Knee patches in the same fabric as the pants are less expensive and the pants can be washed without special considerations. The disadvantage is that fabric knee patches wear out faster than leather ones and have no gripping ability. Self-fabric knee patches are best for lightweight or inexpensive fabrics because they aren't going to last as long anyway.

Suede knee patches are long wearing, give better protection than fabric patches, and do not slip. Suede, especially in a matching color, adds to the expense of the garment. Riding pants with real leather patches also require special care in washing, and the patches will eventually dry out and crack. Nonetheless, real leather is the first choice for full-seat inserts because dressage riders want to be "stuck" to the saddle.

Even though stretch breeches and jodhpurs are made with forgiving fabrics, obtaining a good fit can take some experimenting. The fit will depend on the amount of stretch in the fabric. Different manufacturers often have a different fit. Once you find a brand that fits, you will want to stick with it.

Care and Cleaning

Riding pants made from any fabric containing spandex should not be machine dried. Exposure to heat can cause the fabric to yellow or to wear out faster.

Riding pants with real leather patches or inserts should be washed in cool water with a non-detergent soap (like Woolite®) and line dried. Murphy's Oil Soap® also works nicely if you don't mind the distinctive smell. If your pants are really dirty, you can use warm water, but try not to do this too often. The less you wash leather, the longer it will last. After it dries, the leather will probably be stiff. You can rub it with your hand to soften it; it will also soften as you wear the pants. For riding pants made from other fabrics, simply follow the care instructions appropriate for the fabric.

Shirt

Choose a white (or very light-colored) shirt with long or short sleeves (when showing without a coat the shirt must have sleeves). You need a stand-up collar to wear with a choker or stock tie. Choose easy-care fabrics.

Tie

Chokers can be worn with hunt coats. With dressage coats and shadbellies, white stock ties are worn. The stock tie should be attached with a simple gold (or silver) tiepin, usually a safety pin two and a half inches long.

The white stock tie is a carry-over from the formal dress required for hunting. The stock tie historically served two purposes: as a wind breaker around the rider's neck and chest for blustery winter outings, and as a bandage for either rider or horse in case of an emergency while away from home. The stock pin secured the stock at the rider's neck, preventing it from bulging out of the front of the jacket. It also could be used to hold a bandage in place or to fasten the ends together when the stock was pressed into service as a sling for an injured arm.

In the modern-day dressage arena, the well-tied stock looks elegant and helps preserve the ambiance of an earlier time. A clean, correctly tied stock tie gives the judge the impression that not only do you know what you are doing, but that you also care to do your very best.

"Pre-tied" stocks can be purchased. Some look better than others. Also available are "bibs": a fake shirtfront with a stock tie and Velcro® fastener at the back of the neck. If you are brave enough to tie your own, the step-by-step instructions in figure 8.2 should help.

With a hunt coat, you may wear a choker. Men and boys can wear white, button-down collar shirts and a quiet (one-color) tie, preferably one that matches the jacket or is white like the shirt.

Boots

Knee-high dress boots in black are the most common. Field boots (with laced fronts) are rarely seen in dressage classes and are frowned upon at FEI levels.

Whether you're ordering custom-made boots or buying a pair off the shelf, there are certain rules of fit that you should know in order to get your money's worth. Field boots are fine at the lower levels, and those laces at the instep give a closer fit than you can get in dress boots, making for a longer, slimmer leg look (great for everybody, but particularly helpful for heavy or short legs). Field boots are sometimes easier to get on because the lacing

1. Place opening of tie at the back of your neck and bring the A end through the opening. Pull the end of the tie right around to the front of your neck.

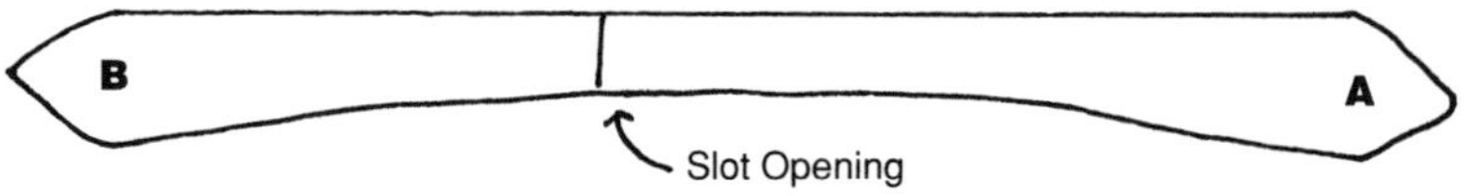

2. Cross the B end of the tie over the A end close to your neck.

3. Now follow the diagrams below.
Turning this page upside down may make this easier for you!

(3a)

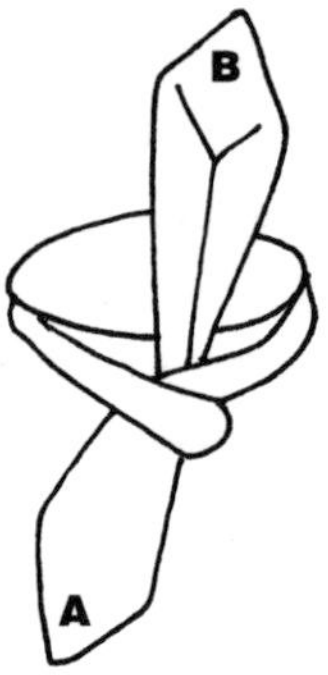

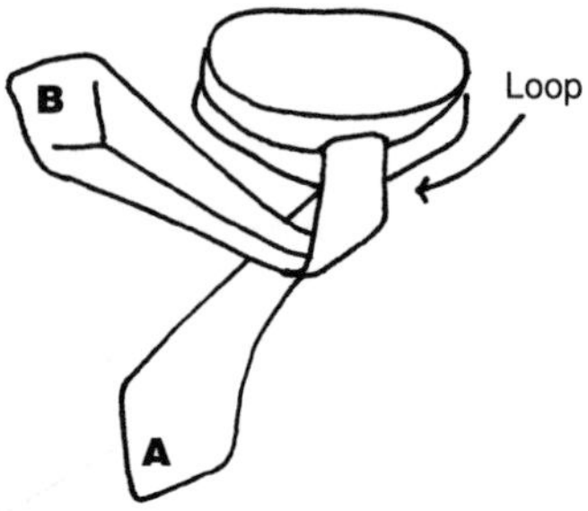

(3b) Create a loop with B end.

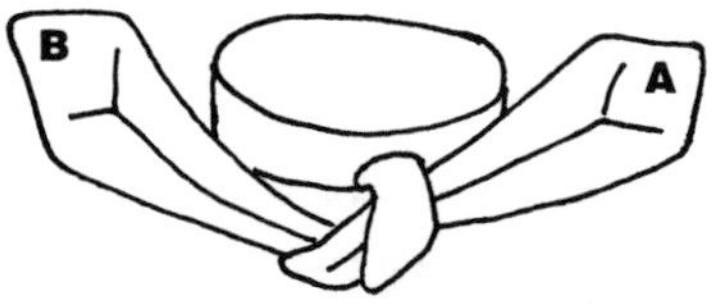

(3c) Pull A end through B.

(3d) Fiddle with the knot so it looks good and is flat in the front. Cross A over B and secure with a stock pin.

Figure 8.2 Tying the stock tie.

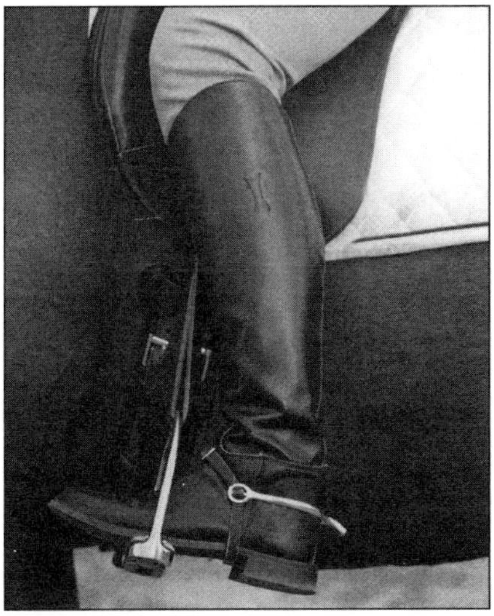

Figure 8.3 Correct fit of boots and spurs. Photo by Charlene Strickland.

at the throat opens to admit the foot and then closes to a narrow fit. Dress boots are almost always black (required at FEI levels) and never have laces.

When the rider is mounted, the boots should rise to the back of the knee. They should be comfortable (not cut off circulation!) but inserting a single finger should make them too tight. The front line should cling closely to the front of the leg (figure 8.3).

Boots will feel a little too tall when they're new and stiff, but will lose height as they break in and wrinkle a bit.

Boots should rise as much as an inch above the knee in front when the rider is standing on the ground because they will be lower when the rider mounts and bends the ankle. Not only does the mounted position immediately lower the boot, but also eventually the wrinkles that develop around the ankles of all boots lower them even more. Brand new off-the-shelf boots will actually hurt the backs of your legs a little when you bend your knee. They'll soon drop, or you can buy extra-high boots and have them lowered slightly behind.

When you mount, the boots should not gap noticeably at the top. If they do, a good shoemaker can sometimes remedy the problem. Most competitors recommend the harder boots that don't wrinkle as much, thus creating a more elegant picture.

Rubber soles (rather than leather soles) add considerably to the life of the boot. Ribbed soles also add to the security in the stirrup (it can be a bit embarrassing to lose a stirrup in a class).

Taking Care of Boots

Saddle soap, Neatsfoot Oil, and specially formulated boot creams can be either over or under-used. The key word to their application is moderation.

Use only specially formulated boot and shoe creams and conditioners. Buff excess polish off your riding boots, as any extra will seal the leather and prevent it from breathing.

Remove all mud immediately, before it dries, or it will dry out your boots. To prevent staining, apply boot cream only to the portion of your boot that doesn't touch your saddle pad, then use a light conditioner on the inside of the boot.

If your boots get wet, wipe off the excess water and immediately clean them with a good glycerin soap or creme polish. If boots get very wet, a little Lexol® is good for reconditioning the leather.

Be careful not to get your boots too oily or they will sag prematurely. To blacken the worn spots, use black leather dye. Shoe polish will usually wipe right off when dampness, sweat, or water touches the boot.

Some manufactures feel wooden trees are the best way to prolong the life of the boot, but they are increasingly difficult to find. Many people simply use a rolled and taped sturdy magazine to hold the boot up. The plastic or metal springloaded trees are not highly recommended, as they can stretch the boot out of shape. All manufacturers agree that you need *something* on the inside of the boots to hold their shape while stored.

Hat

Wear a hunt cap with a hunt or dressage coat, a derby with a dressage coat, and a top hat with a shadbelly.

A top hat is only appropriate when wearing a tailcoat. At the FEI levels it is not permissible to wear a top hat with a short jacket. It is permissable to wear protective headgear (with a dark cover) at any level.

Black velvet is always correct for helmets, although if you're wearing a hunt coat you could wear a brown helmet. If you're wearing a harness, most riders and coaches think clear ones are less conspicuous. Make sure it's snugly buckled (trim off the excess strap beyond the buckle) and properly positioned with the cup under your chin, not so far back that it will hit your throat and irritate you.

Velvet-covered hunt caps seem to attract dust and lint, and brushing sometimes just moves the lint around. For a more thorough job of cleaning the velvet, wrap your hand in masking tape, sticky side out, and stroke the cap sector by sector. The lint will stick to the tape, and your cap will look clean again.

A black hunt cap that has turned rusty brown from exposure to the sun can be freshened up with black leather dye (*not* polish). Just apply a light coat of dye with a piece of rough cloth. When the cap is dry, go over it lightly with a brush to bring up the nap. It's wise to wear rubber gloves when you do this so your hands don't get dyed, too.

Women's hair should be neatly arranged, preferably pinned back or put up under the hat with a hairnet. Judges do not like loose or braided hair hanging below the collar, and long hair will add unwanted movement to your picture.

A hat that fits well is absolutely necessary. You need to find a hairdo that works and a hat that fits — preferably on the tight side. Then always follow the same routine as you prepare your hair for competition. It's a good idea to warm-up with your hat on; then if there's any problem, it can be fixed before entry into the arena.

Women's derbies and top hats should be secured in place with bobby pins. Some riders use an elastic band attached to the sides of the hat that can be tucked under the hair. Others cut a slit in the sides of the lining that bobby pins can be inserted into. Putting folded tissue paper into the lining can sometimes snug up a loose hat.

For men, it's more difficult. Men usually remove the hat for the salute. You must have a hat that fits perfectly and then you still have to sit perfectly so as not to lose it.

Judges like to see riders wear their hats absolutely level. A hat tipped backward makes a rider look like she's stargazing.

Whatever route you choose, do a dry run before the big day. Fix your hair and wear your hat during a routine workout, when it doesn't matter whether or not it falls off.

Accessories

Gloves are required above Fourth Level but are usually worn at the lower levels also. Although white is traditional and required in FEI level tests, black or brown gloves are acceptable in national tests.

Jewelry is frowned upon except for small stud earrings in pierced ears and a very modest stock pin. Judges frown upon sunglasses, so if you must wear glasses, wear clear lenses.

Spurs are required above Fourth Level but are optional at Fourth and below. The spur works differently from the whip. The whip sends the horse *forward,* while the horse will tend to *bend away* from the spur.

Try this experiment on yourself. Try pushing your open hand against your own rib cage (to mimic the action of the rider's leg). The natural reaction is to brace against the pressure. Now poke your finger against your side. You'll most likely bend your rib cage to move away from the pressure — and so will the horse! This is why spurs are usually introduced when the horse is ready for two-track work.

Most judges prefer riders to wear short, blunt-tipped, "Prince of Wales" spurs. A horse won't notice them if his rider's leg is still, but they're useful if he's lazy or strung out. Position them so they sit on your spur rests, and trim straps — leather preferred — just beyond the keepers.

"Spurs must be made of metal, and there must be a shank either curved or straight pointing directly back from the center of the spur. If the shank is curved, the spurs must be worn only with the shank directed downwards. However, swan necked spurs are allowed. The arms of the spur must be smooth. If rowels are used, they must be free to rotate." (AHSA Art. 1920.6)

It is permissible that spurs point down or straight back. A "curved neck spur" (swan neck) is legal, but a spur that turns up when it was not intended to be worn that way is not legal. French spurs, offset spurs, and fixed rowels are not permitted. *"This restriction also applies to warm-up arenas, as well as during competition."* (AHSA Art. 1920.6)

Care of Clothing

Between shows check your clothes and equipment. Do you need to sew on buttons, work out a stain on your breeches, have boots repaired or conditioned? Do these things immediately upon returning home from a show and keep all your show things together. An extra set of everything (or at the least shirt and breeches) can be very useful, also.

Chapter Nine

Making a Good Impression — Rider Position and Posture

In a dressage test, it is the horse that is evaluated. The judge must score the movements only on their quality — in other words, how the horse performs them. However, **your horse can only be as good as you are** (figure 9.1).

If the rider's seat and aids are ineffective or obtrusive, it will be reflected in the horse's performance. Just as a horse's gaits can be improved by good riding, so can they be "ridden away" by bad riding. If the rider sits crooked, the horse can't be straight or move correctly. Changes of speed when going around corners, circles, or figures are often the rider's problem. If the rider loses her balance, the horse will compensate, affecting the score.

Rider faults can affect the score of every movement of the test. The good news is that you can add points to every movement of your test if you pay attention to your position and posture on your horse. While your horse may not have the natural ability to become an FEI dressage horse, you can help him be the best he can be.

The correct dressage position is described as follows:

When viewed from the side, your body should be positioned so that an imaginary line could be dropped straight from your ear, through your shoulder, through your hip joint and then to your heel. Your stomach and back should be flat and your shoulders should be squared. This will help you stay centered in the middle of your horse. Your leg should fall naturally, with a slight bend in the knee, the calves in light contact with the horse's sides. Proper leg alignment is necessary for correct upper body positioning as well as effective application of the aids (figure 9.2).

When viewed from the front or rear, your shoulders should appear squared and level. Don't allow one shoulder to sag lower than the other. Your head should

Figure 9.1 A beautiful "seat" is instantly recognizable. Photo by Charlene Strickland.

Figure 9.2 When a rider is in the correct position, a line can be dropped through ear, shoulder, hip, and heel. Another line will go from the bit through the wrist and elbow.

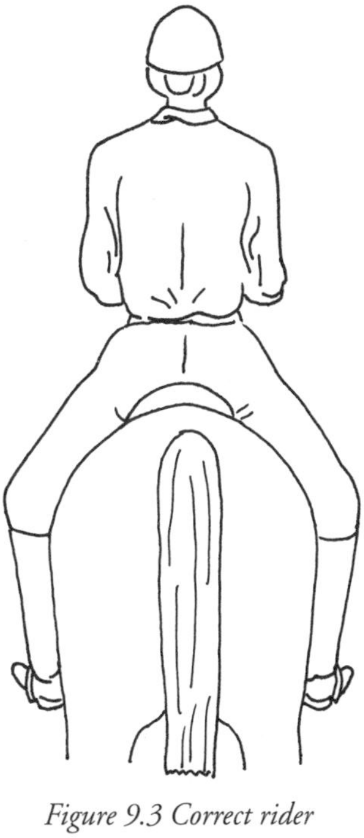

Figure 9.3 Correct rider alignment from the rear.

be straight, not tilted to one side or the chin down. It should be possible to drop another imaginary line from the middle of your head, down between your shoulder blades, through the center of the saddle cantle, and into the center of the horse's backbone (figure 9.3).

Your elbows should lie close to your body, with your wrists aligned with your forearms in a straight line to the horse's mouth. The tension on the reins can be altered by the action of your fingers or by bringing the elbows back — or both. The contact should be elastic, consistent, and sympathetic.

While riders may need to make momentary adjustments to these lines if a horse *is* trying to pull or lean, a good rider can quickly return to these correct alignments.

While most riders know what the correct position is, many times small compromises slip in, then graduate to major faults in posture.

All riders can get so preoccupied with making a horse do something that they become oblivious to their own misalignments. Maybe you are in a situation where you lost confidence and your posture rounds in unconscious apology or insecurity. Or perhaps you misunderstand a correction in your position. For instance, a rider may over-react to her instructor's command to "keep your shoulders parallel to your horse's" and she collapses a hip, or a "lifted torso" becomes a hollow back, or "heels down" puts her in a "chair seat." For whatever reason, you've become crooked, out of position, or out of balance.

Correct body positioning is not only for the horse shows, it's for everyday riding as well. Practice makes perfect: the more you ride using the proper positioning, the easier it will be for you. Remember that you and your horse are a team that is working together. With correct upper body positioning, you'll discover better flowing movement, and a more compatible relationship will develop between you and your horse.

Correcting Posture Faults

Following are the most common posture faults and possible corrections.

Problem: Tension

Tension, or a lack of relaxation, is most often caused by insecurity. If you feel insecure you're probably not sure you can keep your body from being affected by what your horse might do. You worry that if he takes an awkward step during a canter or trot, or spooks at a dog, or takes exception to your aids, you won't have the control you need over yourself to stay with him, hold him together, and give him the support to carry on.

Without security you can't relax; without relaxation, you can't easily control your own body position, and if you can't control your own body, you certainly won't be able to control your horse's. It turns into a vicious circle.

Riders who are not secure instinctively go into the "fetal crouch." This position is characterized by shoulders hunched forward, chest collapsed, stomach tight, and knees drawn up (figures 9.4 & 9.5).

The body language you use while in this position — while trying to stay on top of your horse and keep him going (or keep him from taking off) — sends him mixed messages. Tense, restraining hands hang on his mouth while you clamp with your legs. Your shoulders are going one way and your hips another; you can hardly blame him if his response is confused or startled.

Additionally, if you feel insecure, your muscles will have to work twice as hard to keep you from becoming *more* unbalanced, and as they tense, your ability to feel diminishes even more. Tense muscles can also lead to pain and soreness.

Of course, you have good reason to feel insecure if you don't have the strength and coordination to stay on your horse. You do have to be physically strong and able. You need to

Figure 9.4
The fetal crouch, characterized by shoulders hunched forward, chest collapsed, stomach tight, and knees drawn up.

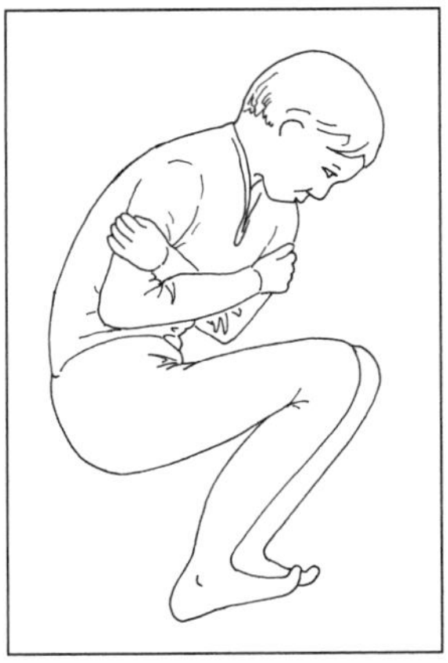

Figure 9.5 Can you see the similarities in this rider's position to the fetal crouch?

develop balance and independent aids. You need the ability to close your legs and keep yourself attached to the saddle without having to think about it. Once the physical strength and coordination are in place, the security these provide will give you the stepping stone toward believing in your skills.

You must develop your mental skills (knowing how to control and influence the horse) hand in hand with developing physical skills. Learn the control points and safety rules for managing your equine friend. This will enhance your confidence and security and therefore your position.

Understand that becoming a "natural rider" does not always mean doing what comes naturally. It can mean changing what you are doing, often in ways that initially feel very unnatural, until the body has regained its poise and security.

If you feel the urge to go into the fetal crouch, raise your chest; shove your hips forward against the front of the saddle and "encircle" the horse with your legs. Toes more or less straight ahead will ensure that you don't "goose" your horse with your heels into unwanted action.

Deep breathing and "soft" eyes are also excellent ways to relieve tension (see Chapter 20, "Dealing with Nerves"). Security is an essential, positive, powerful tool for creating good posture. Almost all position faults are some variation of this instinctive "clutching" position.

Problem: Gripping with the knees or thighs

Do not try to stay on the horse by "gripping." **We stay on the horse by having a leg on each side and keeping the horse going in the same direction we are going.** Gripping with the knees will only push your seat up and out of the saddle. It is like "gripping" an orange with a pair of scissors: The scissors will slide right up and off the orange every time! Your leg must instead become long and enveloping.

First, relax your gripping knees and thighs. Caution: even if you want to relax your knee, you can't if your hip is stiff. To relax the hip joint, simply take your thighs away from the horse for an instant and then let them settle onto the saddle without tension. Allow your hip joints and knees to widen as some of your weight spreads down into your calves. Your knees go down and forward and kneecaps point out just a little (that's why there are knee rolls on the typical dressage saddle). Since the weight of your upper body is on your seat, your thighs rest by their own weight upon the saddle flaps — sort of like heavy bread dough. The weight from the knee down rests on the stirrup. The knees should be flexible, so you can fold them easily as you bring the calves back slightly so that they "wrap around" the horse (figure 9.6).

If your knee is pinching the saddle, you can't sit with the deep, supple seat that encourages your horse to use his back. You don't want your knee flopping loose, but you do want it free to follow the motion of the horse while your leg from the hip through the calf maintains a band of soft contact with his side. Gripping with the knees will also cause the horse to tense his back muscles.

Try this: lock ("grip") your knees deliberately. The change from your soft, following leg will probably cause your horse to stiffen his back, raise his head, or shorten his stride — perhaps all three.

Whenever a horse becomes tense in the back — "clamps" or "hollows" his back — first check that you're not clamping your knees and thighs. If you "pinch" your thighs, it makes your seat hard and unyielding, causing the horse to tighten his back. If you can disengage your thigh muscles, and engage your calf muscles, you can probably disengage the horse's tight back muscles and he should relax. It is rather like holding another person in the circle of your embrace with your fingers pressing on his back but your arms barely brushing his sides. Relaxing your thighs, although it goes against all human nature, will almost always relax the horse.

When your legs are properly positioned, you'll feel that your weight is distributed *around* the saddle, rather than perched heavily on top of it. If you sit too heavily on the horse's back, he can't use it properly to propel himself forward.

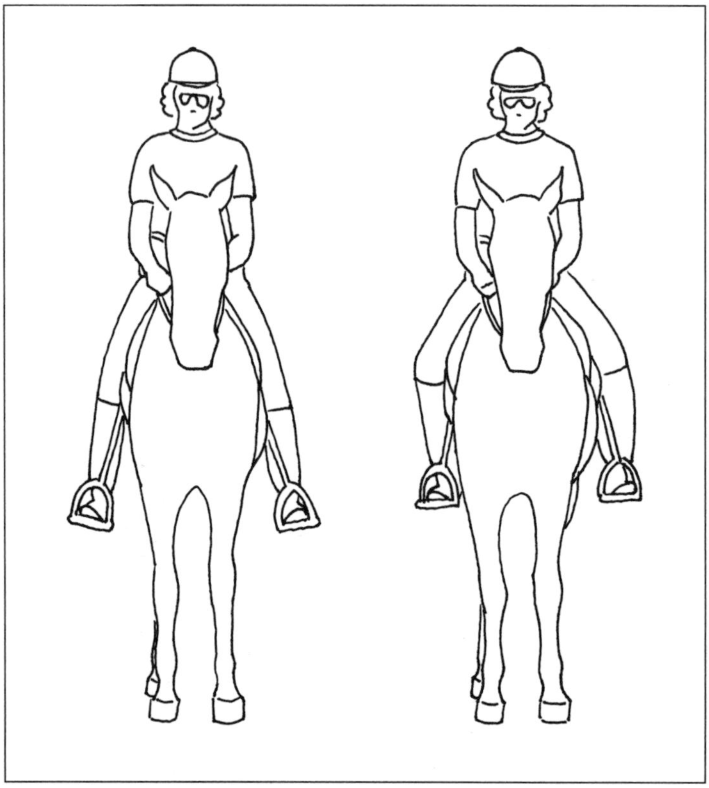

Figure 9.6 Stiff legs (left) push you up and off the horse. Legs "wrapped around" the horse's barrel give you a soft, continuous contact (right).

Problem: Stiff ankles or standing in the stirrups

Riders who habitually press on their stirrups and try to hold a steady leg position, according to some preconceived idea of the perfect seat, invariably *stand in their stirrups*, stiffen their ankles, their knees and their hips, and shove their legs away from the horse.

A common misconception about riding is that in some way the stirrups will help you stay on the horse. The only time the stirrups keep you on is if the horse should suddenly duck sideways. In this case the stirrups are helpful, although if you get comfortable riding without stirrups, you will find you really don't need them to stay on, even if the horse does shy sideways.

The stirrups are there for the same reason that it is comfortable to prop your feet up when sitting in a chair. It helps circulation to flex the ankles a little rather than letting them dangle. Additionally, your nearly level foot will allow your ankle to relax and yet flex in rhythm to your horse's gait, thus provide some shock absorbency.

The ankle must be relaxed so the heel can sink lower than the toe. To lower your heels, raise your toes upward. This firms the calf so it can be used as an aid. If your heels are up, your leg will not be as effective in communicating with your horse.

You ride most effectively with the stirrup iron under the balance point of your foot, which is approximately at the ball of your foot. If it is too far out on your toes or too far under the instep, you lose shock absorbency.

The important point about the level foot (and relaxed ankle) is that if you're artificially forcing your heel down, this action will also send it *forward*. Allowing the feet to go forward puts the rider into the position of a water skier; that is, feet forward, torso leaning back and hands literally hanging on to the horse's mouth for support.

Riding with a forced-down heel creates tension. That heel position means a stiff ankle, which causes a stiff knee, leading to stiff hips — and so on, right up the line. The ankle needs to be flexible enough to sink as needed, as when sitting the trot. This is also why most foxhunting people, trail riders and western riders who work cattle all day ride with a level foot and relaxed ankle, both for efficiency and to prevent stiffness and fatigue.

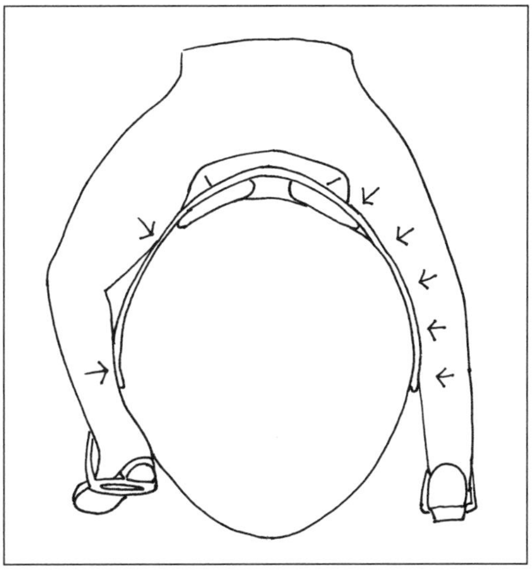

Figure 9.7 If your toes point out, your knees will point out, and you will have very little contact with the saddle.

Problem: Toes point out

Usually, if your toes point out, your knees will point out, which causes a stiff, precariously balanced seat (figure 9.7). Although fashion dictates that the feet should be pointing nearly straight ahead, some people can't keep their feet absolutely parallel to the horse, which demands a degree of rotation in the knee and ankle joints. To find your "comfort zone," stand on the floor with your feet pointed straight ahead and a bit more than shoulder width apart. Flex your knees a little, imagining your horse's barrel between them. Can you still keep your feet flat on the floor? If not and you feel "torque stress" in your knees and your weight shifts to the outside edges of your feet, you'll need to angle your toes out a bit when riding. Do not angle your toes out more than your thighs, however. As you glance down over your knee, you should not be able to see your foot in front of or outside your knees, as is done for clarity in the illustration (figure 9.8).

Problem: Chair seat, hollow back, collapsed back

To have good posture you must have a good, secure base of support in your seat bones and pelvis.

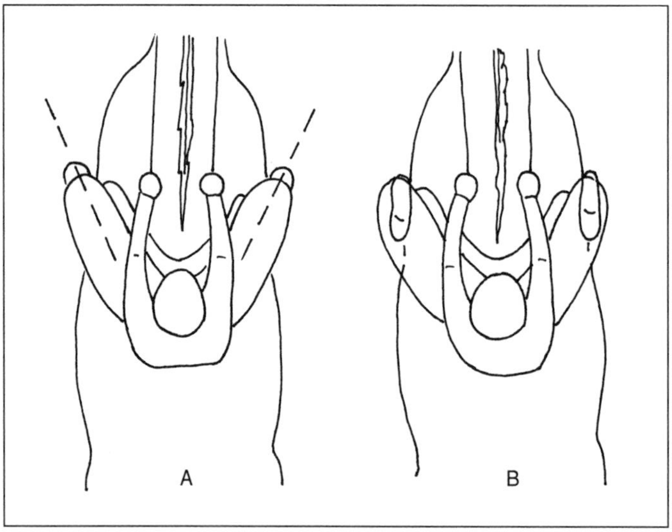

Figure 9.8 It is permissible if your feet are the same angle as your thighs (A). Feet pointed straight-ahead is considered more elegant (B).

The pelvis is a collection of bones that are fused together in a shape rather like a bowl with no bottom. The lower spine is fused into the back of the pelvis at the sacrum. This means that weight from above will be transmitted through the spine and sacrum down the back of the pelvis (figure 9.9). The legs, on the other hand, connect to the pelvis in the hip joints that are located slightly forward of the center of the pelvis. The seat bones are slightly behind and below the hip joints, so, whether standing or sitting, any thrust from above goes down the back of the pelvis and any thrust from below goes up toward the front of the pelvis. When we sit the pelvis quite naturally tilts backward.

The seat bones are shaped a little like sled runners. Unfortunately, they are not very broad or flat but rather somewhat pointed or rounded on the bottom. Therefore they have a tendency to rock forward and

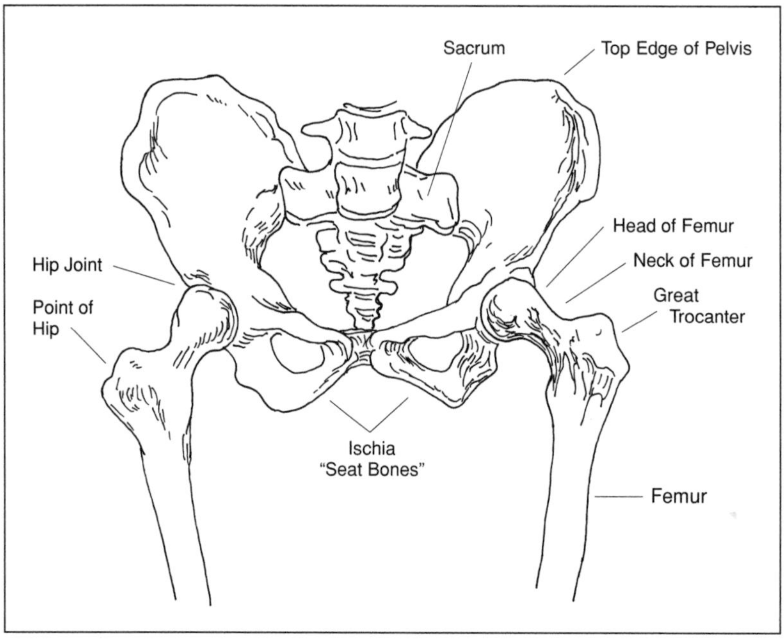

Figure 9.9 Anatomy of the human pelvis. Note how pointed the "seat bones" are.

back. This is good for sitting the trot and canter, but causes difficulties if the rider does not balance on them correctly.

Most riders' natural tendency when sitting on the saddle is to "sit on their pockets," as if sitting on a chair (see figure 9.10B & 9.11A). You should instead "level" the pelvis and position the seat more as it is when standing (figure 9.10A & 9.11C).

To check the "level" of your pelvis, put your hands on your hips, thumbs pointed backward, fingers forward. Now arch (hollow) your lower back. You will feel your pelvis tip forward and down (figure 9.11B). Now tuck your buttocks under ("bow" your back). Your pelvis tips backward as you round your lower back (figure 9.11A). Your pelvis should be level, providing greater stability and keeping your feet underneath you (figure 9.11C).

When the pelvis is correctly "leveled," you will sit on both your seat bones and your buttocks. You should have equal weight on each seat bone. To check this, gently rock side-to-side until you feel equal pressure.

Women often find this position of straightness more difficult than men do. They may have been drilled that good posture is chest out and stomach in, which often creates an arch in the lower back and a chest pointed upward, buttocks pointed backward, position.

Female riders usually need to tuck the buttocks under a little to straighten their spine and level their pelvis. (Without pulling the stomach in, however, which would lower the chest).

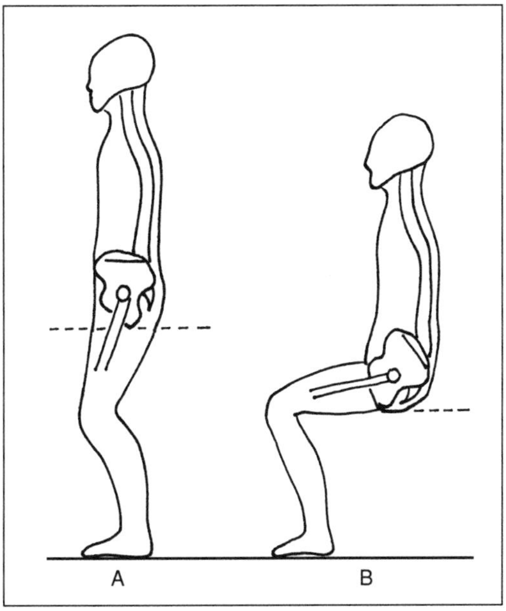

Figure 9.10 The rider must position the pelvis as it is when standing with knees slightly bent (A), not as it is sitting in a chair (B).

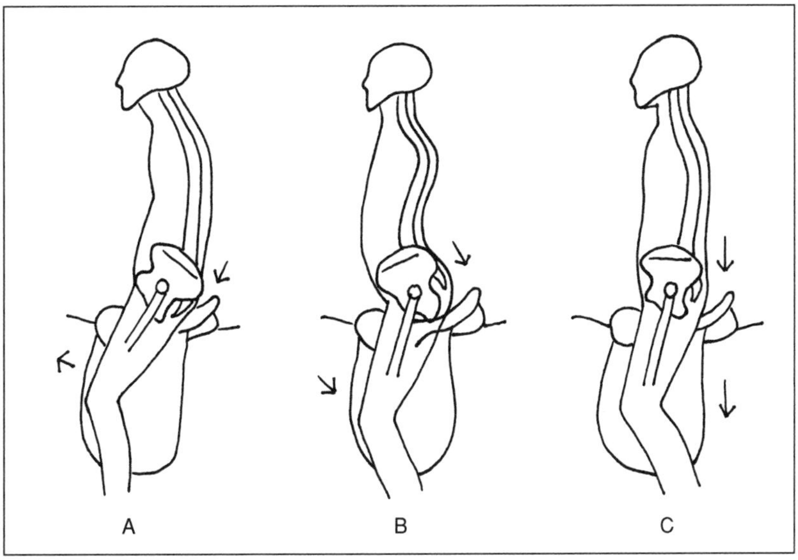

Figure 9.11
When the pelvis rolls backward, it causes a rounded back and shoulders, a collapsed chest, and forward legs: "the chair seat"(A). If the pelvis is rolled forward, it causes a hollow lower back, rounded shoulders, and pinching knees: "the fork seat" (B). A correctly balanced pelvis results in the normal slight curve (C).

It is important to understand the relationship between the pelvis and the rest of your position. If you fall into a "chair seat," your seat bones tilt back, you round your back too much and your legs come up (figure 9.11A). If you try hard to stretch your leg down and "long," it is quite impossible from this position. If, on the other hand, you arch your back too much, you will sit toward your fork (B) so that your seat bones tilt forward and your seat slides to the back of the saddle. The key is to get, and keep, your pelvis level (C).

Problem: Collapsed hip, sitting crooked

In the proper position you will have an equal portion of your body on each side of the horse's spine. If you habitually sit to one side, you probably "collapse a hip" (figure 9.12).

First, check that you have equal weight on each seat bone. To check this, gently rock from side to side until you feel equal pressure on each seat bone. Even better is to have someone periodically watch you from the rear.

If you sit crookedly your horse will move crookedly in compensation. Imagine how hard it would be for you to walk a straight line with rhythmic steps if you had a five-pound weight on one shoulder and a 20-pound weight on the other. Your horse moves just as awkwardly when your weight is unbalanced on his back.

An easy way to correct a collapsed hip is to stretch upward with the arm on the collapsed side (Figure 9.12). For example, if you tend to drop your right shoulder, think of making yourself straighter through the rib cage by stretching your right side. Always make sure each shoulder is directly above each hip joint. If your weight is equal on each seat bone, your shoulders are probably level, and vice versa.

Problem: Poor balance, leaning forward

To maintain an elegant, upright position, your body must be in balance. You need to have your shoulders, hip joints, and ankles in one line. You should look like you would land on your feet if the horse disappeared out from under you.

If any of your body parts are out of alignment, other parts must go out of balance in an opposite direction to keep the whole from toppling over. If you are not in good balance, you will probably teeter forward or back during every transition.

Most riders in poor balance lean forward "over their feet," in order to maintain equilibrium. This will cause

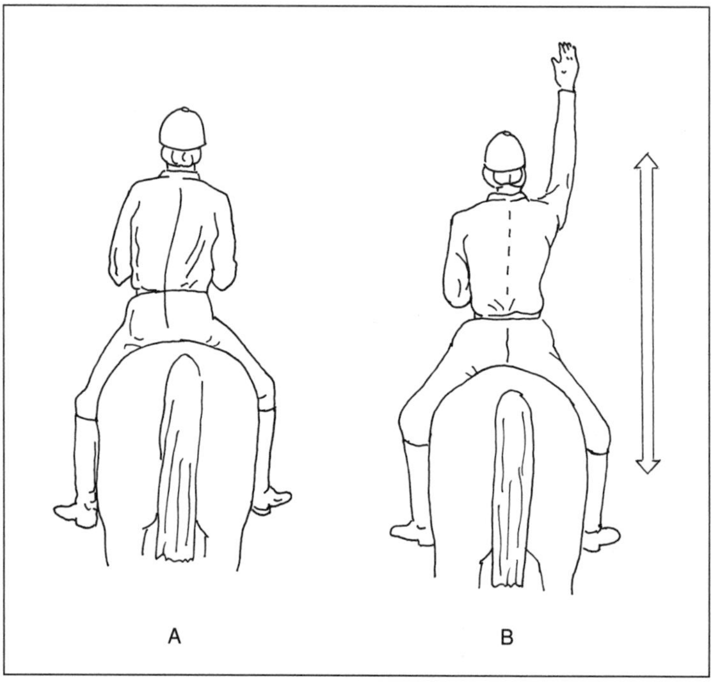

Figure 9.12 Here the right hip is collapsed, causing the seat to slip to the left (A). Stretching up with the arm on the collapsed side helps to correct this unevenness (B).

your horse to go on his forehand and probably quicken his strides.

Here's how to test your balance in the saddle: lean your body forward — notice that it takes muscle effort. Now lean your body back — again it takes muscle effort. The dressage position should be balanced and effortless.

To check your balance on foot, stand sideways in front of a full-length mirror with knees a little bent, imagining you are on your horse. Work your pelvis forward, keeping it level, feet back, shoulders back and in line with your feet; keep working until you get that elegant position seen in photos of top riders. You'll notice that to keep your pelvis forward, you must have *your feet back under your balance point* and your shoulders back — *over your feet.* You'll also notice that it takes some muscle tone to do this (see the next chapter, "Fitness"). All good riders have this muscle tone, although often they don't realize it. It takes some muscle tension in the outer thigh, stomach, and lower back.

Think of what happens to you when your horse begins to trot. Too much relaxation and you flounce around like a rag doll; too much tension and you jerk like a puppet on a string. What you want is something between the two. That is why top riders seem to be so "connected" to their horses. They have become very body-aware and have developed correct muscle tone so they can isolate different parts of their bodies, and they can stay secure yet supple.

Specifically, you want to tone the muscles in your thigh, pelvis, and trunk. When you have enough tone in these muscles, you will be able to control your body and become an effective, as well as an elegant, rider.

Caution: sitting up straight is not the same as sitting *still.* If you try to sit still, the horse will jar you at every step and topple you forward or back every time he makes an unexpected move. Sitting stiff and still will put you out of touch with and "behind the motion" of the horse and makes your position precarious. You'll always be a halfbeat behind, forever trying to catch up to your horse's motion. Try giving a friend a gentle push while both of you are standing up straight and stiff. Chances are, both of you will teeter out of balance. On horseback, any sudden change of speed or direction can easily knock the straight (and still) rider off balance.

Yet another way to get this elegant feeling is to imagine your body being suspended by a cord attached to the top of your head. Stretch your head and chest upward, as if a helium balloon attached to your head were tugging upward, drawing your body along. As you lift your face up, lift your chest up, stretching your spine and "growing" upward. Raising the head and chest strengthens the abdominal and back muscles, so your upper body "carries itself" and relieves the horse's back.

With your chest up, your abdomen should feel like a giant spring being expanded upward in this area. Do not tighten your stomach muscles, and remember to breathe (figure 9.13).

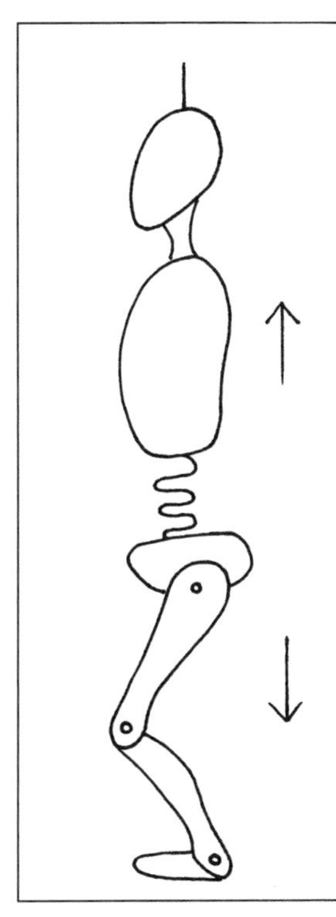

Figure 9.13 Imagine your body being suspended by a cord attached to the top of your head. This will help you to stretch up and down.

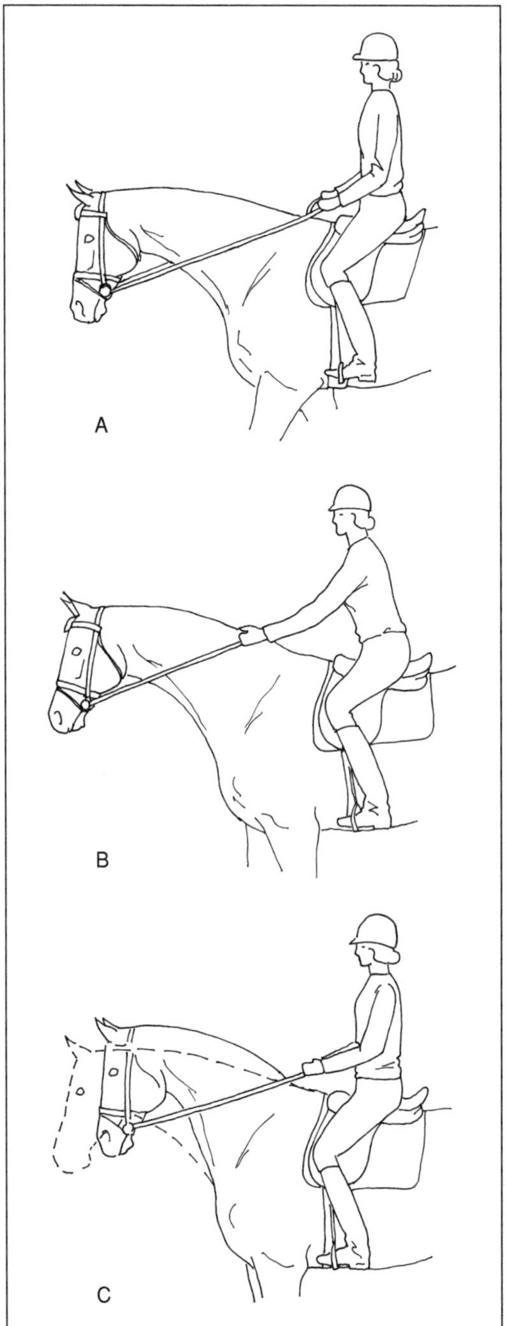

Figure 9.14 The shortening of the reins: The young horse is in a longer "frame," therefore, the reins must be longer (A). Many riders tend to lean forward in order to shorten the reins (B). Bringing the arms forward (from the elbow) will give you a lot of "play" with the reins on the green horse who does not yet have a steady head position. As the horse comes more "on the bit," then the rider can shorten the reins and maintain a better upright position (C).

When you stretch upward, the motion releases your neck and your back. Your lighter seat bones and softer seat invites your horse's back to lift and round, so that his back feels more like a springy cushion and less like a rigid board!

Problem: Leaning back

You may have heard reference to a "driving seat" in dressage. This is not a leaning back of the torso. The rider has to learn to use her back while remaining in balance with the horse. If you lean back, you fall behind the horse's center of gravity.

The "driving seat" is a *momentary* (in rhythm with the gait) *slight* arching of the lower back that "scoots" the seat forward for an instant. It momentarily puts the pelvis slightly ahead of the shoulders. This is followed by a *slight* rounding of the back (then returning to the "neutral" position). It accomplishes a gentle "shove" of the pelvis forward and then back. It is part of a half-halt (see Chapter 11). It has also been described as a quick pulse of the abdominal muscles and forward tilt of the pelvis. During this motion, the rider's shoulders should not change their position.

Problem: Head down or hunched shoulders

The most common fault among dressage riders is carrying the head down and the shoulders hunched forward. This is caused by constantly looking down, in an attempt to "see" what the horse is doing. If you ride with your head bowed down, it rounds your shoulders and puts extra weight on the horse's forehand. Ever notice that the horse almost always nods as the rider bows their head to salute?

To correct this, center your skull onto your spine so your face is looking straight ahead, not up or down. Most experts tell us to "look where you want to go and the horse will go where you look." This is because the horse will be guided by the small weight shifts that correspond to wherever your attention is focused. Additionally, you cannot see where you are going if you are staring at your horse's neck!

Don't ride with your chin poking out or forward, either. This kind of posture creates tension in your shoulders or back. To lower your shoulders, think about squeezing your armpits to your body. "Bring your neck back to your collar" is a visual image that many jumper riders use.

If you must glance down at your horse, do so quickly. Learn to *feel* the horse's movement and your position — seat to mind. Not eye to mind to seat — that takes too long. Rather, seat to mind, to action!

Bringing the arms forward to shorten the reins is another cause of hunched, forward shoulders. This position with the hands forward gives the rider some extra room to adjust quickly as is sometimes necessary with a young or fractious horse.

The position in which you carry your hands will depend on your horse's conformation and stage of training. The young horse is in a longer frame, therefore, the reins must be longer. You must resist the temptation to lean forward as this will put your horse on his forehand. Instead bring your elbows forward (but never totally straight) in order to shorten the reins (figure 9.14).

Don't "pinch" your shoulder blades back to correct hunched shoulders — this will stiffen and hollow your back. Instead imagine your shoulders "growing" out and back. If you still can't get the right feel, pull your shoulders up toward your ears and then let them drop down. After doing this several times your shoulders should settle in the correct position.

Do's and Don'ts of Good Posture

Good posture demands some work and attention — both on the horse and off.

- DO sit and stand up straight (with good posture). If you must sit at a desk or behind the steering wheel for long periods — DO practice sitting up straight. At first, for just a minute or two, then five minutes, then longer. You'll be amazed at how easy and natural it will become.
- DO look at your posture as you walk past store windows or mirrors — walk with good posture!
- DON'T overindulge in unilateral sports, like tennis or golf, that develop one side of your body more than the other.
- DO walk and swim briskly as often as possible for exercise. They're aerobic and bilateral.
- DON'T ever intentionally snap your head back sharply.
- DON'T carry any heavy item in one hand.
- DO carry heavy items in front of, and close to, your body.
- DON'T do any exercise that involves arching (hollowing) the back.
- DON'T ever bend sharply from the waist straight down to your toes.
- DO use a mounting block whenever you can. It's easier on your horse, on you, and your saddle.

Chapter Ten

Rider Fitness and Diet

You've got to be fit to ride well. Since the horse depends on you for directions, it helps his work if the rider is balanced, coordinated, and strong enough to communicate her aids clearly. Aesthetic appeal is also a large part of dressage. A fit horse and rider will look more beautiful and harmonious.

Ask yourself this: Can you work your horse through his daily repertoire (not just hacking) and still feel fresh afterwards? Can you ride through the final movements of a test in competition and know that you are performing as efficiently and stylishly as you were at the beginning of the test? Do you have a nagging suspicion that you could help your horse more and correct him with quicker reactions if you were fitter?

To get more specific, do any of the following scenarios sound familiar?

- When you begin your ride, your horse is relaxed, willing, and moving freely, but gradually his gaits grow choppy and he becomes inattentive and even resistant to your aids. You attribute his change in attitude to boredom or fatigue.
- Although you start your ride with beautiful posture, you find yourself slouching after twenty minutes in the saddle.
- You find yourself huffing and puffing after just a few minutes riding or turn to jelly halfway through a dressage test and exit the arena gasping for air.
- Do you tip forward or back during every transition from one gait to another, or slip to one side during turning?
- After almost every ride, you have a headache or a funny "crick" in your neck. You think your helmet weighs too much.
- The day after a lesson or show are you so sore and stiff you can hardly move?

If you recognize any of these situations, the odds are that something more fundamental than your horse, your helmet, or your saddle is to blame. You're probably out of shape. Many equestrians, for one reason or another, don't want to accept the fact that fitness is a requisite of riding. Success in any discipline, be it reining or jumping, barrel racing or dressage, depends on excellent muscle control, endurance, and flexibility — the rider's as well as the horse's.

If you find yourself huffing and puffing after just a few minutes of riding, you are probably in very soft condition, with muscles unable to work well for even short sessions of activity and effort. As your muscles fatigue, your aids get sloppy, your legs and arms become difficult to control, and your posture suffers. You then become unbalanced and can't react as quickly to the horse's unnatural moves. You're going to be off-center in the saddle, putting strain on his back and making one side of him work harder. Even if your horse is in top condition, your own weariness is bound to cause him confusion and even pain.

Perhaps you assume that your labors in the saddle will keep you in shape. Unfortunately, even if you spend many hours in the saddle every day, riding alone is not enough to make you fit.

Paradoxically, riding is one of the few sports in which the better you are, the less exercise value you get out of the activity. While a novice rider expends a great deal of effort and energy to simply stay on the horse since she may be off balance and using the wrong muscles, the more accomplished rider expends little effort to stay on.

Nor is stable work and other manual work, with or without horses, conducive to good riding posture or fitness for riding. To the contrary, stable work is excellent for producing large shoulders and aching backs. This means unless you are lucky enough to ride three or four horses every day, you need to develop the stretching capacity of the muscles that do the work in riding.

For riding you need shoulder and upper-back muscles strong enough to stabilize you and let you maintain a feel that's both steady and relaxed, without tightening your forearms or biceps. You need lower-back muscles strong enough to maintain your position through transitions — and right afterward provide driving power to maintain the gait. Your stomach muscles have to support your back and keep your pelvis pulled forward so you can drive with your seat, influence your horse's hindquarters, and engage his top line. Your thigh muscles must not only anchor you and keep you secure in the saddle but also energize, engage, balance, and influence the horse's hindquarters and his

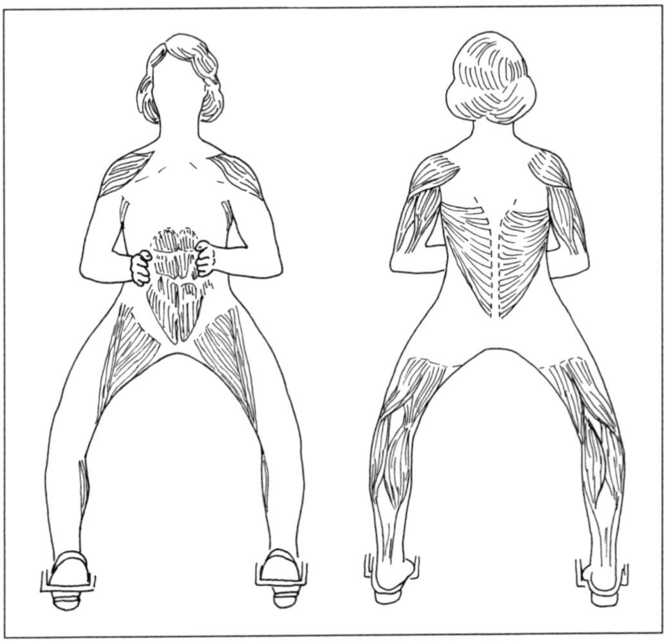

Figure 10.1 Riding a horse uses surprisingly few muscles. However, the ones you do use need to be reasonably strong and elastic (supple). The structures highlighted are those most often used while riding.

middle section, all the way up to his shoulders. And your lower legs have to be strong enough to give his legs energy and make them move. The kind of strength described here only comes from a fitness program (figure 10.1).

There is some good news, however. With a carefully executed conditioning program, your riding will improve and your horse will be more comfortable (and effective). The even better news is that getting fit to ride does not have to be difficult or time consuming.

Although riding can help us shape up, it won't get us all the way there. At the beginning and intermediate levels, riding provides excellent exercise. Riding strengthens some muscles new riders never knew they had. In addition, riding certainly makes a person more flexible. But riders eventually reach a fitness plateau, and only additional exercise will get them beyond it. Perhaps you've worked with your horse for so long that you're not increasing your strength any more. It's like lifting the same bag every day. After a while, you don't notice the weight.

In fact, riders whose fitness depends solely on riding may develop painful problems. Weak or tight muscles force other muscles to compensate, putting the rider at much greater risk of muscle, tendon, and back injury.

The Three Elements of Fitness

Fitness is a measure of how well a body meets physical demands and withstands physical and psychological stresses. Three components affect a person's reaction time, coordination, control, and other physical abilities:

a) Endurance — how many times, or for how long, you can exert force.

b) Flexibility — the range of motion of your joints.

c) Strength — how much force you can exert.

Until the early 1990s, aerobic (oxygen burning) activity was considered the be-all and end-all of physical fitness. But recent studies demonstrate that endurance, strength, and flexibility exercises are also important. These should sound familiar, since they are the same qualities we strive to obtain in our horses!

Indeed, physical fitness not only makes you a healthier person, it makes you a better rider as well. Muscle strength helps you control and guide your equine partner while holding your own body in position; flexibility keeps you in the saddle as your horse gallops, swerves, jumps, and stops; endurance keeps you from "running out of gas" at a crucial moment.

Endurance

Good health and good riding are based on cardiovascular as well as muscular endurance. Although cardiac fitness refers only to the heart — the most important muscle of all — muscular endurance refers to your body's ability to exert itself over long periods of time.

A poorly conditioned cardiovascular system limits a rider's performance capability more than any of the other components of health-related fitness. Moreover, the exercises that improve cardiovascular endurance also improve muscular endurance, the ability of a muscle to perform tasks repeatedly.

To build cardiovascular endurance, your heart and lungs need to work harder than normal for at least twenty minutes at a time. Check with your doctor before starting any new fitness program, and before you begin sweating madly to the oldies, determine the target heart rate you want to reach during your workout.

Breathing is especially important during exercise. If your breathing is shallow and hurried, using quick short breaths, you deprive your body of the oxygen required to enable it to work efficiently (which may explain why you are out of breath when you finish a competition test). On the other hand, if you breathe excessively (hyperventilate) before you exercise, and then hold your breath, you may faint.

What cardiovascular exercise is best for riders? Probably any aerobic activity is going to be all right. Any exercise that gets your heart really pumping will build endurance. The easiest thing to make time for is an exercise that is easily done in your home or back yard. If you're only going to do one thing, you can skip rope. It's probably the best single exercise.

Another very effective exercise option is power walking, which you can do practically anywhere, at any time. You can also easily increase walking's "oomph" by climbing hills, which doubles the benefits without markedly increasing time or distance.

Many top riders recommend swimming as very complementary to riding. It works all the muscles in your body and builds incredible strength and cardiovascular stamina without an iota of stress from impact.

Jogging is a form of exercise that's popular with many riders. It's virtually cost-free, and it develops stamina. Unfortunately it develops thick calf muscles (your riding boots may not fit!) and doesn't really call on the important riding muscles. If you do walk, jog, or cycle (stationary or not), you must include upper-body work and stretching as well.

To get the best out of cardiovascular exercise, work out at least three times a week, with enough variation in the activities to avoid monotony. If you are really cramped for time, instead of riding your horse for the ten to fifteen minutes to warm him up, hand jog him. As with any other form of exercise, start with shorter times and increase it as you become stronger.

Flexibility

Flexibility refers to a joint's range of motion, which is ruled largely by how much "give" the muscles attached to it have.

In order for your joints to work their best, your muscles need to stretch their best. The more flexibility your muscles have, the more efficient the joints will be and the less likely you'll be to suffer strained muscles, tendons, or ligaments.

If a rider can't achieve a full range of motion with her joints, she won't be able to bend the ankles to keep the heels down, or open her hip enough to keep the leg back, or follow the horse's motion at the sitting trot and canter. Women usually have more flexibility than men, but older riders (men *and* women) often lose that freedom in the joints.

Muscles cannot stretch by themselves, they can only contract (shorten). Muscles can be caused to stretch only by (1) gravity; (2) outside tension (something or someone pulling on a limb, for instance); or (3) by contraction of antagonist (opposing) muscles in which one muscle contracts to cause another muscle to stretch.

Actually, any exercise, be it aerobic or strengthening, that pushes the joint to open and close is also causing muscles to stretch. Muscle fibers are very similar to elastic bands, if pulled beyond their ability to stretch, they can tear. The more you stretch a muscle, however, the more the fibers learn to tolerate and the farther the muscle can extend.

This stretching ability increases blood flow to the area and thereby increases not only flexibility but muscular endurance. Slow, methodical stretching exercises might seem dull, but stretching is a great way to improve performance. It's also a good way to warm up. Caution is indicated, however, because stretching improperly could lead to muscle soreness or even microscopic muscle tears. Be sure only to stretch a muscle when it is relaxed.

Many stretching exercises are good to use as warm-up before you mount.

When planning a stretching program, focus on muscles that are more prone to tightness, such as the hamstrings in the back of the upper leg, the hip flexors, the quadriceps in the front of the upper leg, the calves, the

Fitness Cautions

A "warm-up" and "cool-down" phase should be part of any training program as well as the practicing of the sport itself.

While exercising remember:

- Breathe normally—never hold your breath. Inhale before you lift or push, exhale as you lift, inhale again as you return to the starting position.
- Control movements. Flex your muscles smoothly and lower and release a position gradually, so that your muscles get the most out of the workout.
- Don't bounce—you can cause micro tearing of muscles, tendons, and ligaments.
- Lift from the hips—not the lower back. Support heavy loads with the muscles of your legs and buttocks, and keep you knees bent.
- Avoid pain and fatigue. Stop if it hurts—a dull ache is normal, but a sharp pain means you've done too much or are doing it wrong.
- Don't let your muscles get chilled in cold weather. Cold muscles are stiff muscles, and stiff muscles can tear.
- Use moderation. How do you know you are exercising "moderately?" An easy rule of thumb is if you cannot talk during exercise, you are working too intensely, so slow down. If you can sing, you are exercising too slowly, so speed up and work harder.
- Repeat an exercise only as long as it can be tolerated. Exercise to the point of fatigue, but not beyond. And don't work the same muscle group more than once a day.
- While a little next-day soreness (after a workout) is to be expected, stop immediately if you feel pain during the exercise.

Achilles tendons, the lower back, the shoulders, and the chest. Exercises #1 through #7 (figure 10.2) are stretching exercises. You might also use a flexibility-improving discipline like swimming, cross-country skiing, T'ai Chi, or yoga.

Flexibility is more quickly influenced than strength or endurance. According to fitness professionals, by stretching five days a week, twenty minutes each day, you will see a marked improvement in one month. Strength and endurance may take four months or more.

Strength

Strength relates to the muscles' ability to produce force. In many sports, muscle bulk and power are required. This may be in order to throw or kick a ball as far as possible; it may be needed to spring, or to cycle long distances. In riding, this type of muscle building is not required or even desirable. The sport does, however, require the use of many muscles that are not routinely worked in any other form of familiar exercise.

Strength helps a rider mount, pull forward into the jumping position, slow or stop an over-eager horse, perform a half-halt, or sit up elegantly. Muscle tone also builds bone mass, increases metabolism, and lowers the risk of injury.

The *combination* of strength and stretch prevents the "muscle-bound" syndrome that affects athletes in other sports. As muscle fibers develop, they typically shorten, thus inhibiting flexibility and becoming more prone to stress-related injury. Therefore, the effective rider must have the right body *texture*, which is partly genetic and partly acquired.

The fact is that men have about thirty-five percent more muscle fiber than women. They are naturally more sinewy. The rider needs high muscle tone but freedom in the joints. Bulky muscles limit flexibility (suppleness). What you want is "isometric tone." This means the ability to activate muscles on both sides of a joint in order to make the small, frequent changes necessary to match the movements of the horse. This is unlike the large muscle contractions that cause joints to move. Isometric tone stabilizes the joints without making them rigid. Specifically, you want to tone the muscles in your thigh, pelvis, and trunk. When you have enough tone in these muscles, you will be able to control your body and become an efficient, elegant rider. Exercises that are good for muscle tone are floor exercises, weight lifting (moderate), swimming, cycling — actually, almost any exercise that involves movement.

Even if you don't belong to a gym, there are plenty of home exercises to strengthen the muscles that will be used on the horse. Exercises #8 through #16 are recommended for riding strength.

Finding Time

Robert Dover (Olympian and professional trainer, instructor, and competitor) works out two hours a day, six days a week. His fitness regime includes the treadmill, free weights, and exercises to increase flexibility. He simply states, "I'm committed to staying fit, being an athlete and looking like one."[1]

However, that's Robert Dover. If you're like the majority of amateur riders, you're already trying to fit horses into a busy life; you don't have time to do everything!

So take it easy. There's no reason to overdo a fitness program. You're not preparing for the Olympics, yet! If you're a Training or First Level rider, twenty minutes of moderate exercises three days a week should do you well. If you're aiming at Second Level and above, perhaps thirty to forty-five minutes, three to five times a week would do you better. If you ride every other day, do your exercise program on the other days.

For maximum effect, cross-train by balancing a few different forms of exercise. For example, if you can only get to the gym one night a week, power walk another day and swim on the third.

You'll soon be looking better, feeling better, and, more than anything else, riding better. So push yourself, but push within a reasonable, gentle, doable "comfort zone." Remember that after a workout, muscles require downtime to rebuild and strengthen. When you're in your twenties, you can over exert and your body can recover within hours. But if you're older, it takes you longer to recover.

It is also important not to overdo physical training, which should always be progressive and should take into account the rider's age and medical condition. In special cases, medical advice should be sought before a strenuous course of training is undertaken. If you do too much and overexert yourself for the condition you're in, before you know it, you're fatigued, you're injured, you're stressed, or you're just plain burned out.

If you are bored by the very thought of attempting to exercise on your own, play your favorite music, exercise with a friend in front of the TV or on your lunch hour. Always remember to breathe deeply, relax, and laugh often.

Creative time use may mean striding briskly through an airport or mall rather than strolling. When sitting for a long period of time, occasionally flex your muscles. Do things by hand, not by machine (for instance: mow the grass with a walking mower). Walk or climb stairs instead of riding the elevator. It may mean parking a block away from your work place and walking, or biking to the barn instead of driving, or walking for part of your lunch break rather than reading. It may mean tucking your

[1] Robert Dover, interview by Jane Savoie, in *Dressage Today*, April 1995.

Figure 10.2 **Floor Exercises**

These sixteen simple exercises will work all the major riding muscles. Select exercises that will concentrate on the parts of your body that you see as the weak links in your riding, but take care not to overdo any one set. Jog on the spot a little, shake your shoulders, arms, and legs, and move about to keep yourself loosened up between exercises.

(1) This exercise will stretch neck, upper back, and shoulder muscles.

A. In sitting or standing position, interlace fingers and slowly straighten arms above the head. Palms face up, keep chin up.

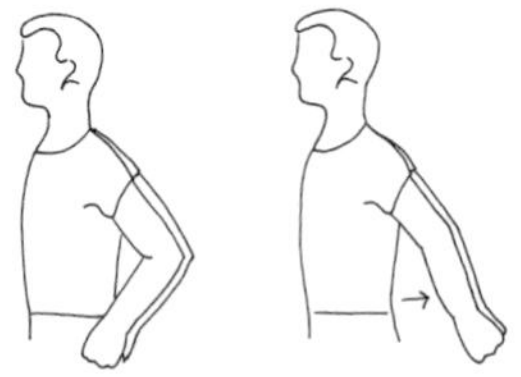

(2) Tones back of arms, straightens round shoulders.

A. Press shoulder blades together, fold and unfold the elbows.

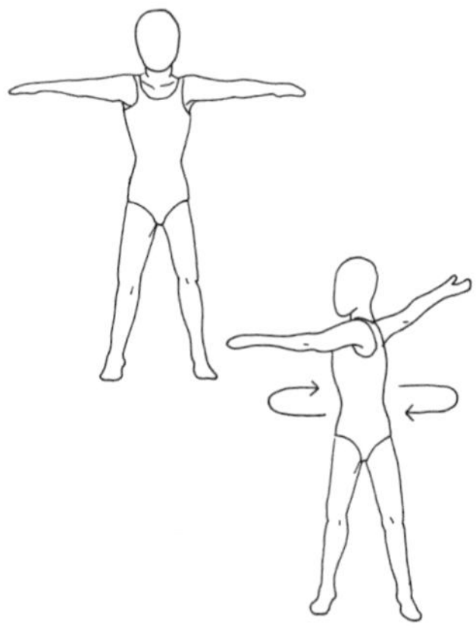

(3) Loosens waist and stretches side and shoulder muscles.

A. Stand with your feet about eighteen inches apart, arms outstretched at shoulder height.

B. Slowly turn the upper body at the waist, keeping the head aligned with the rotating shoulders. Turn first one direction, then the other.

(4) Stretches and strengthens side muscles and helps to correct "collapsed hip."

A. With your feet about eighteen inches apart, stretch one arm over your head and let the other slide down the opposite leg. Hold the position and count, starting with three seconds and increasing the hold daily.

B. Slowly return to upright.

C. Repeat the exercise to the other direction, and hold for the same count.

D. Slowly return to upright, repeating the movements once more each way. Think about your breathing.

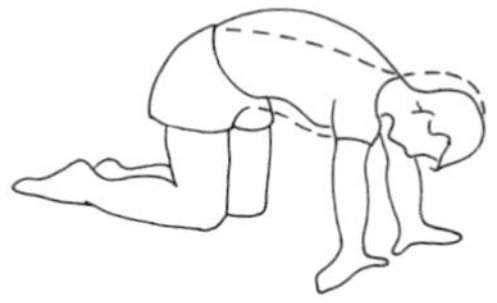

(5) Stretches spine, tones back and stomach.

A. On hands and knees, slowly arch your back, relax, then slowly hollow your back.

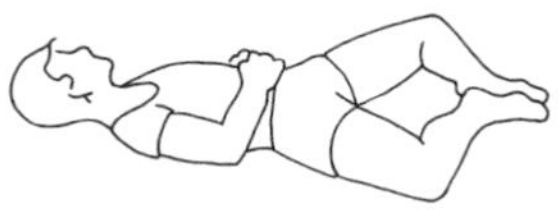

(6) Relaxes and stretches the "grippers"—the muscles on the inside of the thigh that block the pelvis and lock the hip joint. These muscles have to be able to relax (stretch) so they can move in coordination with your buttock muscles.

A. Lying on your back with knees bent and feet flat together, slowly move knees apart while keeping the soles of your feet together. Don't strain.

(7) The muscles that move the pelvis forward and allow the thigh to go back are often too short and need to be stretched.

The right knee rests on the floor (or a pillow), left hand supported on a chair; with the right hand push the pelvis forward and hold for 5 to 10 seconds. Practice on both sides.

(8) Loosens hip, strengthens outside of thigh.

A. Lie on your left side, with your legs straight, one on top of the other. Balance your upper body on one forearm and both hands flat on the floor in front of you.

B. Raise your right leg straight up, away from your left leg, and count to three. Lower your leg and repeat three times.

C. Turn onto your right side and repeat the same upward stretching with your left leg. Repeat three times.

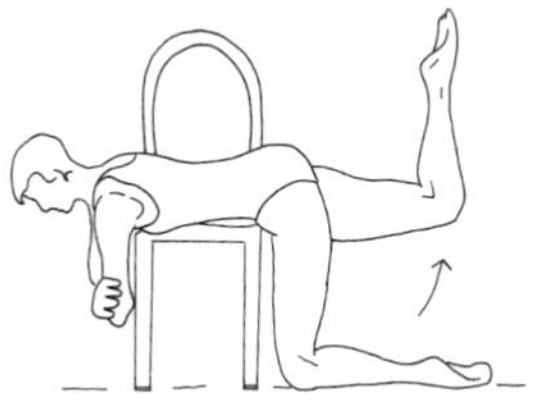

(9) The buttock muscles need to stabilize the pelvis and at the same time work against the muscles of the inner thigh. The buttock muscles open the legs; the inner thigh muscles close them. This exercise strengthens the buttock muscles.

A. With legs bent at a 90-degree angle, while lying on a chair, lift one leg slowly up to the horizontal, keeping the knee at a 90-degree angle; alternate legs.

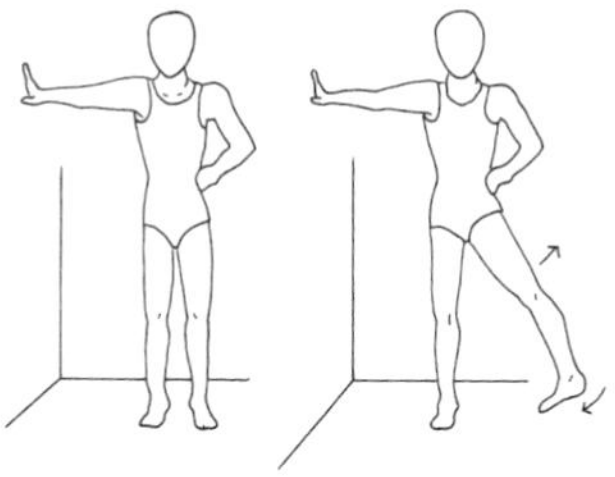

(10) Stretches and loosens hip joints (to "open" the seat), strengthens the thigh of the supporting leg.

A. Balance yourself with a wall or table. Do not lean on the wall.

B. Swing the leg that is away from the wall to the side and point the toes downward, pivoting the ankle.

C. Swing up to eight times. Turn around and alternate legs.

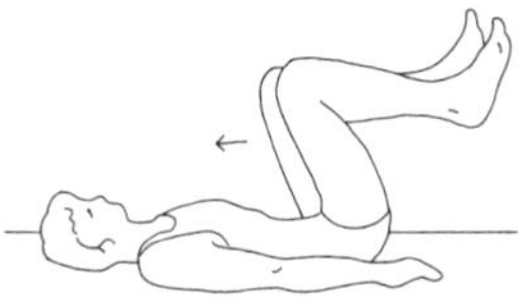

(11) The deep, straight stomach muscles have to be strong enough to naturally lift up the pelvis region and support the trunk. The next four exercises are variations of "crunches," or "sit ups."

A. Lie on your back, legs lifted, arms stretched next to your body; lift up your thighs several times in the direction of your chest, lifting buttocks slowly (not with an "oomph") from the floor.

(12) Strengthens the abdominals, stretches the entire body. The stomach muscles are the ones that "hold" you upright in the saddle.

A. Sitting up, stretch out your arms straight in front at shoulder level, with your legs straight and together.

B. Slowly lower your back to the floor. Take your arms right back and over, with your whole body stretched flat.

C. Now sit up slowly, without lurching suddenly, and continue stretching your arms forward and down with your body.

D. Stretch your arms forward, stretching shoulders and back forward.

E. Slowly return to an upright position and begin once more.

F. Repeat the whole exercise three to six times.

Variation:

A. Clasp hands behind your neck (do not pull on the neck), and sit up and touch alternating elbows to knees. Knees can be bent a little or stretched out on the floor. Repeat six to ten times. Increase to twenty as strength increases.

(13) Fourth variation of "crunches," sometimes called "quarter crunches."

A. Lie on your back, knees bent, lift only the shoulders off the floor. Do not pull on the back of your neck.

(14) Yet another variation of "crunches." Only a totally erect rider can have an elastic pelvis. The muscles on the sides of your body need to be strengthened in order to work as stabilizers. The diagonal stomach muscles also make one-sided weight aids possible, without letting the outside shoulder fall back.

A. Lie on your back, lower legs resting on a chair seat, knee and hip joints bent at a 90-degree angle. Lift your upper body with stretched arms, and move your shoulders sideways by your thighs several times (right/left), slowly rising and going back down.

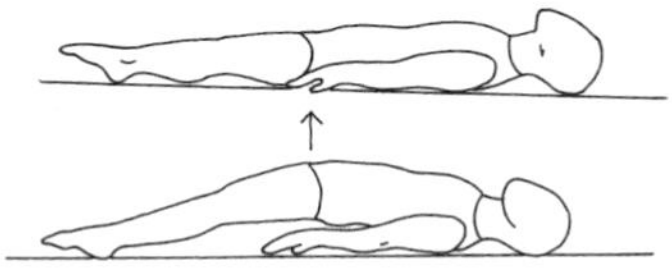

(15) Strengthens the pelvis area to facilitate the execution of half-halts.

A. Lie stretched out on your back, arms at the side, palms down.

B. Raise your buttocks off the floor, keeping the back straight. Hold to count of three, then five.

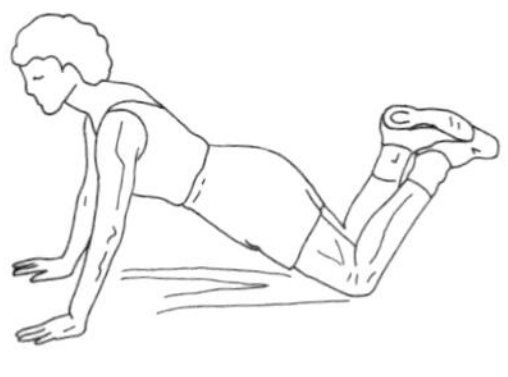

(16) You can't beat push-ups for getting your arms in shape and toned.

A. No need to stretch out your toes, do it from your hands and knees.

B. Touch your chin lightly to the floor, keep your back straight. Vary the push-ups by pointing your hands forward, then try with your hands pointing inward. Repeat as many times as is comfortable.

pelvis underneath you when you're going from the car to the grocery store and feeling which muscles work as you pull your legs through. In the store, it may mean loading your cart with fruit and vegetables and cutting down on the red meat and fat, because a diet that your body can absorb and use easily is better than a diet that loads you down and makes you tired and heavy.

Keep reminding yourself what the rewards are...you'll be more secure, you'll have more strength in your legs, you'll have more stamina, you'll be more sensitive, and you'll do a better job of riding your horse. He in turn will be happier because your strong body will be giving him clean, clear lines of communication.

Diet

It's a funny thing that while most horse owners can tell you to the ounce what they're feeding their mounts, including the chemical composition of that expensive equine supplement, they neglect their own nutrition woefully. Yet "we are what we eat."

Riders not only need nutrition to fuel the body, we need fuel for the brain. Riding events require heightened mental awareness and focus, as well as balance, muscular endurance, cardiovascular endurance, and occasionally strength.

During competition, various factors combine to drain your energy reserves more rapidly than normal, which can lower your performance level:

- Competitors endure an elevated emotional stress level throughout the day, with numerous high-stress peaks when involved in several events throughout the day.
- Events are often spread throughout the day, allowing you little time to leave the grounds for a nutritious meal. The amount of time between breakfast and evening meals is longer. Both factors require your energy reserves to last longer than usual.
- Both hot and cold weather can increase the loss of your body fluids.

Eating for a Healthy Lifestyle

A healthy diet will supply your body with fuel for energy, as well as building materials for growth, maintenance, and repair. These everyday nutritional needs are fulfilled with vital nutrients such as water, carbohydrates (including fiber), fats, proteins, vitamins, and minerals. Ideally, your diet should: (1) provide sufficient and balanced amounts of these nutrients; (2) supply only the amount of calories you need to maintain your appropriate weight and body composition; (3) consist of foods that fit your tastes, lifestyle, family or cultural traditions, and budget.

Most American diets fall short of these goals, containing too much protein and fat and not enough carbohydrates, fiber, and water. You can easily correct this nutritional imbalance and reward yourself with improved health and increased energy, endurance, and mental focus.

Nutrition and the Equestrian Athlete

What is a healthy, balanced diet? You have probably seen the "Food Pyramid" that is published by the U.S. Department of Agriculture. At the bottom, the base or foundation of the pyramid, are the foods that should comprise the bulk of your diet. As you ascend up the pyramid, the foods are just as important, but should be consumed in smaller quantities.

The "pyramid" recommends that you eat at least six servings a day of grain products (breads, cereals, rice, and pasta); three servings of vegetables and two servings of fruit; two or three servings from milk, yogurt, cheese, and other calcium sources, and two or three servings of meat, poultry, fish, dry beans, eggs, and/or nuts. No serving size is given for fats, oils, and sweets, because the recommendation is to eat them as little as possible.

A BALANCED DIET SHOULD CONSIST OF:

• 55 to 60% carbohydrates

As an athlete, you will benefit the most from eating complex carbohydrates because your body converts carbohydrates into energy more efficiently than it converts either fats or proteins. Carbohydrates are broken down into glucose ("blood sugar"). Although the muscles can function without glucose, the brain cannot. Glucose supplies the brain with nutrients that are necessary for quick and clear thinking. Deplete the supply of glucose and you can get woozy or dizzy, or even faint.

Proteins and fats can only provide a limited supply of glucose, whereas complex carbohydrates provide you with a convenient source of prolonged, high-octane energy to supply your muscles and your brain through your workout and throughout your day.

Carbohydrates are found in pasta, breads, cereals, rice and other grains, dried beans and peas, potatoes, corn, and some other vegetables. Many high-carbohydrate foods are also great sources of fiber.

Excess carbohydrates are stored as glycogen. During exercise, the stored glycogen is converted back into glucose to provide you with additional energy as you need it. This is why top athletes "bulk up" on complex carbohydrates the day before — and during — a big event.

• 10 to 12% proteins

The primary role of protein in the diet is to help the body grow new tissue and to repair tissues that have been damaged by day-to-day wear and tear. An adult athlete needs only a small amount of protein in her diet. Although protein is important, excess protein is in fact counterproductive.

Although protein provides some energy, it is in fact an inefficient source of energy and provides practically nothing when it comes to "brain food." Excess protein can also lead to dehydration, as it increases the amount of water required to eliminate your body's waste products.

A diet of 10 to 12% protein (except in the very young) is sufficient to meet all of your health and fitness needs and can be met simply by eating a variety of foods. Protein is found in fish, meats, poultry, beans, peas, soy products, dairy products, eggs, and nuts.

• Less than 30% fats

Fats occur naturally in most food groups, so we seldom need to eat it on purpose. To the contrary, we usually need to attempt to avoid it! Excess fat converts to body fat.

• Six to eight glasses (8 ounces each) of water per day, plus extra for fluid replacement (due to sweat loss) during and after exercise.

Water is the most critical nutrient for any athlete. Water is present in all of your cells, tissues, and organs. It transports your body's nutrients and waste products, lubricates your tissues and digestive tract, lubricates and cushions your joints, and regulates your body temperature. Any equestrian athlete can be prone to dehydration, which is the excessive loss of body fluids, especially in the hot summer months. The initial symptoms of dehydration are thirst, weakness, and fatigue and can culminate in loss of consciousness.

An unreplaced water loss of just five percent can reduce your performance capacity by 20 to 30 percent. Your body loses water primarily through sweating, but you may be surprised to hear that the next greatest amount of fluid loss is through breathing: water is exhaled as vapor.

You should start every exercise session and event hydrated (meaning sufficient fluids in your system) and should replace lost body fluids by drinking chilled water or other liquids. Chilled fluids are absorbed more rapidly and aid in lowering your body temperature. Sodas, coffee, and tea are not acceptable hydrating fluids. They contain caffeine and sugar, both of which contribute to dehydration. Caffeine acts as a diuretic, causing increased water excretion, and sugar requires additional water to be properly absorbed into your body's cells.

Eat a Variety of Foods

Your body requires over 40 essential nutrients (including vitamins and minerals) to function properly. No single food supplies all of these nutrients, so it is important to eat a variety of foods from the five major food groups to attain an adequate nutritional balance.

Eating a varied and balanced diet will normally assure you of sufficient amounts of vitamins and minerals. There is no medical evidence that eating extra amounts of vitamins will increase your performance level. In fact, over-indulgence of some vitamins will block use of other essential nutrients. The key is balance. Minerals do play a critical role in fitness and performance and are affected by prolonged exercise. Strenuous exercise will deplete your body of sodium, potassium, iron, and calcium. On the flip side, exercise will enhance the utilization of the calcium you do ingest. Still, these minerals should be replenished by eating normally after exercise or an event.

Women athletes (especially vegetarians) are often prone to iron deficiency and may find it necessary to supplement iron in their diet. Iron serves to transport oxygen in your blood and your muscles. Iron deficiency anemia impairs oxygen transport, which will decrease your aerobic performance and cause you to tire very easily. If you suspect you are iron deficient, contact your physician for testing. Natural sources of iron are red meat and some vegetables.

Avoid Sodium, Caffeine, and Sugar

Avoid excessive amounts of sodium, including salt tablets and electrolyte drinks. When you sweat, you naturally increase the salt concentration in your body and lower your water content. Excess sodium will absorb additional water from your body cells, causing weak muscles, and will lower the potassium level that is needed to regulate muscle activity. (Excess sodium also means more trips to the port-a-potty!)

The paradox is that many "sports drinks" are high in sodium and electrolytes. This makes them very satisfying in the short term, but they go through your body very quickly so may actually be counterproductive. The solution is to drink plenty of water and natural fruit juices.

A common myth is that it is a good idea to eat sugar before exercise. Ingesting sugar before exercise or an event will not give you extra energy. It will actually hinder your performance by triggering a surge of insulin that will cause a sharp drop in your blood sugar level approximately thirty minutes later and lead to fatigue and decreased mental alertness.

High concentrations of caffeine and/or sugar (soda, coffee, iced tea, candy bars, concentrated fruit juice) can make the rider hyperactive (not good on a sensitive horse!) for twenty or thirty minutes, then depressed and even dizzy as the sugar rapidly leaves the system. These "peaks and valleys" can alternately make the rider nervous and jumpy (called a "sugar high"), then depressed, even dizzy or light-headed — impairing judgment and coordination.

Orange juice meets all the USDA requirements for low sodium, high vitamins and minerals, natural sugars, and healthy nutrients. If you dilute pure orange juice (or any other fruit juice) with 1/3 to 1/2 cold water, you will lessen the risk of a sugar high (and low).

Nutritional Strategy for Competitive Equestrian Events

The typical diet of today's rider-competitor at equine events is inadequate to meet the physical and mental demands of competition. The food offered at concessions and fast food restaurants is usually high in fat, low in fiber and quality carbohydrates, and contributes only cheap calories incapable of sustaining an adequate energy level throughout the day.

As you have probably figured out, your nutritional goal during competition is to maintain a high and consistent energy level throughout the entire day. This will help you remain mentally and physically sharp and will give you a competitive edge in facing the myriad of obstacles you will encounter. You can control your energy level by formulating a successful nutrition strategy:

1. **Begin** by drinking plenty of water at least one day in advance. This will help ensure that you are fully hydrated when you begin your show day.
2. **The evening before** have a high carbohydrate supper, such as rice, pasta, or potatoes.
3. **The morning of the show,** eat a breakfast that is high in carbohydrates and low in fat, protein, and fiber. The reduced amount of fiber will speed up your digestion and help you avoid an upset stomach during your events. Again, drink plenty of water or juices.
4. **During the day,** drink plenty of water before, during, and after your rides. Take frequent small sips of water or other fluid to keep yourself hydrated. If you wait until you are thirsty, your performance level has already dropped.

You should also eat small high-carbohydrate snacks (see sidebar) between your events. As a rule of thumb, you should eat approximately 50 grams of carbohydrates every two hours and drink plenty of water or diluted fruit juice.

Prepare or buy your snack foods ahead of time and keep them on hand in a cooler in a convenient location such as your trailer or tack room. Simple dishes, sandwiches and drinks can be made in large quantities ready to be nibbled on all day long or to provide a noonday meal.

5. **Within ninety minutes after your workout or ride,** you need to eat a small carbohydrate-rich snack to replace the carbohydrate fuel you burned during exercise and to aid in the recovery process necessary after every workout. A glass of juice and some crackers or a piece of fruit will suffice.

Now that you've established an exercise routine and diet program for a healthier lifestyle and improved fitness performance, let's get back to our riding and training routine.

High Carbohydrate Snack Foods

(Recommended 50 grams every two hours)

Food	Carbohydrate/grams
1 apple	32 g
1 banana	27 g
1 orange	21 g
1 pear	25 g
10 pitted dates	61 g
1/2 cup raisins	57 g
1 cup dried banana slices	88 g
5 dried figs	61 g
1 cup cranberry-apple juice	43 g
1 cup grape juice	38 g
1 cup unsweetened grapefruit juice	24 g
1 cup orange juice	27 g
1 cup peach nectar	35 g
4 fig bars	42 g
1 fat-free snack bar (fruit bar or granola bar)	30-33 g
1 bagel (3 1/2 diameter)	35 g
1 pita pocket bread (6 1/2 diameter)	33 g
1 slice whole wheat bread	13 g
1 cup brown rice	45 g
1 baked potato without skin	35 g
1 baked potato with skin	51 g
1 carrot	7 g
1/2 cup corn	17 g
1 cup kidney or black beans	39-41 g
1 cup navy, pinto, or garbanzo beans	43-45 g

Chapter Eleven

All the Horse Needs to Know

This is not a training manual. There are many good books and videos for just that purpose. However, because dressage is "training," and a dressage competition is "a test of training," let's review some of the basic principles so that you can understand the philosophy behind the dressage test.

Any horse can learn "tricks." They can go from here to there, and if someone says go to there sideways, they can do that, too. But, sideways disobedience is not a half-pass, and a wrong lead is not a counter-canter!

Dressage is never "tricks." Each movement or exercise has a purpose and a reason for being performed. When performed properly, the movements make a horse move more beautifully than he did before. But like any other discipline, dressage must be practiced as a science before it becomes art. Just like you must practice the scales before you can play a Mozart concerto, you must practice "the basics" before you can ride a Grand Prix (or even a Training Level) test.

Experienced trainers will tell you that schooling the horse at the lower levels is the most difficult, but that when it is correctly done, the higher levels present no problem. The reverse is also true: if the lower levels are not accomplished correctly, the upper levels are impossible. This may explain why many talented horses never make it beyond Second Level, or if they do, they look mechanical and stilted.

Calm, Forward, and Straight

These words echo down through the decades but remain the cornerstone of dressage training.

First of all the horse must be **calm** if he is to accept our training, our guidance, or even our presence. "Calm" is a state devoid of defensiveness or tension.

Tension can be the result of a horse being over-faced in his work, working out of balance, or resisting the handler or trainer's dominance in the relationship.

Second, the horse must be moving **forward** in order to be influenced by the aids. You can't steer a car or a horse that is not moving. The correction for virtually every problem in our training is more forward impulse.

In Training Level the tests ask for "freely forward." This is indicated by your horse's responsiveness to your light, encouraging driving aids.

The third requirement, **straight**, means that both sides of the horse's body are equally developed for maximum efficiency. "Straight" is a function of the rider's aids; therefore, let's discuss those aids and the horse's responses next.

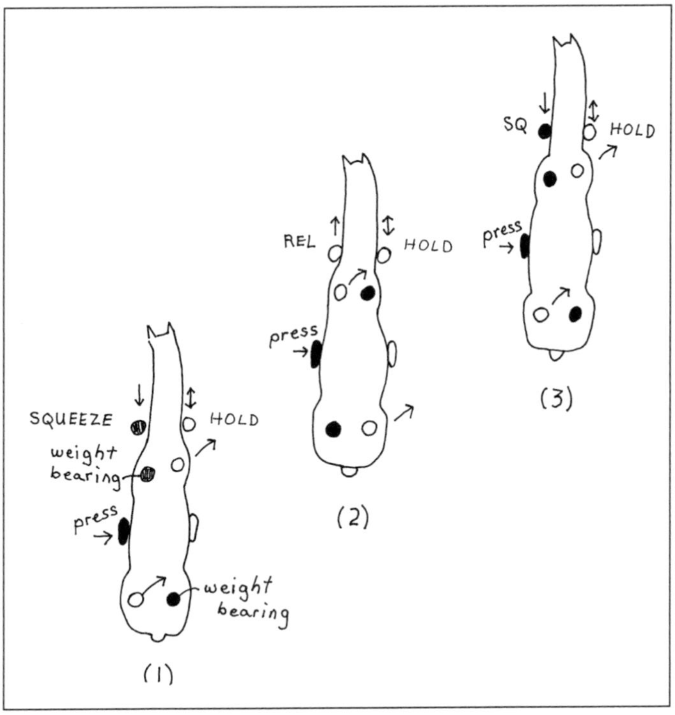

Figure 11.1 Aids for leg yield to the right.
(1) Firmly press the left leg and squeeze the left hand as the left shoulder is back. (2) Squeeze the right hand and lightly press the right leg as the right shoulder is back. (3) Repeat step 1.

All the Horse Really Needs to Know

If you think about it, in order to execute any dressage movement, all the horse really needs to know are two simple responses: (1) **To yield to the rider's hand** (through the bit) and (2) **To move away from the rider's leg.** All dressage movements or exercises are accomplished using various combinations or variations of these two aids and responses. All the other so-called "aids" (weight, seat, bracing the back, etc.) are supplemental and seldom work by themselves.

If the horse is uncompromisingly obedient to the hand and the leg, the knowledgeable (and coordinated) rider can demonstrate even the most sophisticated dressage movement — from shoulder-in to piaffe, and everything in between — on even a comparatively inexperienced horse.

For instance, to get a leg yield we slightly restrain the "inside" of the horse (if leg yielding to the right, the inside is the left, toward which the horse is flexing), while we "push" the horse with our left leg slightly behind the girth. The horse, if obedient to the "forward urge" of the leg and "yielding to the hand," will move in *the only direction open to him*, forward and sideways to the right. The "outside" (right) rein prevents over-bending, and the rider's outside leg is there to prevent the horse moving too rapidly sideways. In other words, we *position* the horse for a movement, and, if he is obedient to the hand and leg, we can ask him to proceed in that "position" for any length of time (figure 11.1).

As "easy" (for the horse!) as this sounds, it should also become apparent that while the horse only has to learn two things, **the rider needs to know, or learn, a great deal!**

The rider needs to learn the pressure points, the natural instincts, and biomechanical laws of the horse. For instance, the rider needs to know that when striding forward, there is only one time (or place) in the stride that the horse can alter direction, speed, or energy to that stride. That "time" is as that particular leg pushes off the ground. Therefore, if we want to increase the length, or energy, or direction of a stride (or strides), we must use our leg aid as that hind leg is pushing off the ground. (Hint: the shoulder on the same side will be coming back.)

So, with our scenario with the leg yield, the rider must apply the inside leg as the *horse's* inside hind leg is striding forward (inside shoulder will be coming back). This is the only time the horse can deflect that leg sideways and/or forward.

If we apply a "pushing" aid as the horse's foot is bearing weight, it is quite impossible for the horse to comply. Never ask the impossible! In so doing (applying the aid at the wrong time or place), we have not only invoked confusion on the part of the horse: "I'm supposed to do *something*, but *what*?" It also teaches the horse disobedience! If you ask for the impossible, the horse quite naturally cannot comply, so why should he ever obey you?

With each gait of walk, trot, and canter, there is an opportune time that the horse can respond to your aids. At the walk, the horse's barrel will swing in as each hind foot comes forward. To get more "impulse," the rider should use the leg aid as her leg swings inward, (that is when the same side hind foot is stepping forward). At the trot, the rider can aid each step or every other step (if rising to the trot). At trot, when the left shoulder is coming back, the left hind is coming forward. At the canter, we aid with our legs offset, to maintain the bent position. Inside and outside legs press at the same time. Using the aids in this way, with the proper sequence and the proper rhythm, there is never any question in the horse's mind as to if we want leg yield at trot, or turn on the haunches at walk, or a counter-canter on a curve.

Of course, the leg aid can be anything from a light squeeze of the calf to a firm "bump," or a sharp jab with the edge of the heel or of the spur. Use the leverage in your knee to put power in your calf.

To check that the horse is listening to your legs try this: Lightly close your legs. If he moves off immediately and eagerly, you're in business. However, if he stands there or just ambles off, resist the temptation to squeeze harder because he'll just get duller, and you'll end up doing all the work. Instead, put him "in front of your leg" by squeezing just as lightly as you did the first time. If, once again, he doesn't respond, give him a sharp "thump" with your heels or tap him with the whip behind your leg or on the thigh (mares don't like being touched in the flank area). Don't humor him by lifting your floppy calf and going "tap, tap, tap": he'll accept you giving a repeated aid and expect it all the time. You want him to know that "If you don't move on the *light* aid, you will get a harsh aid." Believe me, he will prefer the light aid.

Now here's the key. As soon as you get a response — even a disorganized or startled one to the whip or your leg — don't catch him in the mouth. Let him go forward! Allow him to slow down again and then give the *light* leg aid again. If he immediately goes energetically forward, praise him generously with an enthusiastic "Yes!"

If he responds in the okay-to-adequate range but not with a one hundred percent whole-hearted effort, tap sharply or thump again. When he responds, gently bring him back and do the light squeeze again. Your goal? To "whisper" your aid and have him shout his response! Remember, the leg initiates action, the other aids temper or refine the action.

Frequently Used Dressage Terms and Phrases

Contact (with the bit): *"Reins stretched such that they form a straight line, not a loop. Correct contact, or acceptance of contact, is determined by the elasticity of the connection between horse and rider."* The judge assesses correct contact by looking at the outline of the horse. It should appear harmonious and appropriate to the level.

On the Aids: *"Maintaining a good connection, the horse responds instantly and generously to all the aids."* The horse is *"on the bit, in front of the leg, and responsive."*

On the Bit: *"Supple and quiet acceptance of the contact with a stretched neck"* (Horses stretch their necks by rounding (arching) their backs and raising the root of the neck, thereby making a telescoping gesture.) *"and with lateral and longitudinal flexion as required."*

Chewing the Bit: *"The movements of the horse's mouth — gently and softly mouthing the bit — showing mobility and relaxation of the jaw and causing secretion of saliva for a 'wet mouth.' Not to be confused with snapping or grinding of the teeth."*

Take the Reins or Stretching the Frame: *"The horse gradually takes the reins, stretching forward and downward with light contact, while maintaining balance, rhythm and tempo."* (AHSA, Art. 1910.4)

Connection: *"State in which there is no blockage, break, or slack in the circuit that joins horse and rider into a single harmonious unit. The unrestricted flow of energy and influence from and through the rider to and throughout the horse, and back to the rider. See 'Throughness.'"*

Throughness: *"The supple, elastic, unblocked, connected state of the horse's musculature that permits an unrestricted flow of energy from back to front and front to back, which allows the aids/influences to freely go through to all parts of the horse, (e.g. the rein aids go through and reach and influence the hind legs). Synonymous with the German term 'Durchlaessigkeit,' or 'throughlettingness.'"*

Uberstreichen/Release of the Rein: *"The brief release of the contact, wherein the rider in one clear motion extends the hand(s) forward along the crest of the horse's neck, then rides for several strides without contact. Its purpose is to demonstrate that, even with loose rein(s), the horse maintains its carriage, balance, pace, and tempo."*

Italics are from the *USDF Glossary of Dressage Terms*

Obedience to the Hand

Just as horses must be taught to respond to the rider's legs, they must be taught proper response to the bit. Because the snaffle bit is a fairly mild bit (see Chapter 7), horses can easily learn to ignore it. The solution is not to get a more severe bit, but for the rider to *learn how to use the bit effectively.* In order to fully understand how to shape and influence the horse and achieve the various responses we require from him, we must know something about his anatomy.

The "Yes" and "No" Joints

Just behind the poll is the junction of the skull and the first vertebra of the neck (the atlas). This joint only allows "nodding" (longitudinal flexion); hence, it can be called the "yes" joint. Behind the "yes" joint is the junction of the atlas and the second vertebra (the axis), which allows side to side movement of the head and can be called the "no" joint (figure 11.2).

In order to get the horse to yield at the poll, we must *first* get him to say "no" — to yield at the "no" joint — and then *he* will say "yes" (flex or yield at the poll).

The easiest way to understand the function of these two joints is to stand beside the horse's neck and experiment by manipulating the horse's head with the snaffle reins. If we take hold of both reins evenly and attempt to

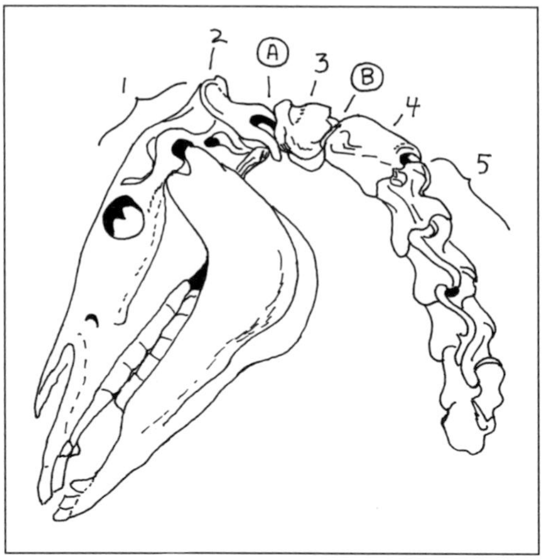

Figure 11.2 Location of the "yes" and "no" joints. Only "yes" (up and down) movement is possible between skull and atlas. Only "no" (side to side) movement is possible between atlas and axis.

1. Skull	*(B) "No" Joint*
2. Poll	*4. Axis*
A) "Yes" Joint	*5. Cervical vertebrae*
3. Atlas	

flex or arch the horse's neck by pulling his chin straight back towards his chest, we will meet quite a bit of resistance: it will take a good deal of "pull" to convince the normal untrained (or even trained) horse to yield at the poll. Moreover, once you do manage to get the horse to arch his neck towards his chest — or at least bring the face to perpendicular — you will find that it is *almost impossible* to get the horse to bend laterally (sideways). It is as though he were "locked" in position, which, essentially, he is! You have "jammed" his vertebra together, which allows him to brace his whole muscular neck against your hands. Many times what rider's perceive as a "hard mouth," is really the horse's locked spinal column.

If instead (after letting the horse relax and stretch his neck back to a natural position) we take hold of one rein and bring the horse's neck to the side, encouraging the horse to bend his neck evenly toward you (you may have to press or lean on his shoulder to prevent him stepping toward the rein), you will find that the horse will not only "give" or yield very easily to the side, he will at the same time flex at the poll, lowering his neck and tucking his chin; in other words, he will come onto the bit! (figure 11.3).

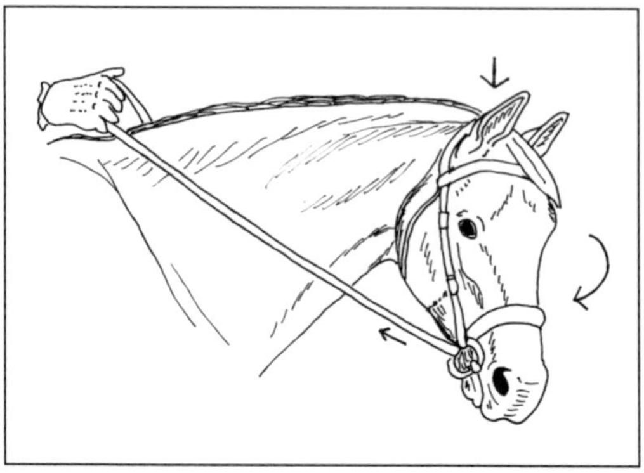

Figure 11.3 By bending the neck a little to the side at the second joint, it is almost impossible for the horse to "brace" against you.

The explanation for this is that the first joint (between the atlas and skull) can only bend longitudinally (up and down) and if it is bent first, it "locks" the next joint (the axis), preventing easy lateral bend in the horse's spine.

If the horse is forced to bend laterally with his poll "locked," he will bend at the third vertebra or at the withers, both of which are undesirable. If, on the other hand, we bend the axis first (sideways), it frees the atlas (and all the other vertebra) to flex and yield.

Even traveling in a straight line, we can keep a little sideways flexion at the poll, called "positioning." This is just enough bend at the poll (not the entire horse) that the rider can see the horse's inside eyelash. The horse should stay light and receptive to your aids (figure 11.4).

It is quite acceptable to ride the horse "in position" in the lower levels. As the horse becomes more confident in the show atmosphere and more reliable about "staying on the bit," we can ride him straighter and straighter.

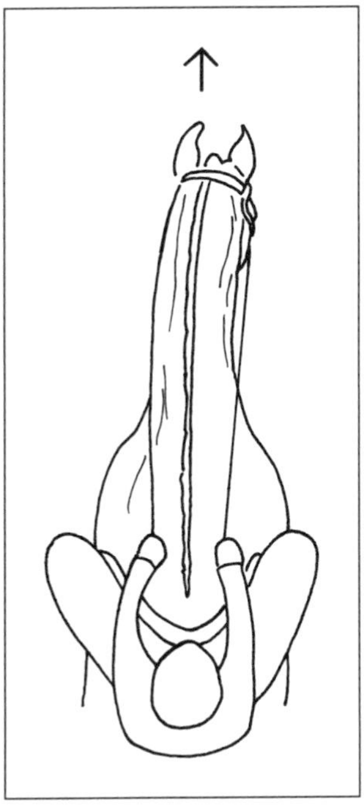

Figure 11.4 "Positioning" is keeping just enough bend at the poll so the rider can see the horse's inside eyelash.

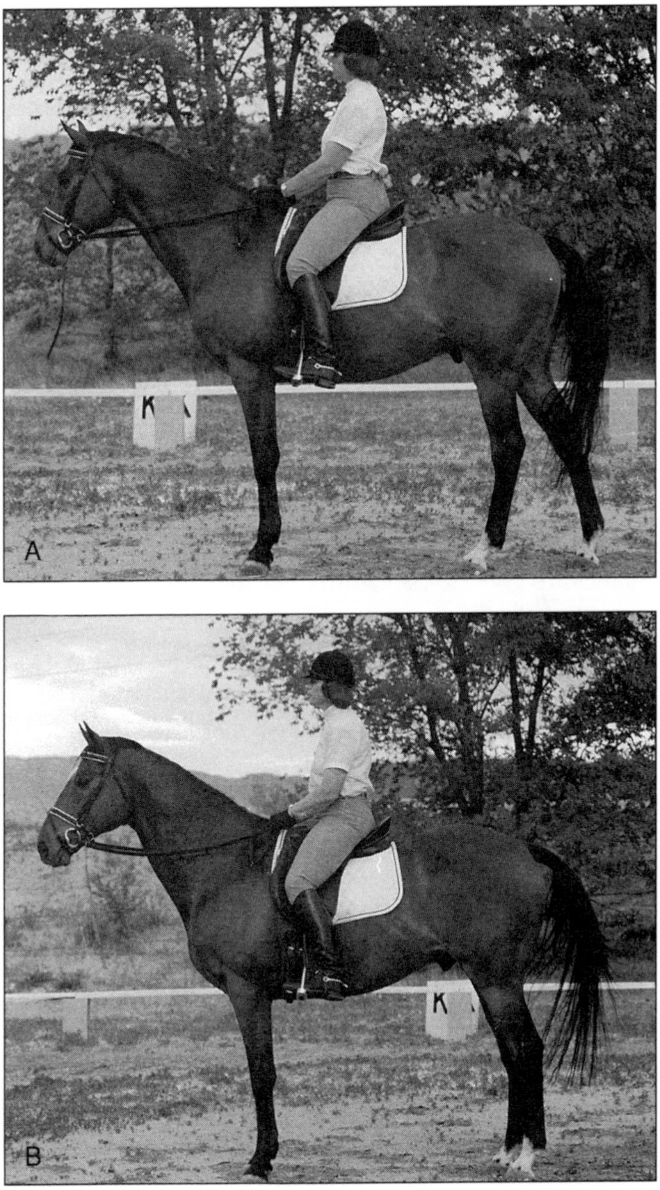

Figure 11.5 A typical untrained halt where the horse leaves a hind leg trailing (A), and a "square" halt where the horse has stepped up under himself squarely with both hind legs (B). Photos by Charlene Strickland.

The Right Time and Place

Just as with the leg aid, there is a time and place where the horse can most easily respond to the rein. Most people instinctively try to halt a horse by pulling back on both reins at the same time. They are asking the horse to stop in mid-air! (Actually mid-stride.) This is very difficult for the horse to do, so he often resists. The horse then realizes he "got by" with a sloppy, sprawled-out halt, so why should he ever be obedient? If the horse *is* obedient, he will stop in mid-stride with his legs separated (figure 11.5A).

Here is the proper way to teach and practice a "square" halt:

First, bear in mind that while going forward the horse moves his limbs in a definite sequence of movements. To complete a stride, the horse must be able to complete the entire sequence of the movements of individual limbs that go to make up such a stride or strides.

We want to communicate to the horse that we expect it to stop "square" — that is, with the legs at the four corners of the body, with the weight equally distributed over all four. Many judges comment that this is a "balanced halt" (figure 11.5B).

To accomplish a square, balanced halt, the hands should not pull together, which would cause the horse to stop in the middle of a stride or resist. Instead, there should be a sequence of signals: (1) establish contact with the mouth; (2) retard the left hand to slow/stop the left side of the horse; (3) retard the right hand to slow/stop the right side of the horse; (4) retard the left side again for the last *half* step to allow the horse to "round off" his stride. It may be necessary to assist the impulsion ever so slightly with a push of the leg at precisely the right moment to get that last half step. At the same time, stop the following motion of your seat by stiffening your back and thighs during the down transition.

Initially it will take at least three motions and a minimum of two- and one-half steps of walk to reach halt and possibly more. Eventually, even from the trot and later the canter, it will still take two motions that will become so subtle that they almost blend together.

When halted correctly, the horse is balanced on his four feet and ready to advance, turn, or rein back without going through any preliminary fumbling to get his legs in position. You can use the principles just described to figure out how to achieve smooth up or down transitions in the other gaits.

Straightness

One often hears the judge's comment that "the horse was not straight." Straightness means the hind feet follow the path of the front feet, whether on a straight line or on a curve. On a circular path, the horse will of course have to bend his spine (however slightly) in order to have the hind feet "follow" the front. This is also called "straight" (figure 11.6).

Most pleasure riding horses are not taught to be straight. Consequently, when we begin schooling for dressage, we must show the horse how to be more efficient, more balanced, and more brilliant in his gaits. We must teach straightness.

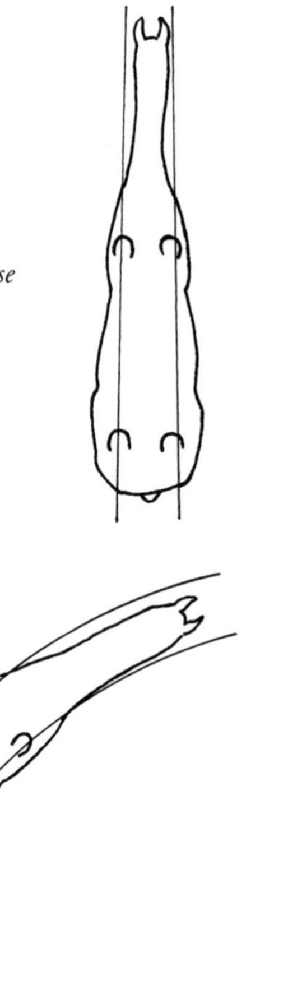

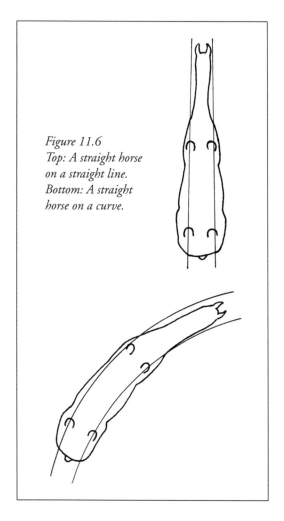

Figure 11.6
Top: A straight horse on a straight line.
Bottom: A straight horse on a curve.

Many times if we simply concentrate on riding the horse in a straight line, we can achieve a measure of straightness. However, many inexperienced horses will tend to cant their necks in one direction and "drift" their bodies to the other direction. A horse that is bent to the right and "drifts" to the left is said to be "falling over his left shoulder" (figure 11.7A).

The first correction for this problem is to turn him toward his bulging shoulder. In other words, ride an arc in the direction to which he is drifting. If you are in a fenced arena, ride several feet inside the fence so that you can turn

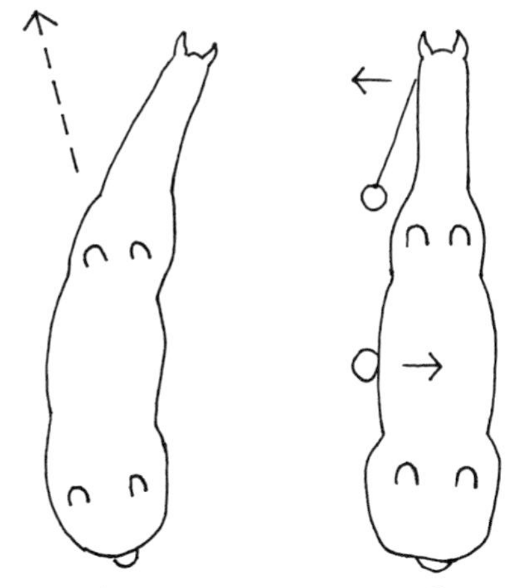

Figure 11.7 A horse bent to the right, drifting left (A); the correction: bring the forehand in line with the haunches with an opening rein and strong left leg (B).

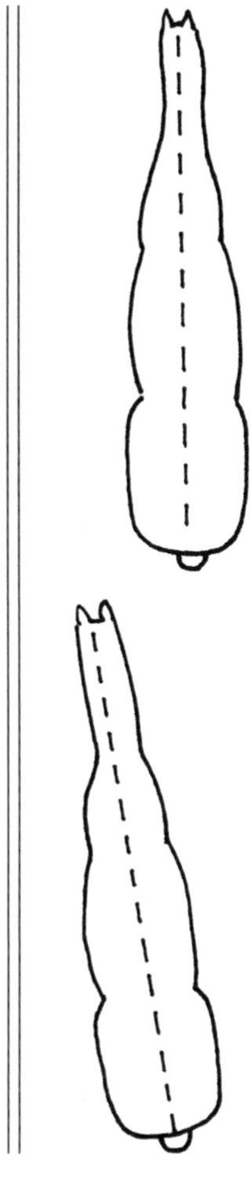

Figure 11.8 "Leaning on the wall." Top: A straight horse, with his backbone parallel to wall. Bottom: A crooked horse, with his shoulder is too close to the wall, which makes it impossible for the hind feet to follow in the track of the front feet.

in either direction. The next correction is to add enough leg to improve the forward impulsion. It is difficult to steer a horse that is moving too slowly (figure 11.7B).

Another cause of "lack of straightness" is the horse's tendency to "lean on the wall." Horses tend to keep their shoulders and haunches the same distance from a wall or rail. However, because the horse's haunches are usually wider than his shoulders, the horse's spine will be angled toward the rail instead of straight on the track. To correct this, you need to move your horse's shoulders away from the rail, the same way you corrected his "drifting." The judge will consider the horse straight if the *inside* legs line up when going down the rail and the spine lines up coming up the centerline (figure 11.8).

Practice absolutely straight lines by turning down the centerline or the quarterline and focusing on a marker at the end. This will also work going down the rail — look up and find a marker to ride toward. Your horse will never be straight if you constantly look at his neck!

Put the horse in a "channel" between your two hands and your two legs. After you perfect the centerline, work on the diagonals, remembering that the rail or fence will "pull" your horse toward it and may encourage crookedness those last few steps. Only if the horse is straight will he push off evenly with both hind legs.

Other than poor steering, a major cause of slight "crookedness" in horses is that virtually all horses have a "hollow" side and a "stiff" side, with more pronounced muscle development or coordination on one side than the other. In humans, it is called left- or right-handedness.

The "crooked" horse travels slightly sideways. It is estimated that 85 percent of horses are "a little crooked." In some, it is caused by the already mentioned stiff and hollow side, in others by the rider sitting to one side, and in a small number by physical differences in the horse's structure.

Crookedness can (and often does) lead to uneven muscle development. Crooked horses often favor one canter lead over the other or move with a shortened stride on one side. The horse becomes strong on one side of his body and correspondingly weak on the other side. When well-confirmed, the horse will take a shorter stride with the weak hind leg, and sometimes this is mistaken as lameness (figure 11.9).

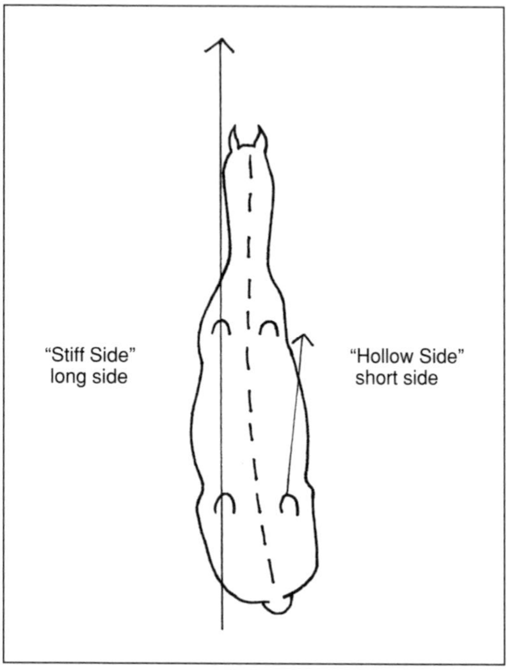

Figure 11.9 The "stiff" side cannot bend because the "hollow" side cannot stretch.

Minor crookedness or unevenness can often be corrected with appropriate work and exercises. That is why it is important to have your ground person occasionally observe the horse from behind to check the evenness of development.

The correction for an unevenly developed horse will involve various lateral exercises at all three gaits. Like a tree branch, if you gently bend it opposite the tendency, it is likely to spring back to "normal," or nearly straight.

To even up the horse, the rider has to try to stretch the muscles on the hollow (short) side and loosen the muscles on the stiff (long) side. (It's called "stiff" because the horse has difficulty bending *toward* that side.) The easiest way to correct this is gently bending the horse on circles or serpentines.

It may sound contradictory that we work on straightness by bending the horse, but "straightness" means the even development of both sides of the horse's body so that your horse's hind end follows his front end. Even on a circle or bending through a corner, he must be "straight" — not like a plank, but sort of like a train, whose every car follows the ones before it on a track.

By bending on a curve, a horse works his back muscles (actually every muscle in his body!). If the horse bends his body from poll to tail, he will stretch the muscles along the outside and compress those on the inside of his spine (inside being toward the inside of the curve).

The alternate bending and stretching of the horse's body has the same effect on him as a person's exercises in a gymnasium: it will strengthen the muscle systems involved, in this case the back, the croup, the belly, and the loins. As the horse gets stronger, he will be able to push off more strongly and carry more weight with his hindquarters.

At first, you will have to make a lot of corrections to keep your horse straight, but it will get easier. To avoid unevenness, work your horse equally in both directions, whether under saddle or on the longe. Work on straightness is important, because only a totally straight horse will be able to achieve good lengthenings of stride or extensions.

Transitions

Probably the most important innovation to competition dressage of our century is the riding of transitions. A "transition" is the movement from one gait to another gait. Transitions are the key part of any test because they connect the movements. Transitions are the most difficult and revealing part of a dressage test. It is the ability to shift from pushing power to supporting power; from supporting to pushing power; or from straight to lateral movement.

Many people think Training Level Test One, with its thirteen little movements, is dull as dishwater, but nearly half of those movements are upward or downward transitions, which favor the horse that is supple and responsive to the aids.

The American Horse Shows Association tells us that transitions *"should be quickly made yet smooth and not abrupt. The cadence of a pace should be maintained up to the moment when the pace is changed or the horse halts. The horse should remain light in hand, calm and maintain a correct position."* (AHSA, Art. 1907)

What this means is that the horse must show clear rhythm before, during, and after the transition. The transition should be prompt but calm and smooth, with no intermediate steps of any other gait or pace than required (for example: directly from canter to walk, or walk to canter, with no trot steps in between). Each step should be well-balanced and engaged (relative to the level). The horse should not tip onto the forehand nor throw his head up during a transition.

You've Got to Have Rhythm

Not only do you need a good sense of rhythm and tempo to show your horse's gaits at their best, you need rhythm to execute smooth, obedient transitions. A very rudimentary way of describing the aids for transitions might be that when going from walk to trot, for example, you would squeeze with both your legs simultaneously, *in the horse's trot rhythm.* However, don't expect the horse to take the trot on the first squeeze. The first squeeze alerts the horse; at the second squeeze, he should be prepared to trot; and by the third, he should be in the trot — already in the proper rhythm. If he hasn't taken the trot by the third squeeze — get your whip out!

The transition from trot to walk is accomplished similarly. With our hands, we retard the horse in a one-two motion (one side of the horse, then the other). As soon as the horse comes down to the walk, we are ready to use our legs alternately to maintain impulsion and rhythm in the walk. Canter to trot is a retardation of the outside rein as the head goes down (the hind legs are about to land), repeated if necessary on succeeding strides.

Using the aids in this way, with the proper sequence and the proper rhythm, there is never any question in the horse's mind as to what we want; therefore, we avoid confusion and accompanying resistance.

You can figure out the routine for other transitions, always remembering to: (1) prepare the horse (call him to attention with a half-halt or preparatory move); (2) give the aids in the proper rhythm and sequence; and (3) demand he do the movement promptly (be ready to back up your command with hand, leg, or whip).

In all the levels, and especially Training Level, a smooth transition is more important than an accurate one (exactly at the letter). An effective way to initially practice smooth transitions is on a 20-meter circle. The horse is less likely to "fall" on his forehand or stiffen if he is bent on a generous circle.

To shorten or lengthen strides, keep the timing the same, pulsate the legs and shorten or lengthen the stroke of the following hands to shorten or lengthen the frame (outline) of the horse as appropriate. When going from lengthening to collection you might raise the hands a little (because the horse's neck should rise), but keep the energy (and rhythm) with your legs. When going into a lengthened or extended gait, lower the hands a little.

Remember, the key to the modern dressage tests (all the way up to and including Grand Prix) is transitions. Time spent practicing transitions will reward you with excellent scores throughout your test.

The Half-Halt

Mention "half-halt" and most dressage novices will exclaim: "Oh my, will I *ever* be able to do one properly?"

Well, guess what — if you have been following the commentary on the previous pages and practicing transitions, you are *already* executing half-halts!

Transitions done in rhythm and therefore "in sync" with the horse's movement automatically lead to half-halts. In other words, the execution of proper up and down transitions teaches the horse (and rider) how to half-halt.

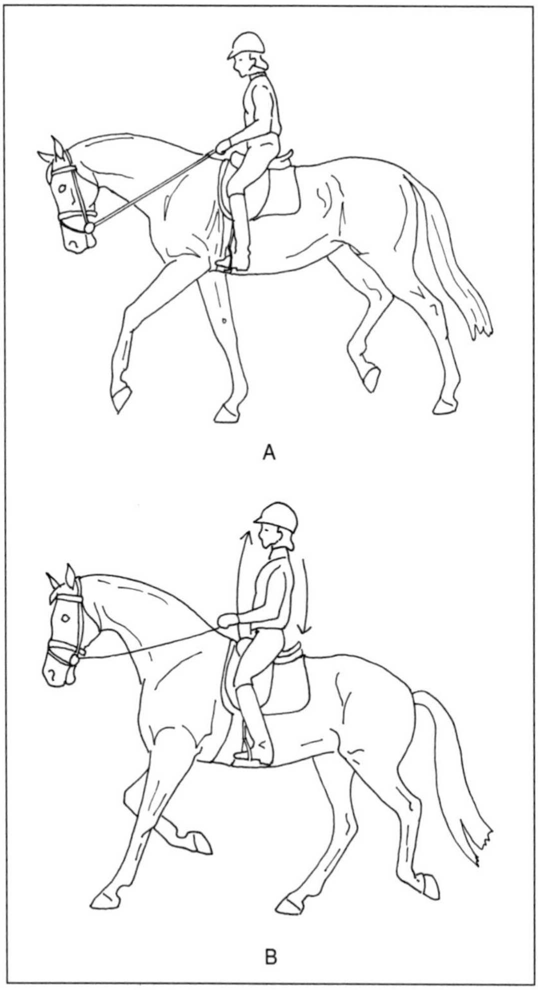

Figure 11.10 Re-balancing the horse with a half-halt: A horse leaning on his forehand (A), the rider squeezes with her legs, grows taller, and redistributes the horse's energy (B).

A half-halt is a momentary, almost invisible rebalancing of the horse. Half-halts are used to "call the horse to attention," to collect and to rebalance whenever he tends to lean on his forehand or needs to increase engagement (cause greater bend in the hind leg joints), for instance in preparation for a change in direction, position, or pace.

The progressive training of the horse aims to encourage the hind legs to step further underneath the body towards the center of balance and thus relieve the front legs of some of the load. This makes the horse "lighter" on his feet and easier to maneuver. In simple terms, a half-halt persuades the horse's forehand and front legs to *wait* while the hind legs catch up and step more underneath the horse's body. The half-halt is the most often-used exercise in dressage.

A half-halt is executed by momentarily increasing the "drive" of the seat and leg into a "regulating" hand. The length and tension of the reins directs the horse's impulse more upward, resulting in a shorter, more upright frame (figure 11.10B).

We begin doing "baby half-halts" — even in Training Level — whenever we do a down transition. Remember, a down transition is not a *slowing* down from one gait to another, it is a change of leg sequence or frame. The resulting gait, even if that gait is walk, must be full of impulsion — right from the first stride. In other words, the horse changes his *shape*, not necessarily his speed. If you keep your legs "on" while doing a down transition, you are in effect doing a rudimentary half-halt.

Dressage is all about movement, and because balance is a fluid state, it is necessary to rebalance constantly. The only way of doing this is by understanding and mastering the half-halt technique.

Chapter Twelve

What are Working Gaits?

In Training and First Level the tests call for "working" gaits (except walk, which is presently termed "medium"). Therefore, what exactly, is a "working gait?"

Working gaits could probably be described as "the best gaits that horse is capable of." You see, the most important principle of dressage is that the horse not only retains his absolutely pure gaits, but that they are actually improved.

This is because the quality of all the dressage movements depends on the quality of the gaits. A flying change can only be as good as the canter that preceded it. A shoulder-in or half-pass depends on the quality of the trot, a turn on the haunches depends on the quality of the walk, etc. If riders will pay more attention to these rules, we will not see so many faults in the movements.

Of course, we cannot hope to improve upon nature. The horse must have correct gaits to start with (see Chapter 6, "The Horse"). But dressage is all about *improving* the horse's natural gaits. The things that we can improve are the balance, self-carriage (to a point), suppleness, and consistency (steadiness) of the gaits.

Why are they called "working" gaits? Possibly because it takes a little "work" to present them at the horse's best.

The Medium Walk

Although much emphasis is placed on how beautifully the horse moves at the trot (in stallion advertisements for instance), *all three gaits are important.* In fact, there is a coefficient for most walk movements in the AHSA tests, underlining how important it is considered.

A good medium walk (required in Training Level) will show the horse stepping into or slightly past the hoof prints of the front feet. The head carriage will look fairly still but the rider can feel the neck lengthen and shorten at each stride.

The main visual check of the correct walk is the "V" we see at one point of the stride (see figure 6.2, page 51). If the legs get out of sequence, for instance if the two legs on the same side start moving together, the walk is said to be "lateral" or "pacey," an almost automatic "4" (insufficient) or below in scoring a test. If the diagonal legs start striding together, the gait becomes a "jog" or "jig" — it imitates, or actually becomes, a slow trot. This will usually be phrased as "broke gait," or "jigged." While either conformation or tenseness can cause a lateral walk, a jog is almost always caused by nervousness.

The medium walk is close to the horse's "natural" walk. It is described as: *"a clear, regular and unconstrained walk of moderate lengthening. The horse, remaining on the bit (a light contact with the bit), walks energetically but calmly with even and determined steps, the hind feet touching the ground in front of the footprints of the forefeet. The rider maintains a light, soft and steady contact with the mouth."* (AHSA, Art. 1903.4.3)

The medium walk should be in a natural carriage but with even contact on both reins. The lack of restraint is a point frequently overlooked by riders in their efforts to maintain a contact. In all the walks, the rider must encourage the horse to use his neck and body, while indicating the length of stride and amount of impulsion shown by increased bending of the joints.

Many novices don't understand how to achieve a good energetic walk without causing the horse to "break" or jig. The walk is a four-beat gait that moves the rider forward and back and side to side in a somewhat complicated manner. At the walk the horse's barrel will swing (or move) your calves in and out as he moves his hind legs alternately forward and back. Your right leg will swing in as he pushes off with his right hind and your left leg will swing in as he pushes off with his left.

You will also feel the rhythm and sequence of the walk in your hips and thighs. As your right calf swings inward, your right hip and thigh will "dip" forward and down. As the left calf swings in, the left hip and thigh dip. You can regulate the length of the stride by restricting or accentuating the range of motion of your hips. Caution: do not allow your hips to swing side to side; that may cause the horse to start "pacing" (a lateral walk). Instead, concentrate on a forward and back motion.

To ask for more energy, you simply accentuate the inward swing of your alternating legs: right, left, right, left, and so forth. You do not want the tempo to change, so you maintain it, even during transitions of lengthening or shortening.

The other way to adjust the length of the stride is with your hands. The horse's head and neck should stretch forward and down at each stride. If this motion is restricted, the sequence of the gait is interrupted and the horse will either stop or jig (or worse, go lateral). Let the horse take your hands forward at each stride.

An effective way to condition your hands to react properly is to imagine your arms as inanimate "side reins." These "side reins" are attached at your shoulder; the elbow is the elastic piece that allows stretching and retraction. Your hands are attached to the ends of these imaginary side reins and the fingers can shorten, lengthen, and adjust the reins. With this bit of imagining, you can allow the horse to "take" your hands (and therefore arms) forward, and the weight of your "inanimate side reins" (arms) will bring the reins back without pulling. Allow the process to be repeated at each stride to the horse's proper rhythm.

To shorten the strides, shorten (but do not stop completely) the forward stroke. In other words, the longer the stride, the more your hands will move forward and back — the greater the "range of motion." The shorter the stride (as in collection) the shorter the stroke.

A "Going Somewhere" Walk

The most common reason for low scores or inconsistencies at the walk is lack of correct practice. Many books and trainers tell us that "too much" work at the walk will ruin it. Riding the walk will only ruin it if we ride it badly! If the rider is sensitive to the motion of the walk and while maintaining contact does not interfere with that motion, the walk should show improvement, not deterioration. So let's see how to produce the best walk your horse is capable of.

Whereas walking on a loose rein with a long, downward stretched neck should be the reward after the daily lesson or for rest periods, if we only use the walk for rest periods the horse will soon develop a very lazy, boring walk. If the competition ring is your goal you must develop a marching, "going somewhere" walk.

A lot of this "enthusiasm" for the walk is created by your attitude. First, you must discover what your horse's best walk is, then work to recreate it in the dressage ring. You can put your horse on the lunge line and experiment until you see his best walk (see Chapter 6, "The Horse"). Probably an even better way is to take the horse on a trail ride. Coming home, most horses will show their best walk (that is unless they habitually jig). You want that long-strided, swinging the whole body, going somewhere, walk.

Back in your practice arena, you can "program" your horse so that he knows that when you ask for the walk (as described above), you expect that long-striding, energetic, marching walk. Only when *you* relax can he relax.

When you are asking for a medium walk or free walk, look up and ride your horse straight towards your "goal" (the next letter or the far side of the arena).

Having established a good straight line, ask for a more energetic walk. As you give the leg aids, make sure there is no restricting pressure on the reins that could block his forward movement. Urge him forward with your legs in rhythm with his stride, timing your leg aids to the side-to-side shifts of his barrel. *Count out the rhythm* so it is perfectly even. If your horse responds promptly, reward him with a verbal "Yes!" (This seems to inspire enthusiasm in my horses.) If your horse gets tense or rushes, calm him by rubbing your cupped hand up the crest of his neck.

If, on the other hand, you find that you're applying an enormous amount of leg and not getting a result, apply your whip immediately behind your leg, in time to the stride, as described in the last chapter. Ask again for a forward walk, first with your legs, then again with the whip if necessary, until he walks forward at a brisk pace. Remember, you want that same walk he is capable of when he heads back to the barn after a good trail ride.

Some horses have a tendency to get "lateral" in their walk (the legs on the same side of the horse move forward together — like a pace). This is usually caused by conformation and may become more of a problem as you go up the levels. At Training Level it can usually be sufficiently corrected to be at least adequate.

To correct the lateral tendencies, whenever the horse is walking on contact keep him bent through the body and moving a little sideways. This "breaks up" the lateral pairs of legs into the correct four beat sequence. Bend to one side and leg yield or shoulder-fore for several steps, then bend to the other side. Eventually it will take less obvious efforts to maintain the correct walk. At the free walk, horses are less likely to go lateral.

The Free Walk

What distinguishes the different paces of walk is the comparative length of stride and outline (frame) of the horse.

The definition of the free walk is *"a pace of relaxation in which the horse is allowed complete freedom to lower and stretch out his head and neck."* (AHSA, Art. 1903.4.5)

Figure 12.1 A hollow back (left) versus a rounded back (right).

The *Rule Book* no longer dictates the length of rein (it used to state "long" or "loose") but "complete freedom" implies "no contact" on the reins.

In the free walk the horse should stretch his head and neck down (a few inches below the level of the withers) and forward. It is a fault if the face comes behind vertical. The back should visibly "swing" as each hip comes forward, and the horse should overstep the front tracks by at least six to eight inches.

In a test, the free walk must never look lazy. "Relaxation" here indicates *mental* relaxation whereby the horse stretches his head forward and down and proceeds determinedly across the diagonal with no restraint (no contact) from the reins.

There should be a difference in the length of stride between the medium walk and the free walk. If a horse with a limited natural walk can lengthen his stride at all, it will be when he is stretching forward and down and arching up his back, allowing the haunches to step through more.

Correcting the Jig

If a horse is tense or if he is pushed beyond his physical ability to take long strides, he may break gait or jig. Horses that are tense often need to be reassured. They try too hard or they don't understand what is expected of them. You can calm the horse by speaking in soothing tones (at home!). Say "Eeaasy," or "Slooow." It doesn't matter so much what you say, it's the tone of voice. Or you can give light but insistent tugs on the rein to slow the horse.

At home or in the warm-up arena, you can run your hand up and down the horse's crest in a pushing motion. This usually prompts a stretching and relaxing forward reach of the neck and body. If the rider relaxes her body, this will definitely help the horse. (See Chapter 20, "Nerves," on how to relax horse and rider.)

Confirmed jiggers may have to spend several sessions *just walking.* Don't get upset with the horse. Walk him on a long rein for as long as it takes to convince him you are not going to do anything exciting until he walks. If he breaks into a jog, quietly (but insistently) bring him back to a walk and then continue on a long rein. Eventually the horse will figure out he may as well relax and walk because there is nothing else to do.

The Working Trot

The typical trot of an unschooled horse under saddle is rather stiff and short because the back is usually held rigid or slightly hollow, neck stiff and a bit high, and the hind legs "pushing" more than "lifting." Such a horse could be described as "trotting with the legs alone." In the course of training, we want to encourage the horse to move with his whole body, not only making a more comfortable gait, but "saving" his legs as well (figure 12.1).

Though it's difficult (even for judges) to disregard a spectacular trot, even a so-so trot can be improved. The trot is in fact the easiest gait to improve. We can make it more brilliant through efficient use of energy; we can make it more regular by perfecting and maintaining a pure rhythm; and we can make it lighter and more elegant by teaching the horse to better balance himself. Every horse's trot is capable of improvement through training, and indeed must show improvement as the horse progresses up through the levels of competition.

The working trot shows more efficiency of movement than the horse's "ordinary" or natural trot. Ordinary gaits may suffice to warm up or to limber up the horse before serious demands commence, but they are far too "ordinary" to be aesthetically pleasing or totally efficient.

The working trot *"is a pace between the collected and the medium trot in which a horse not yet ... ready for collected movements shows himself properly balanced and, remaining on the bit, goes forward with even, elastic steps and good hock action. The expression 'good hock action' does not mean that collection is a required quality of working trot. It only underlines the importance of an impulsion originated from the activity of the hindquarters."* (AHSA, Art. 1904)

This description is a little vague. The working trot might be described as that particular horse's "best trot" (for his stage of training).

At the working trot, you want to encourage the horse to "track up;" that is, place the hind foot exactly into the track left by the front foot. If your horse is not blessed with a nice long stride, you will have to be especially sure he is relaxed so he can stretch into a longer stride.

For all the muscles to work properly, you must achieve the right balance of relaxation and energy. Drive the horse forward and bring him back with half-halts until you achieve his best trot.

Some horses simply cannot track up without straining. A tense horse will take short, quick steps. Get the longest, springiness stride you can with your horse moving energetically but not straining or rushing.

There must be an elastic contact on the bit. If you just drive the horse forward, he will "run" — take fast (rapid) short steps and topple onto his forehand.

In order to round the back and engage the hind legs, the horse must accept a contact on the bit and allow the rider to "push him up to" that contact. This will cause his back to react just like a whip that you push against your hand; it will arch upwards, creating a springy "bridge" on which the rider can sit in comfort and which the horse can efficiently lift and push with his hind legs. The bit must regulate the amount of roundness in the horse's back and the tempo of the strides. In fact, the working trot is often described as being "on the bit with impulsion" (figure 12.2).

In the working trot, we strive for a rhythm that is comparatively slow for the ground covered. In other words, long, slow strides are most efficient. Too fast a rhythm is called "hurrying" or "running" and wastes energy.

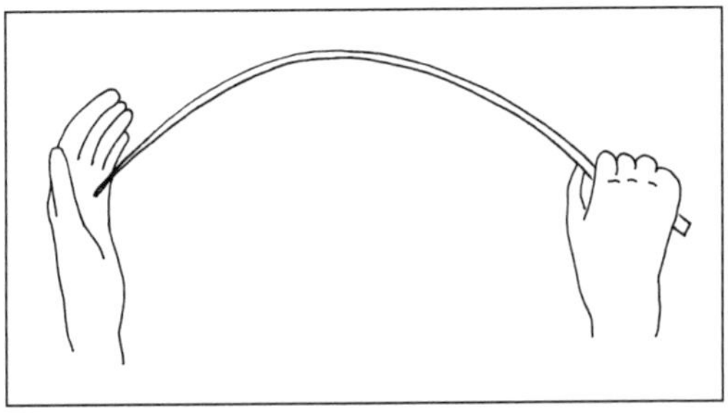

Figure 12.2 Your goal is for your horse's back to become a springy bridge. Take a flexible whip and push it into the palm of your hand and it will flex like a bow. Think of your horse's back as the bow.

Under saddle you can influence rhythm with your hands, legs, and seat. The horse will not maintain rhythm completely by himself; the rider must do it.

If the horse is moving short and "quick" (too fast a tempo), try to slow his tempo by slowing your rate of posting (or sitting) motion. Urge him gently forward (with rhythm) into the appropriate length of rein to "arch" his back. If he is still taking short, stiff steps, he may be mentally tense. (See Chapter 16, "Warm-Up," for further suggestions.)

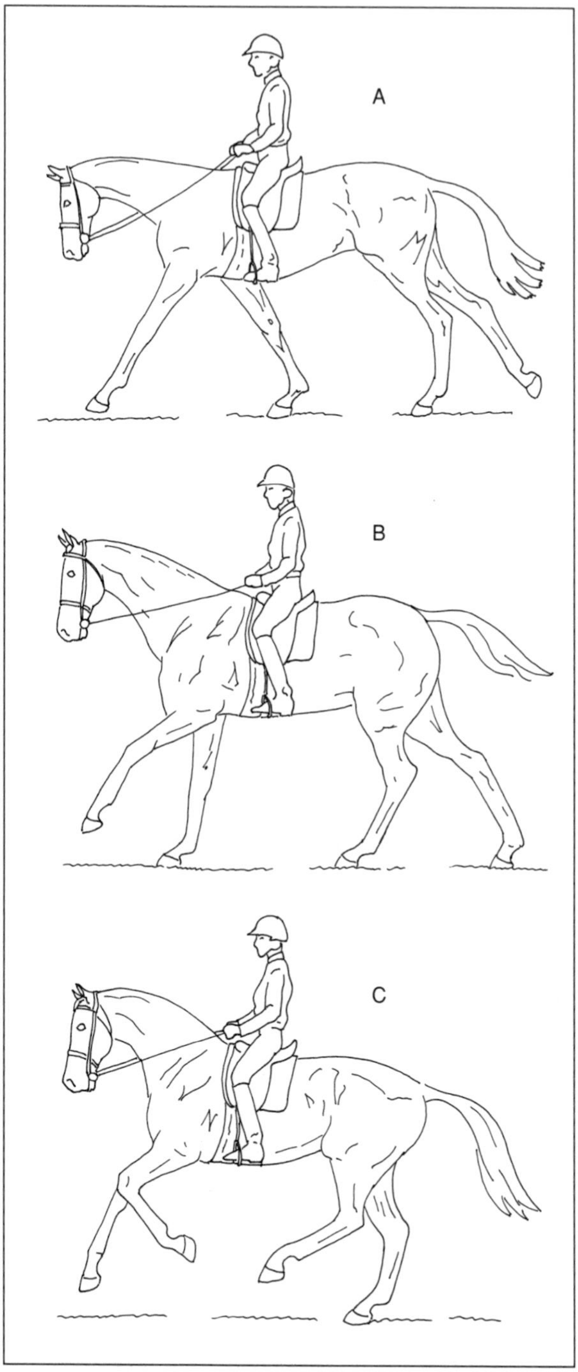

Figure 12.3
(A) A "downhill" canter. (B) A level canter. (C) An "uphill" canter.

A Word About Sitting Trot

Sitting the trot is 50 percent the horse and 50 percent the rider. If the horse has a stiff or sagging back, it will be almost impossible to sit to anything but a slow jog. If the rider attempts to "sit it out" despite the discomfort, the horse will stiffen even more. The horse must have a raised, swinging back in order for even a very accomplished rider to sit it properly.

The rider's 50 percent of the sitting trot is that she must know how to *move with* the horse's trot. Moreover, at a really good working trot, it will take a little effort on the rider's part.

There is a lot of motion from a horse's body to be absorbed at a working trot. Most of this motion can be taken up by the free use of the waist, hip joints, knees, and ankles. If any of these joints are stiff, the horse's motion goes up through the rider's body and produces a kind of pogo stick effect, making the head bob and the shoulders jump, causing the rider to pound her own and her horse's back. The horse understandably does not appreciate this, especially at stronger tempos, and therefore tightens *his* back in defense, thereby creating *more* bounce, and so forth.

When to Sit, When to Post

In some Training Level tests, the rider may ride the trot either rising (posting) or sitting. Discuss this with your trainer or coach (or ground person) — it depends on how your horse goes best.

Even though sitting or rising is optional (in some tests, not all), riders are cautioned to be reasonable. Do not post three or four strides, then sit three, or the like. Such a practice would be disruptive to the flow of your ride. The sitting and posting periods should be conducive to showing the horse at his best.

There is no AHSA (or FEI) rule dictating which posting diagonal is required (the leg to which the rider rises). Therefore, this is another matter you need to take up with your coach or trainer. (The common practice is to rise as the outside foreleg goes forward.)

Trot and Canter Complement Each Other

Learning obedience and rhythm at the trot improves the canter. However, a horse that is trotted too much will become stiff in the back, and the canter may become very stiff and choppy. Cantering loosens the back and thus softens the trot.

The Working Canter

The *"Working canter...is a pace between the collected and the medium canter in which the horse, not yet trained and ready for collected movements, shows himself properly balanced and remaining on the bit, goes forward with even, light and cadenced strides and good hock action. The expression 'good hock action' does not mean that collection is a required quality of the working canter. It only underlines the importance of an impulsion originated from the activity of the hindquarters."* (AHSA, Art. 1905.4.2)

At the canter, you always want a clear three beats, then a moment of suspension (all four feet off the ground). The hind feet always overstride the prints left by the front feet by at least 12 to 18 or more inches. Ideally, the horse should appear to move "uphill" by bending the joints of the hindquarters and bringing the hind legs well forward. Even the Training Level horse should not appear to be cantering "downhill," which would indicate that the balance is "on the forehand." The Training Level horse should be able to canter at least "level" (figure 12.3).

Actually, the canter is not a natural gait for most horses. The "natural" gait is a four-beat gallop with its flat and fast groundcovering strides. Admittedly canter and gallop merge into one another as the pace increases or decreases. Over the centuries, some breeds have been bred to have a natural three-beat canter. If you possess one of these, you are lucky. If not, you must teach it.

The main difference between the four-beat gallop and three-beat canter is the straight versus bent body. In order to show three beats, the horse must be slightly bent through his

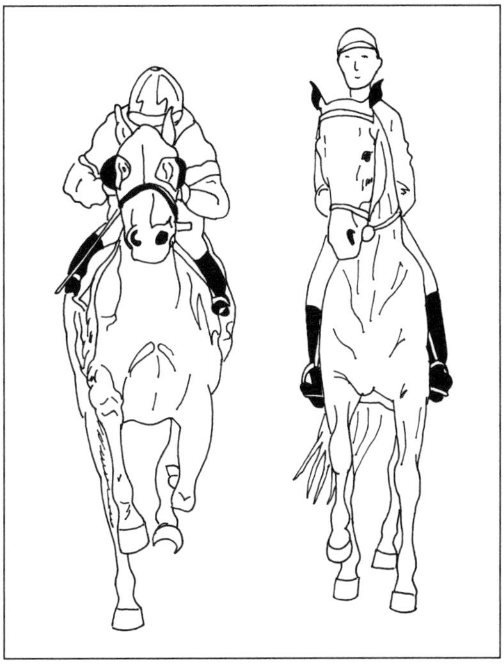

Figure 12.4 At a gallop the horse is biomechanically straight (left), but at the canter, a horse with a slight bend is "straight"(right).

body. Thus, the canter is considered "straight" if the hind feet are in line with the front feet but the body (the spine) is slightly curved (bent) toward the leading leg (figure 12.4).

In order to be able to achieve the maximum push forward, the racehorse keeps his spine straight on his line of travel. In a true canter, the horse "lifts" more than pushes (or at least should); thus the gait gains less ground for the amount of energy expended. If the horse does not bend his body — if he keeps his spine quite straight — his canter will tend to be either lateral or four-beat, like a slowed-down gallop.

There are some clues to look for to judge the correct amount of bend for the canter: the inside legs (front and rear) should be in line with each other and the horse's outside ear should be in the middle of the track (figure 12.5).

The canter is not correct if four hoof beats can be heard (or seen), which happens when the inside hind leg is put down separately from the corresponding diagonal foreleg. The most common causes of a four-beat or a lateral canter are: the horse loses impulsion and does not canter with sufficient elevation; or the horse is too straight (in his spine); or is tense (stiff) in his back.

If the horse is stiff and tense, bending will make him easier to influence. On the other hand, if a four-beat canter is caused by laziness (sometimes described as "labored"), the rider must inspire the horse to more activity. Move him out more to build impulsion and then if he has not settled into three beats, bring him back with half-halts, which should put him more on his hindquarters and produce the three-beat canter.

Like the working trot, the working canter is a bit more collected than an "ordinary" (or "natural") canter. In addition, like the working trot, the horse will seldom come to this more balanced and rounded canter by himself.

In order to produce the desired elevation of the canter strides and to maintain the rhythm, it is often necessary to have an almost continuous interaction of driving and restraining aids. You ask for greater engagement from the animal's hindquarters while slowing the front end, and some of his weight will shift rearward.

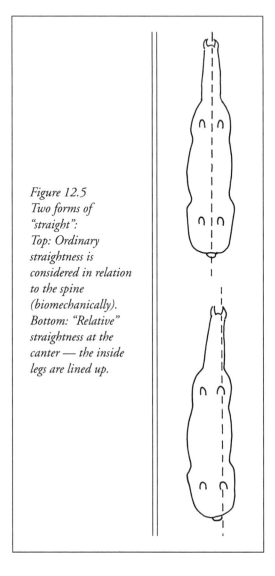

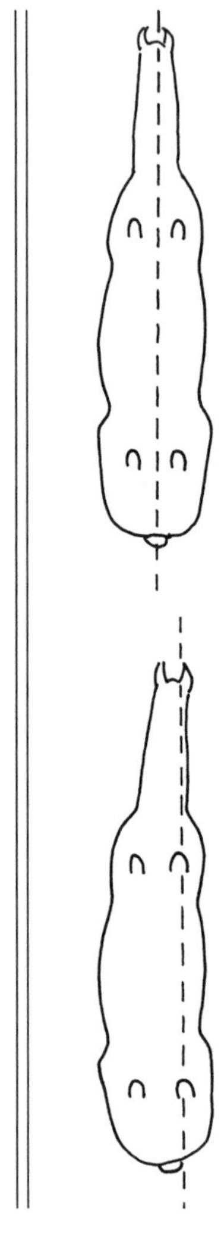

Figure 12.5
Two forms of "straight":
Top: Ordinary straightness is considered in relation to the spine (biomechanically).
Bottom: "Relative" straightness at the canter — the inside legs are lined up.

You do not "slow" the front end by restraining equally with both hands, however. That will only encourage the horse to lean on your hands and possibly go faster! Being bent toward the leading leg is what produces the collection and engagement and "uphill" appearance of a good canter. This takes coordination and a sense of rhythm from the rider. It is an almost simultaneous drive and restraint at the right moment in the canter stride. As the head comes up (horse rocks back), restrain more with the inside hand than the outside, and at the same time drive with both legs (inside leg at girth, outside leg slightly back also encourages bend), then release as the head goes down. The result should be to drive the hind end under while slowing and elevating the front. This is what allows you to shorten the horse's base (collect him), enabling him to bring his hind legs further under his center and "leverage up" the forehand. It's like pulling on a bowstring; the more tension you can generate, the more bend you will get. Cantering on a 20-meter or smaller circle will encourage this bend and engagement (bending of the hind leg joints). When you go down the straight side, do not lose the bend you have achieved. You want to feel the horse's hind legs reaching forward under your seat and lifting you at each stride.

You must be especially sure to balance a horse going around corners. Left to his own designs, a horse is most likely to round a turn by leaning his shoulder to the inside and bending his head and neck to the outside. This balances him against the centrifugal force of moving on a circle. The faster he takes the turn, the more exaggerated this action becomes. To help the horse balance more back on his hindquarters, drive and bend him on curved lines. Insist that he bring his hind legs forward by keeping him bent and energetic (figure 12.6).

It is also a fault if the horse brings his haunches too far to the inside at the canter. The correction is to bring the inside legs in line by putting the shoulders in front of the haunches (figure 12.7).

Too Fast or Too Slow

Bending also makes it easier to control the speed of the canter. Young horses canter fast because they are usually stiff in the body and balanced

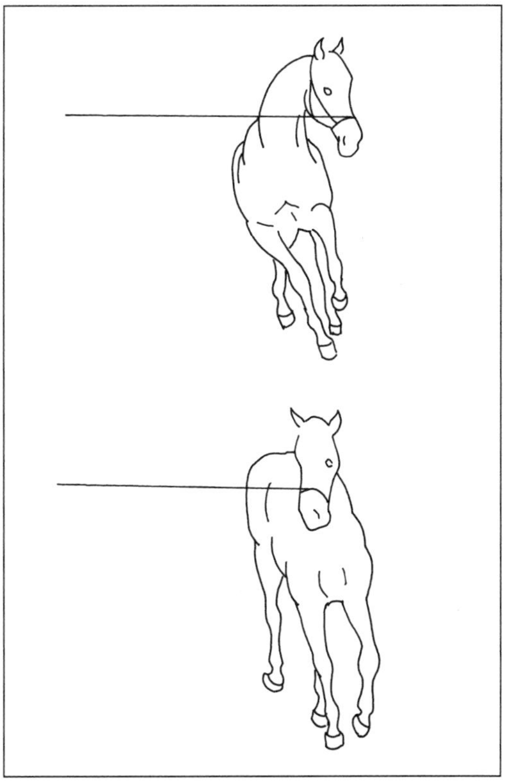

Figure 12.6 Top: This is how a horse naturally balances on a turn at speed — head and neck to the outside, "leaning" on inside shoulder. Bottom: By "driving" the horse into a taut rein, the horse with bend can balance upright.

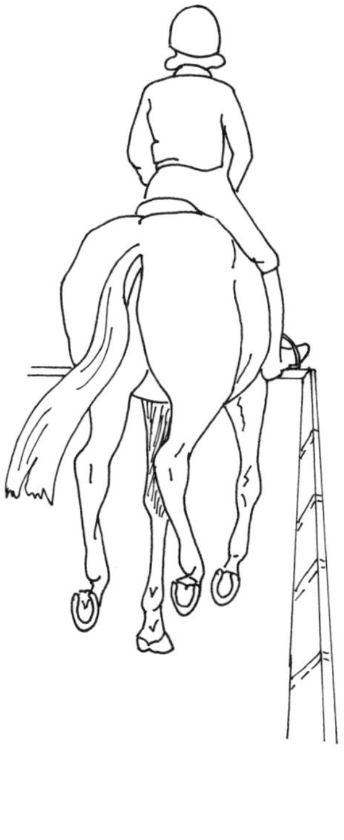

Figure 12.7 Most horses have a natural tendency to carry their haunches to the inside at a canter.

on the forehand. Ex-racehorses canter fast for the very same reason.

The key to turning a strong canter into a brilliant canter is never to pull back equally on both reins. If instead you bend the horse's poll slightly to the inside while still maintaining contact on the outside rein (so he doesn't just turn his neck and gallop over his shoulder), the horse will be powerless to resist you. *Slow each stride* until you get the desired effect. Use the same rein action combined with lots of leg on horses that are dull or try to lean on your hands.

Attempting to slow the canter with too much rein action and not enough leg may turn the horse into a "leg mover." This horse steps out the leg sequence (more or less) with almost no body movement or without the hind legs coming truly forward. These horses are extremely difficult to correct because they are "behind the rider's aids." You may need to get professional help for this problem.

Leads

A major concern is correct leads. On the right lead the horse is bent or curved to the right; on the left lead, bent to the left. Very often the horse has a "good" lead (takes it easily, stays balanced), and a "poor" lead (difficult to get, or awkward when the horse does take it). This discrepancy is usually caused by one side of the body being more developed than the other.

During the normal process of training, the rider has to try to even up the two sides of the horse. Minor unevenness can often be corrected with appropriate work and exercises. Horses that are "one-sided" (a term meaning chronically bent to one side) are an especially difficult problem. They will have difficulty picking up one lead or maintaining it. You may need to put the horse on the longe line; correct (maybe strengthen) your canter aids; or get a trainer to help you correct this problem.

Chapter Thirteen

At What Level Should You Compete?

The AHSA tests (Training through Fifth Levels) can be purchased by writing to the American Horse Shows Association. The United States Dressage Federation publishes the tests for Introductory Level (walk and trot) and Freestyle (First through Fourth Level). The tests are usually changed every four years, so be certain you have the correct tests.

"The levels of dressage are offered as a means of evaluating a horse that is changing." (AHSA, Art. 1922.6.5)

The dressage tests allow a knowledgeable judge to get an accurate assessment of the correctness and deficiencies of your training and your riding in roughly five to ten minutes. The tests are not designed to teach the horse anything. They are composed primarily to demonstrate the shortcomings and strong points of the horse and rider team at any given stage of training. Therefore, always remember that since the tests do not teach your horse anything, simply programming your horse for a given test or competition will not lead very far in training for advancement.

The AHSA dressage tests can be used as *guides* to training, however. The order of the introduction of the movements and figures can be used as a sort of "road map" to training. Some of the exercises are good training tools; some are strictly to test that the training is there.

Of course, not all trainers and competitors agree with the order in which each movement and figure is presented. New tests always provoke heated discussions among riders and trainers not only as to progression, but sometimes even as to whether certain exercises should be included in the tests at all. These latter ones are usually exercises that are useful in training but are not deemed suitable by some people for a public presentation.

There is an effort made for each test within a level to be slightly more difficult than the one before, as well as to make each level more difficult than the one before. The tests are therefore designed to be a workable blueprint for the correct, systematic, step-by-step training of a horse. Even if you live miles from the closest trainer, you can rely on your scores to tell how your training is going.

The Object or Purpose of the Levels

"The purpose of each test is printed on the cover (and in the Rule Book), and the horse shall be considered in light of the degree of training it should have achieved to be shown at that level." (AHSA, Art. 1922.6.5)

Training Level is for novice horses or riders, although there is no requirement that you must start there! Each succeeding level increases in difficulty and sophistication, until one reaches (we can always hope!) Grand Prix level.

The tests and levels follow the "Training Scale," which is:

The Dressage Training Scale

TRAINING LEVEL:

1. Rhythm
2. Suppleness/looseness
3. Acceptance of the bit

FIRST LEVEL:

4. Pushing power/thrust
5. Straightness

SECOND LEVEL:

6. Impulsion/engagement
7. Collection

In Training Level, you must attain the purity of natural rhythm (which the horse may have lost when introduced to a rider) and keep the horse loose (relaxed) and supple. In First Level, you develop pushing power and thrust, along with straightness. In Second Level, you introduce collection, engage the horse behind to carry more weight, and require greater accuracy of the movements.

A horse is allowed to enter two consecutive levels at a given competition. Therefore, you usually have six to eight different tests to chose from at any one competition.

To decide what level and test to compete in, first look at the objective of the level and test you wish to compete in. Next, look at the *movements* (such as leg yield, shoulder-in, lengthened trot or canter); the *figures* (the size or shape of circles, figure eights or serpentines); and the *transitions* (between gaits) of the individual test. Does your horse fill all those requirements sufficiently at home? Would he rate at least a 5 or 6 on all movements? If so, this is where you should probably begin.

Many instructors and trainers will tell you you should be schooling your horse a level above what you are competing in, the reason being the more sophistication you show in a particular test, the higher your scores. This is

Over-Performance

You will occasionally hear the buzzword "over-performance," or something like, "That is a Fourth Level horse; what's he doing in Second?"

Although over-performance is not defined in the *Rule Book*, judges are given guidelines on how to deal with it. Officially, they are told that "over-performance" means performing a movement not called for in the test; for instance: a collected trot instead of a working trot should be scored down, but if there is a refined movement, reward it. In other words, if the test called for working trot and a very *good* working trot is shown, it should be rewarded.

It often remains an ethical question, for there is no "rule" that once a horse has been trained or shown to a certain level, it cannot compete below that level. While superior training should not be penalized, the judge can penalize *wrong* movements.

why you will find many trainers competing at a higher level at the schooling shows, then "dropping back" a level at the recognized shows.

Many of us are guilty of practicing tests and forgetting the real purpose as we get lost in the details. The judges use the definitions and the "Objectives and Standards" as outlined in the *Rule Book* as the guiding criteria for scoring. The Objectives of the Levels are designed to direct competitors in the correct development of their horses. Although the tests are changed from time to time, the "Objective" of the levels remains pretty much the same. You can use these to judge for yourself if the horse is truly ready to enter a specific level or move up. Let's start with the Objective of Training Level, as stated in the *AHSA Rule Book.*

Training Level

Objective: *"To confirm that the horse's muscles are supple and loose, and that it moves freely forward in clear and steady rhythm, accepting contact with the bit."* (AHSA, Art. 1918.2)

Let's see what this means in simple English:

"Muscles are supple and loose": The *USDF Glossary of Judging Terms* defines "suppleness" as "pliability; ability to smoothly adjust the carriage (longitudinally) and the position or bend (laterally), without impairment of the flow of movement, or of the balance."

In other words, suppleness is the easy bending of the horse, and the horse's ability to shift his center of gravity forward, backward, or side to side. A horse that leans in or throws his haunches out on circles or corners lacks suppleness. At Training Level the circles and corners are large, so the horse should have no trouble bending and keeping his balance.

"Looseness" refers to the horse's relaxation. Relaxation is relative: Too much relaxation will show as laziness. Too little relaxation will show as tenseness, resulting in short, stiff steps.

"Moves Freely Forward": "Freedom" is the "amplitude of range of motion of the fore and hind limbs." (USDF) Freedom is also a lack of restraint. The horse should take long steps and swing his shoulders and hips freely. If the horse looks restrained, the neck is contracted and this will impede the mobility of the shoulders. If the horse is stiff or tense he is not moving "freely forward," and this is often reflected in a shortness of steps. This is not to imply the horse must have overstep (although it is always an advantage); it implies the horse must look diligent and purposeful. "Forward" refers to the horse's desire to move on when directed by the rider.

"In clear and steady rhythm": "Rhythm" is the correctness of the beat — four-beat walk, two-beat trot, and three-beat canter. It is a major fault to have an incorrect rhythm. The rhythm must be "clear" ("correct") and "steady": no speeding up or slowing down.

"Accepting contact with the bit": is the horse's unresisting willingness to allow the maintenance of a steady contact and the application of the aids. "Acceptance" is "lack of evasion, resistance, or protest..." (USDF)

Accepting the bit is not the same as "on the bit," but rather the absence of resistance to the bit. Types of resistances often seen are: stiffening the jaw, pulling against the hand, bracing against the bit, and going above the bit.

At Training Level, many of the transitions between gaits are between letters. This takes into consideration that the balance of the horse has not yet been perfected and allows the rider time to prepare her horse for the transitions.

A Training Level "Frame"?

Although judges are cautioned not to use the phrases "Training Level *frame*," "First Level *frame*" (because conformation as well as training, dictate the frame or "outline" of the horse), for the rider or competitor, these are very descriptive phrases.

The Training Level frame might be described as a fairly natural carriage, without

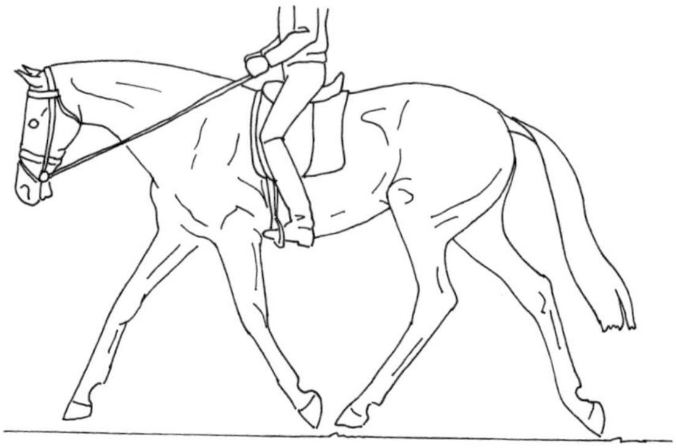

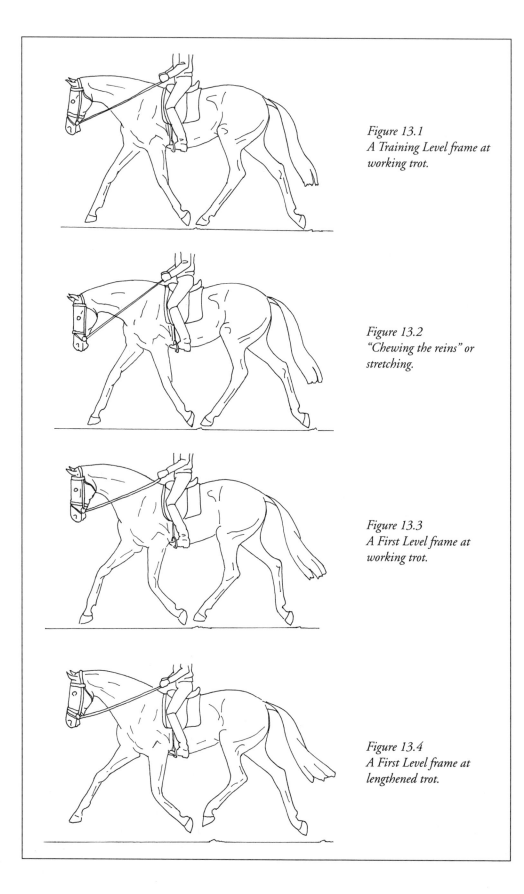

Figure 13.1
A Training Level frame at working trot.

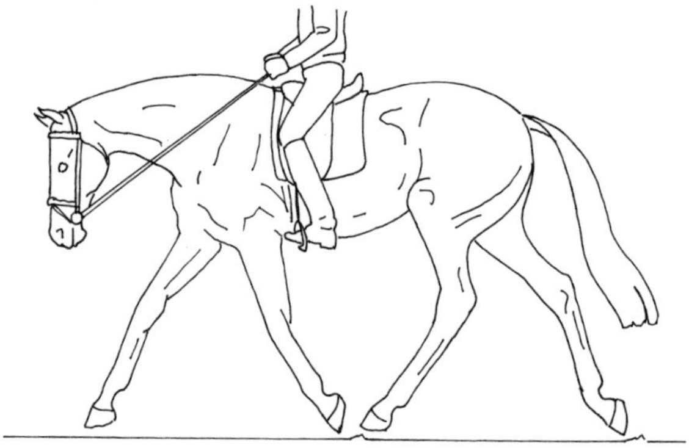

Figure 13.2
"Chewing the reins" or stretching.

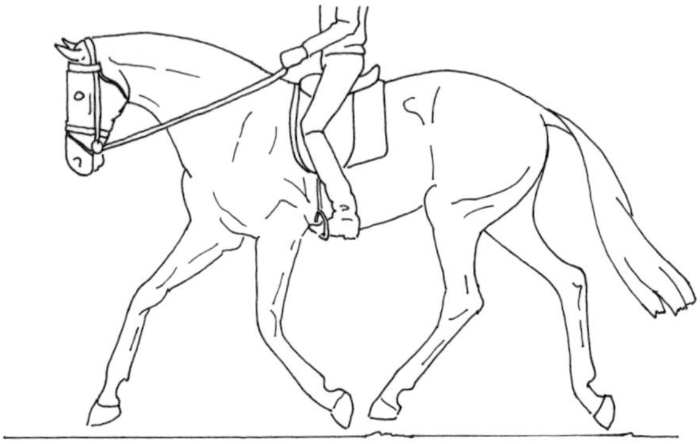

Figure 13.3
A First Level frame at working trot.

Figure 13.4
A First Level frame at lengthened trot.

excessive weight carried on the forehand, with the horse moving freely forward in the shoulders and haunches (figure 13.1).

Due to the proportion of the Collective Marks versus the movements in Training Level, a horse that is a super mover, presents a pleasing outline (frame), and has good impulsion will usually be the highest scoring horse in the class. This is not as true in the other levels where the movements are more difficult.

The movements required in Training Level are:

- Medium walk
- Free walk
- Working trot
- Halt from trot (through the walk)
- Working canter
- 20-meter circles at trot and canter
- Stretch into the rein at trot

Stretching the Frame

This exercise was added to the AHSA tests in 1995. In Training and First Level it is called "letting the horse take the reins out of the hands." It has a variety of other names: "down and round; long and low"; "showing the horse the way to the ground"; and "chewing the reins out of the hand." "Stretching" is the name that makes the goal of the exercise clear (figure 13.2).

Note that the rider must keep a soft contact with the horse's mouth throughout the exercise; the reins are not released. The horse's poll angle should remain approximately the same as before the stretching.

The horse should stretch over his back, reaching down and forward with the head and neck, seek the bit, and remain in a steady tempo. The rider must continue riding forward or the horse will also quit. The rider must work to maintain the rhythm, engagement, and suspension of the pace; only the outline of the horse changes.

When the horse is stretched to about where his mouth is level with the point of his shoulder, stop feeding the rein and allow him to trot on, stretching into the bit and lifting his back underneath you.

If a horse quickens his rhythm, he has lost his balance forward. If the horse loses rhythm or puts his nose in the air, loses contact with the bit, or simply does nothing, it is insufficient (scored 4 or below). Some attempt and some stretch would probably be a 5; more stretch and unchanging tempo would probably be 6 and up.

To bring the horse out of the exercise, increase the driving and half-halting aids, without losing the flexion and roundness of the neck and back.

First Level

Objective: *"To confirm that the horse, in addition to the requirements of Training Level, has developed thrust (pushing power) and achieved a degree of balance and throughness."* (AHSA, Art. 1918.2)

From this level on, the requirements are either added onto, or are a refinement of, the previous level (figures 13.3 & 13.4).

"Has developed thrust (pushing power)": "Thrust" or pushing power is demonstrated in the lengthened trot and canter. Here the horse is expected to push its body more into the air from the hind legs. The First Level horse should also have developed at least a small degree of "cadence" (a springy accentuation of the rhythm and tempo).

"A degree of balance": "Balance" is the "relative distribution of the weight of horse and rider upon the fore and hind legs (longitudinal balance), and the left and right legs (lateral balance). The horse is in good balance when the weight is distributed evenly left and right, and sufficient toward the rear legs that it can easily manage the task at hand. Loss of balance means the sudden increase of weight onto the forehand and/or to one side." (USDF)

Balance is demonstrated on the 10- and 15-meter circles without leaning in or out and in the lengthenings by not "running" onto the forehand.

Even though the above quotes do not say that the horse must be carrying more weight on the hind legs than the front at this point, this weight distribution is a necessity if the horse is to achieve correct lengthenings of stride. The horse does not really step more "forward" with the hind legs; rather, he does not trail them as much behind the vertical.

"Throughness": is defined as "the supple, elastic, unblocked, connected state of the horse's musculature that permits an unrestricted flow of energy from back to front and front to back, which allows the aids/influences to freely affect all parts of the horse (e. g. the rein aids go through and reach and influence the hind legs)." (USDF)

Prompt and fluid transitions at the letters, as well as the transitions from working to lengthened strides and back, demonstrate this quality. Clear transitions between and within gaits challenge your horse's balance — and by so doing, improve it.

To have the lightness and ease of movements called for in the Collectives at First Level, the horse needs to be very accepting of the bit most of the time ("let the rein aids go 'through'").

Although the Collective Marks for First Level are the same as for Training Level, they are divided among more movements, so each one has less weight.

The movements of First Level are:

- Medium walk
- Free walk
- Working trot
- Lengthen stride in trot
- Halt directly from trot
- Working canter
- Lengthen stride in canter
- Simple loop at counter-canter
- Change of lead through trot
- 10-meter circles at working trot
- 15-meter circles at working canter
- Leg yield at trot
- Stretch into rein at trot

Lengthened Strides

Most horses find it almost impossible to lengthen correctly before they have learned to shorten the stride. Therefore, it is necessary to teach the horse to be able to carry himself in a shorter stride in order to put the hindquarters in a position where they can propel him forward without difficulty.

Once the hindquarters are under the horse (engaged), he can be asked to "push off" and show some length. It is a mistake to make the horse stretch too far before he is ready as it may cause him to put his hind legs out behind him or to "spraddle" behind.

It should be clear that the lengthening of strides is very different from what might be called a "pleasure horse extension." English pleasure horses do lengthen their strides and over track, but they also markedly speed up their rhythm and usually brace against the bit.

At the lengthened trot, the horse should cover more ground by pushing off strongly with his hind legs and producing a *longer* period of *suspension*, which results in some over track. He must not "topple" onto the forehand, which would be revealed by quicker strides. The lengthened trot or canter is not necessarily faster (m.p.h.) than the working gait, because speed is not the motive for lengthening. What we are seeking is greater engagement and impulsion, with a slight lengthening of frame, thus preparing the horse for medium and extended gaits.

Lengthening the canter is not running; it is coming from behind; it is the scope of the stride. At the lengthened canter, the number of strides per minute should not change, but each bound should be bigger. If the horse lacks thrust at the lengthened canter, the strides will "flatten" because the horse falls on the forehand. To achieve this, think of asking for upward thrust rather than speed.

Any free-moving horse can easily lengthen the canter, but an important part of judging the lengthened canter is the down transition. Do show a down transition *before* the corner. Many riders make the mistake of letting the corner slow their horse. When you do this and the transition is a separate score, the judge could almost give you a "0" for no transition!

Many horses lose their balance on the transition to working canter as evidenced by their haunches coming to the inside. This can be corrected by using half-halts to balance your horse.

Leg Yield

This movement has been in and out of the tests several times in the last decades. Although some trainers do not consider it a proper classical movement, it is a useful preliminary to the more difficult lateral exercises to follow. Its purpose is to teach the horse to move away from the leg and accept the outside rein.

The horse is kept almost straight, except for a slight positioning at the poll away from the direction in which he moves, so that the rider is just able to see the eyebrow and nostril on the inside. The inside legs pass and cross in front of the outside legs.

Leg yield is usually performed on the diagonal, in which case the horse's body should be, as closely as possible, parallel to the long sides of the arena, with the forehand just slightly in advance of the hindquarters. If performed along the wall, the horse should be at an angle of about 35 degrees to the direction in which he is moving (figure 13.5).

Figure 13.5 Leg yield to the right.

Common faults are: too much bend, resulting in "falling" over the outside shoulder; lack of crossover; loss of balance, regularity or alignment; variable tempo (quickens or slows the pace); leading with the haunches; trailing the haunches.

Second Level

Objective: *"To confirm that the horse, having demonstrated that it has achieved the thrust (pushing power) required in First Level, now shows that through additional training it accepts more weight on the hindquarters (collection), shows the thrust required at medium paces and is reliably on the bit. A greater degree of straightness, bending, suppleness, throughness, and self-carriage is required than at First Level."* (AHSA, Art. 1918.2)

"Accepts more weight on the hindquarters (collection)": Although collected trot and canter are called for, this is only a little more collection than in First Level. The collection is demonstrated by the transitions in pace, the 10-meter circles, and the shoulder-in (figures 13.6 & 13.7).

It is the horse's strength of topline that determines when he advances to this level of difficulty in dressage. The hind legs thrusting

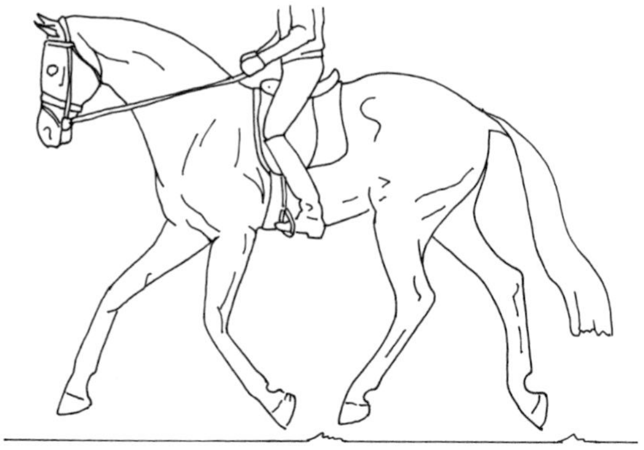

Figure 13.6
A Second Level frame at collected trot.

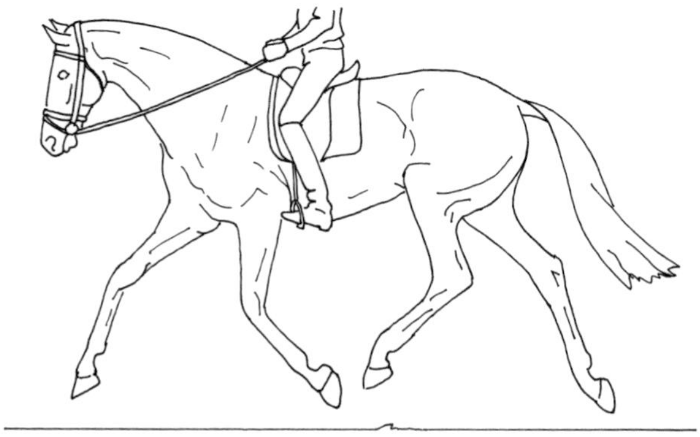

Figure 13.7
A Second Level frame at medium trot.

into elastic hands develop a topline that results in self-carriage. When he has a solid topline, the introduction to lateral work will not suffer loss of impulsion.

Shortening of the reins does not produce collection — increased engagement does. At Second Level, your horse must begin to lower his hindquarters, lift his withers, and bend the hip, stifle, and hock.

More weight on the hindquarters and collection require a degree of "engagement." "Engagement" is "increased flexion of the joints of the hind legs and the lumbo-sacral joint (the spinal joint immediately in front of the peak of the croup) during the moment of support, causing a relative lowering of the croup/raising of the forehand, with the hind legs supporting a relatively greater proportion of the load." (USDF) This cannot be done if his topline is weak. If the horse is forced to do this work without muscle tone, unsoundness can occur. In addition, if the horse lacks suppleness, he will also lack engagement. From Second Level up you can't have impulsion without engagement.

The collection and engagement are considered sufficient for the level if the horse can perform the movements without losing his balance — forward, backward, or sideways.

"Shows the thrust required at medium paces": The definition of medium trot and canter is "a pace at which the horse shows a length of stride between that of collection and extension, and a more uphill balance, more forward and upward thrust, and more reach than in his working pace. The movement produced is rounder than that of extension." (USDF) Medium paces require impulsion, which is defined as "thrust, releasing of the energy stored by engagement." (USDF) It is demonstrated by lift, springiness, and suspension.

"Is reliably on the bit": actually, "on the aids," which is "maintaining good connection, the horse responds instantly and generously to all the aids." (USDF)

"A greater degree of straightness, bending, suppleness": These requirements will be demonstrated by the increased difficulty of the movements.

(A greater degree of) "throughness and self-carriage": "Self-carriage" is the "state in which the horse carries itself without taking support or balancing on the rider's hand." (USDF) Again evidenced by the horse not losing his balance in the movements.

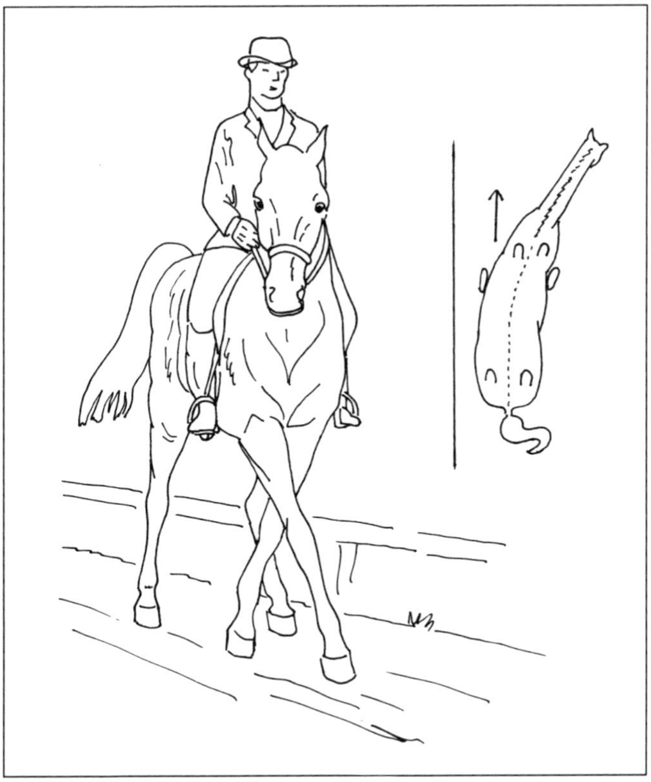

Figure 13.8 Shoulder-in: the judge's view and a rider's view.

In the Collective Marks, the terms "engagement of the hind quarters" and "suppleness of the back" have been added. Here lightness of the forehand begins to equal "engagement."

The required movements of Second Level are:

- Medium walk
- Free walk
- Collected trot
- Medium trot
- Halt from trot
- Canter from the walk
- Collected canter
- Medium canter
- Counter-canter
- Change of lead through trot
- 10-meter circles at collected trot
- 10-meter circles at collected canter
- Release the inside rein at canter
- Shoulder-in
- Rein back

Shoulder-In

Shoulder-in is both a collecting and engaging exercise. In a correct shoulder-in, the horse is slightly bent around the inside leg of the rider. The horse's inside foreleg passes and crosses in front of the outside leg; the inside hind leg is placed in front of the outside leg. At every step, the horse must move his inside hind leg underneath his body. The hind legs track straight down the track, the front legs cross. The horse is looking away from the direction in which he is moving (figure 13.8).

Common faults: loss of rhythm; loss of tempo; lacking bend in the body or too much bend in the neck; leg yield instead of shoulder-in (straight body); too much angle; tilting head; lacking engagement (bending of the hind legs); not taking enough weight with the inside hind leg; loss of impulsion.

Guide to Test Selection

The most important consideration is that the test should be suitable for your horse. Points to consider are:

- Horse's level of training
- Horse's behavior away from home (trailering and at the show grounds)
- Horse's degree of fitness and the amount or type of warm-up needed per test
- Rider's skills
- Rider's ability to present a test (this is different from being able to produce a movement)

Now look at the test with the following points in mind:

- The content of the test(s): kinds of movements such as medium trot, shoulder-in
- The sequence of movements (structure)
- The placement of the movements in the arena. Avoid tests with awkward sequences of movements; this only teaches your horse to worry and to resist.
- The length of the test
- How well the test incorporates your horse's strongest movements (look at the coefficients)

Remember that there is no way to tell what your horse will do tomorrow. Assess today's skills and match the test content to those skills.

Rein Back

The horse should step back with alternate diagonal pairs of legs in a straight line without any sideways deviation of the hindquarters. The feet should leave the ground with distinct steps.

Common faults: horse refuses to back; hollows his back; opens his mouth; leans on the forehand; leans back; goes behind the vertical; drags the feet; braces the neck; takes uneven steps; or the hindquarters deviate to either side.

Choosing Your Tests

The test is not meant to be an obstacle course to trip up a rider and horse. Ideally, it gives the rider the chance to show off the horse's correctly achieved basics and to allow judges to reward the rider's efforts.

Pay careful attention to the Objective of the level and test you are entering. Do not choose a test if your horse cannot perform one or more of the requirements. If your horse needs "show experience," you are still better off picking the tests he will be most comfortable with. This practice avoids cramming the horse through a sequence of movements that will make him tense because they are at the very limits of his skills. This tension will most likely show up in the score and placings. No need to add rider frustration to a horse's first time show nerves.

In addition, you should be aware that most horses "lose" part of their training when in a show atmosphere. This is why knowledgeable dressage competitors try to have their horses trained a little beyond the bare requirements of a level or test.

The dressage levels and the tests within the levels are progressive, so that there is no sharp demarcation in difficulty between tests. Training Level, Test 4 is almost imperceptibly different from First Level, Test 1 requirements. This provides an easy transition up the levels.

You should try the test at home before you decide. A rule of thumb here is that if the test seems to "happen" too fast — your horse (or you) have trouble preparing for a movement, and then the next movement is already there — you are probably not ready for that test. If the test rides easily, you are probably ready.

Also, look at the test's coefficients. Because these double the score, it is especially important to be proficient with these movements. Yet another consideration is how important the placings and scores or awards are to you. Are you experimenting to see how well your horse will do a certain test under pressure? Or do you want to be assured of a good score or placing? Depending on the section of the country, your horse may not be "competitive" (placed in the ribbons) unless he is in the 6-7-8 score range, but this should not prevent you from *schooling* at that level, if that is your goal. Once a horse's performance at a particular level or test is consistently in the 6 and 7 range ("satisfactory" to "fairly good") he is probably ready to move up.

Chapter Fourteen

Memorizing and Visualizing Tests

Although you are allowed to have a reader or "caller" for your tests, it is a very good idea to have the tests firmly in your mind so you know how to prepare for the movements. Just like the performing pianist does not look at musical notes but plays by heart, so will the accomplished dressage rider ride her test from memory. While it is perfectly acceptable to have your test called, you must know the test well enough that you ride the horse to his very best.

You've probably been told your horse can only think about one thing at a time — guess what, that also applies to you! It's essential that you know your test so well that you can do it on autopilot. After all, when you're in the arena, you want to concentrate solely on riding your horse and not on where you go next. Many riders lose points unnecessarily because they don't know where they are in the ring. It's hard enough to be perfect at an event without fumbling to remember what movement comes next.

If you don't know what movement is coming up next, you can't properly prepare for it. If you are momentarily distracted, you could lose track of where you are (and maybe miss what your caller read).

In the low levels, the tests are fairly simple to memorize, and in finals or championships and all FEI and freestyle tests, they must be ridden from memory. So study your tests at home, not on the horse's back. Concentrate on learning the patterns as well as learning the narrative. Then rehearse the test in some way that is helpful to you.

Here are several suggestions to help in memorizing the tests.

1. Geometric Memorization (memorize the design):

Some people can remember pictures better than words. To do this, draw the tests on paper, a section at a time, and memorize the geometric patterns you see. Carry this slip of paper ("cheat sheet") with you at all times (figure 14.1).

You need only mark the letters that are in odd (unexpected) places. Visualize whether you are riding toward the judge or away from the judge. Picture the test as a series of symbols (a diagonal, a circle, a serpentine).

The entrance and exit are so standard that they do not have to be especially memorized. ("A - Enter at (gait), at "X" halt, salute, proceed at (gait)." All that is necessary is to memorize what gait you enter at and which way to turn as you approach "C". The exit is also similar for all tests: "Down the centerline, halt and salute at either "X" or "G", and leave the arena at a free walk on a long rein."

For the body of the test, you might find, for instance, that two diagonals immediately following each other look like an hour glass; that a 20-meter circle is either "at the end" (at "C" or "A") or "in the middle" (between "B" and "E"). You can mark smaller size circles by writing the size (15 or 10 m.) within the circle; shoulder-in can be curved lines along

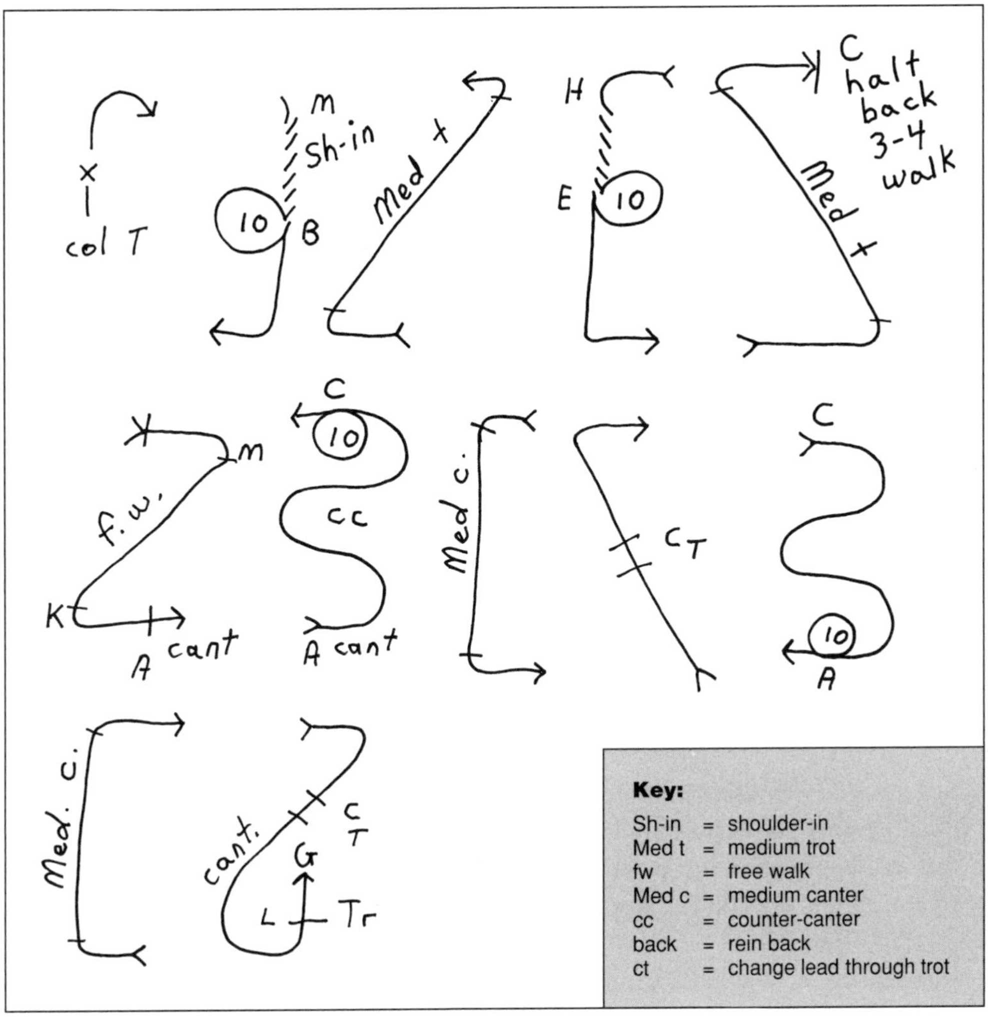

Figure 14.1 A "cheat sheet."

the rail and half-pass or travers (haunches-in) are appropriately placed slash lines. A lengthened trot rising could be dashed lines or the initials "Len. T."; a figure eight should indicate which circle is first and second. Develop your own codes and you will soon become expert at picturing your test on paper and in your imagination.

Reduce a copy of the drawn test on a copy machine to approximately 3½ x 5½ inches, fold it, and put it in your coat or shirt pocket so you can refer to it while practicing at home or warming up at the show. You can also recite the test while you are driving, or at a break at work, or anywhere. If you are not sure of a part of the test, refer to the "cheat sheet."

2. Act it out:

Some riders find it helpful to walk the test out, the way three-day-event riders walk the cross-country course. Acting out the test helps imprint it on the mind.

One way to do this is to draw an arena, complete with letters, and push a paper clip around it. Or run your finger around some other imaginary arena. Some competitors do the test on foot on a sidewalk, using the lines in the pavement to mark the ends of the arena. The small arena is two pavement squares, the large arena is three. Or mark off a section of your living room with some kind of markers to simulate letters and walk, "trot," and "canter" (on the correct lead of course!) around your imaginary arena. Always keep in your mind's eye where you are in relation to the judge — "toward the judge," or "away from the judge" — so that if you get turned around in an actual test, you will realize it immediately.

It is also a very good idea to imagine the aids you will be using as you practice each movement. This establishes a physical "memory" in your psyche.

With repetition, you will learn where all the letters are and they will become second nature. "A" is always at the entrance, "C" is where the judge sits, the corner letters are "K", "M", "H", and "F"; "B" is the center long side to the right of the entrance, and "E" is on the other side. This just leaves the "odd" letters that are in the Standard (large) arena only. A simple way to remember them is, starting at the judge's left, they are: R-S-V-P. Isn't that easy to remember?

3. Memorize the Narrative:

If drawing patterns or acting out doesn't work for you and you're better at memorizing sentences or phrases (for instance, you do well memorizing speeches or poems), here is a technique that might work for you.

Break the test down into separate maneuvers, then abbreviate each maneuver to the gait or the figure it makes. Using the same test as above, memorize the sequence as follows:

Enter collected trot; X halt; turn right; immediately shoulder-in; 10-meter circle at B; continue down rail; diagonal medium trot; shoulder-in; circle at E, diagonal medium trot, and so forth.

It may help you to verbalize the patterns — recite it to your trainer or friend, using your personal narrative while they follow on the actual test sheet.

4. Sequence Memorization:

It may look daunting, but this technique is nothing more than a systematic version of the narrative test. It has proven very successful for riders at the upper levels (Second and above). It does presuppose, however, that you have also memorized the test in segments. In other words, you memorize the trot section, the walk section, the canter section, and so forth.

Conceptualizing the test in this way helps keep beginning Second Level or above riders from thinking of the upper level tests as a monumental task that they may never master.

Using a Second Level test as an example,

simply memorize each section, then remember the order of the segments. For example: collected trot segment, then walk, then canter and finish with trot.

Sequence Memorization

This is a sample Second Level test — all trot and canter work is collected unless otherwise stated.

A Enter collected trot	
X Halt, salute,	
proceed collected trot	**7 trot elements:**
C Track right	turn right
M-B Shoulder-in right	sh-in
B Circle right 10m	circle 10
K-X-M Medium trot	med
M Collected trot	
H-E Shoulder-in left	sh-in
E Circle left 10m	circle 10
F-X-H Medium trot	med
H Collected trot	
C Halt, rein back 3-4 steps,	**4 walk elements:**
proceed medium walk	halt
M-X-K Free walk	rein back
K Medium walk	walk
Before A	free walk
Shorten the stride (of walk)	
A Collected canter left lead	**9 canter elements:**
A-C Serpentine of 3 loops	serpentine
width of arena,	circle 10
no change of lead	med
C Circle left 10m	dia. trot change
H-K Medium canter	serpentine
K Collected canter	circle 10
F-X-H Change rein, at X	med
change of lead through the trot dia.	trot change
C-A Serpentine of 3 loops	turn on CL
width of arena	
A Circle right 10m	
K-H Medium canter	
H Collected canter	
M-X-K Change rein, at X	
change of lead through the trot	
A Down centerline	**1 trot element:**
L Collected trot	L trot
G Halt, salute	G halt
Leave arena free walk	

5. Photographic Memory:

Some riders have a knack for memorizing a "movie" of their test. In this age of video, it is very easy to implement this technique. Simply have yourself and your horse videotaped in the test and watch it, as many times as necessary to commit it to your natural mind-progression process. Just as self-talk helps some people, so does self-picturing.

MORE TIPS FOR MEMORIZING TESTS

- Most Training Level tests go: trot, canter, trot, walk, trot, canter, trot, and finish.
- Some tests have a pattern — a circle for example — on one rein (one direction), then a diagonal, and the pattern repeats on the other rein or some other "mirror image" formula.
- Listen to the tests on tape. You can make your own tapes and pause between each movement to give yourself time to say the next movement before the tape does. Then carry these with you in your car and listen while you travel.
- When you are walking your horse during your warm-up, walk through the test.
- If there are several riders before you as you sit at the ingate, watch them ride the test and call it to them in your mind.

You must be able to recite the test without pausing and thinking about it. You must be able to pick up the test at any point and continue. Don't worry about the letters in most cases: for example, instead of "K-X-M", think "diagonal."

Multiple Tests

If you are doing more than one test at a show, it may help you to memorize them in the order you will ride them. After you ride the first test, eliminate it from your mind so you can focus on the next test. To do this, take a short break away from the show ring. Find a quiet place and recite your next test. If your classes are close together, don't hang around the arena and watch the rest of your class. Make any necessary tack changes, freshen up your horse, and concentrate on your next test. Don't let someone hover around who insists on telling you everything you did wrong in the last test; focus on things you can improve in the next test.

Whatever your memorizing technique, incorporate self-talk into it — it is the "white noise" that takes your mind off distracting stimuli. Give yourself quiet time to organize your test in your mind before you enter the show arena. Believe that you will remember the test and believe in yourself and your horse.

Visualizing the Test

Visualization is the ability to imagine yourself successfully or unsuccessfully completing an act. When you visualize, you can "see," "feel," and "experience" the act before you actually do it. What is even better, *you* control the outcome during visualization.

Many studies have proved that visualization, done properly, is a valuable form of *practice*. If the rider, even if sitting quite passively in a chair, *thinks* — or says out loud — a specific instruction, or a scenario, her nervous system will "fire off" the appropriate muscles in the proper sequence of the movement. For instance, a person can think about hitting a tennis ball and the muscles will fire off in the proper sequence even though outwardly the person doesn't move at all. This phenomenon, if utilized as a form of visualization, can add hours to your practice time.

Visualization cannot replace learning the fundamentals of training (or riding). Mastery of the basic techniques and skills of riding are necessary *before* visualization can be used effectively. Your best results will be attained by *supplementing* your training in the saddle with positive visualization.

Jane Savoie (dressage teacher and trainer, reserve rider for the 1992 bronze-medal U.S. Olympic dressage team, author of *That Winning Feeling!*) has said, "Your subconscious mind hears and believes everything you say and think and strives to achieve your thoughts. So be sure you program your mind carefully and thoughtfully."[2]

You can get a lot of "practice" by simply visualizing a well-ridden test. "See" your ride in your mind in vivid detail. Execute every stride, every corner, and every transition gracefully and flawlessly.

Ms. Savoie likes to say, "It's not true that practice makes perfect. In actuality, *perfect practice makes perfect.*"[2]

When you practice "in your mind," you can actually practice many of the appropriate "moves," thereby engraining correct habits.

Whenever you get nervous about an upcoming show or test, run through your visualization of the "perfect ride." If you're going to lose sleep the night before a competition, you might as well make use of the time!

In your mental rehearsing, practice not only all the "right" moves but practice what to do if things go wrong. If your horse loses energy, if he gets tense, if he shies. You must practice your game plan often. If you have your game plan down pat, it will leave you more time *during* the competition to pay attention to your horse's mood and make little corrections during the test. Having a plan set clearly in your mind frees your reflexes to act quickly, instinctively, without having to stop and think.

Visualize the test and practice without the horse. Close your eyes and mentally ride through the pattern, picturing yourself on horseback actually "seeing" the markers from that perspective. For instance, picture yourself entering the arena, trotting toward the first marker, then preparing your horse for the halt.

[2] Jane Savoie (a motivation talk at Rainbow's End Farm, El Paso, Texas, April 19-20, 1997.)

If you can, ride with attention to the "feel" of the test and to establish a kinesthetic "memory" for the sequence of moves. Mentally ride through the rest of the test and develop a strategy.

Also, include emotion in your mental rehearsal. Maybe you are the type who needs to get charged up to perform well or maybe you need to feel quiet, calm, and inwardly focused.

This method must also involve rehearsing the test according to how your horse thinks. You might want to take a blank dressage test and write out how you are going to ride the test, keeping in mind how your horse thinks in a test at a show. It has to be based on your horse's stage of training at that time. Naturally, the results will vary as the green and inexperienced horse becomes more seasoned. For example, horses that anticipate — the "electric" horse — may be clever about jumping into the canter too soon. Consequently, when practicing, the rider needs to keep her mind on the trot (or walk) until the exact moment to ask for the canter.

The more phlegmatic type horses are always thinking that "F" to "X" (half the diagonal) is long enough to do lengthened trot and do not like to make the effort a-l-l the way to "H". So, at home it is necessary to think "F-X-H to corner," still asking for lengthened trot until the diagonal is finished.

Here are a few tips for effective, positive visualizations:

- Find a quiet and calm place to perform your visualization. Close your eyes and visualize your test from start to finish, as if you were riding it. If your mind starts to slip, you know you're not concentrating. Think about the surroundings. When you're going across the diagonal in lengthened trot, what are you looking at? When you're doing lengthened canter, where are you going? What are you seeing? Always remind yourself where you are in relation to the judge. Imagine every transition and bend and how you need to aid your particular horse; be aware of all feelings and sensations. Visualize yourself in great detail and in the process of accomplishing your goals. Create very vivid images by involving all of your senses. Hear the rhythm of your horse's footfalls, smell the clean, fresh air. See your horse's markings. Feel an elastic contact with his mouth.
- Visualize yourself being in complete control of your performance. Break down your performance into small, individual steps. Work out each segment of the test. Remind yourself how a really good transition felt or the power of a good lengthening and try to recapture that feeling. Concentrate on reliving the experience from the inside, as though you're watching a movie.
- Develop a "coping rehearsal." Imagine corrections to anticipated problems: (and work out solutions before hand) a shy at the judge's stand, a slowing in the corners, or coming out of circles. Allow yourself to admit you're worried about something, but then make sure you work out the solution.
- Focus on affirmations of the skills you want to improve on or the test you want to memorize. Visualize tips that will improve your test. For example: "Keep my heels down, stay balanced and centered in the saddle, and keep my eyes up." (Don't make too lengthy a list! "Eyes up, heels down, stay centered," would be better.)
- Symbolic visualization can assist you in your performance. If you are trying to prevent your chest from collapsing and your shoulders from rolling forward

during the canter depart, perhaps you can imagine your chest being pulled skyward by a string from the clouds and your shoulders being gently pushed back by a summer breeze as you canter. This assigns you a definite task so you can accomplish your specific goals.

- It may be helpful to develop phrases such as "bury him in the corner," or "sit on the inside seat bone for the canter depart." You can think these phrases during the test when you need a reminder.
- Always end your visualization on a positive note. If you make an error, correct it before you conclude.
- Practice this exercise at home before every lesson and show. You may also find it helpful to practice the exercise while sitting outside the arena gate, just before you ride your test.

Remember, you can imagine anything you want to — it's your own private movie!

Are You Ready?

Until you can visualize every aspect of your test, you are not ready to show. You must be able to ride each movement in connection with the next movement. When you compete, you are doing it to show off yourself and your horse. Give yourself every advantage.

Chapter Fifteen

Practice Makes Perfect (Almost)

You have chosen your tests for your entry into "competition dressage." Now it is time to practice the specifics of those tests.

In your day to day riding, you will concentrate on developing the general qualities of your horse. You may want to review the chapters on how the horse should walk, trot, and canter, contact the bit, carry his head and neck, and use his back. Reread the sections on the rider's seat and aids. After you and your horse have mastered these points as well as can be expected at this stage of training and you have memorized your test(s), you are ready to practice riding them.

Always remember that without a freely moving, relaxed horse and proper contact, perfect geometry is worth very little. An accurate ride on a horse with erratic paces and tense, short strides will score lower than a smooth, sweeping, slightly inaccurate ride by a properly moving horse. Of course, if the level of competition is high, the winner will have to display good gaits *and* accuracy. So, you do need to spend some time practicing the test before a show. If you have to search for the letters, or fight to keep your horse round on the circles or straight on the straight-away, your test is going to be interrupted by mistakes and irregularities. "Seat of the pants" riding will not get you extra points.

A Practical Arena

Once you have memorized the test so that you can recite it and also do it without hesitation with your pencil on paper or in your mind, you come to the problem of finding a place to practice it on horseback. Very few of us have a Standard arena to work in, so we have to improvise something. The most obvious solution, which requires only an assortment of jump poles (or scrap boards), buckets, barrels, milk cartons or some type of markers, is a suitably level area so you can practice.

The show arena is usually enclosed with a very low fence (about 12 inches high). You can use poles laid on the ground or the type of border fence used to edge flower gardens. One of the easiest to set up is 54 10-foot-long 2x4's set on a like number of 16-inch cinder blocks. It costs about $300 but should last forever, is portable, and costs less than the commercial arenas. If you do not have sufficient area or materials for a "real" fence, at least mark a set of corners and one or two 20-meter circles. Although you may use "feet" and "inches" when marking off your practice arena, during practice you need to get used to *thinking in meters.*

Whatever you use for a practice arena, it should have a very low barrier, be fairly level and have good footing. If your horse is only used to working in a fenced arena, he may not have respect for a low fence. You need to find this out before the show!

When you leave the rail and try your new arena with its low sides, a strange thing will usually happen. The horse will feel like a different animal. The purposefulness may have gone out of him. He just will not see any reason for doing these strange maneuvers out there in the middle of nowhere. In fact, until he is on the bit and going with impulsion, it may be rather discouraging. The circles may not be as round or as even as when you had a fence for a guideline. You may also find when you first try it that a 66-foot (20-meter) circle is an enormous thing. It is hard to find the correct curvature, and sometimes the circle tends to get smaller and smaller. After a while you will begin to get your bearings and your horse will begin to listen to you for directions.

A short geometry lesson about the space you will be competing in is a good place to start. Many beginners (and experienced riders too!) lose unnecessary points in the accuracy department because they don't have a good working knowledge of the dimensions of the dressage arena (figure 15.1).

All levels of dressage competition, from the Introductory Level (USDF walk-trot tests) to the highest (Grand Prix Special), take place in a rectangular arena enclosed by a low fence (sometimes a row of poles on the ground). A Standard arena is 20 meters wide (approx. 66 feet) and 60 meters (approximately 198 feet) long; a Small arena is 20 meters by 40 meters (approximately 132 feet). Letters around the perimeter mark precise points on a grid. (No one can explain the origin or placement of the various letters, however.)

A good way to learn the geometry of the arena is to take a piece of graph paper and use each square as one meter. Draw out your arena 20 meters wide and 60 meters long. "A" is at the entrance in the center of one short side, "C" is at the center of the opposite short side. Starting at one corner (the one to the left of the judge), "M" is 6 meters (approximately 19½ feet) from the corner; "R" is 12 meters (39½ feet) from it; "B" is another 12 meters and so on to the far corner. You will notice that the Small arena is exactly twice 20 meters long and the Standard arena is three 20-meter segments (figure 15.1).

To square your corners, use the Pythagorean Theorem (see figure 15.2 inset). To do this you need three stakes, one or two 50-foot (or longer) tape measures and several hundred feet of string. It is also helpful to have another person to help you. Begin by driving a stake where you think your first corner will be. Attach a length of string to the stake and measure out to 30 feet; place a second stake here. Now attach another piece of string to your corner stake and measure out 40 feet. If you have a helper, have him hold his string at the 40 feet mark until you walk to your second stake with your tape measure. Adjust the two strings until you can stretch the 50-foot tape measure between them, then drive your third stake at

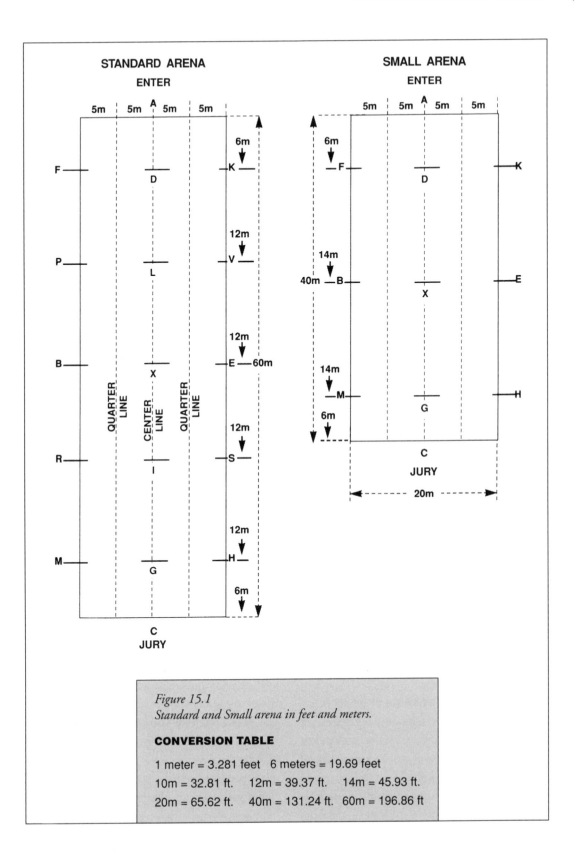

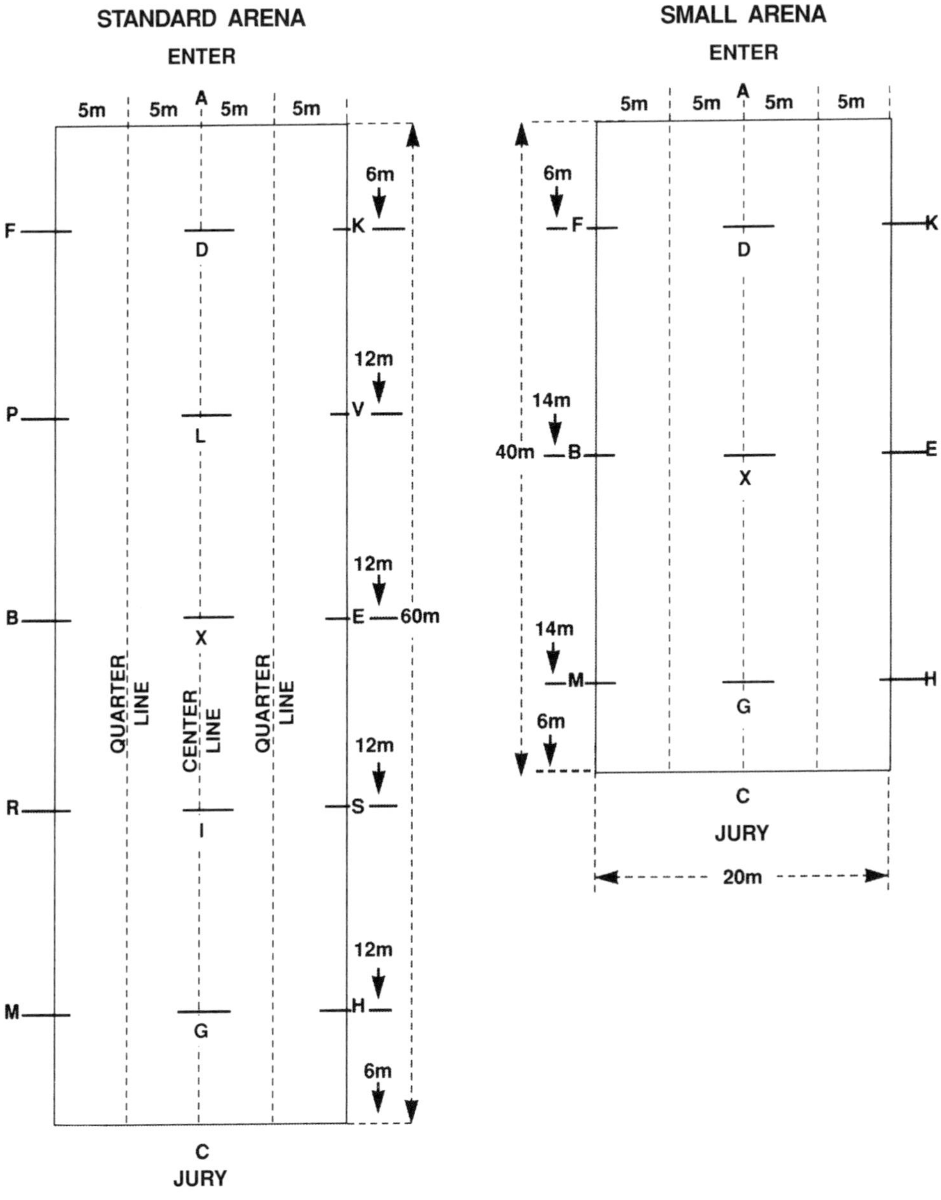

Figure 15.1
Standard and Small arena in feet and meters.

CONVERSION TABLE

1 meter = 3.281 feet 6 meters = 19.69 feet
10m = 32.81 ft. 12m = 39.37 ft. 14m = 45.93 ft.
20m = 65.62 ft. 40m = 131.24 ft. 60m = 196.86 ft

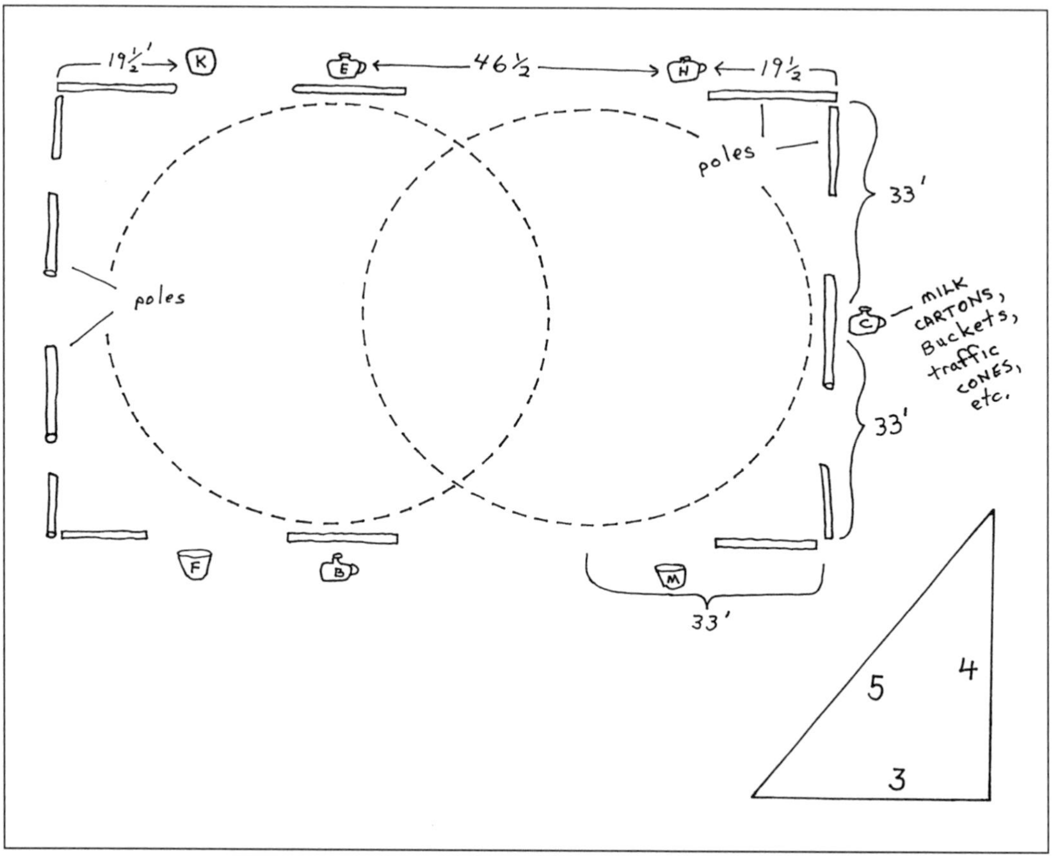

Figure 15.2 A "makeshift" arena. Minimum requirements: 65x100 feet of level area; eight buckets, plastic milk cartons, traffic cones, or similar objects; plus at least ten poles, boards, border fence, rows of rocks, or similar barriers.
Lower right: Pythagorean Square: any combination of 3-4-5 will give you a right-angle "square" corner.

the juncture. You can now extend your two sides out to 66 feet. (or 20 meters one direction and 198 feet (or 60 meters) in the other. Measure out your second corner the same way. Any combination of 3, 4, 5 will give you a perfectly square corner.

When practicing a test, know exactly where the "outline" of the circles and figures are in reference to the markers in the arena. For instance, a "serpentine of three loops width of arena," is three 20-meter half circles connected by a straight segment as you cross the centerline. Note where, in relation to the letters, you need to cross the centerline and where you need to touch the rail.

Accuracy

Accuracy must become a way of life for the competition dressage rider. Always ride accurately around the arena — that is, straight down each side — as far into the corners as the training of your horse allows and just as straight along the short side.

It is a fact that you can gain or lose points on accuracy of the figures and movements. Circles are one example, but even the straight lines need to be truly straight. For instance, if the horse is not absolutely straight on a diagonal, he will lose some stride that he might have had at the very least, or be so crooked that he becomes irregular at worst. Inaccuracy will detract from the scores of every movement where they occur.

In the *AHSA Rule Book,* judges are cautioned that: *"Accuracy (moderate) should be a factor only if the inaccuracy avoids the difficulty of the movement, i.e. a larger circle avoids the difficulty of a 10-meter circle..."* (AHSA, Art. 1922.6.2) Judges are required to take off points if the inaccuracy makes the movement easier, but will seldom raise the score if the inaccuracy makes it harder (as in a circle that is too small).

Concentrating on accuracy reinforces your training. You give the horse a definite direction, frame, and path to follow, and you know for sure if he is obedient or not. If you just let the horse pick and choose his path and his speed, you are not really training; you are letting the horse make the decisions, and you are being a passenger. If he "chooses" to go the same direction you intend, you are in luck. If he chooses a different direction, it is not his fault — you gave him that choice!

Accuracy is the rider's responsibility. If your horse is being "obedient," the accuracy is totally up to you! (If he's *not* being obedient, that's up to you also!) Remember, a dressage test is a test of training; that training is "tested" by demonstrating improved gaits and accurate figures.

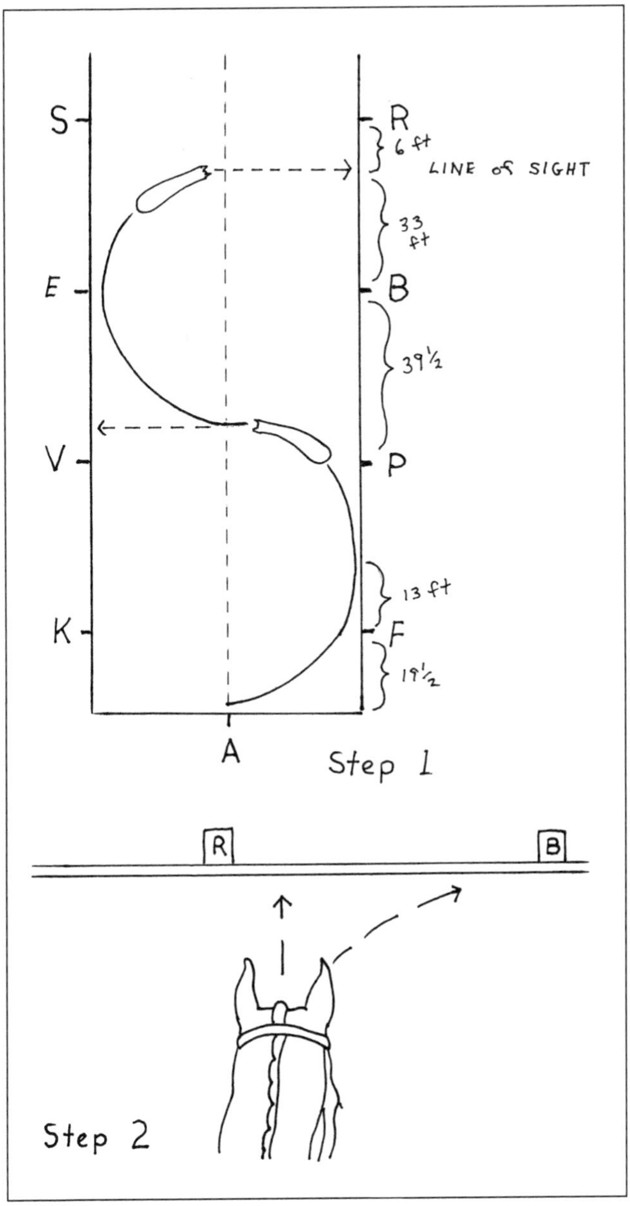

Figure 15.3 Step 1. Imagine your path of travel, on graph paper if necessary, noting your "line of sight" for each movement. Step 2. "Line of sight" from on horseback.

Performing perfectly round and precise circles or figures demonstrates the control of the rider as well as the acceptance of that control by the horse. By riding a "perfect" circle, or straight line, or accurate transition, you demonstrate that you are deciding where the horse should go, and the horse is obediently obliging (figure 15.3).

Being accurate also trains you to keep your horse straight and even between your reins and legs. By keeping your legs against your horse throughout your test, you can deal with it smoothly and quickly if a problem arises. If you have been riding with your legs "off" and you suddenly come down on your horse's sides with your legs, you are likely to startle him into a rough transition.

One of the biggest helps in keeping your ride accurate is to **look where you are going**, so your eye connects to the arc of the optimum route to the destination. If you don't look up, you won't know were you are, and since the horse will go where you look, that's how you'll get there. Sight each new marker early, beginning with the judge as you enter at "A". Using your eyes may seem like a little thing, but it will make you sit better as well as improving your accuracy, and that means better marks for every movement.

Transitions

"In a movement which must be carried out at a certain point of the arena it should be done at the moment when the competitor's body is above this point." (AHSA, Art. 1922.6.2)

Transitions from one gait to another, or the beginning or end of a circle or figure, should be executed as the rider's shoulder passes the letter. At the lower levels, some of the transitions are done between two letters. This gives the green horse more time for preparation, because the *most important* part of a transition is the smoothness and purity of the gait(s). As the tests progress up the levels, the accuracy of transitions becomes more and more an issue, as accuracy denotes obedience of the horse.

An abrupt transition shows the horse losing his balance, popping his head up, or stiffening through his body. An abrupt transition usually occurs if the rider has given his aids too suddenly and without sufficient preparation. As a result, many critical elements, such as balance, rhythm, head-carriage, may be lost.

As you are practicing, try to think ahead. For example, while you are doing a circle, think what comes next. Do not keep concentrating on the circle until suddenly you come to the end of it and instantly have to whip your horse onto the straight track.

Throughout the training the rider should aim to make all transitions as smooth as possible. During training at home, when introducing a new movement, you may want to wait until the horse is "ready" before you ask for a transition or change of position, as from a circle to a straight line, or the transition from trot to canter. When preparing for competition, however, transitions, figures, and movements must be performed at specific markers. For instance, the strike off at canter at the letter "M" (right after the corner), might proceed like this: The rider will start his young horse — or an older horse who may not be reliable about his leads — in the corner, to help him strike off on the correct leg. When the aid is understood by the horse, the rider must begin to make the strike off in other places and then finally at a precise point. The rider must make the horse very obedient to the lightest of aids so that with only a minimum of preparation she can ask for complete obedience and get the strike off where she wants it.

To achieve this, there are several factors the rider must take into consideration.

First, the rider must allow for the time lapse, however small, which occurs when her thoughts have to be transferred to her muscle system, and in turn, to the horse's brain and muscle system. This varies from horse to horse and from rider to rider.

Each horse has a different "response time," a different length of stride, and varying degrees of flexibility. The rider must learn how far in advance she needs to give the aid so the strike off (or other movement) will occur "on the mark" (as the rider's shoulder passes the letter).

Secondly, the rider must prepare the horse and warn him that something is going to happen. These "warning" aids are called half-halts (see Chapter 11). If the horse is correctly prepared for the transition, the rider should be able to take the horse from one gait to another, or one figure to another, or from straight to bend and back to straight, with accuracy.

How to "Draw" a Circle

If a circle is not round, is it because the horse could not be steered around the path? Or is it because the rider did not know how to "draw" a circle? Either way the judge will mark it down *as poor training*.

Here is a suggestion on how to "draw" a circle:

Begin by marking the four outer limits of your circle, as illustrated here. This can be measured on the ground with a tape and the four points marked with sawdust, traffic cones, or something similar. Now you simply ride a curved course between your markers. With experience you can line up with the markers on the sides of the arena, and you will also be able to judge the amount of bend required by your horse for each size circle (figure 15.4).

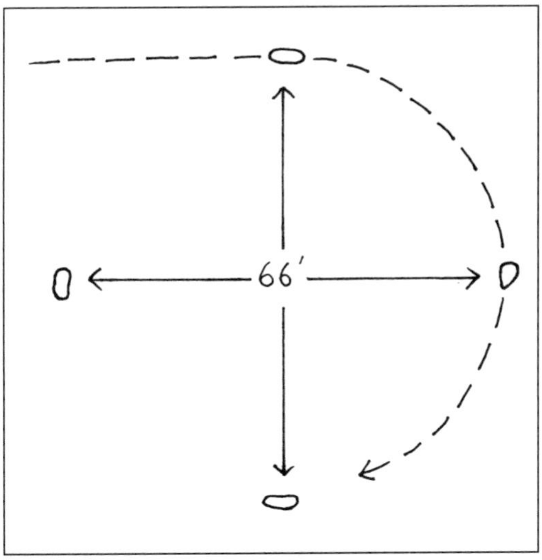

Figure 15.4 How to "draw" a circle: Put markers on the ground, then practice riding around the pattern.

A common mistake, especially with the larger circles at the low levels, is for the rider to "square off" the sides. For a 20-meter circle at "C" or "A", you must make your circle distinct from the corner before and after the circle. When riding your circle, do not go into the corner. After finishing the circle, do go into the corner (figure 15.5).

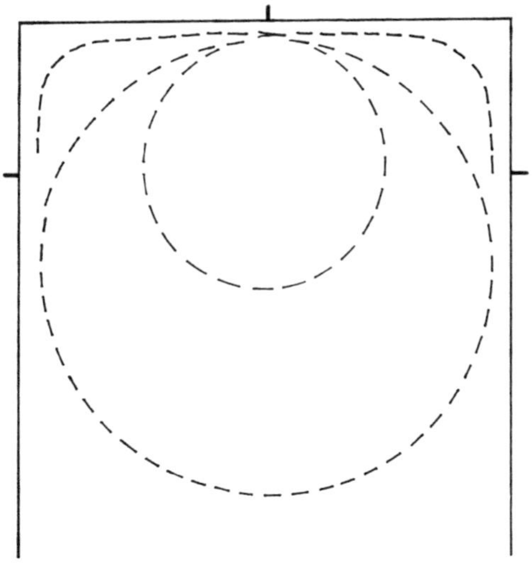

Figure 15.5 Correct circles and corners at "A" or "C".

At home you might want to set up markers for each new figure required in a test: for instance, the serpentines, figure eights, corners, diagonals, half circles, and so forth. Don't get overly dependent on these markers, however, because you won't have them at a competition! You need to learn to judge distances between existing letters of the arena. For instance, for a 10-meter circle at E or B, it's between the rail and the centerline. As you curve toward "X", line up with "C" or "A". A 15-meter circle is from the rail to the quarter line; a 10-meter circle at "C" or "A" is centered between the quarter lines — you get the idea.

The 10- or 15-meter circles at "C" or "A" present a very tricky problem for the rider. The quarter lines are not usually marked in a competition arena. Even the judge has to "guess" where they are! One way to practice is to make a square of 10 or 15 meters with ground poles (or traffic cones) and ride inside this to give you an idea of how tight it really is. As the next step, place a marker or traffic cone on each quarter line (on the rail) and 4 meters beyond the corner letters. These are your "sight lines" for the exterior of your circle. The final phase is to ride the circles without any markers. If you can do this on fresh raked sand, you can go back and check your accuracy by looking at your tracks.

Corners

Every corner is (or should be) one-quarter of a circle. The size of the corner will depend on the level of training of your horse. A young or unconditioned horse cannot be expected to bend as deeply as a supple, well-educated horse, but at any level the corners, the circles and the figures must be *round.* It is required that you ride the corners at least as small as the smallest circle required within that particular test. Example: in Training Level the circles are 20 meters in diameter, so in theory your corners can be one quarter of a 20-meter circle — although you will get better scores if you make them smaller, say 12 to 15 meters. At First Level, your corners must be at least one quarter of a 10-meter circle at the trot and 15 meters at the canter. At the FEI levels, the horse should describe one quarter of a circle of approximately 6 meters diameter at collected gaits, and at medium and extended gaits one quarter of a circle of approximately 10-meter diameter. Whenever turning a corner, the horse should be correctly bent and balanced.

"Cutting corners" refers to the degree that the rider takes or does not take when riding her horse into the corners of the arena. It is just as bad a fault to ride too deeply into the corner and turn sharply to get out as it is to waste a lot of the arena by not going anywhere near the corner (figure 15.6).

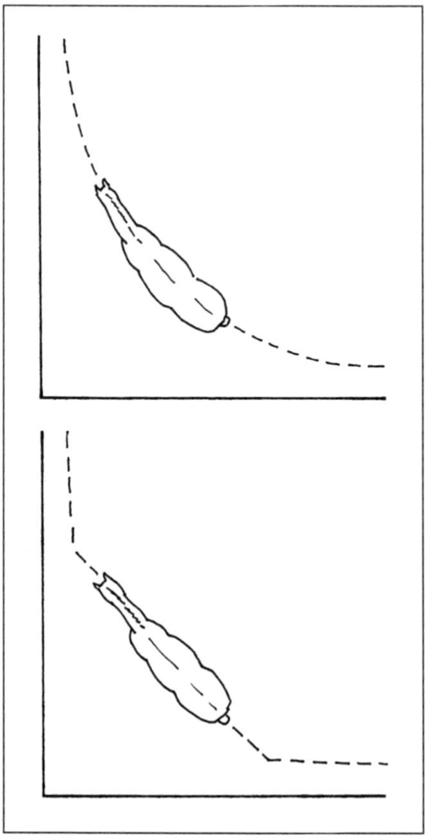

Figure 15.6 Top: A correctly "bent" corner. Bottom: "Cutting" the corner (no bend).

A rider must bear in mind the stage of training of her horse. Obviously, the more supple and trained the horse the deeper the rider can go into the corner.

To practice corners: two poles laid on the ground can give you an idea of correct approach and execution if you don't have an arena. A guide to riding an "accurate" corner is as follows:

Visualize a point on either side of the corner and ride a true curve between them with the horse bent in the direction he is going. A wrong bend (counter bend) or no bend at all is incorrect.

Figure of Eight

"This figure consists of two exact circles of equal size as prescribed in the test joined at the center of the eight. The rider should make his horse straight an instant before changing direction at the center of the figure." (AHSA, Art. 1910.3)

The most common problem with this figure is that riders tend to make two loops instead of two perfect circles joined by a period of straightness. If the figure begins and ends at "X", be sure you are parallel to the judge when crossing the apex. If it is two 10-meter circles between "E" and "B", make sure you are straight on the centerline at "X" (figure 15.7).

The Figure "S"

This is phrased in the tests as: "B to X half circle right 10 meters, X to E half circle left 10 meters," or the reverse (figure 15.8).

Starting at "B" (in our example), you must be able to ride an accurate 10-meter half-circle so you end up exactly on the centerline. If you don't have enough bend, you will over shoot the centerline ("half-circle too large"). If you produce too much bend, you will under shoot the centerline ("half-circle too small"). The change of bend is on the centerline, exactly lined up with the judge. What happens all too often is that when the rider and the front of the horse reach the centerline and change position, the rider forgets that the horse's haunches are still on the first circle. They end up crossing diagonally and never being straight on the centerline.

Never forget: your horse cannot bend two directions at once! You must have at least one stride of straightness between the two half circles. Ideally, these straight strides will be exactly on the centerline and directly facing the judge. Take note that the judge at "C" will have difficulty seeing how many strides (unless excessive) it takes to straighten and then bend to the new direction. Of course, the smoother and fewer strides on the centerline, the better the score should be — depending on the degree of training. The better the training, the fewer steps and more accurate the change should be.

Next, you have the half-circle in the other direction. Very few horses bend equally well in both directions. If you misjudged your first half-circle, the whole movement will be lopsided. You may be able to compensate as you straighten on the centerline; if not, take note to work on more bending, or more accuracy, or better control of the energy. If the horse is going too fast or on his forehand, the circles will be too large; if the horse is going too slow the circles may be too small.

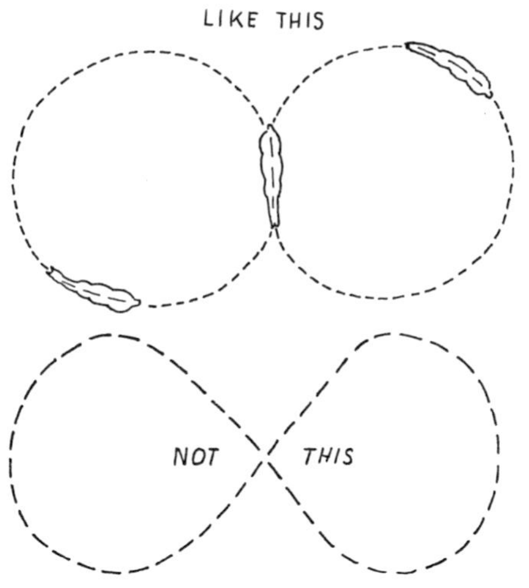

Figure 15.7 A figure 8.

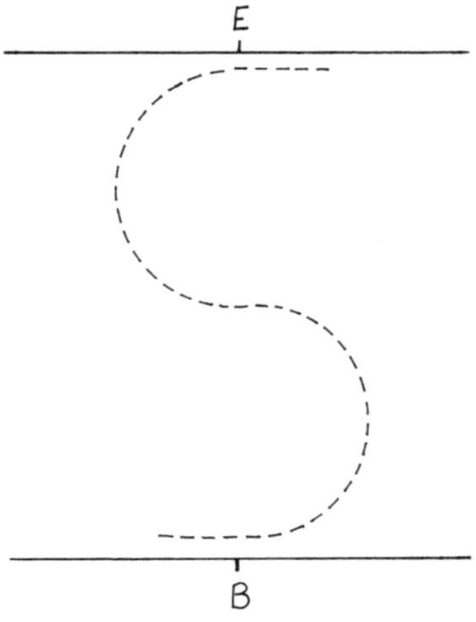

Figure 15.8 A figure "S".

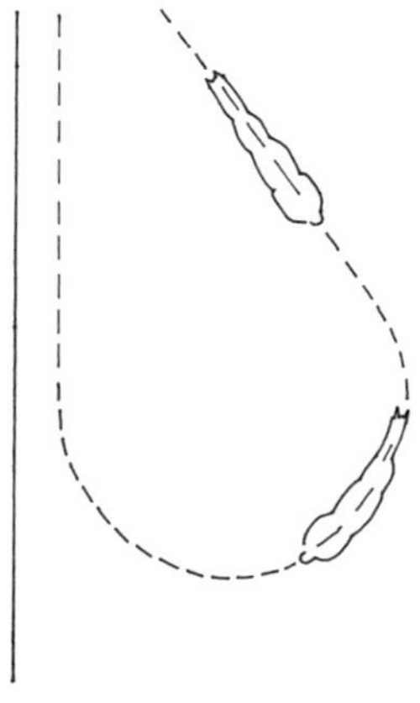

Figure 15.9 A half-circle and return to the track.

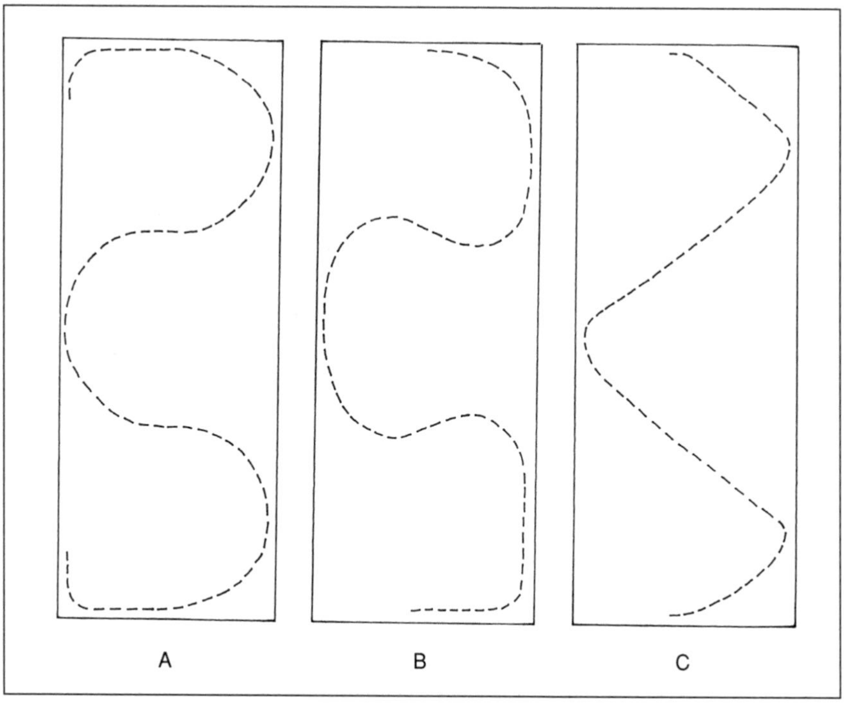

Figure 15.10 The serpentine: (A) correct, (B) incorrect, (C) incorrect.

Serpentines

"The serpentine consists of half-circles connected by a straight line. When crossing the centerline the horse should be parallel to the short side. Depending on the size of the half-circles the straight connection varies in length." (AHSA, Art. 1910.2)

The first loop of a serpentine is started by curving away from the middle of the short side of the arena, and the last loop is finished by curving towards the middle of the opposite short side. Before and after the serpentine you ride into the corners (figure 15.10A).

What should not be seen in serpentines is incorrect bend (bend to the wrong direction), lack of change of bend, indirect rein, or any sideways movement. Judges are looking for the bend and the change in the bend.

The loops should be of equal size. How long should the straight line be? That depends on the horse. Be sure to center your second loop on "E" or "B".

Again, the rider is responsible for the size and equality of the loops. Often they are not ridden equally because the horse turns more easily on one rein than the other. Most horses do find work easier on one side just as people are right- or left-handed. The very reason for the exercise is to see that the horse can perform well on both reins and that his muscles are evenly developed. Riders should be aware that they themselves are stronger on one side and weaker on the other and must be careful when schooling not to have the wrong effect on their horses.

Change Rein

When a rider is going around the arena clockwise, she is said to be "on the right rein"; going counterclockwise, "on the left rein." When she changes direction, whether through a curved line or by traversing the diagonal of the arena, she is said to "change the rein."

When you change rein across the diagonal, the important things to remember are that it is preceded by a corner; that the line across the diagonal should be straight; upon completing the diagonal line the horse should be "aimed" a half stride before the letter so the rider passes the marker; and finally, the movements should be finished with a neat, rounded corner. At Training Level, most judges will not penalize you if you come to the letter a little early so that you can execute a smooth turn onto the rail and into the appropriate corner.

Enter, Halt, Salute

Except for the USDF Introductory tests, every dressage test begins: *"At A, enter (gait), X halt, salute, proceed..."* Although this is only one movement, it is a very important one, for it is the judge's "first impression." The score for this movement often sets the mood for the rest of the test. For instance, if the judge awards you a "5" for the entrance (barely sufficient), it will be more difficult for her to go up with the scores. Whereas if you can get a "7" or "8" for the entrance, the judge will hesitate to drop more than one or two points for mistakes, unless they are severe.

Remember, practice, practice, practice!

At home you can set up cones or poles on the ground for an entrance (if you don't have an actual arena), complete with the letter "A" placed 12 to 15 feet (5 meters) from the center of the entrance. Later you can vary the distance so you are prepared for every eventuality (figure 15.11).

You want to have your horse "on the bit" and in the proper "frame" as you round the end of the arena (remember "first impression"). Glance at the ground exactly in the center of the gate. You want to ride your horse exactly over this spot (because you can't see the letter behind you).

You want to be straight on the centerline when you enter and proceed straight to "X". The halt should not be abrupt. (Please refer to Chapter 11, page 113 to review the correct aids for the halt.) At Training Level, you are allowed two, or at most three, walk steps before and after the halt. At halt the horse should be straight on the centerline (parallel to the long sides), square (forefeet even with each other and hind feet even with each other), still (immobile), and should maintain a contact with the bit (optional at lower levels) during the salute. Ideally, the hind cannons should be vertical. Shift the reins to one hand, salute by nodding briefly or by removing the hat (men only), smile

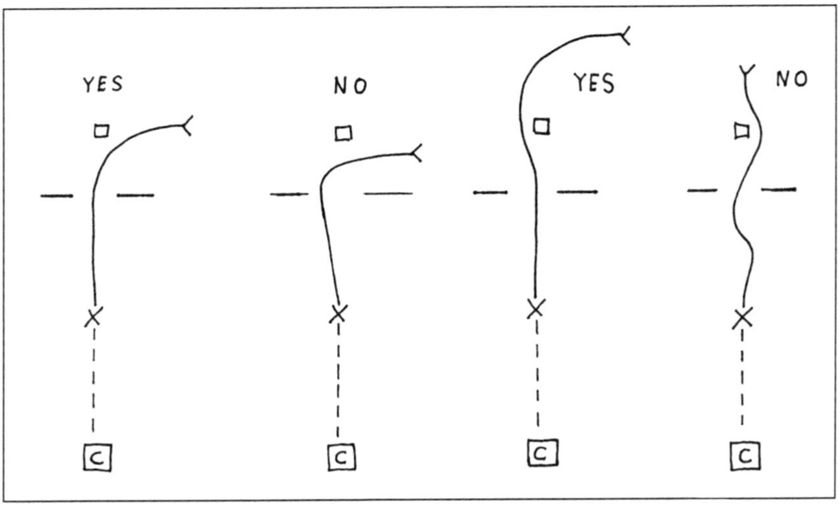

Figure 15.11 The entrance at A.

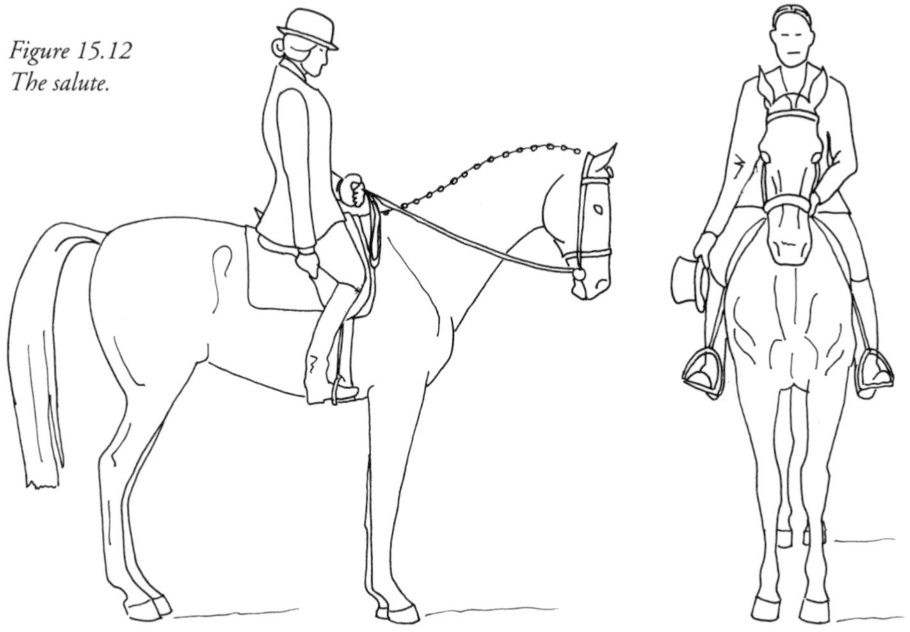

Figure 15.12
The salute.

The Salute

"At the salute riders must take the reins in one hand. A lady rider shall let one arm drop loosely along her body and then incline her head in a slight bow; a gentleman rider shall remove his hat and let his arm drop loosely along his body or may render the salute as does the lady rider. The military salute is only permissible when riding in uniform." (AHSA, Art. 1922.2)

The unwritten protocol here is that the palm of your saluting hand is facing away from the judge at "C" and that for gentlemen the crown of his hat is facing towards the judge at "C" with the open part facing either toward the horse or rearwards. Also, if the rider is carrying a whip, the whip should be transferred to the non-saluting hand before the salute, so that the saluting hand is empty in the case of lady riders and only holding the hat in the case of the gentleman rider.

at the judge, and as soon as she acknowledges your salute, shift the reins back into two hands and proceed. The horse is expected to step straight forward.

At the lower levels, Training Level especially — before the horse is firmly on the bit — your entrance may not be very straight. Horses like paths and rails, and if there are none, they tend to wander. This can be corrected with a good impulsive trot forward, keeping the horse firmly between your hands and legs. Try to establish your good trot and a good frame as you round the last corner before "A". Map your path past "A" directly over the center of the entrance; as soon as you are lined up with the center of the entrance, look up, and aim directly for "C". If the judge is in line with "C" (as she should be), make eye contact and ride briskly forward. Your horse is more likely to stay straight if you are looking at a reference point straight ahead.

Glance out of the corner of your eye for "E" or "B" (parallel to "X") and apply the aids so you will halt at "X". Keep in mind a smooth halt, if not exactly on "X", is better than an unbalanced, jerky one exactly on the spot. A judge at "C" cannot actually see if you are exactly in line with "E" or "B", although a judge at the side could. If you have to drop the contact so your horse will stand still, do so — although it is better if you can maintain a light contact with your rein hand while saluting.

If the horse does not stop straight or square, do not fidget or attempt to straighten him in the test. Above all, do not let him step backwards — that is an automatic fault. Not being straight means that his haunches shift to one side a little as he slows down and stops, so that he is not quite parallel to the long side of the arena. This is something to work on at home. Some horses always shift the same direction. If the haunches always shift, say, to the right, you may be able to hold them straight with a stronger pull on the right rein.

Stopping "square" means that the four feet are at the four corners of a rectangle. To do this, the horse must take a half step with the last foreleg to bring it up to its mate and also with the last hind leg. In time, you must teach your horse to halt square. It is not so important at Training Level, but as you proceed up the levels, it becomes not only more important, but more difficult as the halt is performed at first through the walk, then directly from the trot, and finally, at Fourth Level, directly from a collected canter.

When you move forward after the salute, again the horse may not move exactly straight ahead. Some horses tend to move slightly to one side, usually the same side to which they are "hollow" (see Chapter 11). Correct this as best you can, and proceed directly towards "C".

After you salute and move off, you will either "track left or right at C". This means, quite simply, "turn left (or right)".

The turn at "C" should be a precise one half of a 10-meter circle. Many riders wait until they are too close to "C" before starting to turn. A perfect half circle would start one meter before the line between "H" and "M" — or sooner if you could tell that your horse disliked the judge's umbrella, or the flowers, or whatever, and was not going to get very close to them. Judges are tolerant about this, especially at the lower levels.

If your horse does spook at the judge's stand, get him past as best you can and proceed with your test. Do not make a big fuss about getting past "C", just get on with your test. When you come around to "C" again (during the test), be prepared to have your horse more on the aids so you can get past with a minimum of interruption.

The USDF Introductory tests have no initial halt and salute. The idea is to not break the horse's momentum coming up the centerline so he does not become suspicious of the judge's box. There is a halt and salute at the end of the test.

These Introductory tests are for beginning riders — they are not intended for experienced riders who wish to use them as warm-up tests.

One last word about halts. When they are in the body of the test and the test reads "halt four (or five, or whatever) seconds," here's a little tip: halt, then count (to yourself) one-thousand, two-thousand, three-thousand... and your timing should come out pretty well.

For a "Halt and rein back," come to a solid, square halt; pause only a second or two, then rein back. After the rein back (usually three or four steps), immediately and smoothly proceed forward. There is not a "halt" after the rein back, so don't expect (or allow) your horse to "square up."

Chapter Sixteen

Developing a Warm-Up

One of the critical preparations for competition is developing a warm-up. In Europe, this is called the "Riding in" period. It is the time and regime you use to prepare a horse for his test in competition. The "warm-up" must be completed at a certain time in order to ride the optimum test.

Dressage tests can be won or lost in the warm-up arena. While this statement may be considered a bit exaggerated, there is no doubt that the fashion and manner of the warm-up are, to a large degree, deciding factors in the success of the test. Therefore, it is very important that every rider is fully aware of the purpose of a warm-up and how it should be organized and performed as far as both time spent and content.

Similar to every other phase of preparation for competition, the warm-up is developed at home. When you ride at home, pay attention to how much warm-up your horse needs. How much canter? Lateral work? What did you do to get him to do his best? That's what you'll need to do at a competition, except he'll probably need 10 or 15 minutes longer at the show. These strategies are easily modifiable; just use them as a starting point. You must have in the back of your mind what portions of your routine will be appropriate at a competition.

Definition of "Warm-Up"

The purpose of a warm-up is to prepare the horse mentally and physically for the task at hand. That "task" may be a training session at home or at a clinic, a jumping session, or a test at a competition.

A warm-up session also sets the stage for your horse's relaxation and willingness to work for you; in other words, it focuses his attention. Since we must get into the horse's mind by controlling his body, let's discuss the physical aspect first.

Everyone knows that a runner goes through warm-up exercises before he sets off on his run. These exercises are designed to relax, stretch, and loosen muscles. An explanation of how this works is that muscles work by contracting and then relaxing, contracting and relaxing. Blood flows to the muscle in the "relax" phase; the muscle contracts, burning the "fuel," and then must relax again to allow the expended fuel (waste product) to flow away and new fuel to enter. Thus, a muscle that is working in a rhythmical way is evenly and thoroughly fed. "Stretching" the muscles (during the relaxed phase) allows more blood flow into the muscle and out again, thus increasing efficiency when you ask for more exertion.

In a tense or cramped muscle (as in a tense, nervous horse), the blood vessels are pressed together, thereby providing less nutrition. If the muscles are constantly contracted, no new blood or fuel is permitted into the muscle tissues and the waste products build up and poison the muscle (which is what happens when you get a "Charley-horse"). Basically, the same thing happens if the muscles are pumping too fast — that is, the rhythm or tempo is too fast. There is not enough time between "beats" for adequate fuel and waste assimilation and the muscle becomes exhausted.

Over a period of time, a muscle worked in this way cannot be strengthened and will actually degenerate. This explains why horses that are improperly worked often look thin and depressed after a short time. In addition, a tense muscle is subject to tearing or cramping. Warming up your horse properly is one of the best ways to protect him against injury.

To relax the horse physically, make him comfortable. An uncomfortable horse will not listen to your aids. An uncomfortable rider cannot communicate clear aids.

Relaxation is accomplished by first giving him a short play period if he needs it (on the longe or free), then riding with a balanced seat; working with rhythm; changing gaits (or exercises) often (so that one group of muscles is not overworked); and by not asking for a movement that the horse is not physically prepared for.

You will find that relaxing the horse physically will relax him mentally as well (and vice versa).

To relax the horse mentally, be consistent with your aids; work with rhythm (the repetition has a calming effect), and keep your routine "interesting" so the horse is attentive to you.

Also, remember that fatigue blocks the learning process (because energies must be directed by the brain to maintain motion). Thus, an exhausted horse will "tune you out." This is the horse that we say is "running on nerves." An interesting point is that strenuous exercise, *followed by a rest*, will relieve mental stress by forcing the brain to relax. This is why some horses compete better if they are worked hard *the day before* a competition (rather than at the competition). Beware that if the horse is "soft" (unfit), he may be sore and cranky the day after exercise. Solution: "Know thy horse."

Ride the same at home as you intend to ride at a show, and ride the same at a show as you ride at home. A horse will be calm only when he knows what to expect from the rider. Don't surprise the horse with your aids, and always use your aids in the same manner. Your aids may get stronger or lighter as the horse's mood demands, but the sequence and the timing must be the same. To change the signal is to confuse the horse and a confused horse cannot relax. Repeat exercises until they are habit; repetition breeds confidence and confidence makes a calm horse.

Warm-Up Routine

Now let me give you a very basic warm-up routine with variations for specific cases. These are suggestions, not to be taken as hard and fast rules.

- Turn out: Most horses do well with a turn out so they can play and kick up their heels. On the other hand, some older, quiet horses perform better (more brilliantly) if they are confined for a good part of the day.
- Longeing is good for the horse that is a bit too exuberant to ride comfortably, but don't just stand out there and let the horse charge around at his own pace. What will happen is the horse may go all out for a few minutes, then he'll slack off and relax, and then go in fits and starts.

You will "take the edge off" in a shorter period, and much more predictably, if you make him pay attention and work at your direction. Make the horse trot or canter or walk to a specific rhythm and at a specific energy level for several minutes at a time. He will warm up quicker if you make him concentrate rather than speeding up and slowing down at his own whim. Longeing as part of the warm-up is just that, a time to stretch and slowly warm up muscles and get rid of tensions. Note whether your horse "revs up" or calms down during longeing. One more caution: "play" on the longe line does not include bucking or running out of control. If the horse is allowed to buck on the longe line, it is very likely he will at some time buck under saddle, for the same reasons and in the same manner. Try to wean your horse away from daily longeing because it isn't always possible to longe at a show or clinic.

If you have a horse that needs to be worked down at a show or competition, don't build up his endurance at home. Turn him out a lot and only longe the minimum (if at all) at home. Try to keep your working sessions to 30 or 40 minutes at most. If you have a really hot horse that's used to a couple of hours of work at home, you are in for a long, hard hassle at a show. After a horse becomes accustomed to the hustle and distraction of being in strange surrounds, then you can build more muscle and endurance if they need it.

- Grooming: Before saddling up, always give your horse a good grooming session. The young horse should enjoy it and appreciate the fact that "work" is not all that you do with the horse. For the older horse a vigorous grooming session serves to stimulate and massage stiff muscles. At a competition, an enjoyable grooming may relax the horse.
- Work under saddle should always start by walking the horse until you feel him soften in your hand and any initial stiffness disappears (or at least lessens).

Start with a relaxed walk on a fairly long rein. On an especially timid horse, you should keep a light contact, to let the horse know you are there. Try not to restrain or inhibit forward movement, however.

Your horse should know that he will not get to do anything else until he walks properly; even if you have to spend a whole riding session walking.

Horses are not as excitable at the walk. Usually the spookiest horse will accept a strange sight if you let them really look at it and see for themselves that it does not move, or it does not attack. Horses have great imaginations. If they run from something, they imagine it is chasing them! The way to break this habit is to make the horse look at something for as long as it takes him to understand it is not chasing him.

With a small number of horses, a show warm-up will consist of nothing but walking. It may take these horses 30 or 40 minutes of walking before they are calm enough to trot or canter. Other horses are very self-assured and you don't want to give them an excuse to shy. This kind of horse you walk for only a few minutes (until they stretch and relax), and keep it very business-like. Keep the horse's mind on you by keeping his head in front of him (no gawking around for these fellows), and if you see something ahead that you think might give the horse an excuse to "let's see if we can scare the rider," turn him away, or take a gentle contact on his mouth and pull his head first one way then the other. This is not a see-sawing punishment. It is a gentle to and fro movement of the bit that reminds the horse, "Hey, I'm here and I will put your body (and your mind) where I want it."

Whatever the technique of getting the horse to walk, you must have it in your mind that you *will* walk — no matter how long it takes. To transmit this attitude to the horse, sit balanced but "heavy" in the saddle. A tense, "ready for anything" rider puts the horse on guard. If you sit with your legs long and "ooze" down and around the horse, you will be very secure because you can feel the horse much better than if you sit tensely. You will be ready to react if you have to and actually will be in better tune with your horse than if you sit tightly or rigidly.

Walk until you feel the horse get loose and a little sloppy, then ask for a longer strided but still relaxed swinging walk. A lazy type horse you obviously will not walk for a very long period, and you will ask for energy at the walk very soon. Still, wait for that loose, swinging feeling in the horse's back that tells you he has relaxed and released his muscles. Only when you feel he is ready should you pick up a relaxed, forward, ground-covering trot.

Most trainers prefer the trot as the main warm-up gait because the horse always has two diagonal legs on the ground, bearing equal amounts of weight. Allow the horse to stretch forward and down with his head and neck (but not to invert or "hollow" his back).

The purpose of this phase is literally to warm the tissues by increasing blood flow, which enhances elasticity of the soft tissues — a must for dressage riding. Before you can make the muscles supple, you must loosen them.

"Loosen" means relaxing — without getting sloppy. If your horse is tense or over eager, do not hold him down to a tense, jarring trot — encourage him to stretch. Control the tempo with your posting. If the horse gets too strong, pulsate your hands to the proper rhythm and turn some of that energy into cadence (yes, that's how you get that high, floaty, cadenced trot) by channeling the energy upward at each stride, not by restraining and therefore stifling the horse's gaits.

Again, don't tense your body and fight the horse. Many rider's panic when their horse does the most beautiful trot, and they ruin the horse's desire to ever do that trot again — such a pity. If you feel you are losing control, come back down to a walk and see if you can ease him back into a calmer trot a few minutes later.

Relaxation cannot be "forced" on the horse; it can seldom be accomplished by simply working (wearing) the horse down or exhausting him. This is because fatigue channels blood away from the brain — an exhausted horse is not listening to you, he is "running on nerves," and he is oblivious to everything around him — not a very safe situation.

On the other hand, if your horse is the stoic type, take care that he doesn't get sloppy with his hind legs. If your horse tends by nature to trail his hind legs behind him, use an energetic working trot on a circle. To wander around without making an effort to round the horse's back is not kind. It presumes that the horse will somehow adjust. The trouble is, of course, that most of the adjustments — high head, hind end out behind, short steps — are all detrimental to the horse's well being and physical and mental conditioning.

Following several minutes of active forward trotting, add some suppling exercises, starting with gentle turns and large circles, serpentines and leg yields. Make big, generous circles, figure eights (20 meters each circle), and loopy serpentines in both directions. The bending lines will automatically supple your horse more than straight lines.

- Now, check yourself: toes in; heels down; shoulders, hips, and heels vertically aligned. Keep the really good, solid, effective upper part of your calf on your horse's side, and make sure that the rest of your leg is "there" to support him — not to hold him up, but to be a part of him so he has confidence in your presence. Keep a soft hand and elastic back and arm. Elastic means on contact without restricting, so he has both reins to move into not because he's leaning on you, or because you're pulling his head in or sawing at the bit, but because his hind legs are propelling him into roundness. Sink down into the saddle; keep your lower back supple; hold your upper arm parallel to your side; flex your elbow to create a straight line from elbow to bit; and tell yourself, "drop my elbows." Go ahead, just lower them. Your chest and shoulders will pull up, and you'll relax and softly become part of his back.
- Check your horse: is he coming forward from behind so he can step farther under his body, bend and compress his joints, lower his haunches, shift his balance back, and elevate his forehand? Is he straight, so his hind legs follow the track of his front legs, his spine conforms to the line he's traveling on, and exactly half his body is on one side of the line and half on the other? Good! That means you can create even contact by riding his right hind through his right side and his left hind through his left side for that wonderful feeling we call "connection": the energy you put in with your leg, you feel evenly (via the bit) in each hand.
- Always pay attention to accuracy — to ensure the horse is straight (whether on a circle or on straight lines) so he can engage his hind legs evenly.

As you do the suppling exercises — large circles, serpentines, and the like — when you feel any initial resistance to this degree of bending diminish, gradually reduce the size of the circles and serpentines and start collecting and lengthening stride (a great way to stretch ligaments and muscles gently). Walk between exercises as needed.

How long should you trot? Until you feel some relaxation. Just before the horse gets sloppy, begin bringing him onto the bit, in degrees. If the horse tenses up, backs off the bit, or gets too quick (short-strided), encourage more length to the trot and try gradually bending the horse on large circles. Bending will usually bring the horse onto the bit more quickly than trying to force a stiff horse to flex.

He should be rhythmic, as if he has a metronome deep inside, and supple, giving you the feeling that you're drawing the bit into a wet sponge. He should stretch long and low on command, and he should be "through" (see page 134 for a discussion of "through") so he accepts — even draws in and absorbs — your leg, seat, and rein aids and allows you to fine tune and manipulate his body with a total freedom from resistance. Now you're ready for your work session.

Save canter work for after the horse is "warmed up." If you go to the canter while he's still distracted and a little tense, he'll pull, or maybe "crow hop" — not from spite, but because he's not warmed up enough to rebalance his weight from his forehand back to his quarters. If you wait until he's soft in your hand at the trot, you'll rarely find yourself in a pulling match at the canter.

It's best to have your horse on the bit before asking for a canter. Here again you must know your horse. An excitable horse especially should be completely on the bit before you ask for a quiet, semi-collected canter. Canter for short periods, usually on circles, then drop back to the trot; get the horse to relax again at the trot, then canter a circle or two the other direction. Short canters will often do more to keep a horse quiet (they figure out they're not going anywhere) than trying to "wear them down" with long, barely controlled gallops. Although a soft horse will tire fairly quickly at the canter (they can trot much, much longer before they tire), if you use this as a frequent strategy, the horse will build up endurance fairly quickly, especially an ex-race horse who will be reminded of his more exciting days.

Some horses get "mad" if you hold them down too much at the canter. Remember, a horse must be able to reach forward and down at each stride of the canter. A horse with a big bold canter that can't seem to contain himself at a more collected pace will sometimes relax more quickly if you let him canter and stretch on a large circle.

To control the canter, take a firm hold on the outside rein, then give and take with the inside rein, keeping the horse bent through his body. Use the same rein action combined with lots of leg on horses that are dull or those that try to lean on your hands.

The warm-up will reflect your training program from its humble beginnings (large 20-meter "Training Level" circles, easy changes of bend at a natural working trot) to your present level of training. Only after you have established your "foundation qualities" (rhythm, equal bend, acceptance of bit and leg) will you move on to more sophisticated bends and lengthening and shortening his frame, until you reach the horse's present "level" of training. Even the Grand Prix horse starts his warm up with "Training Level" movements!

- The warm-up gradually focuses the horse's attention on you and the task at hand. You should expect the horse to be attentive to you at all times. Horses that are "left alone" too much (not given specific instruction) either get headstrong (they assume they are the boss and act the part) or they get insecure and begin to shy, fidget, or bolt.

This is because horses are herd animals. It has nothing to do with the horse "loving" you or even loving his work. Some horses will always be testing to see if they can be the "leader" and do what *they* want to do. Others *want* a leader: someone to tell them where to go, what to do, and that the world is "safe."

Horses also fall into definite "personality" classes (see Chapter 26). Excitable, timid horses need a lot of walking and work in a small area, around and around and around. The boring aspect of the repeated movement and familiar surroundings will calm even the most scatter-brained beast. The horse with the active, self-assured personality needs variety and frequent changes of scenery, but still must be taught to pay attention to his rider.

The horse that is prone to dullness should be put on the aids rather quickly and given brisk trots and canters on smallish circles, followed by lengthening and shortening, changing direction and gait often. After he is warmed up, all his work must be done briskly. His work is designed to "wake him up," not wear him down.

Use the warm-up to assess your horse's mood. Attach a "label" to your horse's mood so you can develop a strategy to deal with it. Use labels that are descriptive and positive or neutral, such as "flighty," "stiff," "distracted," or "mellow." Labels that are vague, judgmental, or couched in human terms rather than equine ones ("nasty, "out of sorts," "vindictive," "stupid," "crazy," "lunatic") give you little to act on.

Go for the cause, not the symptom. For example, if you've chosen "lazy" as the label, this is a symptom of a bigger issue: ignoring the leg. Get the horse to listen to your leg by strengthening your aids or using the whip once, and the "lazy" goes away. "Distracted" is another label with an underlying cause, probably "worried." By quietly and firmly riding a horse through a "worried" moment and bringing his focus back on you, you fix the "distracted."

If the word is "spooky," get the horse's attention. If he's paying attention to you, he won't notice the things he wants to spook at. Put the horse on a pattern that will settle him and get his attention, such as figure eights over and over. If the description is "bored," work on variety. If the horse is excited, "hot" or "fidgety," it can often be fixed by walking the horse or using a pattern that will "lull" him to quietness. Sometimes the "hot" horse needs to be ridden vigorously forward to take the edge off.

Accept your horse's resistance as input. He's telling you, in the only way he can, to be supple and elastic, clear in your aids. He's saying, "Tell me what you want in clear and proper terms." Always analyze the cause of a resistance. Always be willing to go back to basics. Your training will proceed a whole lot faster.

Don't always blame yourself. Check yourself out first, but if you think you are riding properly, then figure out why the horse is evading. Is he being lazy? (Horses can be lazy.) Is he tired or sore? Is he just "testing" you to see if he can get his way? You need to take in all the data available to you and figure out the solution.

You'll notice that to do all this, you keep up a conversation with your inner self and with the horse. What to do, how to correct. Is the horse balanced? Is he in self-carriage? Is he rhythmic? If any of the answers are "No" or "Not quite," figure out *what to do* to get him balanced, responsive — everything you know he should be. Your inner voice should keep asking questions and making suggestions while you're riding a test or an exercise. It will help you make corrections and learn to solve problems.

You will know your horse is "warmed-up" when he lengthens, shortens, and bends his frame in response to your aids and he delivers up the amount of energy you are asking for, showing that he is supple and responsive in mind and body. Intersperse your work periods with rest periods of working on a long rein (at any of the three gaits). Too much collection or concentrated work can make a horse "muscle bound" and cause him to shorten and stiffen his gaits. Also, the horse's concentration span is notoriously short, with a maximum of about twenty minutes, so give his *mind* an occasional break also by taking all aids "off" (riding on a loose rein).

With your warm-up at a show, you also need to plan rest periods so that your horse can concentrate *during* the test. As you work at home, formulate in your mind how you will warm up at a show.

A Sample Show Warm-Up

- **5 to 10 minutes walking** around the warm-up area so your horse sees everything there is to see — longer for the timid or inexperienced horse.
- **5 to 10 minutes trotting,** to stretch and loosen. With a timid horse, keep his attention on you without getting strong or exciting him. The dull horse you can let be a little sloppy at first while you loosen the muscles so the blood gets flowing. Save his energy for the test.
- **2 to 5 minutes walking.** Alternate medium walk and an active free walk.

  If you are warming up for a clinic, you should now be ready to go in for your lesson. The clinician will direct any further warm-up. If you're at a show, continue:
- **3 to 5 minutes trotting** smaller circles and developing a good working or collected trot for the level you are showing.
- **When ready, "test" the horse's canter.** If he tends to rush or get excited, stay on

20-meter circles and canter short periods. If dull, liven up his canter with smaller circles (to engage), and lengthen and shorten it to inspire enthusiasm. Canter both leads. The *last* canter should be the lead you will use *first* in the test (and in the same pattern).

- **Walk again.** Let him cool down and relax again. Let him "off" the aids for at least a couple of minutes so his mind can relax. Even a timid horse should be adjusted to the surroundings by now.

You may want to do one more trot and/or canter session. If at a show, you might practice one or two test movements now. Not to train, but to alert the horse to what is coming. If you are at home, this is when you would work on refining your training or adding an element of a new exercise. Time elapsed: 35 to 45 minutes.

Dress Rehearsal

It's also a good idea to "rehearse" your warm-up at a friend's house or a schooling show to find out just what works and what doesn't. Horses are always more on edge (as are riders) away from home or in unfamiliar surroundings. Every competition horse (and rider) needs a few "miles" on them before they are ready for serious competition.

Remember, your warm-up is as important (if not more so) as how you ride the test in front of the judge. Don't enter at "A" unprepared.

Chapter Seventeen

More Practice

By now you have memorized your test, developed your warm-up, and practiced the various elements of your test(s). Now it is time to put everything together.

You need to learn your test(s) inside out, so that riding them will be mostly automatic. That way you can concentrate on your horse, knowing full well that you are prepared for whatever decision you might face in the show ring.

Lower level riders sometimes tend to avoid riding through the test before the show. They do every movement, but they can't fit the pieces together. You must practice the test at home until all the movements blend smoothly. To wait until the day of the show to try to put the test together clearly portrays you as an inexperienced competitor. You do not have to drill the complete test every day. You can practice your trot work one day and your canter work the next day. (That keeps your horse from getting sick of the test.) It's okay if your horse starts to anticipate the test a little (for instance cantering in the corners). It's not okay to go to a show and look like you have never ridden the test before.

Let us now consider how to practice the tests, as well as some last minute preparations.

Practicing Tests

Well before a show, you should review the tests you plan to ride, pick out the elements in them that you may not have been working on, and give them extra attention. Perhaps you have not been doing "trot, walk, halt, trot." Or maybe you have not been alternating periods of rising and sitting trot with attention paid to keeping the rhythm unchanged, or crossing the arena from "B" to "E", or doing lengthened trot sitting, or doing canter departs on straight lines.

If you have been making transitions when you felt the horse was just right, you had better make sure you can do them at pre-selected points. Try to have the horse "right" when you reach the point you have decided on, but make the best transition you can whether you and the horse are ready or not. These are the things you need to know, and practice, before the show.

If you do not have an arena to practice in, you will have some special problems. You could set up "parts" of an arena to practice segments of your test. For instance, set up an "entrance" with a couple of poles laid on the ground and a marker for "A" and another at some distance to aim at as "C".

Initially, practice pieces of the test so you know exactly how many strides it takes to get a transition or exactly how much bend a certain size circle requires. Know what to do if your horse tenses up or gets out of the proper frame. Perfect the individual movements to the best of your horse's abilities.

After perfecting individual movements,

The Test Caller or Reader

Being a good test caller is not difficult, but it does require concentration and attention. If you plan to call dressage tests, the most basic requirement is a good clear voice that carries well. This is particularly important for the outdoor competitions, where wind, rustling leaves, and various show and schooling noises can only hinder good communication between the caller and the performer. It is not necessary to shout, but you must be able to make yourself heard.

When calling a ride, look at the rider while speaking. You should be well enough abreast of the movements to know what comes next and what you have to say without constantly looking down while saying it. If necessary, raise the paper to chest level and speak over it. Speak from down in your chest rather than up in your throat so the sound carries.

Behind "E" or "B" is the most commonly preferred place to stand, with your back to the wind if possible. The test sheet should be on a clipboard or in a stiff book, so the papers don't wave about. It is wise to step back a stride or two from the ring as the horse and rider approach, as some horses are intimidated by having to trot or canter past a person standing close to the rail.

The caller should know the test she is calling. She should be familiar with the sequence of the movements and the amount of time required for each. Calling the movements too soon is as bad as calling them too late. Keep your finger on the line so you can read it, look up to see where the rider is, then go right to the correct line for the next call. When the rider is approaching the right spot to prepare for the next movement, call it out.

The letters "C", "B", "E", "V", "P", "D", and "G" all sound alike (so do "K" and "A") when called out. To avoid confusion, wait until one soundalike letter has been passed before calling another. For instance, if a movement is to be performed at "B", wait until the rider has passed "P" before you call the next movement.

Don't repeat letters or movements unless absolutely necessary. Read exactly as it is written. Repeating movements or rearranging sentences can be construed as "unauthorized assistance" by the judge. If it is clear that the rider did not hear the command (perhaps an automobile went by), judges will allow repeating. Many callers have a system that requires the rider to look directly at them if a letter was not clear or not heard, which can get them out of trouble when repetition is absolutely necessary. No extemporaneous or creative additions to the text are allowed, no matter how greatly needed they may be.

If the rider gets "off course" and the judge does not seem to realize this, stop reading! Eventually the rider or the judge will realize they are lost. The judge will blow the whistle and instruct the rider where to start again. Listen closely and as soon as the rider is in position, read that movement again.

The most important thing of all is for the caller to pay attention to her job not the rider's! The caller's job is to read the test clearly, with the proper timing. Let the rider worry about riding it. She needs you to read the test, not to fret anxiously if the horse blows up. Just tell them where they're supposed to go. Your worry, consolation, or congratulations will be appreciated after the ride is over, when it is appropriate.

practice the complete test. If you plan to have a "caller" (the person who reads your test), it might be a good idea if they practice with you once or twice before the show. Have them read the Sidebar "The Test Caller or Reader" if they are inexperienced.

You may find that the first couple of times you ride a complete test you need to simply concentrate on getting from letter to letter without losing track of where you are (if you are riding from memory). If so, do it. Eventually the test must become imprinted in your brain so you can concentrate on *riding the horse!*

A dressage test should not appear laced together from different movements. Rather it should be one continuous statement in rhythm, energy, and continuity.

A helpful hint to riding a successful test is to have a checklist of priorities in your mind. This is a sort of list of the ingredients of each movement of the test. The checklist prevents errors like: "the circle was round but lost the forward movement." A typical list might be:

1. Rhythm
2. Energy
3. Contact (the "feel" of the horse in your hands)
4. Follow the test (listen to your caller and prepare for the next movement)

As you ride the test, click off the checklist (silently of course): 1, 2, 3, 4, and then start over again. As you move up the levels, your "list" will become more sophisticated, and you will focus in depth on each transition and movement. For instance, to get a really round and balanced circle you might say to yourself: "10-meter circle = sit on his inside hind," or some other phrase that you have "programmed" into your test ride. These little phrases will remind you how to get the very best from your horse.

You might compare it to putting together a jigsaw puzzle. Gradually you assemble all the various pieces (movements) and eventually you have a completed picture. Then you just have to make sure none of the cracks show — make your transitions smooth, your "flow" continuous.

At first, the constant changes in direction and gait may startle your horse. If he gets too upset, ride half the test and then trot or canter on straight lines for a couple of minutes to settle him. Gradually you will learn to correct your horse (rebalance him, straighten or "soften" his outline) *while riding the test.* This is another advantage to memorizing the tests. If you come across a problem, you can repeat it (at home — not at the show!) until you "get it right." You must learn to *ride the horse,* not just mechanically do the patterns.

Ride the test through once and assess what needs the most work (what would make the largest impact on the scores). Remember, gaits are most important, then figures, then transitions. Make those things work well and the details will fall into place.

You may find that if you get yourself all "psyched" up — "We are riding a test, it *must* be perfect" — your horse will get all frantic, even at home. Learn what "energy level" works best in your particular case. Also, consider that the horse's sensitivity level may be heightened in strange surroundings.

When schooling test movements, try to understand the purpose of putting that particular movement at that particular place and strive to achieve that purpose. For example, the entrance: the important things are straightness on the centerline and submissiveness (smoothness) of the halt. The horse's energy level is not as important as those two points.

The key to preparing for a test is — again — planning. Most mistakes happen at home many times before they happen at the show. You know your horse will probably lose his bend here or rush there, so iron out the mistakes: correct them before they happen. Make use of your practice of visualizing (Chapter 14) and avoid your usual mistakes by preventing them. By the time you ride down the real centerline, after weeks of mental and actual practice your plan is there to follow. Because you have ridden it a hundred times in your head, things will keep coming to you that you need to do to prepare for the next part of the pattern.

Focus on overall planning rather than on individual movements — in mental rehearsals, warm-ups, and right through the test. Have a plan before the judge rings you in. Know how many half-halts to practice down the long side. If your horse sometimes hollows his back and lifts his head when you ask for leg-yield at home, have a plan in case he does it in the test. Instead of just riding the test, you'll ride the horse.

The centerline and halt are the first and last impressions to the judge. You must practice them. Go down the centerline and halt, then stay there — teach the horse to stay still until you are ready to move off. Salute when you halt — take the reins back after the salute and don't move off right away — *make the horse wait.* In a test you will halt, transfer the reins, salute, pick up the reins, and then move off. You must teach your horse to wait for the cues.

Also, practice turning onto and off the centerline, from both outside and inside the arena. Use practice at home to discover which side of the arena to enter from, because some horses do better entering from a left turn, others from a right. (Depending on whether they are easier to straighten after a right or left bend.) It is not necessary to have an arena to practice centerlines: pick a rock, weed, fence post, or whatever and decide that is "X" and ride a straight line to it. You must learn to ride the horse accurately.

When practicing canter leads, you must learn to "feel" which foreleg is leading in the strike off so that you know immediately that the horse is correct (or incorrect). If the horse fails to make the correct strike off, you must quickly (but with finesse) bring him back to the trot, check the balance, and try again.

The free walk is not a gait of rest. Every step of the walk must be the best you can make it. Go for marching energy (a "going somewhere walk"). In your practice, push the horse to the maximum of his ability. Probably in the actual test, you will have to sit a little quieter. After the free walk, when you pick up the reins again, some horses get cranky. This is something you should find out at home and work on finding ways around it.

Anticipation

Most seasoned competitors will tell you that any horse will memorize any test if they do it often enough. So, you may as well practice the tests at home. Most horses already know where "X" is. If you practice the test at home you can work on the horse anticipating and teach him to wait for you. If your horse anticipates the halt at X, simply ride past "X". Most of the canter departs in First and Second Level are at either "A" or "C" right after the free walk diagonal. You may have to walk your horse past the letter — at home — or trot instead of canter, so that the horse will do it *at the letter* in a competition. If they anticipate, correct it at home.

You should know your test so well that you are able to stop in the middle (at home, not at the show!) and continue it after an interruption. If your horse starts anticipating a test pattern, test yourself by riding the test in reverse!

Don't over-practice the full test. Horses that go through tests over and over again get dull and lose their "oomph." Sadly, we often see horses at shows that are obedient but have lost their sparkle and suppleness. Work instead on parts of the tests to keep your horse progressing in his training as well as preserving his enthusiasm.

One more thing: you should practice your tests in both small and standard arena sizes so you know exactly where your "reference" points are for your figures and circles.

If it sounds as though you must think of everything at all times and remember half a dozen things at once, remember that this is only an ideal. You cannot, of course, think of everything at once, but you can work on all aspects of the performance at one time or another. Gradually more of them will become automatic, you will be able to concentrate on more and more details, and your scores will get better and better. Dressage schooling is a matter of skill, persistence, intelligent planning, and concentration. The only one of these your teacher can give you is skill. The others must come from within you.

Dealing with Distractions

Dressage horses, if properly trained, should not have to be ridden in a sterile environment. Indeed, one of the main objects of dressage is to make the horse *"confident, attentive* (to the rider) *and keen, thus achieving perfect understanding with it's rider."* (AHSA, Art. 1901) Competition is a "proving ground" that the training has been successful.

At a show, you and your horse will be bombarded with hundreds of distractions. You can best prepare your horse by trying to imagine every possible scenario and working on a plan or preparation. The inexperienced or timid horse needs to be desensitized to what can be expected in the competition arena by repetition, repetition, repetition.

It is a good idea to work a horse in places where there are distractions. Start with one thing at a time: things like other animals, a dog, other horses milling about, then umbrellas, blankets hanging on a fence, people sitting at ring side, tables with papers flapping at ring side, flags, anything you can think of to get the horse accustomed to before show day.

Although the young horse may be startled to begin with, he will gradually learn about all these things. As he becomes trained he will learn to ignore them, so long as his rider is firm and does not let him look around too much and as long as the rider's aids are interesting and keep the horse's attention.

The Judge's Stand

An important thing to get your horse used to (at home) is riding up to parked, open horse trailers, tents, and tables. At many dressage competitions, the judge and scribe sit in an open two-horse trailer. Park one where you can ride directly up to it and past it. That's one more distraction you can resolve at home.

The Shying Horse

Shying or spooking is a special problem with dressage horses. It can break a rider's concentration and ruin a whole test; but it doesn't have to be that way.

Every dressage horse must learn to keep his attention on his rider. If his mind is elsewhere, his attention will be on finding the spooky things.

Most horses shy because they are either inexperienced or inherently timid. If the horse is excessively timid, *you* need to learn how to be brave! You must evoke confidence in the horse that you will never hurt it or allow it to get hurt. If your horse is the aggressive self-assured type, again you need to be brave and decisive about what you want from the horse.

This chapter is mainly about the timid or totally inexperienced horse. If you have an aggressive or dominant-type horse that is a "phony" or violent shyer, you may have to get professional help to teach you how to deal with it.

The timid horse lacks confidence, and unless guided by the behavior of others, either herd companions or his rider, he feels insecure. This horse needs a definite "leader" image to follow and have faith in. The rider must assume this "leader" role. To do this you must first of all *believe in yourself.* This is because what you think is what you transmit through your "body language."

For example, you see something up ahead that your horse *might* spook at. If you tense up, preparing for the "inevitable," the horse senses your tension, searches for the cause and "says," "Let's get out of here!"

On the other hand, it may be windy and the horse is getting nervous. *Don't say,* "Oh my gosh, he's going to spook," because he will! Instead, say to yourself, "It's windy and the wind feels good on my face." The horse will feel your inner peace and be calmed by its effect.

You must assume the position of the brave guardian of your herd of two. At the first sight of something that might be scary, you should turn your attention in that direction. Then, within seconds, relax and *tell the horse why* there is nothing to fear. Tell the horse — out loud if necessary — what the thing is and why it can't possibly harm you. For example, "That's just a rock, it can't hurt us." If you are truly confident about the object, you will transmit this confidence to the horse.

The only way to deal with these intrusions is to accept them as facts and deal with them without emotion. Soften your eyes, breath deeply, and go back to your riding. Having dismissed it from your mind, you can get back to the business of training and riding, and your horse will most likely be thinking along the same lines. He will gain confidence in your apparent "bravery."

If the horse suddenly comes to a stop facing some terrifying object, do not get all frantic in an attempt to force the horse forward. You'll probably scare him more. Instead, sit there for a moment so he can see that it is not threatening. Hold the horse as still as possible — if he turns away and attempts to run, he will imagine it is chasing him! Hold the horse still, but sit heavily and deeply and relax your body as if to say, "See, it's nothing, I know that for sure and I'll wait here until you believe me." After you have successfully demonstrated this "guardian" type behavior several times, the horse will gain trust in your judgment.

To overcome the anticipation of riding a chronic shying or timid horse, you must constantly be thinking ahead of your horse and setting up positive situations. To do this, assign yourself tasks, envisioning what you want to do and how you are going to do it. If you concentrate on a task, you will encourage the horse to concentrate on you. If he's paying attention to you, he won't notice the spooks.

Exercises that will usually focus the horse's attention, without exciting him, include: changes of bend or direction (as in serpentines or figure eights over and over again; frequent but clear and "soft" up and down transitions and some lateral movements (especially if done at a walk). Accurately guide your horse on

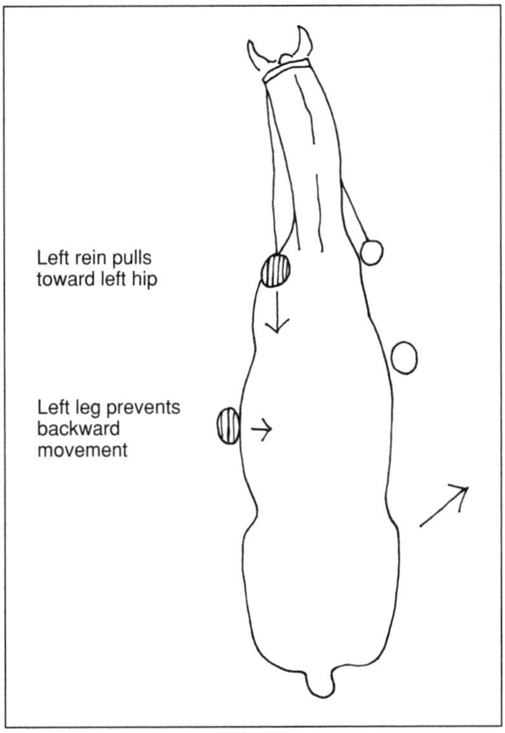

Figure 17.1 Aids for the (left) rein in opposition to the haunches.

straight lines and perfect figures rather than randomly "wandering around." If *you* concentrate on the pattern, your horse is more likely to concentrate *on you.* If you get into a bind where the horse doesn't seem to understand what you want, don't get in a fight, which will frighten the timid horse; *change the subject* — do something you know your horse can do confidently.

Learn to divert a shying horse by using "the rein in opposition to the haunches." This is a powerful aid to prevent shying or to recover when a horse does shy. It can be applied either on the moving horse or on the horse standing still (figure 17.1).

You may want to practice it once or twice in each direction so you understand its concept.

While standing still: to shift the horse's haunches to the right, the *left* rein is drawn toward the rider's left hip, acting against the horse's left haunch, while the right rein prevents excessive bending. The left leg presses enough to cause the horse to shift away from it. The right leg need press only strongly enough to prevent the horse from backing up. Result: the horse will move his quarters to the right and his head to the left, pivoting more or less on his center. It is a very strong aid and the normally trained horse will find it almost impossible to go against it.

To angle the horse sideways while moving: (To divert his attention away from some object for instance). *Both* legs keep the horse up to his bridle and maintain movement. The left rein bends the horse slightly toward the left (away from the object of his interest). Do not let the horse overbend at the withers or he can "run" over his shoulder and escape your control (figure 17.2).

Result: The horse will move obliquely forward with his forehand slanted to the left and haunches to the right (which has got to be better than ending up at the far side the arena!).

The rein in opposition to the haunches can prevent the quarters from moving over against its effect and can also move the quarters over to the other side by its effect. In other words, the horse can be angled away from the object of his attention and essentially forced past it.

When you've learned these skills, you'll have new tools for getting his attention and controlling him when he's spooky and for making him lighter in your hand. That means a more relaxed and controlled ride for you both.

AN OUNCE OF PREVENTION

Can we prevent the shy from actually happening? In many cases, we can. Try this: When your horse is completely relaxed and undistracted, a light squeeze then softening of your inside hand and leg is normally enough to make him give you his attention. (Remember the "yes" and "no" joints in Chapter 11?) Under normal working circumstances, light leg and what most trainers call "vibrating" the inside rein — quietly squeezing, then softening your fingers

Figure 17.2 Rein in opposition.

against your palm — should keep his inside ear checking back on you every few seconds.

When your horse is nervous and spooky, though, you'll need to gradually turn up the volume on leg and rein aids until you can get and keep his attention. Say a dog is lying down next to the ring and your horse wants to stop and stare. Sit evenly on both seat bones, focus up ahead (*not* on the dog), and breath evenly, so your tension doesn't build his fear like the music in a scary movie. (You know the dog won't hurt him.) Keep him moving forward by resting your outside leg quietly behind the girth and tapping your inside leg with fairly sharp, buoyant pressure at the girth. Don't thump, which will alarm him if he's the sensitive type, and don't clamp, which will create tension or dull him. Keep your hands low, even if his head is in the air, and firmly draw his nose to the inside, elastically maintaining contact with your outside hand as you withdraw your inside rein until you can see the lashes of his inside eye. Relax your shoulders and sit "heavy" (to convey confidence). Squeeze and soften the inside rein; insist on a response from your inside leg.

If your horse is still paying more attention to the dog than you, increase your pressure on the inside rein, turn your inside toe out, and tap your leg more emphatically; if necessary, tap him sharply with the back of your heel. If he still ignores you and doesn't go forward, put even pressure on the inside rein and nudge or kick him with your heel or spur.

Anytime he "gives you his ear" (angles it toward you), or his nose comes to the inside, reduce your aids a notch — if you had to tap with your heel, for example, switch to pressing with the back of your calf — and encourage him to soften through the throatlatch (alternating squeeze and release of your inside hand) to keep his attention. As soon as he softens in his jowl, relax your leg to its normal working contact and quiet your hand, showing him that when he pays attention, you reward him. Continue around the track, check his response occasionally with the lightest of aids, then next time around, talk to him in confident praising tones and bend him slightly before he spots the dog and you lose him.

Use of the Voice

"The use of the voice in any way whatsoever or clicking the tongue once or repeatedly is a serious fault involving the deduction of at least two marks (and possibly more if the judge chooses) *from those that would otherwise have been awarded for the movement where this occurred."* (AHSA, Art. 1922.3)

The use of the voice is usually shown on the test sheet by a line drawn through the score for the movement where the voice fault occurred and then a new score reflecting the deduction put beside it. Another method is by a "-2" (or -3) written beside the score. Most judges indicate "voice" in the comments section.

If you are in the habit of using your voice, you can see that you can lose a lot of points if the judge hears you. Whenever you are practicing tests, refrain from using your voice.

Although the voice is useful in training (horses react more to the tone than the actual word), it is an aid for the benefit of the rider — not necessarily for the horse.

In Chapter 14, it was pointed out that if the rider thinks or says out loud a given word or command, her nervous system will "fire off" the appropriate muscles in the proper sequence of the movement — even though she does not move.

In this way the voice (or your thoughts) can inspire enthusiasm or calm, or even reprimand the horse. So, you can achieve the same effect if you *think* the word, or phrase, in place of saying it out loud. Your body language, the tension or relaxation of your body, will convey what you are thinking — so "talk" your horse through the test — silently!

Preparation, Preparation, Preparation

- Do your training at home. Don't expect to teach your horse anything at the competition (except that it can be an enjoyable experience).
- Make sure your horse has all the basics firmly in place, including reasonable loading and traveling behavior, long before you go to the show (or clinic).
- Horses usually become more prone to misbehavior when they're away from home (this is partly due to their own nerves, but probably also due to their handlers' nerves), so do all you can to keep your mount calm both before and during the event.
- Stick to all your standard management routines leading up to the event. Don't try out a new farrier or shoeing technique, and don't change the feed or change equipment adjustments the week before. Horses thrive on the familiar and an abrupt change can leave them nervous, uncomfortable, and even colicky.
- In the weeks prior to the event, train your horse to relax on command. Certain physical motions and sensations help horses release muscular tension, and you can make the response nearly automatic with training. One is walking on a long rein; another is stretching into the rein at the trot or canter.
- Avoid over-training your horse in preparation for an event. The last thing you want is a sore or sour horse. Give him a day or more off, or go for a trail ride in the days before an event so he can "refresh" himself.
- Pack some "security blankets," such as feed, hay, water, and treats from home. This will come in handy if your horse is not the kind who'll eat and drink anything away from home.
- Ride your horse at different times of the day so that he is not surprised by being tacked up at an odd time of the day or evening.
- Arrive early. Even if your horse trailers like a dream and is perfectly at ease in new situations, he needs plenty of time before the first session to acclimate to the bustle and new surroundings.
- Take a capable helper, someone who can walk your horse and run errands for you. This will lower your anxiety level and subsequently that of your horse.

Home Away from Home

One last preparation: trailering and tying your horse. Make sure your horse will load and quietly travel in a trailer — *before* the day of the show.

Even for short trips, you'll want to outfit your horse for travel. Bell boots and shipping boots will minimize the chances that he'll suffer nicks and bruises during loading and hauling. A protective padded helmet might be a good idea for a particularly long or rough route (or a high-headed horse). Also make sure that your trailer ties come with panic snaps so that you'll be able to release your horse quickly, should the need arise.

Some horses bond to their trailer mate or stable mate. Often these horses behave badly when they are separated from their "buddy." Find out before the show if this is the case and ask to stable that horse away from his friends at the show. This might be inconvenient, but it is better than trying to get through the test with a hysterical horse.

Standing Tied

Standing quietly when tied seems like such a basic behavior that it is disconcerting to see adult horses who can't be tied. Horses are tied because that is the safest way to control them in public (and private) situations (figure 17.3).

Horses should be secured with unbreakable halters and unbreakable ropes to immovable objects. Having been successful at freeing himself sometime in the past by pulling back and breaking free is the main reason offered as to why an adult horse might have such a problem. If you are not sure your horse will safely tie, begin by doing so in a very secure situation, free of obstacles and at the proper height, to an immovable object, like a stout post or hitching rail. If you suspect a horse will pull back when tied, it is not safe to tie them to a small two-horse trailer; if hysterical enough, they can pull a trailer over.

Learn to tie a "quick release" knot so that if the horse does tighten it, you can still get it loose when the need arises.

If an adult horse "sits back" on a rope, speak calmly, decisively, and stay out of his way. If the horse gets into a trapped predicament (foot over the rope, for example), a quick release knot is the only salvation. Try not to let the horse know it "got away." Speak calmly and try to hold the horse still until he calms down. Never, never tie a horse to something that could break away, such as a loose board, or a gate, or truck mirrors. Even the most sedate equine will be panic stricken if a board starts chasing it across the pasture or parking lot.

There will be times when you need to tie a horse and leave it unattended. Most one-day schooling shows do not have stabling, so the horse must be tied at the trailer.

Practice leaving the horse tied (preferably to your own trailer) at home. Groom, saddle, and feed your horse there and let him become accustomed to being tied for a half-hour, then an hour, then perhaps two. Like everything else, it will become comfortable to your horse and he will look on it as a little part of "home." This is especially helpful for the horse's first show away from home.

If the horse must be tied for a long period, as at a clinic or schooling show, provide a hay bag to keep him occupied and unconcerned about what is going on around him. Remember nets sag badly when emptied. Whether a bag or net is used, tie it up high so there can be no possibility of a pawing foot becoming trapped. Also, check the horse frequently and renew the fly spray or move him to shade if insects are becoming a bother.

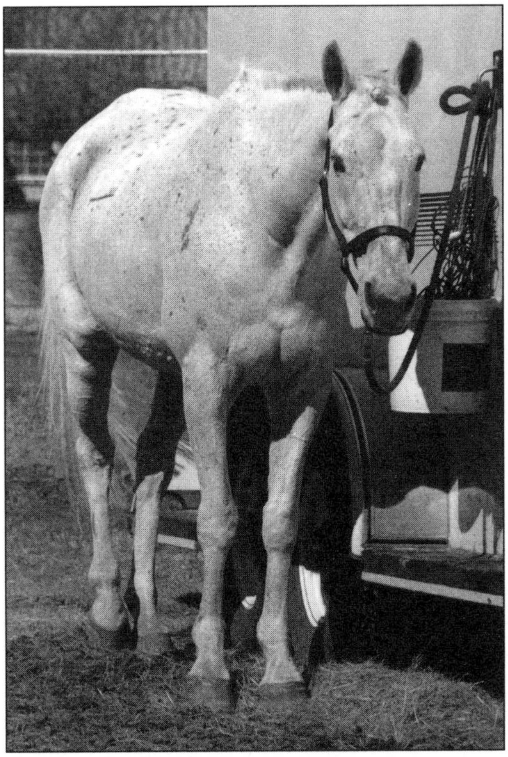

Figure 17.3 Home away from home. Be sure your horse will tie safely if no stabling is provided. Photo by Charlene Strickland.

Cool Down

Whether at home, at a clinic, or at a show, always take the time and care to cool your horse down. Cool down includes ending your ride on a good note — with a success and a reward. If it is appropriate, a dismount "on the spot" and return to the stable, or a long walk are good rewards for a particularly difficult movement well done.

For the end of your schooling sessions, allow your horse to stretch and finish the way he started — loose and relaxed. This allows the muscles to return to normal temperature and the horse to return to the stable calm and comfortable for the next day's session (or the next test).

During exercise, the circulation focuses outward, sending blood into the muscles; after exercise, it takes a big shift back toward the gut. If the shift is too sudden, the muscles could start to spasm, compressing the soft-walled blood vessels and blocking them from carrying away oxygen-depleted blood and lactic acid (the waste product of exercise) out of the muscles. It is residue lactic acid that makes muscles sore and stiff after a workout.

If you habitually work your horse up to a sweat, leave the ring, bring your horse into the barn, and stand him in cross ties (even if you put a cooler over him and don't feed or water him), the damage that lack of gradual cool-down does to his muscles can accumulate to the point that it predisposes him toward "tying up" (chemical residue in the muscles) and arthritis (from chemical residue in the joints). To avoid these problems, always walk your horse until he's cool (he doesn't have to be dry, but the sweat should be sticky).

Keep in mind that heavy-muscled horses (such as some warmbloods and Quarter Horses) take longer to cool down because of their muscle mass. With the heavy-muscled horses, walk the horse until he starts to dry, then five more minutes.

In summer, you can wash the horse down. Hose his neck, chest, and between his legs with cool water. Always use lukewarm water on his back. Scrape the excess water off and then walk him until he's dry enough to put away. In the cool months, never leave his wet back exposed to get a chill. A chill in the back will delay his training program several days or weeks because of painful back muscles.

You always want to leave the horse happy and comfortable so he will look forward to his next ride.

Chapter Eighteen

Grooming the Horse

The best way to make sure the judge takes you seriously at a dressage show (or any show, for that matter) is to look the part. Good show grooming reflects a winning attitude and can give you that extra edge when you enter the show ring. Judges and spectators alike expect to see an exquisite test when a bright horse and a polished rider trot toward "X".

When you take the time to polish your boots, whiten your whites, and ride in on a horse with a sheen to his coat, neat braids, and a tail that flows, you are demonstrating that you appreciate the efforts of the show committee and you are telling the judge, "We're proud to be here." The judge cannot help but respond positively, and that certainly gives the well-groomed team at least a slight advantage in the competitive arena.

The Well-Groomed Dressage Horse

The only rule on the grooming of the horse is: *"Any decoration of the horse with unnatural things, such as ribbons or flowers, etc., in the tail, etc., is strictly forbidden. Braiding of the horse's mane and tail, however, is permitted."* (AHSA, Art. 1921.6)

Neatness and cleanliness are expected and show pride in your presentation. Although it is not required, a dressage horse usually has his mane braided. If yarn is used, it should match the horse's mane color. White adhesive tape can be wrapped around the braids. Horses with long manes, such as Arabians and Morgans, may have their manes braided French style, basket weave, or left free. The tails are usually left long and unbraided, but are often trimmed or braided at the top and "banged" (cut off straight) at the bottom.

These matters vary according to the taste of the rider and breed of horse,

Figure 18.1 A well-turned-out horse.

since there is nothing compulsory. Of course, horses should always be clean and neat (figure 18.1).

Preparing for the day of the show can be a monumental task. All of your attire either goes in the washing machine or to the dry cleaners so that it is bright, clean, unwrinkled, and ready to go. Your horse, however, cannot be transformed into a swan in just one day.

Although the following tips will help you put the final polish on your show horse, you can't neglect your horse's coat, mane, and tail on a daily basis and then expect to put together a winning look the day before the big show.

Maintaining a thorough daily grooming regimen will make preparations for the show much easier, freeing you to focus on the details of packing and preparing for your test. Your daily grooming routine should leave about two hour's worth of necessary show-grooming finishing touches.

Daily Grooming Routine

A shiny coat and flowing tail start with good food and are maintained with large doses of elbow grease.

- Feed good quality hay and grain — supplements will not make up for a poor feeding program. A quarter cup of pure corn oil in the daily feed will help add natural oils to a coat depleted by frequent baths or harsh climate conditions.
- Hygiene is important. Work on the body and neck with a soft rubber curry to break up dirt and stimulate healthy skin. Then use a hard brush or vacuum to remove the loosened dirt.
- On the face, legs, and body, use a soft brush and rub rag to lift surface dirt.
- Carefully pick out the tangles in the tail and occasionally add conditioner to keep the hairs supple and healthy. Brush a long tail very carefully.
- Attend to the feet. Clean, brush, and apply dressing to the sole, heel, and coronary band as needed to maintain correct hoof texture. Don't overdo hoof

dressing, it can soften the wall. Keep the horse well shod.

- Maintain the bridle path, muzzle hairs, ear edges, and fetlock areas with regular trims. In the early spring, before the horse starts to shed, clip the long hairs around the face, throat, elbows, and belly.
- Carefully clean and dry the pasterns and under the fetlocks, because dirt concentrates in these areas and scratches (grease heel) can occur.
- Occasionally clean the sheath of geldings and stallions.

In Warm Weather

- Clean between the jawbones, inside the ears, and under the belly because these are favorite areas for bugs.
- Check the mane and tailbone for ticks.

In Cold Weather

- Consider body clipping horses in training so that when they sweat, they don't have cold, wet hair on their warm muscles.
- A horse can be "towel bathed" in cold weather by soaking a terry cloth towel in hot water (as hot as you can stand on your hands, no hotter), wringing it out so it's barely damp, then rubbing against the hair. Repeatedly rinse the towel until you need to replace the water. Do a small section at a time and don't get the hair too wet. By repeatedly toweling, then (when dry) currying again, you can get a horse fairly clean.
- Do not clip the fetlock hair short in the wintertime — horses need the hair to keep moisture away from the heels in cold weather.

Preparing the Mane for Braiding

The mane and tail require special attention. If you intend to braid the mane, you will need to thin and pull it to a uniform length and thickness. This is the only practical way to thin a short mane so it will lay flat and/or is thin enough to produce uniform braids.

Begin preparing the mane about three months before your projected show debut. If the mane is really long, use scissors or a knife blade to shorten the mane to the approximate length you want (four or five inches, usually). You can use a sharp pocketknife to shorten the mane. Take a swatch of mane firmly between thumb and forefinger and cut from underneath out. Once you get to a workable length, then pull three or four hairs out at a time until you get the mane the thickness you want, using the following procedure:

Wrap four or five hairs at a time around a comb or your finger and pull them out by the roots. This will not hurt the horse if you go at it in stages, working up and down the mane for about 15 minutes at a session. You will find that your fingers get sore long before most horses start complaining! If your horse *does* complain, pull a couple of hairs, give him a carrot, pull a couple more hairs, give him a carrot, and so forth. Keep pulling to thin the mane until you get it to two-thirds the thickness you want for braiding. A month later, pull out another one-third. The week before the show, pull the remaining third and any remaining long hairs. This method will insure that as the mane grows back, it will always be tapered in thickness and not have a clump of extremely short hairs at the base. The mane grows about one inch per month so you need to factor this into your grooming routine.

When you have the mane the thickness you desire (each braid can be about one-half inch in diameter and an inch apart to look good with tape), you can even up any long ends with a comb and scissors or a knife blade.

If the mane is especially thick, and after you have pulled as much as you think you dare, you can use a pair of tooth-edged thinning scissors designed just for that purpose. Cut from underneath about two inches from the crest and don't overdo with the scissors. Horses that have thick crests usually have thick necks, so they can have bigger braids.

If you decide not to braid, but want a short and tidy mane, braid it tightly with setting gel three or four days before the show, then take it out the day before and wet it down. When dry it should lie pretty flat.

A Long Flowing Tail

A long luxurious tail requires even more work and attention than the mane. It takes years to grow a long, full tail. To encourage growth in a short tail, carefully brush from the roots to the end with a soft body brush. This stimulates the roots to grow and distributes the natural oils through the hair. If the hairs are brittle, *do not* brush. Use a natural conditioner (remember, horses are outside most of the time and chemical conditioners can "burn" the hair in sunlight). If the tail is thin, it may be because it is being caught on bushes or weeds, or brushed against fences or the stall walls; or the horse may be stepping on it when he lies down; or other horses (or animals) may be chewing on it. If your horse's tail is naturally thin or is losing hair for whatever reason, you probably should braid it up and put it in a bag to protect it (see below). The tail can grow at the rate of about an inch or less a month, so if a large "hunk" gets pulled out or broken off, it can take as long as four years to re-grow a long, full tail.

To keep a long tail full, the tangles should be picked out carefully by hand, never brushed, and the tail should be braided and kept in a sock or tail bag to avoid hair breakage. To do this, wash the tail in either a specially formulated equine shampoo or a human one. Do not wash the tail (or body) of the horse in detergent. Detergents will strip the natural oils and cause the hair to become brittle and damaged. If the tail is very tangled, use liberal amounts of conditioner to allow you to sort out the individual hairs. Get the hairs as tangle-free as you can, then rinse out the excess conditioner. If you leave too much in, it causes dirt to stick and the braids to shift and mat the hair.

Wait until the tail is dry, or almost dry, and then take three strips of cotton cloth (an old bed sheet torn in three inch wide strips is good), separate the tail into three sections, and, having tied the cloth strips together at one end, braid the cloth and hair into a simple three-strand braid. Tie the ends of the cloth braid in a simple knot. Cut the leftover cloth strips to a length of about 18 inches. These will serve as "fly swatters" (figure 18.2).

Next, fold the tail braid upward, and thread one of the cloth strips through the braid and tie it off. Do not tie it around the tailbone — you could cut off the circulation and cause an infection. Slip a sock or a cut-off denim pant leg over the tail and tie two of the tabs through the tail (see figure 18.2). The denim holds up to beating against fences or stall walls. Remove the bag and re-condition and detangle the tail every two or three weeks.

One or two days before the show, take the tail down, wash, and detangle it. Rinse most of the conditioner out (too little and you get static, too much and you have a heavy clump of hair). Once you have all the tangles out, cut the bottom of the tail off straight (at least two inches above the ground). If you do all this the day before the show, it should only take a few minutes to groom the tail at the show.

One Week to Show Time

Any necessary body clipping should be done at this time to give the hair a chance to grow out a little and look natural. For example, clip any stockings or white legs to about 1/4 inch. This will remove the unavoidable manure stains and expose spotlessly white markings.

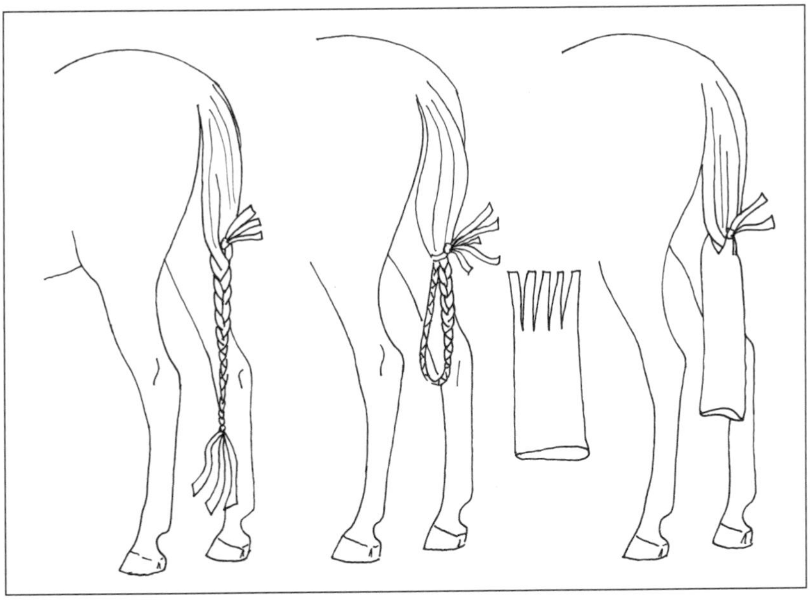

Figure 18.2
Putting up a clean, long tail.

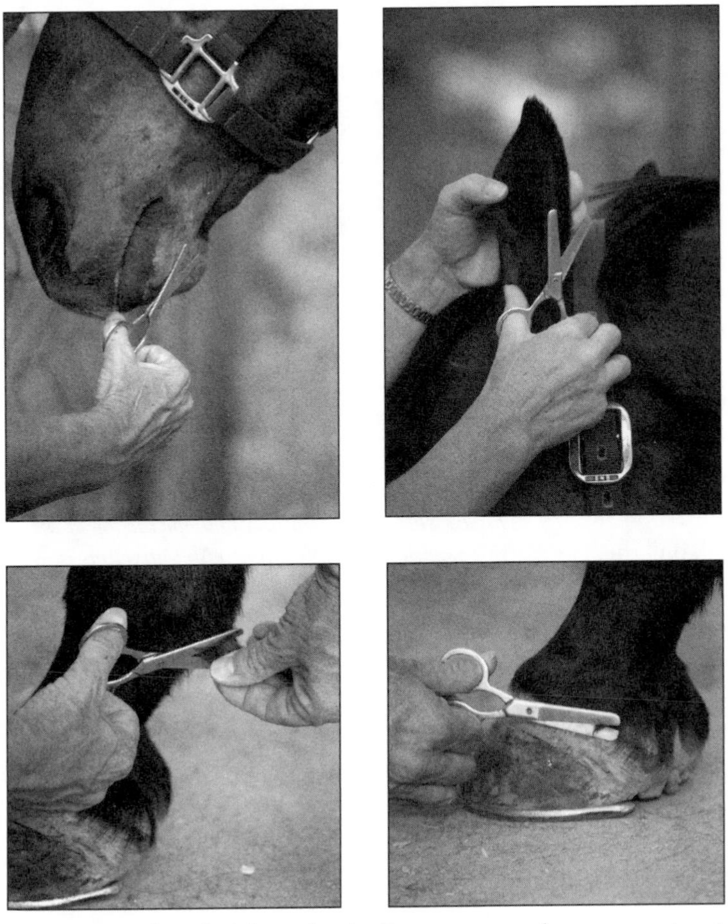

Figure 18.3 If you don't have electric clippers, you can do necessary trimming of the muzzle, ears, and legs with scissors. Photos by Charlene Strickland.

Trim the bridle path, the muzzle hairs, and the edges of the ears. Remove any straggly hair under the chin, at the elbows, back of pasterns, or on the belly (figure 18.3).

Peel the chestnuts off as neatly as you can.

Trim the top of the tail if desired. This can be done with clippers, but this is risky because if you slip, you're in trouble. Scissors work best (figure 18.4).

The purpose of trimming the top of the tail is so it stands away from the hindquarters and the judge can see if the quarters are doing their share of the work. (If the judge *can't* see the hindquarters, she may assume they are not working.)

To find the correct length or shape for the top of the tail, braid or bandage about six inches of the top of the tail to give the basic outline of the way it will look after it is cut. Longe the horse or have someone ride it and see how it looks. Horses carry their tails at different heights while in motion, so what looks good while standing may not look good on the move (figure 18.5).

Once you have decided how far down to trim the top, you now clip each side of the tail, tapering each side so it follows the natural contour of the tail. Lay the scissors against the skin and clip a little off one side then the other so you end up with a very even finished product. You will probably have to cut or pull a few hairs on the very top so they lie flat.

To "bang" the end of the tail, pull the hair straight down, hold it in one hand very evenly, and cut it with scissors straight across the bottom. Cut just a couple of inches at a time, step back to see how it looks, then trim more if the tail is still uneven or is still too long. The tail of the dressage horse should not drag on the ground. Besides, you don't want the horse to step on it and pull hairs out.

This is also the time to give the mane a final thinning and shaping. If you're not really good at braiding, you might want to do a "dress rehearsal" now to see what style will work best for your horse. If you find you can't do a good job of braiding, you might be better off going *au natural.*

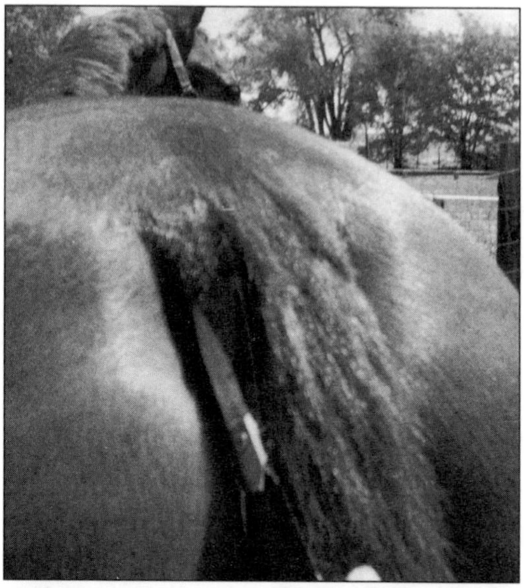

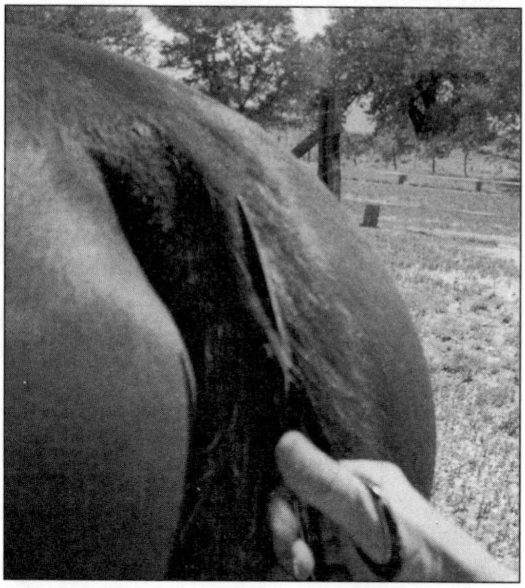

Figure 18.4 The safest way to shape the top of the tail is with scissors. You can finish with clippers if you wish.

Twenty-Four Hours and Counting Down

The eve of show day is the time to give your horse a bath and to clip his facial hair

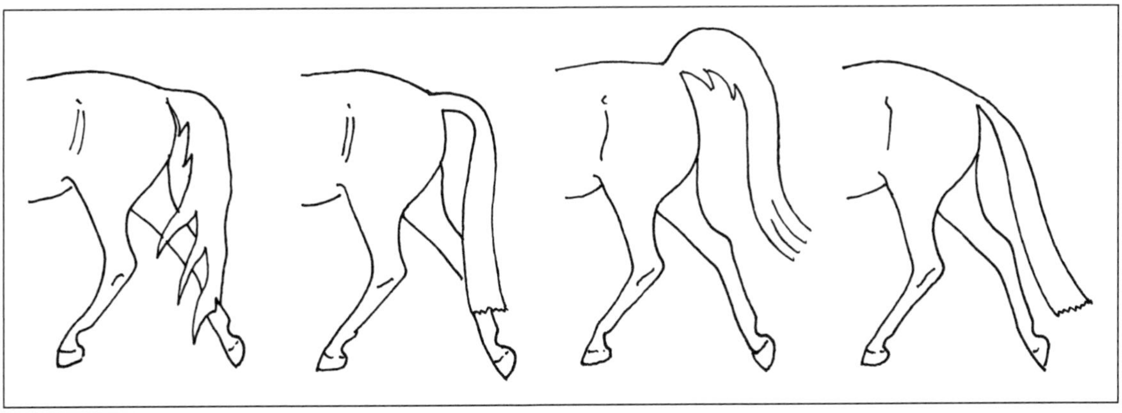

Figure 18.5 Which tail style suits your particular horse?

(whiskers) one last time. Bathing the horse removes all the deep-down dirt so that on show day, even if the grounds are dusty, a quick wipe with a towel will remove the dust. If the horse sweats, a damp sponge will wipe the sticky part away.

Bathe your horse with a good-quality equine or human shampoo. Wash and rinse the horse one segment at a time, starting with the face and working from top to bottom, front to back, and one side then the other side. This prevents the shampoo from drying on the horse.

Use a damp cloth instead of a sponge on the face because you can't get the soap rinsed out as well with a sponge. Take a damp cloth and go down inside the ears very gently to clean out dirt, hair, or residue. Then, dilute a little bit of shampoo, put it on your hands, and wash the whole face.

Ivory® liquid works well for white leg markings. Wet the leg down, scrub the soap in with a brush or your fingers, and then rinse well. Squeeze excess water out with your hands and dry with a towel to prevent chaffing in the back of the fetlock.

Completely rinse the horse again, even if you rinsed as you went along. With this rinse mix one cup of white vinegar in five gallons of water and sponge down the horse's body to cut any missed soap film. This also helps repel flies.

Scrap off excess water using your hands or a rubber-edged scraper and apply a mist of silicone-based grooming product to the neck, hindquarters, legs, and tail, avoiding the saddle area and the mane, if you plan on braiding it. This will act as a gloss and dust repellent. Once this is dry, dust can be easily wiped away by using a dry cloth.

It will take approximately one hour to "let down" a long braided tail, 30 minutes for the bath and another hour to braid the mane. You should also clean, disinfect, and organize the grooming kit that you will take to the show. There's no sense in grooming a clean horse with dirty equipment!

To Braid or Not to Braid?

There is no requirement for braiding the horse for dressage. Many breeds (Arabians and Morgans are two examples) are *required* to have a "long, natural mane" in some of their show divisions. This requirement of the breed division makes it impossible for you to shorten your horse's mane to what would be a workable length for a traditional "hunter braid."

Braiding gives the horse a neat, "finished" look and makes it very easy for the judge to see the carriage of the neck. Judges like a clear outline (silhouette) of the neck, because they don't have to guess whether the horse has a properly developed and functioning topline under an unruly or "fly-away" mane. Finally, braiding is practical in that it keeps the mane out of the way of the reins.

There are many styles of braiding you can use. While some are breed-oriented, you should use the style that most enhances the individual horse.

French Braid

This is sometimes called the Viennese braid, as that is where it was first used. It is ideal for heavy-crested horses. It is very simple to do, and requires no thinning or shortening of the mane (figure 18.6.B).

Basket-Weave

This is a favorite for long-maned Arabians. You can use braiding rubber bands or tape to separate the sections. On a white mane, you can use black tape, on a chestnut or dark horse, white tape (figure 18.7).

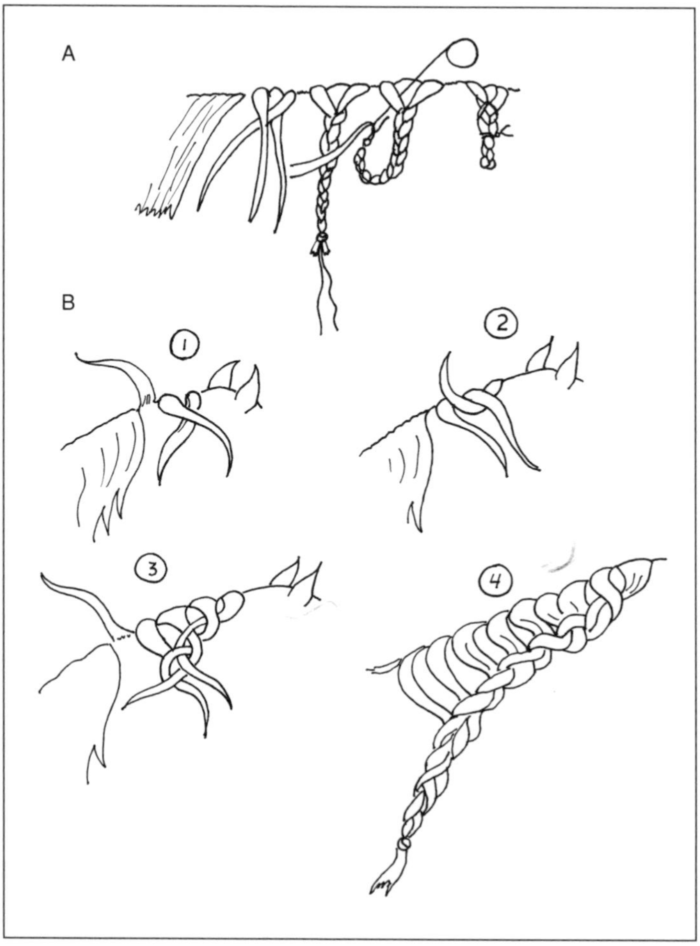

Figure 18.6 Two of the most common mane styles: (A) Hunter braid, (B) French braid.

Figure 18.7 A basket-weave pattern looks especially attractive on Arabians. Photo by Charlene Strickland.

Hunter Style

This is the current fashion for dressage. Actually, there are several styles, but for all the mane must be shortened to three or four inches in length and thinned so that the braids are small and neat. The yarn, thread, or rubber bands used should be the same color as the mane. Colored yarn is forbidden, as are ribbons, flowers, or pompoms. White tape is appropriate for First Level or above. Do not use tape unless your braids are very neat and

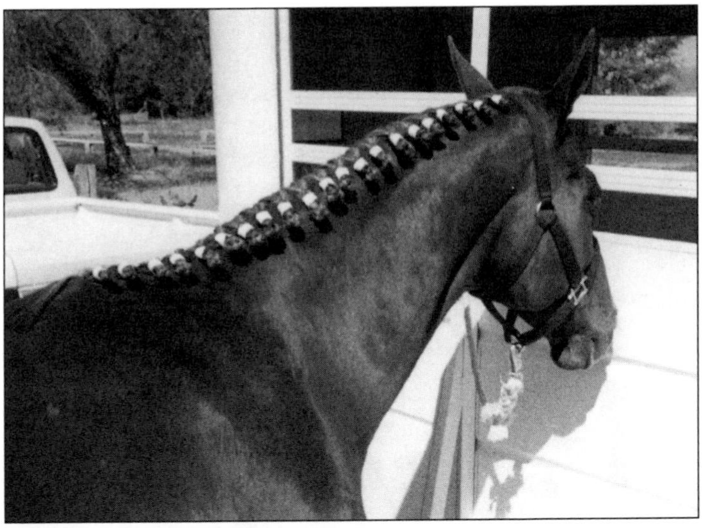

Figure 18.8 In the upper levels, taped hunter braids are popular.

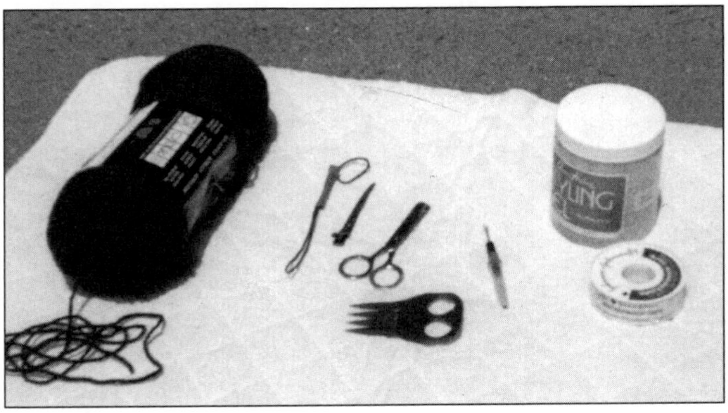

Figure 18.9 Braiding equipment. Note the pull-through second from the left. Below: A closer look at a pull-through.

even and your horse has a beautiful neckline (figure 18.8).

Before beginning to braid, the mane must be the right length. Review pulling the mane under "Daily Routine, page 181."

Do not shampoo your horse's mane right before you braid, because this will make the hair slick and difficult to handle. Either wash it with plain water or bathe the horse *after* you braid.

For braiding, you will need the following items:

- coarse-toothed comb
- large hair clip or clothes pin
- pull-through
- yarn or thread
- styling gel
- half-inch wide, water resistant, white adhesive tape — this is optional (figure 18.9).

Start behind the horse's head and work toward the withers. Use the comb or clip to separate a one and a half-inch section of hair and clip the rest of the mane out of your way. Work the styling gel into this section and divide it into three equal parts. As you braid, keep steady downward tension on the hair as you go. The braid can be secured with yarn that has been braided in (start it about midway down the braid's length) or with a small rubber band looped on to the very end.

Braid and tie off each section all the way down the neck. This insures that the braids will be even in size. Then go back and pull each braid up with a specially designed braid pull-through or a thick wire that has been bent to resemble one.

Tie off each braid with a second rubber band or the ends of the yarn. Tape can now be added if desired. If you braid the day before a show, take your braiding kit with you in case you need to redo one or two braids that get rubbed out overnight.

It's Show Time!

Before you load him in the trailer, go quickly

Grooming Tips

Every top show groom has a bag of tricks out of which they pull some secret technique to make their horses stand out. Here's a list of some tips to help you shine on show day:

1. For really white socks or stockings, dust them with baby powder, cornstarch, or French white chalk right before mounting. Do not allow the stockings to get wet or you will have to completely wash and dry them before re-applying the whitener.

2. To cut down on static in the mane and tail, use dryer sheets. One wipe-down through the hair will help eliminate static. Endust® will also work on an especially wispy tail, but be sure to wash it out after the show.

3. Rubbing a dab of baby oil along the bridle path or the top of the shaved tail will get rid of that chalky, just-clipped look and make it shiny.

4. Use setting gel when braiding to help keep any stray or short wisps in place in the braids. Hair spray right after you braid will do the same thing.

5. Wash your horse a couple of days before the show so that the oils of the coat have time to work to the surface for a natural shine. Keep a light sheet on to keep the coat clean until show day.

6. To remove yellow stains from white legs, first clip them with a number 10 blade (to about 1/4-inch length). This will often remove the stained portion of the hair. To remove an overnight stain, mix a half-and-half solution of rubbing alcohol and Vetrolin® liniment; then dip in a sponge, rub the mixture into the spot, and repeat until the stain is gone. Rinse with water and dry with a towel, then brush smooth. This won't work very well on long hair, where stains are pretty much permanent. To prevent a white tail from getting stained, keep it in a bag.

7. If you choose not to braid a horse's mane, lay a dampened towel over the neck whenever you groom to help the hairs lie down smoothly.

8. If the horse leans on the trailer butt bar, wrap a bandage (carefully) around the top of his tail.

9. Instead of using rags to wipe down your horse, purchase inexpensive knit gloves and apply Endust® or fly spray directly to them. When you are finished, they can be washed.

10. For coarse tails, use a hot oil treatment in addition to your regular equine conditioner to soften the hairs and make them flow.

11. For a thin tail, try braiding many tiny braids into the length of the tail, using liberal amounts of setting gel. When you take it down and lightly pick the hairs apart, you should have more "volume."

12. Spraying Listerine® mouthwash on finished braids can help minimize itching and rubbing. It can also prevent rubbing the top of the tail.

13. If your horse gets shavings in his braids, use a small, short-bristled brush to gently remove them without damaging any of your work.

14. If you keep the horse's tail braided up most of the time, when you take it down swish it around so he can *see* it — *before you mount up!*

15. If you clip the inside of your horse's ears, place cotton inside to prevent hairs from entering the ear canal and also to deaden the buzz of the clippers.

over your horse with a medium brush and get any sawdust or manure stains that he may have acquired overnight. Then upon arrival at the show grounds, after he has accepted his surroundings and before you saddle up, give him a good going over. Although you need to do some grooming at the show, never sacrifice a good performance in order to avoid a little sweat or dust. After your horse becomes more predictable in the show atmosphere, you can add more polish to your presentation.

At least a half-hour before you mount up, take the hay away from your horse. Nothing looks worse than green slime oozing around the bit!

With a medium brush, completely brush

the body and legs, then use a fine finish brush on the entire horse, including the face. Brush, comb, or handpick through the tail. Flatten yesterday's braids if the horse has rubbed them. You can spray them with hair spray and cover them with a towel until the braids have dried. Clean the ears, nostrils and around the eyes using pre-dampened towelettes or a wet cloth. You can apply a coat conditioner for extra gloss. Give black legs an extra dose of spray silicone, and if the socks are still clean, spray them also (it will repel dirt from the white areas and make dark colors glisten). Do not put a silicone-based coat product underneath the saddle area. It can cause slippage of the saddle pad and can be quite detrimental. Clean under the tail with a dampened towel. If any stockings or white areas need to be washed, you will need a minimum of 45 minutes for them to dry.

Finish the hooves by scrubbing off any dirt and dust with a short, hard bristled brush, followed by an application of hoof lacquer if you want extra shininess. If you do not have a rubber mat or concrete surface to stand your horse on while the lacquer dries, use a stiff piece of cardboard or skip this step altogether.

If needed, spritz with fly spray. Use a water-based, not oil-based spray, because oil attracts dust. Don't spray heavily, and make sure you put some on the face and under the belly. Do this to keep your horse from stomping at flies or being concerned about them during your test.

Have your groom bring some supplies to the warm-up area: a towel, a hoof pick, a coat brush for *your* coat, and a comb for the horse's tail (figure 18.10).

In Between Classes

To help keep the horse's coat clean between scattered classes, cover it with a clean sheet. Brush the coat and the mane and tail if they are loose. Reapply coat conditioner if the coat starts to dull. If the horse gets sweaty, sponge him off with a damp sponge. Sponge under the saddle and dry with a towel each time the horse is untacked.

Figure 18.10
The groom gives the horse a final touch-up before entering the arena. Photo by Charlene Strickland.

Chapter Nineteen

A Rider's First Show

You are ready to enter your first show! It shouldn't be a large or prestigious one to start. Better to enter a small one, preferably a schooling show close by. And don't enter your first show with hopes of winning prizes; think of it as a chance to test you and your horse against others of equal ability and to learn what needs improvement for the next time. Pick your classes carefully and make sure you know what each class is judged on and what is required of the horse and rider .

How Many Tests and Classes Should You Enter?

This is totally at the discretion of the exhibitor. Usually a horse can enter any test in two consecutive levels at a competition, though some classes may be restricted by age or status.

Training Level horses can usually handle three tests in a day. Second Level and up usually go in no more than two tests a day. Fourth Level and up rarely go in more than one class in a day.

Training Level tests are usually the first in the show, so plan on them being early. If you have a really green horse, consider your first and maybe second test a "warm-up." Even some older horses can not be relied on to settle in the first test of the show, so plan accordingly.

Things Every Exhibitor Needs to Know

Before you fill out that entry form, let me give you a little background into the etiquette and rules of a dressage competition.

Pre-Show Planning

One month before:

- Send in entry fees and forms
- Check that the trailer and vehicle are in good working order (tires, brakes, lights, floor, ties, and latches)
- Update your horse's worming and vaccinations
- Find a friend to groom for you and agree on what you'll be asking her to do

One week before:

- Call the show secretary to ask for ride times, directions to the show grounds, parking, longeing areas, warm-up areas, and the number of competition rings

The day before:

- Check the trailer again
- Touch up clipping (face, ears, bridle path); groom tail
- Bathe horse
- Braid mane (optional for schooling shows)
- Clean tack; polish riding boots
- Pack everything that can be packed the night before
- Clean your horse's stall before you leave the barn to help keep him clean

Show Officials

A recognized show has a hierarchy of officials. You should know whom to go to (and who *not* to approach) should you have any questions.

GROUND JURY

The ground jury is the presiding judge or judges. Judges must be selected from the current Roster of American Horse Shows Association (or FEI) licensed dressage judges. Exhibitors cannot speak to the judges without prior approval.

SHOW MANAGER

The manager and show committee are responsible for the operation of the competition and enforcement of the rules of the AHSA from the time entries are admitted to the competition grounds until their departure. Management is responsible for collecting AHSA fees, keeping records, hiring the necessary judges and officials, and documenting eligibility of entries. They are also responsible for rules pertaining to eligibility, conduct of the competition, wearing of coats in hot weather, illegal equipment in the warm-up arena, changes in riding order, and so forth.

You go to either the manager or the show secretary with questions about entries, eligibility, scratches (withdrawal from classes), time problems, and stabling.

SHOW SECRETARY

The show secretary processes the entries and performs other duties as assigned by the show committee or the manager. See the show secretary with questions about entry or time schedule.

TECHNICAL DELEGATE

At all recognized dressage competitions there must be a technical delegate (T.D.) selected from the current Roster of Dressage Technical Delegates. An AHSA steward may officiate at a regular or local member show offering classes at Third Level or lower. (An exception is the Arabian division, where a steward may officiate through Fourth Level.)

At combined training events, the T.D. has authority to make changes to courses and rule on enforcement of the rules. At dressage competitions, the T.D. can only advise, consult, and report, while the judge is the ultimate authority.

The technical delegate is the representative of the AHSA on the show grounds, whose duty it is to report violations of the AHSA rules and to advise management, the judges, and the competitors as to what the rules require and how to interpret them with respect to things that happen on the show grounds. For instance, a question about the legality of certain articles of tack would be directed to the T.D.

Basically, the judge enforces rules inside the competition arena; management enforces rules outside the arena; and the T.D. makes sure *everyone* is following the rules. The T.D. can advise management to expel a person or a horse, or advise someone on how to lodge a protest against another exhibitor or against management and help them fill out the forms.

The T.D. interacts with everyone, with the goal of seeing that both show management and equestrians follow the same rules and safeguard the well-being of the horses.

RING STEWARD

Show management must appoint ring stewards to spot check saddlery at the direction of the technical delegate. At a recognized show, the bit and saddlery may be checked after the horse exits the ring — so be certain your bit and equipment are legal. The ring steward may also have the duty of making sure competitors get to the in-gate on time.

GATE PERSON

Some shows assign someone to open and close the arena gate behind each exhibitor. However, there is no regulation that the gate must be closed, so you should practice at home with an open gate so your horse doesn't think that open gates are an invitation to leave.

SCRIBE

A scribe sits with the judge and writes down the scores and comments. The scribe must be quick, accurate, and silent, not interrupting the judge.

SCORER

This person works in the office and totals the scores on the judge's test sheets, posts the scores, and possibly passes out completed tests. If you find an error in your test, do not go to the scorer; go to either the show secretary or manager.

Rules You Need to Know

Rules facilitate the conduct of the competition and insure equity for all competitors. If you are not sure what the rules are at a non-recognized dressage competition, assume AHSA rules will be used for dress, equipment, and protocol.

WHO CAN COMPETE

"To be eligible to participate as a rider, driver, owner, handler, lessee, agent or trainer at Regular Member Competitions...persons must be Individual Members of the Association...or if not a member, must pay a registration fee as provided in Art. 207." (AHSA, Art. 1504)

Various rules affect the eligibility of a horse to be shown under certain judges; among these are:

"A judge may not be an owner of any competing horse, except that horses may be ridden Hors de Concours in classes where the owner is not officiating." (AHSA, Art. 804.17 & 1919.5)

No horse that has been sold by a judge or by her employer within a period of three months prior to the competition may be shown before that judge.

No horse that has been trained by a judge or a member of the judge's family may be shown before that judge unless the trainer and client relationship has been terminated 30 days prior to the competition. This includes riding in a clinic.

No judge's trainer or any of the trainers' clients may compete as exhibitor, rider, owner, or lessee in any division, unless the relationship was terminated 30 days prior to the competition.

No rider may compete in an equitation class before a judge by whom she has been instructed, coached, or tutored, with or without pay, within 30 days of the day of the competition.

In all these instances, it is the *exhibitor's* responsibility to withdraw if any of these scenarios occur. (See AHSA, Art. 804)

In addition, *"A dressage competition manager may not compete at his or her own competition. However, he or she may ride 'Hors de Concours' if he or she designates an assistant in charge while he or she is riding."* (AHSA, Art. 1919.5)

"Hors de Concours means that: "Scores for these entries will not be published or recorded, nor shall they count towards any prizes, placings or year-end awards... Only with the permission of show management may a horse/rider combination enter a class Hors de Concours." (AHSA, Art. 1919.4)

By signing the entry form... *"Every entry at a recognized competition shall constitute an agreement and affirmation that all participants... (1) shall be subject to the Constitution and Rules of the Association and the local rules of the Competition; (2) represent that every horse, rider, driver and handler is eligible as entered; (3) agree to be bound by the Constitution and rules of the AHSA and of the Competition, and will accept as final the decision of the Hearing Committee on any question arising under said rules, and agree to hold the Competition, the AHSA, their officials, directors and employees harmless for any action taken..."* (AHSA, Art. 1502.4)

THE DRUG RULE

A drug fee is charged exhibitors at AHSA recognized competitions. A portion of the fee is used to cover the costs of research, inspection, and enforcement of drug rules.

AHSA permits each breed and discipline to choose between two drug and medication rules. The Dressage Committee uses the "Therapeutic Substance" rule, while the FEI permits "No Foreign Substance." The latter rule is in effect in any competition operating under FEI rules.

Under the therapeutic substance provisions, certain medications may be used for a "therapeutic purpose" only. The rule accommodates the use of a forbidden substance for the diagnosis or treatment of illness or injury only.

Any product is forbidden if it contains an ingredient that might affect the performance of a horse or pony as a stimulant, depressant, tranquilizer, or local anesthetic or that might interfere with drug testing procedures ("masking substances"). There is a long list of "forbidden" and "masking" substances (of which a couple of wormers are included). You can call 1-800-MED-AHSA for more information.

If a forbidden substance is administered for any other purpose (for example, for clipping, shipping, or training) the animal must be kept out of competition until the forbidden substance can no longer be detected in the animal's blood or urine sample.

If a horse or pony has been administered any product containing a forbidden or masking substance (for instance, if he had to have stitches a few days before the competition), the exhibitor must file a written *Medication Report* before the animal is returned to competition, if the possibility exists that the drugs may still be detectable in the horse or pony's urine or blood. New forms must be filed at each competition the horse or pony is scheduled to compete in for as long as the drugs may remain detectable.

Under the therapeutic substance provisions, three medications are classified as "restricted": phenylbutazone (Butazolidin® or "bute"); flunixin meglumine (Banamine®); and methocarbamol (Robaxin®). This means that the rules establish maximum acceptable plasma levels for each.

There are guidelines published for the recommended dosage of each, but adherence to them does not guarantee compliance with AHSA rules, since the responses of individual horses and ponies will vary. Nor will reliance upon the guidelines serve as a defense to a charge of violation of the AHSA rules in the event of a positive drug test.

While "bute" is allowable in small doses and at prescribed time limits, a horse that must be constantly on an anti-inflammatory medication probably won't be able to get enough training time to compete.

The use of any so-called herbal or "natural" products that are purported to affect the performance of a horse or pony in either a calming (tranquilizing) manner or energizing (stimulant) manner is expressly forbidden by the AHSA Drug and Medications Rule (Art. 401). Even if such a product is ineffective, its use constitutes unsportsmanlike conduct, in that its purpose is to achieve unfair advantage and dishonest gain.

Horses and ponies are randomly tested for either blood or urine at AHSA recognized competitions. Nobody knows ahead of time if there is going to be drug testing at a particular show. Owners, trainers, and employees or representatives of the owners or trainer must cooperate in the collection of blood or urine samples or face criminal charges.

DIVISIONS

Recognized dressage competitions usually offer "divisions", or separate classes, by age or experience. Usually one cannot "cross enter" divisions. For instance, if you enter Training Level Test 1 *junior*, you *cannot* also enter Training Level Test 1 *Open*, but there are exceptions, so read the prize list carefully.

The typical divisions offered are:

Junior Rider: *"For the purposes of competition in the Dressage Division: Individuals are eligible as Juniors until the end of the calendar year in which they reach the age of 18."* (AHSA, Art. 1919.3)

Young Rider: *"Individuals are eligible as Young Riders from the beginning of the calendar year in which they reach the age of 16 until the end of the calendar year in which they reach the age of 21."* (AHSA, Art. 1919.3)

JR/YR: Designates Junior and Young Rider are combined.

Adult: *"For competition purposes, in the Dressage division, competitors shall compete as Adults from the beginning of the calendar year in which they reach the age of 22."* (AHSA, Art. 107) For the other AHSA divisions, an adult or senior is an individual who has reached her 18th birthday as of December 1st of the current competition year.

Amateur: Many people think "amateur" designates "beginner" and "professional" equals "expert." This is not so. Many amateurs are experts and some "professionals" are not. The designation represents a monetary one only. A professional rides for remuneration, pure and simple. There are many "expert" amateurs who ride, train, and show their own horses.

"Regardless of one's equestrian skills and/or accomplishments, a person is an amateur for all competitions conducted under AHSA rules who after his/her 18th birthday, has not engaged in any of the activities which would make him/her a professional." (see Art. 808 of the current *AHSA Rule Book* for a list of what a person can or cannot do and still qualify as an "amateur.")

"Every person who has not reached his/her 18th birthday is (classed as) an amateur and will not be issued an amateur certification.

"Every person who has reached his/her 18th birthday and competes in classes for amateurs under AHSA rules must possess current amateur certification issued by the Association. This certi-

fication, ... must be renewed annually, ...and must be available for inspection...(by the show committee). *Forms may be obtained from the Association."* (AHSA, Art. 809.2)

Open: If you do not fit, or do not wish to enter in another designated division, you must show in the "open" class. Again, at most shows (but not all), you may show in only one division for the same test. If some tests are offered in JR/YR, Amateur, and Open and other tests are only offered in Open, obviously you can show Amateur in one test and Open in another.

Other Classes

Musical Freestyle Ride

The rules for FEI level freestyles are in the *AHSA Rule Book,* while the United States Dressage Federation publishes the rules and tests for First through Fourth Level freestyles. See Chapter 24 for suggestions on composing and presenting a musical freestyle.

FEI score sheets can be obtained from the AHSA office, and USDF (First Level through Fourth Level) score sheets and rules are obtained from the USDF. The current FEI and USDF score sheets must be used, and any changes made by the FEI or USDF will come into effect at the time of their being released, at which time those changes will supersede the previous score sheets.

PAS DE DEUX

This means "a musical ride of two." It is not a recognized class but some shows offer it, either as a competitive event or as an exhibition. Guidelines are published by the USDF.

Dressage Equitation Class

To provide incentive for riders to develop correct seats, the concept of dressage equitation classes was reinstated in 1995. Participation in the classes is encouraged for Juniors, Young Riders, and Adult Amateurs and can be held at all types of shows, including regional championships, with the goal of a national championship comparable to hunter equitation classes (figure 19.1).

Dressage equitation classes are usually open to riders who have never competed above Second Level in recognized competition. Classes may be divided by age, sex, and level. If entries warrant, separate classes may be held for Junior/Young Rider and Senior exhibitors. (See AHSA, Art. 1931.)

The class is shown as a group at medium walk, working trot, and canter both ways of the ring. The riders are judged on position, seat, and the correct use and effect of the aids (as demonstrated by the horse's responses) that are required by the Training and First Level dressage tests.

The movements are performed by the exhibitors simultaneously; however, the judge may ask for independent execution of certain tests. In judging the seat and use and application of the aids at the working gaits, judges should include the following tests: (a) transitions from one gait to the next both ways; (b) transitions from walk to halt and vice versa. Judges may also ask to see transitions from trot to halt and vice versa with or without stirrups. No change of horses shall be required. Whips and spurs are allowed, and horses must be shown in a plain snaffle (figure 19.2).

AHSA/USDF Qualifying and Championship Classes

Rules stipulating special conditions or requirements for championships, in the *AHSA Rule Book,* are intended to refer only to AHSA/USDF Championships, not local, regional, and other championships. If any region or group is hosting their championship at an AHSA recognized competition, they must print all special rules and requirements for those championships in their prize list, and must be sure that exhibitors are aware of all applicable local rules before the classes begin.

Figure 19.1 **Dressage equitation guidelines for the rider.**

	GOOD	MINOR FAULTS	MAJOR FAULTS	ELIMINATION
Seat/Upper Body	Continuous, complete contact with the saddle; keeping the spine vertical and in the center of the horse; relaxed thigh and supple back; upper body balanced over seat and leg; proper alignment of rider's head, ankle, hip, and shoulder; head balanced over shoulders with chin up.	Rounded back; swayback; lacking appropriate muscle tone; tense or floppy; leaning out or in; not in middle of horse; collapsed hip; rocking at the canter; shoulder moving excessively with each stride; balance too far forward or too far back.	Bouncing out of the saddle; tight in the thigh or muscles of buttocks; or pumping with seat; excessive body motion; chair seat–legs too far in front of the pelvis; crooked.	Falling off horse.
Legs	Correct heel/hip alignment at all gaits (heel under hip); correct angle in hip and knee to ankle joints; quiet, steady position; correct stirrup length; heel level with or lower than toe; stirrup on ball of foot.	Too much weight in stirrups; incorrect alignment; angles too open or too closed; stirrups too short or too long; unsteady leg position; pinching with knee or thigh; heels higher than toe; bringing up knee and heel when using leg aid.	Kicking; spurring every stride; toes out; gripping with calves; losing stirrup; heels thrust down with excessive weight in stirrups, especially if out in front of thigh.	
Hands/Arms	Arms hanging naturally at side with relaxed shoulders, elbows, and wrists; direct line between elbow, hand, and horse's mouth; thumbs up or at a 45° angle; quiet, steady, light contact; able to maintain consistent head position; hands held in front of pommel over withers; effective half- halts.	Reins too long or too short; unsteadiness; hands held too wide apart, too low, or too high; losing contact with the mouth; elbow angle too open, too far back, or lacking elasticity.	Pulling on reins; constantly fussing with reins; gaits compromised by heaviness or bumping hands; continual seesawing to keep horse's head down; horse's mouth gaping.	
Effect of Rider's Aids	Able to influence balance, show horse to best advantage; able to maintain consistent frame; smooth and prompt transitions; able to demonstrate submission and impulsion; demonstrate ability to coordinate seat, leg, and hand aids for control. Rides clearly from back to front.	Breaking from walk to trot; resistance to aids; ineffective use of ring; not clearly riding the horse forward from back to front.	Missing leads; breaking from trot to canter or trot to walk; horse above the bit; failure to rein back; lack of impulsion; lack of submission; use of voice.	Resistance of longer than 20 seconds; rider not having his mount under sufficient control.
General & Overall Appearance	The rider should have an elegant, but effective, appearance, conforming to AHSA rules on dress and equipment; tack clean and appropriate to horse and rider; consistency of form and control in harmony with horse; good attitude toward horse and judge.	Dirty boots and tack; ungroomed horse; unbraided horse; lack of suitability of horse to rider.	Equipment not according to AHSA rules; not dressed according to AHSA recommendations; bad attitude toward horse; lacking harmony between horse and rider.	Illegal equipment; broken equipment that the rider cannot continue without fixing; horses's tongue tied down; horse leaving arena; cruelty; marked lameness.

By Heather Bender. Reprinted by permission of Dressage Today *(Feb 1997, Vol. 3, No. 6)*

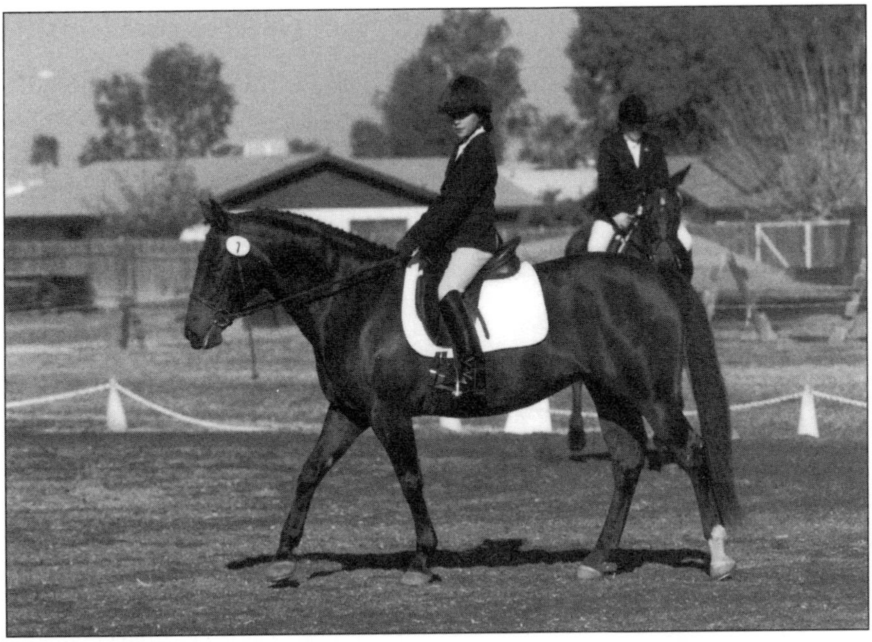

Figure 19.2 In an equitation class, the judge may ask for individual work. Photo by Charlene Strickland.

"The AHSA recognizes special competitions for Dressage Championships. Recognized Dressage competitions wishing to hold qualifying classes for one or more of these Championships should request information from the International Disciplines Department at AHSA or from USDF." (AHSA, Art. 1927)

Some of the conditions that apply to AHSA/USDF Championship classes (including qualifying classes) are:

- All Championship and Qualifying classes must be ridden from memory
- Whips may not be carried
- A horse must be ridden by the same rider throughout the competition (AHSA, Art. 1927.5)

Regional Championships

A single Regional Dressage Championship program organized by the USDF and recognized by the AHSA is held yearly in each of the nine USDF Regions. In addition, Alaska and Hawaii may each hold state championships.

Beginning in 1995, there is one qualifying system with nationally standardized minimum percentages. To qualify for the Regional Championship, horse and rider combinations must earn two qualifying scores in official AHSA/USDF Qualifying Classes, at two different AHSA/USDF recognized competitions, from two different judges.

Riders enter official AHSA/USDF recognized competitions that offer the AHSA/USDF Qualifying Classes. The AHSA/USDF Qualifying Class is the highest test of each level.

All qualifying competitions for AHSA/USDF Championships are open only to horses that have been recorded with the AHSA and ridden by Junior, Senior, or Life Members who are United States citizens. Competitors must also be Participating Members of USDF. Applications and fees for the horse's recording and rider's required memberships must be received by the AHSA and the USDF on or before the first recognized day of such competition. Qualifications are not retroactive.

Show secretaries usually require a photocopy of all required registration certificates and memberships. Qualifying classes may be offered at Training through Grand Prix levels, including USDF and FEI Freestyles. Championships may be offered for Open, Adult Amateur, and

Junior/Young Rider divisions at each level, including freestyles. Yearly specifications for AHSA/USDF Qualifying Classes and Championships may be requested from the International Disciplines Department of the AHSA or from the USDF. If a rider intends to enter an Adult Amateur Championship, she must be an Adult Amateur by AHSA definition and must provide proof (amateur card) to show management.

In the fall of the year, Regional and National Championships take place at designated AHSA/USDF shows. A horse may not be entered in more than one AHSA/USDF Regional Championship show in the same calendar year. Having won an AHSA/USDF Regional Championship, a horse and rider combination may no longer compete in AHSA/USDF regional championship competition in that division at that or a lower level (Grand Prix Level excepted).

At no time during a AHSA/USDF Championship competition may any horse entered in that Championship competition be ridden by anyone other than the rider entered in the Championship competition on that horse. Further, any horse entered in a Championship competition, even if entered at two levels, must be ridden by the same rider throughout the competition.

Specifications for Qualifying and Championship Classes may be requested from the AHSA office or from the USDF. (See AHSA, Art. 1927)

Suitable to Become a Dressage Horse

A mounted group class. *"Open to horses that have not competed in any test above the First Level that are under seven years of age. To be shown at a walk, trot and canter both ways of the ring. To be judged on the horse's potential to become a dressage mount."* (AHSA, Art. 1930)

Dressage Sport Horse Breeding

The purpose of these classes is to encourage the breeding of horses suitable for dressage and to provide an opportunity to demonstrate the effectiveness of breeding programs. A breeding division for dressage may be held separately or in conjunction with a recognized competition.

Classes are open to any horse without regard to size, breed, or origin. Classes for ponies or specific breeds may also be included and must be clearly specified in the prize list.

Horses' quality shall be evaluated as to potential for dressage sport horses or breeding stock. In in-hand classes, horses are shown individually on "the triangle" (figure 19.3).

For additional information, refer to the *USDF Dressage Sport Horse Breeding Guidelines* and *AHSA, Art. 1933.*

Reading the Prize List or Show Premium

When you receive your show premium, read it through carefully. The main source of communication between you, the rider, and the competition organization is the show premium (also referred to as the prize list). This document will explain any special conditions or requirements. Be sure you understand the various class definitions and eligibility restrictions. If you have any questions, call the competition secretary whose phone number will be listed in the premium. Send in your entry form and all fees on time. Be sure you are aware of Coggins test or health certification requirements of the competition and local and state laws.

Virtually all dressage shows have a closing date: the date the entry must be postmarked or received by. The reason for advance entries is because at a dressage show all the rides are scheduled. Due to time constraints (a maximum of about 60 rides in eight hours), rides must be scheduled ahead of time. Management usually accepts entries "first come — first served." If entries exceed time slots in the show,

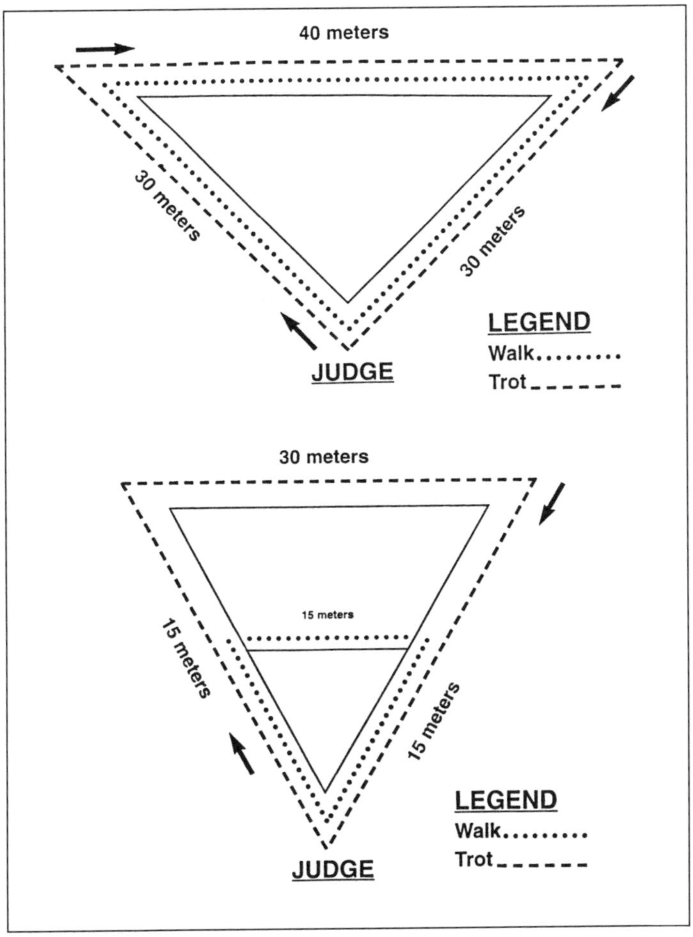

Figure 19.3
The two versions of "the triangle" pictured in the AHSA Rule Book. *Entries in the class approach the judging area one at a time, walk to the apex of the triangle, and await the judge's instructions to proceed on the triangle. The handler will lead the horse on the perimeter of the triangle at walk and trot, returning to the apex to stand the horse for conformation judging or to repeat any movement at the judge's request. Handlers are permitted to have one assistant, with a whip, if necessary. Repetition of all or any part of the movement on the triangle may be allowed at the judge's request only. At the completion of the judging, the handler will lead the horse away from the judging area. The judge may elect to judge conformation either before or after judging the horse's movement on the triangle. (Reprinted by permission of the The American Horse Shows Association)*

postmarks or "received by date" provide a cut off point, and excess entries may be put on a waiting list (to use in case of scratches or withdrawals) or may be returned when the show is full. Some shows return entries if they are missing information. If this happens close to the closing date, a rider may miss out on the show because the classes will be filled before the entry can be resubmitted.

If the premium has an "opening date," this means don't send entries in before this date. "Post entries" are entries received or accepted after the closing date. This is usually on a "space available" basis.

At recognized competitions, a tentative time schedule must be included in the prize list (premium). If the show committee changes this schedule and a competitor cannot show due to a change in the day she must ride, her entry fees must be refunded. After closing of entries, organizers will prepare a time schedule that includes all rides, called a "program." Competitors are notified of their riding times in advance if possible. Time intervals must be allowed between rides for judges' breaks and award presentations. The time schedule should be posted in a conspicuous place by noon the day before the competition. Most competitions mail out each exhibitor's personal ride times or provide provisions (in the prize list) for how to obtain ride times before the competition.

The announced order or time for classes may not be changed (at a recognized competition) unless at least twelve hours notice of such change is given to each exhibitor and judge affected. Provided the order of events is not changed, the show committee may call any class up to 30 minutes ahead of its scheduled time, provided exhibitors are given one hour's notice. (AHSA, Art. 309.1-2) If it becomes necessary to interrupt a dressage competition for any reason (most often because of weather), the unfinished portion may be recommenced and rescheduled for the same or the following day, at the option of the show committee with the ground jury's consent. All scores recorded before the interruption will stand. (Art. 311.7) Note: Interruption of Procedure rules differ when dressage classes are part of a regular or local member show. (None of the provisions of Art. 309 or 311 apply to combined training events.)

Some shows have "mandatory work time" for exhibitors. This is being used by more and more competitions because of the difficulty in getting volunteers (for scoring, gate, scribe, runners, and so forth). Sometimes you can pay a fee rather than work — sometimes not.

Filling Out the Entry Form

To save yourself any extra charges, nasty notes, or rejected entries, take a few minutes to read the Premium thoroughly, and fill out every blank of the entry form, including all required signatures. Include copies of membership cards as requested and correct payment and send it in well ahead of the deadline.

Rider, owner, and trainer must each sign the entry form. If they are one and the same person, the name must be signed three times. You cannot use ditto marks or print "same" in place of signatures. A "trainer" is an adult who has responsibility of care, custody, and performance of the horse during the competition. The trainer must be an AHSA member (or pay the non-member fee) and must be on the show grounds. The trainer is directly responsible for the horses under her care at the competition.

A minor (under 18) cannot sign as "trainer." In cases in which a Junior does not have a trainer to sign the entry blank, his or her parent may sign on the trainer line and write "parent" after their name. In this case, the parent does not have to be an AHSA member and need not pay the non-member fee. (This does not apply to the owner signature — if a parent is the owner of the horse, she must be an AHSA member or pay the non-member fee).

AHSA membership numbers for rider, owner, trainer, and horse (if the horse is recorded with the AHSA) are not required in order to compete, unless they are required by the specific class. Non-member fees must be paid for each if numbers are not supplied. A photocopy of the current AHSA membership card must accompany the entry form. Note that riders, owners, and trainers who enter only USDF Introductory Level tests, Pas de Deux, or Quadrille classes are included in those participants who are exempt from AHSA membership requirements. This means they do not have to be members or pay a non-member fee.

Chapter Twenty

Dealing with Nerves

Do you find yourself falling apart before a show? Does your mouth go dry, your palms get wet, or your heart start to pound as though you'd just run a race? Everything about your preparations seems overwhelming, and you don't have the nerve to continue?

You are experiencing pre-performance anxiety. There's hardly a competitor alive who doesn't suffer somewhat from nerves. A little anxiety is good — it sharpens the senses, pumps the adrenaline, and allows us to give "all we've got." Too much anxiety can indeed cause you to "choke" — that is, to lose your focus and fall apart mentally and physically. As you may have experienced, when this happens you lose your ability to perform at your best — or at all.

It's All in Your Head

There's only one part of your body that distinguishes between the human conditions of fear and anxiety — your brain. Fear is a painful emotion excited by danger, alarm, or apprehension of danger or pain. Anxiety, however, is a response to a *perceived situation.*

Sometimes called "stage fright," anxiety is triggered when a situation is interpreted as threatening or overwhelming. Unlike fear, anxiety continues until you convince yourself otherwise. In the meantime, your body is in a prolonged state of "fight or flight," which can last from hours to days. At the very least, this is extremely tiring. At worst, it causes loss of sleep, headaches, nausea, irritability, a feeling of extreme tiredness, heart palpitations, and maybe (no pun intended) nightmares. It can leave you wondering if you ever want to go through this again.

Anxiety symptoms may be responsible for the headache you get as you fill out the entry blank for the next show or what causes your breathing to quicken as you load your trusted mount into the trailer for the long ride to the competition grounds. The drain on your body may make your muscles cramp or leave you feeling nauseated as you wait at the in-gate. Once your anxiety has escalated to that degree, no amount of rationalization is likely to restore your composure in the few minutes you have before your test.

Identifying Performance Anxiety

The initial clue to performance anxiety can begin up to several weeks prior to the actual competition. Learning to recognize this initial clue will enable you to identify mounting tension in the early stages and take positive action to alleviate it before it gets out of hand and evolves into a destructive pattern of self-fulfilling prophecy.

Start with Self-Analysis

The first step on any road to change is to identify the cause of your problem.

1. Though it may take some soul-searching for you to realize that you **fear failure**, recognize that possibility. If you stop to think about it, there's no real logic to this fear. No one at the show is saying, "Look at her, she's terrible!" and the judges won't run you out of the ring if they're displeased. (Unless you commit some rule infraction.) Let's face it, unless the spectators are all family and friends, they really don't care.

The other riders are there for themselves, not to watch you. Generally, there are very few spectators, and if there are, they probably won't know if you did it right or not. Besides, everybody will have forgotten about it by the time the next person is in the ring.

None of the spectators are going to go look at the score board and exclaim, "Oh look, here's the score for that terrible ride we saw." Even other competitors only look to see where they placed, or who is *ahead* of them in the placings, not "who they beat."

Even the professionals occasionally "mess up" — they, too, go off course, experience a spook, or forget to take the leg wraps off. It's how you deal with it that counts. If you have a bad test, let it be a lesson on what you need to improve for the future.

2. Another bugaboo of first time competitors, is **fear of the unknown**. No matter how prepared you are, you can't foresee every incident. You need to trust that when the unexpected comes up, you will be able to deal with it safely and prudently. Remember, dressage is a *learning experience* — no show, no test, is the be-all and end-all of your career — unless you choose it to be.

3. Do you fear **the competition will be better than you**? What if it is? You are showing your horse at his particular stage of development. Don't compare your horse or your situation with others in the class. Each horse, each rider, is an individual. The judge is going to compare you to "the standard." How you place with the other riders in your particular class is coincidental.

Been There, Done That

However, let's say you're not a beginner to the horse show world, and despite all your best efforts, show day arrives and you feel a mini-disaster unfolding. Perhaps it is four or five hours before your event. You have plenty of time, yet you are feeling irritable, and you snap at a friend for an insignificant mistake. You become a little disoriented and your memory is fuzzy. You're feeling dizzy, so you sit down for a moment. You fail to notice that your breathing has become more shallow; you begin to sweat; your head pounds.

It is one hour before your event. You begin warming up your horse. You're worrying that the competition is tough, the arena is a little soggy, and your horse is not performing the way you want. Tension is building in your muscles, resulting in a lack of flexibility throughout your body. Of course, your horse immediately senses your inflexibility and your tension build-up and reacts negatively by tensing up himself. You soon notice your horse is not warming up properly and you become more tense, and again your horse senses this and responds with increased tension, which you notice and so on.

It is fifteen minutes before your test. Now you notice that your stomach is starting to feel really queasy, and soon your lunch is doing things never intended for the human body. You make a mad dash for the nearest bathroom. You're increasingly tense and inflexible, your mouth is now completely dry, and you're sweating as if you were doing the tango in a sauna. You're developing a splitting headache, and it's become impossible for you to concentrate — this is no time for a memory loss! Your breathing is becoming increasingly short and shallow, your heart is beating rapidly, and the only thing you're visualizing is you and your horse doing the worse "crash-and-burn" this horse show has ever seen!

Predictably, you go off course, and then your horse shies when going past the judge. By the end of your ride, you are almost in tears, and salute the judge apologetically. Your ride went poorly — to say the least! You feel a loss of energy and you are unable to remember any good parts of your ride. You are thinking only of all the things you and your horse did wrong.

Can this scenario be turned around? Of course, it can.

There are ways to control, or at least moderate, these symptoms so that competition becomes fun and exciting. (In a *positive* way!) Not everyone is able to maintain a cool head at all times, but with a little practice and preparation, you can manage your reactions to previously "scary" stimuli and put your nervous energy to positive use.

It is possible to climb out of negative destructive practices and realize a better performance by listening to your body, identifying mounting tension in its initial stages, and taking positive action to conquer your anxiety.

Be Kind to Yourself

While you cannot and do not want to avoid certain stresses, you can learn to develop a healthy perspective and deal with them productively. Facing the problem is far healthier than denial or running away. When you are stressed and your emotions are running high, the best strategy is to be kind to yourself.

1. Recognize your own limits of time and energy resources. Establish priorities and eliminate the low priority tasks. Use realistic scheduling. Give yourself enough time to accomplish your goals.

2. Remind yourself about the positives in your life. It may help to sit down and write out a list of the good things about you and your horse. This gives you something to refer to when your resolve fails.

3. Avoid negative thoughts. Negative self-talk can turn into a self-fulfilling prophecy. Instead think about what you can do to turn things around.

4. Slow down and allow yourself to relax. Tackle one task at a time.

5. Don't deny the existence of your problems. Recognize them and take constructive steps to deal with them by looking at your problems objectively, setting goals, and developing a rational step-by-step problem-solving strategy.

6. Set realistic expectations. Expectations that are too high can lead to frustration and depression. It's healthy to strive for perfection as long as you accept the final reality that you can never achieve it (and neither can anyone else!).

7. Seek out and discover the logical, productive lesson from each situation. You can

learn and benefit from any situation, good or bad.

8. Try for a grander perspective on it all. You're not judged on any one class or show. The picture you create as a rider is bigger than that.

Recognize that there are many, many ways to demonstrate your riding skill and to show your *self* through your riding. It's all in how you present yourself and how you present your horse, how you treat him, how you speak about your wins and losses, the grace with which you handle a wrong lead, a refusal, a spook, an elimination, a bad lesson, a bad show. A *winning* rider is not always the one with the blue ribbon.

Stress Management

Whatever its source, you need to learn to manage your anxiety so it doesn't interfere with your performance. Note that it is "manage," not "overcome." If you eliminate your anxiety completely, you'll lose your edge — that heightened state that pushes you to perform at your highest possible level. While too much anxiety can make you quit, at a lesser degree it can keep you going even when you're tempted to quit.

Anxiety management begins with adequate preparation — for both you and your horse. To better prepare, follow these five steps:

1. **Get physically fit.** This will not only make you a better rider, but also help you manage your stress more effectively — because you will know you are doing the best you can.

2. **Eat a proper diet.** You may wonder what diet has got to do with anxiety, but what you eat affects you not only physically, but also mentally. Proper diet can help you concentrate better (see Chapter 10).

3. **Practice scenarios.** As your show date nears, set up the same criteria, expectations, and pressure in your home arena that you'll encounter at the show. For example, work to hit every transition, every circle and corner, right on the mark; you'll not only ride better, you'll have practice dealing with the pressure to perform at your absolute best. If necessary, ask friends to sit in as an audience, and practice a dress rehearsal. (See Chapter 17.)

4. **Attend as many shows as possible as a non-competitor.** This will desensitize you to the show atmosphere and help acquaint you with protocol and the performance level of the other exhibitors. If your horse is new to showing, taking him to a couple of shows and just riding him around the grounds will prepare *him* for competition.

5. **Know when you're ready.** Do your "homework" (training and preparing your horse) well ahead of time so you can approach the competition with the following philosophy: "My work is done for this particular show. I'm as prepared as I can be. My horse and I are as trained as we are capable of being at this point. This ride is just one of many in a long line of tests. I won't attach greater importance to it than it deserves."

Having taken the pressure off yourself, you can just relax and have fun. You'll also enjoy the show more and reduce your horse-show jitters if you concentrate on your *efforts* rather than on the *results*.

Cause and Cure

It is possible to effectively control and overcome your anxieties by improving your mental self-awareness and by developing preventative mental techniques. You need to start by knowing what it is that triggers your anxiety. Following are some possible causes of anxiety that can (and should) be resolved. They range from the frivolous to the serious.

Is the competition psyching you out?

If watching other riders makes you nervous, don't watch them! Focus on your own ride instead.

Are you a timid rider? Do you find yourself tensing up anytime your horse tenses up, preparing yourself for the inevitable shy? Do you feel insecure because you believe you don't have enough control of your horse? Do you find it especially difficult to relax at a horse show or clinic? Have you ever been so frightened by a horse that you have "lost your nerve?" These are the "symptoms" of a timid rider, and no matter how hard you try to "look confident," bystanders — and even more importantly, your horse — will notice. The first step toward overcoming this problem is to find its cause.

1. Are you afraid of being hurt? Everyone working around horses should take safety precautions seriously. There is no way to completely prevent mishaps around horses, but safety consciousness can greatly reduce your chances of getting hurt. Always be aware — not anxious, but relaxed and attuned to your surroundings — while riding and working with horses.

Laziness, negligence, and hurried short-cuts are the biggest causes of injury in the horse world. Re-evaluate and improve the safety condition of your facilities, fencing, tack, and equipment. Wear your riding helmet if it makes you more confident, and dress in clothing that will not put you at risk. Head protection and appropriate footwear are two of the most important precautions.

There is a fine line between being safe and being paranoid. You don't want fear to take over, but neither do you want to let yourself become careless. By behaving in a focused, methodical manner every time you're with horses, you'll reduce the opportunities for injury.

2. Do you feel you don't have enough control of your horse? You can learn control strategies from your instructor or books on training. (And you are "training" every time you handle your horse.) Another important strategy is to always *tell your horse what to do.* Timid riders tend to sit back and "wait and see" what the horse is going to do, then get scared when the horse takes the initiative or does the unexpected. Don't wait for the horse to decide what he wants to do; *tell him what you want,* in fair but firm commands. If you initiate the commands, your horse will not have time to come up with his own ideas.

Sometimes timid riders get paired up with a timid horse. The result can be downright scary. The horse spooks, the rider tenses, and the horse takes the rider's fear as confirmation that there really is something to worry about. See Chapter 17 for suggestions on dealing with shying horses.

3. Does your horse "act differently" at a show or clinic? A major reason horses act differently at shows or clinics is that we act differently! Your horse is an incredibly sensitive creature and as a herd animal is bound to react to *your* emotions.

While this seems so simple as to be absurd, many of us get uptight at a show, clinic, or other event, and this affects how our horses behave. You're not going to be able to put in an accurate, confident, controlled, and harmonious ride if you can't control your own mental state.

Begin by developing a good warm-up (Chapter 16) and carrying it through at the show. Your show warm-up should be comprised of exercises that you use at home, so as not to surprise the horse. You may need to use exercises to sharpen his responses, keep him in a relaxed state, or to focus his attention on you. Only experience will tell you what the horse needs.

If you're still not sure why you're riding or behaving differently at the shows, set up a "make believe show." Groom, bathe, and braid your horse, then trailer to a friend's house. Have some friends act as judge and spectators. You might want to video the warm-up and test(s). If you still can't figure it out for yourself, ask your friends what they think you are getting nervous about. Are you concentrating too hard on the test instead of the horse's performance? Are you trying too hard and making yourself stiff in the process? Analyze your horse's actions and your own, and try to find a solution to your problems.

4. Do you feel insecure in your riding position? If so, executing a death grip with your knees will not help — in fact, will hinder — your security. If you get so tense that you "freeze," the horse can "bounce" you right off his back! Consult a riding instructor on how to improve your position and security on the horse (also see Chapter 9). Two ways to overcome tension are correct breathing and "soft eyes."

Breathing

Breathing well — using the full expansion of the lungs and controlling the speed of breathing — can contribute at all levels to riding a thoughtful, panic-free test.

In humans, holding one's breath is a sign of anticipation or anxiety. It is very common to hold one's breath unconsciously at the start of something challenging, such as approaching a line of jumps or beginning a difficult dressage movement, or maybe during warm-up at a show. In animals, though, holding the breath is part of the "startle reflex." When your horse feels the rhythm of your breathing suddenly stop (or become shallow), he assumes you're worried about something and that he should be, too! The result is performance loss, frustration, and *more* tension.

If instead you breathe slowly and deeply — as if your lungs were located in your feet — and in a regular rhythm, you will *relax* your horse. Why? Because he feels the calming in-and-out of your breathing. Also, because breathing deep and low down lowers your center of gravity through imagery, making you feel more secure in the saddle, which makes *him* feel more secure about you. Deep breathing reduces tension, on the horse or off. Tension can raise your center of gravity as high as chest level and make you unbalanced.

Now that you know why you should breath deeply, try this in the saddle: Breath in a calm, deliberate way while walking your horse in the ring or hacking out. If necessary, count to yourself: 1-2-3 inhale; 1-2-3 exhale, and so forth. You should feel your horse swinging along freely and confidently. Keep going for several minutes, establishing a nice, regular rhythm. Then without changing your position or leg pressure, draw in your breath and hold it. You may feel a change immediately as his stride shortens and his back stiffens. If he's very sensitive, he may even stop or look for something to shy at! Now begin breathing from deep down again and feel the improvement. In times of stress, you may have to deliberately *tell yourself to breathe!*

Soft Eyes

Sally Swift, founder of Centered Riding®, coined the phrase "soft eyes." "Hard," narrowly focused eyes make you tense, and that makes your horse tense. To release this tension, "soften" your eyes, not by unfocusing them but by widening their view, so that instead of homing in on one spot — your horse's mane or a trouble spot ahead — you're aware of your whole environment and what's going on all around you. With "soft eyes" you should be able to see the sides of the arena as well as *feel* every part of your body and your horse's.

It is difficult to understand the concept of soft eyes until you have tried it. As an exercise, as you are riding along at the walk, focus your eyes hard on an approaching object — a stone, or a jump standard, or a similar distinctive object along the path. Nine times out of ten your horse will hesitate to go past it — he may even shy. By staring at the object, *you* appear concerned with it, so *he* will be concerned with it also.

Remembering these two little details, breathing and soft eyes, should come in handy in the warm-up arena when you feel either your horse, or yourself, tensing up.

Take Control of Your Emotions

For most of us, learning to control our emotions takes some positive steps. There are three mental strategies that can improve your chances of competitive success, or at the very least make the experience more enjoyable. Set realistic goals. Use positive visualization. Tell yourself to relax!

1. Set realistic goals. When individuals choose idealistic goals and do not attain them, they typically feel unhappy, then chastise themselves for failing or for not working hard enough. This quickly evolves into a negative cycle that results in self-defeating behavior and *increases* performance anxiety. An obvious example of an unrealistic goal is "I want to win every horse show." This goal seems extreme, yet some competitors feel that they have failed unless they take first place, achieve certain scores, or win certain awards. You must *accept that you cannot control everything.* You have no control over show conditions, bad weather, spooky occurrences, your horse's soundness, subjective opinions, and a myriad of other factors. It's not enough to be good; you have to be *lucky* as well.

To develop a healthy perspective toward competition, you must establish realistic goals. These goals will form the foundation of your mental practice program. Choose specific (and attainable) goals that you can control and realistically attain. For example, divide your goal to "succeed at horse shows" into more specific goals such as:

- To be relaxed prior to and during your performance.
- To maintain correct riding posture — lengthening your legs, lowering your heels, and keeping your eyes forward — whatever you know you always have to work on.
- To be precise in your seat and leg cues.
- To keep your horse straight and forward.

Now visualize how you can successfully complete each step toward your goal. Also consider time management — have you allotted enough time to accomplish your goals?

You can gain useful insight into your goal development by asking for your trainer's input. What is her opinion on the goals you've established? Also, observe your peers who are at a similar level of preparation and expertise. Ask them how they reached that level of success.

You could keep a brief daily riding log or log of test comments (see Chapter 23). This will assist you in creating a more complete view of your goals, help keep you focused on the facts, and keep you in touch with specific tasks — as well as let you know when you have achieved a specific goal.

2. Positive visualization. Visualization can be defined as the ability to imagine yourself successfully or unsuccessfully completing an act (see Chapter 14).

Whenever you feel yourself getting uptight, try visualizing a solution to an anticipated problem in your test or warm-up. Go over the test in your head, doing a run-through geared to your particular horse — whether he's lazy, hot, nervous, timid, whatever — to prepare yourself for what might happen.

You can even visualize your test while driving to the competition. Although you can't close your eyes while driving, in the quiet of the car you can go over your visualized test. The solitude of the road gives you plenty of contemplative time to focus on a specific goal, relax your mind, and adjust your attitude.

At any time during the days (or nights) before a test you find yourself getting anxious, take a few minutes to visualize a successful test or a successful warm-up. You can do this right up to the last minute as you sit at the in-gate waiting for your turn. Bystanders will know by your blanked out expression that you are "psyching up" for your test and will leave you alone.

Establish your own visualization routine. Only through consistent practice will you become proficient at these techniques.

3. Tell yourself to relax. Whatever you say (or think), your body will believe! Remember it goes even further than that; your horse picks up on your emotions — sometimes before you do! So, you really can *tell yourself to relax!*

Your body continually organizes its actions around your thoughts and ideas. This can work for or against you. For instance, if you keep remembering what went *wrong* when you struggled to get your horse on the left lead in your last riding session (or test), you're potentially programming yourself to *repeat* that same problem in your next ride. But if you take control of the process by replacing that picture of failure with a plan of action, your body will try to program *that* ride instead. You are much more likely to achieve success.

Don't talk yourself into being nervous. Keep your attitude positive. Exclaiming, "I'm nervous!" "He isn't acting right!" "I can't do this test," will only feed your nerves.

4. Don't talk yourself out of a good time. If someone asks you how it's going, reply with a confident "Just fine," or "So far so good." Before you know it, you'll believe it!

5. Don't demean yourself with modesty. Saying "Oh, he's not very talented," or "He's acting terrible today" will only give you an excuse if you don't do well — keep it positive!

6. Give yourself credit. Sometimes people develop a "habit" about how they see themselves. They have accepted that there are limits to what they and their horses can do, and they don't test to see whether it's true or not. They have stopped exploring the options, because their feelings and opinions about themselves get in the way.

7. Cut out the negatives. Negatives, such as "never," "won't," "don't," and "not" don't register in the unconscious the way specific, descriptive (positive) verbs and nouns do. If you're thinking something negative like "I'm *not* going to get tense today," you *will* get tense, because you're not telling your body what to do!

To establish a positive approach, envision what you want to do and how you are going to do it. This phenomenon is called "trigger phrases" and can be used in many ways. You can actually program your mind to connect relaxed feelings to a word or phrase. Then if you repeat that word (or phrase) later in a stressful situation, it helps the body remember how that more relaxed or "in control" state feels. It utilizes the same characteristics of our mind that cause an old song or perfume to bring back memories and emotions. If it is used properly, it can be very powerful. The body can learn to produce a relaxed feeling simply by

Are You Creating the Problem?

I am often amazed by the negativism that some riders fuel at shows. I was just at a show in Albuquerque, New Mexico, that was held in a closed pavilion. It was one of those places where the ring is low and the stadium rises above it. Fortunately, the walls of the ring were low enough that the horses could see over them. We were able to ride in it a day prior to the show and my horse was fine, but I was surprised by everyone else's reaction. Back at the barn or at the warm-up, people kept telling each other how bad it was and how frightened their horses were. It was interesting to me because when these people went into the ring, they had blow after blow. Instead of realizing that it wasn't so bad, they believed it was, and their horses believed *them!* Rather than being swayed by other riders' impressions, I relied on my own good sense that my horse would not think it was scary if I did not think it was scary.

repeating a word.

Try different words or phrases to discover which one works best for you. Some suggestions are:

"We can handle this."

"We are going to be fine."

(Say "we" because you must always include your horse in here. It is never "you against the horse.")

"Take it one step at a time."

"I've survived much worse than this."

"This is not as bad as..."

"We're going to do the best we can and it *will* be good enough."

If your horse has a history of acting up, you might think up some phrases or words to help you handle the situation. For instance, if you're riding a young or spooky horse, instead of wondering whether he's going to run off or buck you off, think, "sit deep." *Your body will do what you tell it to do.*

On the other hand, if the horse is being lazy, say to yourself "Go," and believe it or not, your "go" muscles will kick in and should inspire the horse to move. (See Chapter 14, "Memorizing and Visualizing Tests.")

There is a multitude of ways to mitigate the problems associated with the anxious mind. Stress management systems, popular with many corporate executives, can work wonders for equine endeavors as well.

Remember these important points:

- Your self-esteem is never dependent on winning (or getting a high score). You are a good rider whether you win or not.
- Reward yourself and your horse on your improvements. Keep sight of your long-term goals. Patience is invaluable.
- There will always be another horse show. Myriads of variable conditions exist that you cannot control, but you can choose to try again.
- You never fail until you stop trying.

As you explore the options for controlling your nerves, remember that you have chosen to add this stress to your life — it should be an enjoyable experience.

Chapter Twenty-One

The Horse's First Show

This chapter gets the horse and rider to the show, through the warm-up, and poised at the in-gate for the best test they are capable of.

If you know what to expect at the show, you can more easily keep your horse calm and focused on the task at hand. You will be able to focus on your riding if you have a thorough and detailed plan for the entire show day — from morning feeding to stepping into the ring, including how you will navigate high-traffic warm-up arenas and how you deal with an anxious horse.

A plan will give you a calmer horse who'll compete better because you warmed him up properly; an on-time, collected arrival at the arena that will impress the judge; and a day that'll be more fun and relaxed than you could imagine.

You need to plan ahead so that you will be calm and organized upon arrival at the competition grounds. Prepare a packing list (see Sidebar) for horse, rider, and trailer. Clip and bathe your horse and do most of your packing the day before the show. Make sure your horse is properly shod. Don't depend upon a farrier at the show grounds, and don't expect that a wash rack will be available.

Part of your plan is estimating when you need to leave home. Call for your ride times (refer to the show premium for information on how to get your times). If, for example, your first test is at 10:00 AM, from there calculate *backward* to what time you need to get going by using the time table sidebar, adapting it to whatever start time you're assuming. (Note: Training Level tests are usually first, so if you and your horse are not familiar with the show grounds, plan on being there very early.) If you are riding more than one test and you end up arriving a little later than hoped, you can use the first test as part of your "warm-up."

Packing List

Go to the event prepared! A well-organized packing plan and a timely arrival will go a long way toward avoiding last minute pressures. The following list may be helpful to get you started on your own. You may not need everything, or you may need more. I've provided you with a handy checklist — feel free to photocopy it for repeated use.

	Papers
	Copy of show premium and photocopy of your entry form
	Copy of time allotment from show secretary
	Test diagrams or USDF test booklet
	Copy of Coggins test and health papers
	AHSA Rule Book
	Pens or felt markers, note pad, Score Reporting forms
	Stable card indicating the horse's name, owner, hotel & hotel's telephone number, and room number
	Copies of AHSA and USDF registration cards for horse
	Copies of AHSA and USDF registration cards for rider, owner, and trainer
	Road map and directions to show grounds
	Shipping Outfit
	Tail bandage (optional)
	Four leg wraps and cottons or ready-made shipping boots
	Adhesive or masking tape to secure bandages
	Four bell boots to protect coronet bands
	Heavy-duty halter and protective head cap for shipping (don't leave the horse in a stall with a nylon halter — they don't break if caught on something)
	Full hay net and carrots or tidbits
	Two lead lines, one with a chain, and extra halter (preferably leather)
	Longe line and long whip for difficult loaders
	Blanket or sheet, depending on climate
	Equipment for Stalls
	Hammer
	Pliers to cut wires and remove nails from the stall
	Screwdrivers
	Assorted size nails
	Several screw eyes (various sizes) for feed bins, stall guards, etc.
	Electrician's tape and baling twine or wire
	Several double-ended snaps
	Length of rope
	(This all fits neatly in an old flight bag that should be the first item at hand when you arrive on the show grounds. The first chore is to fix the stall for your horse before unloading him.)
	Stall guards (two if possible)
	Two water buckets per horse
	One feed bucket per horse
	Manure fork, scoop shovel, broom
	Wheelbarrow if space allows
	Shavings enough for two full nights, minimum four bags
	Ant spray, particularly in the South
	Insect repellent
	Peppermint drops: if your horse refuses to drink water in a new stall, get him used to the peppermint flavor at home so he won't notice the difference at the show.
	For stallions: plywood panels for stalls
	Tack Room
	Saddle stand, tack hangers
	Removable hook for clothes hangers, mirror
	Flashlight
	Card table and chairs
	Blankets
	Regular sheet or blanket, depending on season
	Cooler or fly sheet
	Rain sheet, as needed
	Grooming
	Brushes, curry comb, towels (cloth and paper)
	Hoof dressing and hoof pick
	Braiding kit (extra yarn or rubber bands) and milk crate (or mounting step) to stand on
	Grooming spray, fly spray

Packing List *continued*

	Skin bracer (liniment)
	Clipper and/or scissor set
	Wash bucket and sponges (don't mix up with feed and water buckets), sweat scraper
	Ivory® soap liquid (for white areas) and horse shampoo
	Medical Supplies
	(Be sure your horse has all vaccinations — tetanus, rhino, influenza, encephalitis, etc.)
	Telephone number of your vet at home
	Liniment, poultice, and Mineral Ice®
	Wraps & bandages other than for shipping
	Cottons for under the leg bandages
	Antibiotic ointment
	Azium® in case of food or other allergies
	Rubbing alcohol or Vetrolin® bracer
	Cotton, gauze bandages, elastic bandages
	Thermometer, twitch
	Electrolytes
	Tack
	Saddle, two girths, extra set of stirrup leathers
	Two saddle pads for each day, white or stable color (the colored one is for warm-up)
	Two pairs of reins: one leather for good weather, one canvas fabric or rubber for rain
	Extra bridle (in case of breakage)
	One whip four feet or less (leave any whip longer than four feet at home; it could cause your elimination)
	Longe line and longe whip
	Saddle soap and sponges
	Tack repair kit, Swiss army knife
	Galloping boots (for warm-up in bad footing)
	Feed
	For one-day show, take your own drinking water for horse from home
	For multi-day shows: Proper feed mix for sufficient feeding, plus one extra meal for anticipated length of show. (Put each feeding of grain/pellets in a heavy paper bag — then it's already measured and ready to dump. Cut it in half if horse is nervous.)
	Carrots and tidbits
	Hay, two times the normal amount for duration. (Keeping hay in front of the horse most of the time will help him relax.)
	Clothing
	Two pair white breeches for each day
	Two white shirts with sleeves, short or long, for each day
	Stock ties, stock pin — at least two
	Riding jacket in a clothes bag
	Clothes brush, spot remover
	Hunt cap (or hat) in box or hat cover
	Gloves: one pair with leather for good weather, one pair with rubber for rain
	Rain gear (clear or conservative rain jacket, hat cover)
	Coveralls or wrap-around skirt, to protect white breeches
	Show boots, boot jack, boot hooks
	Rubber boots (or rubber slippers)
	Spurs (only if needed)
	Powder for boots (to get on if wet)
	Extra boot socks
	Miscellaneous
	Personal grooming kit and mirror — you must look just as neat, cool, fresh, and collected as your horse
	Sunscreen, broad-brimmed hat
	Jacket if cool
	Combination lock for tack trunk to leave your valuables, jewelry, or a few dollars you may want for refreshments
	Comfort
	Folding chairs
	A cooler with cold drinks or hot coffee, depending on season; snacks, noonday lunch

This list can obviously go on indefinitely and everybody has her own ideas; however, if you go through this, you probably will not forget too many of the essential items.

Show Day Time Table

(Assuming first test at 10:00, 45 minute drive):

5:15	Feed; hook up trailer and load last-minute supplies (cooler, sandwiches, etc.); eat light breakfast (55 minutes)
6:10	Quick groom, wrap legs (20 minutes)
6:30	Load horse onto trailer (30 minutes)
7:00	Leave for show (45 minute drive — allow 1 hour)
8:00	Arrive/unload, check in at show office; check out grounds (30 minutes)
8:30	clean up horse (30 minutes)
9:00	Tack up horse (15 minutes)
9:15	dress yourself (10 minutes)
9:25	Mount up, walk to ring (5 minutes)
9:30	Warm up (30 minutes)
9:55	Final preparation before you go into ring (4-5 minutes)
10:00	Test time

You will note that there is extra time in the schedule for loading and driving to the show grounds. If you arrive ahead of schedule, you won't have to rush through your saddling and warm-up.

Arrive at the Competition

When you arrive, swing into your plan of action to ensure yourself plenty of time to get to the ring. Fight the desire to stop and chat with acquaintances or watch a few rides. *Get organized first;* then do your visiting if you have time before your class — or afterward, when you can relax.

Here is the "order of go" for you and your groom after you arrive on the show grounds:

1. Find a good parking place in the designated area (assuming this is a show where you'll show out of your trailer, not a stall). There may be someone to direct you to a parking place, especially if the grounds are cramped. Remember to allow room on one side of your trailer or the other to tie your horse(s). Do not park so close to another trailer that other people's horses can kick, or be kicked, by yours.

2. Unload your horse, tie him securely, give him a hay bag, and have your assistant keep an eye on him while you go to the show office.

3. Report to the show office as soon after your arrival as possible. Pick up your competitor's packet and verify your ride times, classes, and stabling arrangements (if applicable). Set your watch to official competition time.

Check that the ride times you were given match the ride times you had already received. If there are any discrepancies in your entry, you need to straighten them out now.

Your competitor's packet should contain your exhibitor number and a show program (schedule of rides). Verify your ride times, classes, and rings. After the competition begins, any change in the schedule needs to be worked out with the management in a timely manner. Scratches and substitutions need to be officially processed by management. It is also an AHSA rule that you must obtain permission from management before withdrawing a horse from the competition or removing it from the show grounds prior to completion of all its classes.

If you arrive the day before the show, you must ask permission before entering a competition arena. Management may sometimes allow schooling in or around the competition arena, but do not assume that this is permitted without asking. Sometimes the prize list will address this issue.

4. On the way back to your trailer, take a quick survey of the grounds, checking out locations of your competition ring(s), your schooling area, longeing areas (if necessary), rest

rooms, the water faucet, and a shady area where you can take your horse between workouts. Check out the ring you will be riding in. If there are rings side by side, should you listen for a whistle or a bell? Check with the gate person or paddock master, who'll be standing near the in-gate, most likely with a clipboard. Double-check with him if the rings are running on time and where the official clock is. If the show is running early, you are not required to ride before your official time, unless you want to.

5. Back at the trailer, check your horse and give him water. Unwrap his legs and organize your tack. Hang up your bridle, put your saddle, saddle pads, and girth on a saddle rack. Keep your saddle covered if the sun is intense (or if it's raining). Organize your coat, hat, gloves, and so on within easy reach.

6. Groom your horse (according to your time schedule). Don't fuss with him too much if he's not used to it. You want to keep everything as routine as possible so your horse (and you) stay calm.

7. Tack up your horse at your scheduled time. Allow at least 15 minutes for tacking up.

8. Dress yourself: boots, hair net, tie, and hat on; don't forget your spurs and/or whip.

9. Put the horse's show number on. You can put his number on the bridle (if its the small round kind, make sure it's secure), or safety pin it to the saddle pad (if you have a square one) or to the back of your coat. If it's hot you'll probably have your groom carry your coat to the warm-up area (turn it inside out so it stays dust- and hair-free), gloves in the pocket, or if it's cool, put your coat on before you mount. If you use a mounting block, have your helper put it out of the way after you mount.

10. Head for the warm-up area. Keep telling yourself you have plenty of time. *Your number one priority* is to make this a good (comfortable and safe) experience for your horse. There will be many more shows in the future. If this is your first show, you want to set the precedent with your horse that this is an enjoyable, stress-free experience that the two of you can look forward to.

If You're Late

If, despite your planning and best intentions, you're late for your first (or any) class — maybe you had a flat tire or you had trouble loading your horse — *don't panic.* If you can get your horse saddled and to the ring on time, by all means do it. You've paid your entry money, just "school" the test (ride your horse as passively or calmly as you can so he gets some positive ring experience). Look at it this way — you get some warm-up time without the hassle of the other competitors getting in your way!

Above all, don't put yourself or your horse in danger by rushing. This is just one day, one show, one class; you have a lot more classes and shows in the future. You could end up with a scared horse that runs away with you because he wasn't warmed up properly. If you can school confidently and calmly under time pressure, then try to make the class. However, if you feel rushed and distracted and you can't be sure of warming him up safely, you'll do better to scratch. If you don't have time to let the office know, tell the gate person.

How Long to Allow for Warm-Up

Most competitors seem to want a definitive, black-and-white answer to that question. There is no definite answer beyond "it depends." You must be sensitive to each horse's needs. One horse may require a long warm-up, while another needs only a few minutes. It may take several shows to figure out what is the optimum time for your particular horse.

A good rule of thumb is to allow 45 minutes to an hour for your first warm-up at your first show. If you don't need all that time, you can always walk or let your horse stand for periods of time. "Normal" warm-up time is probably 45 minutes, and this allows for five minutes to "spruce the horse up" before the test and be at the in-gate as the competitor ahead of you is riding her test.

Upper-level riders typically warm up for 45 minutes to an hour then put the horse away for an hour or two. They then bring the horse out again 20 or 30 minutes before their test.

Tacking Up

The restrictions on bits, bridles, and equipment (see Chapter 7) *"also apply to warm-up areas and other training arenas, however, nose covers, running martingales, boots, and bandages are permitted in the warm-up. Side reins are permitted only when longeing (mounted or unmounted). Horses competing at Fourth Level and above may be warmed up in a snaffle if the rider so chooses."* (AHSA, Art. 1921.7) Horses warming up for a Third Level test may not warm up in a double bridle. At recognized shows, the horse must wear his competition number whenever out of the stall.

Do not change your equipment or your demeanor at the show. The horse needs to be gently reminded of what he is expected to do without any harsh discipline or signs of nervousness from you. This includes being led, groomed, and saddled for his warm-up.

Grooming and tacking up are important times for you to reassure your horse with familiar and comforting actions and words, and to remain patient and understanding even if the horse gets fussy. This time is important and can really affect the horse's mood and attitude in the arena.

Should you Longe?

What do you do if you get to the show and your horse is a bundle of nerves? Say it's cold and windy, or there's a lot going on? You can try to get him a little tired and not so fresh by longeing, but this is best kept as a last resort. Though at home longeing a fresh horse is usually fine, stay away from longeing in a show situation, where — because the horse tends to be distracted and therefore susceptible to injuring himself — longeing could do more harm than good. Also, you can't longe in the warm-up rings. You have to find somewhere else to go if you need to let the horse buck and play. Some shows set up a separate area for longeing.

It's better to wean the horse away from longeing. At the show try to relax him and get him listening and responding by using an energetic rising trot and doing lots of figures — circles, figure eights, half-circles in reverse — or anything else that will get him physically working and mentally paying attention.

The Warm-Up

At a show or clinic, your warm-up not only consists of a period of relaxing and loosening exercises for you and your horse, it also allows the horse to look around and get accustomed to his surroundings. At a competition, the warm-up may take *longer*, but it is still composed of the same *elements* you use at home: walking, bending exercises, up and down transitions, and the like.

The purpose of the warm-up is to have the horse ready, at a prescribed time, to work his very best. This is not the time to train — that should have been done at home. Use the warm-up to get the horse supple, listening, and *happy*. You don't want to go into the arena with the horse or yourself in a bad mood. A good "competition horse" should go into the arena to show off.

How a horse reacts in strange surroundings depends on his inherent personality or temperament. A competition atmosphere puts a heavy demand on any horse's concentration, and since his ability to cope with that atmosphere can only be worked on at a competition, you need to take your horse out to shows and events as soon as he is ready to go. Some horses are more vulnerable to the atmosphere than others, and you have to get to know your horse so well that you can predict how he will react to certain things. Then you can develop a specific system of warm-up to suit your horse.

Here are some things you should seek to discover *before* you arrive at your first show or clinic:

1. Know what the horse does right the first time and don't school it in the warm-up.

2. Know what the horse worries about if you work on it and limit this in the warm-up.

3. Don't drill either the good or the bad things.

4. Know what you need a few tries to get right, then stop it in warm-up just before it is right.

5. Know how to warm up *your* horse. Some need lots of walking, some need to be left alone, some need to warm up early then be put up, then just worked fifteen minutes before the class — whatever *that* horse needs.

6. Traveling will often make a horse stiff, so if you haul into a show, you may need to plan on a little extra time to loosen the horse.

Some horses change at shows from how they are at home. Many horses who are lazy at home become a far more explosive ride at a competition, and this demands a change in tactics from the rider. In this case, you must be prepared to change your game plan. Always remember, the most important thing is to *make this a pleasant experience for the horse,* so that he (and you) looks forward to the next show as a pleasant place to be.

There are two common reactions to the show atmosphere. One is that the horse comes out like a lion and wants to take on the world, but he will usually wind down and relax with the more work he does. The other type is the horse that starts out fairly relaxed, but then becomes more and more excited, so that the more you work him, the worse (more nervous) he becomes.

A "Normal" Warm-Up

It is important to know your own horse and have him sufficiently worked so that he is at his best for the few minutes that he will be competing. Some horses need a lot of work, an hour or more, to get them settled down and working properly; others need only a few minutes to kind of "wake them up" before entering the ring.

A "normal" warm-up will follow very closely the warm-up you have developed at home (see Chapter 16). Again, if this is your (or the horse's) first show, be very aware of his reactions. Usually, you can see what kind of attitude your horse has by his manner while being unloaded.

Use the warm-up to **assess your horse's mood**. Attach a "label" to your horse's mood so you can develop a strategy to deal with it (see Chapter 16). Use labels that are descriptive and positive or neutral: such as "flighty," "stiff," "distracted," or "mellow." Labels that are vague, judgmental, or couched in human terms rather than equine ones ("nasty," "out of sorts," "vindictive," "stupid," "crazy," "lunatic") give you little to act on.

Deal with one issue at a time. This can be difficult, especially when you're preparing for a test on a new horse with only 30 minutes to work with. It forces you to cut through the distractions and deal with the one dominant issue in your horse's life at that moment. For instance, as you walk your horse out to the warm-up area, a piece of paper innocently blows by. Your horse stares sideways at the paper, he snorts and blows, jumps sideways, almost unseating you, and prances the rest of the way to the ring. The last thing on his mind is work, and the only thing on yours is the prospect of watching your plans go up in smoke as you visualize him "blowing" the whole test.

It doesn't have to be that way. Temporarily put your plans on hold and tap into your horse's mood, work with it, and quickly and efficiently guide him back onto a track where you're both comfortable and productive. Instead of asking, "Will we be ready for our test in 20 minutes?" you'll ask, "What's on his mind and what will it take to turn him around?"

Go for the cause, not the symptom. For example, "distracted" is a common problem at a competition, but "distracted" is a symptom of a bigger issue: probably "worried." By quietly and firmly riding a horse through a "worried" moment and bringing his focus back on you, you fix the "distracted."

If the problem is "spooky," get the horse's attention. If he's paying attention to you, he won't notice the spook! Put the horse on a pattern that will settle and get his attention. If the word is "bored" (yes, horses can get bored at a competition, when they know exactly what is going to happen every time), work on variety. If the horse is excited, "hot," or fidgety, it can often be fixed by walking the horse or using a pattern that will lull him to quietness. Sometimes the "hot" horse needs to be ridden vigorously forward to take the edge off.

Above all, don't get frustrated, don't get discouraged, and don't get mad. Be patient. Try to figure it out. You're training your horse, and whether it's good training or bad training, everything you do goes directly into his memory banks.

As you work with your horse, remember that he is exposed to many new things: different horses, lots of activity, and strange surroundings. Although you must gently enforce your horse's manners and obedience, rough handling can undermine his confidence. If your horse indicates nervousness, pat him, speak to him in a soothing voice, and give him a treat to reassure him. Some horses will be too nervous even to eat a carrot, but do what you can to reassure yours.

Start your warm-up as you always do, probably by walking. This gives the horse the opportunity to look around and become used to his surroundings. Give him as much time to settle as he needs. If he becomes restless at the walk, it may be he is becoming bored and thinking of things to do to entertain himself or express his nervousness, which will irritate you and increase the likelihood of a confrontation between the two of you. Use your best judgment on when to move on to the trot.

The trot is the best gait to settle as well as get the horse's attention on you. The canter, on the other hand, tends to excite an already nervous horse. One of the most effective methods to relax a horse in the warm-up ring is a business-like, steady trot. Horses relax more quickly when asked to trot in a business-like manner, interspersed with short walking breaks.

To prevent boredom or focus the horse's attention at the trot, do large circles, half-circles, and serpentines, making each change of direction easy and on a normal contact. The size of the figures depends on your horse: small, tight work and short turns increase mental energy and excitement in a horse. Larger figures should calm him. Keep his attention by giving him a definite direction to go. A good exercise is large figure eights at the trot. The constant yet quiet changes of direction focus his attention on you while suppling his body in both directions. If you are having a hard time getting or keeping his attention, try work on a square: on the arena floor, pick out markers — a clump of weeds, a jump standard, or a certain fence post — and do perfectly straight lines and precisely rounded corners (geared to your horse's level of training). The clear, concise aids will keep your horse "on track," both mentally and physically.

When your horse starts to simmer down, you can throw in some walk-trot transitions and canter circles. And when you feel that you have his full attention and he's balanced and listening, go on a 20-meter circle and let him do some stretching (Chewing Out the Reins — see Chapter 13).

It is important that you remain relaxed

while riding. Your horse will respond to the lack of pressure and to your casual, easy manner, gradually softening his back and his mind as he begins to look around and take in his surroundings.

When you feel the horse is ready, try a little canter. If he gets "strong," keep him bent on a circle and turn that "strong" canter into a "brilliant" canter.

Walk the horse often so he doesn't get sweaty. At the walk, let the horse relax both physically and mentally. If you have a lot of extra time left before your ride time, occasionally trot or canter the horse to keep him "primed" and ready for his test. Your horse's mind may need to be occupied with your gentle but constant requests. In an organized and logical manner, ask your horse to perform transitions, turns, and movements, keeping him attentive, but calm. Avoid rushing or hurrying to change gait and direction, but keep your instructions consistent.

The "Hot" Horse Warm-Up

Particularly challenging to a rider is the nervous horse, who requires more patience and effort to ride and teach than does the steady horse. A horse who is fearful, anxious, nervous, or rattled at a competition needs an extra dose of friendship and understanding.

Horses have so many ways of expressing their nervousness. If you can learn to recognize them, you can manage each individual and learn how best to react to each expression.

With the horse that becomes "hotter" as you work him, it is no good just battling on in the hope that you will gradually wear him out. By the time he is fit for showing, especially if he is an event horse, he will have enough depth of stamina that you will find it difficult to drain his reserves.

Only in extreme cases should you try to "wear a horse down" to prepare him for a competition. A tired horse is exhausted both physically and mentally. While some horses need the "edge" taken off, others get mad and irritated when they get tired, and while you may have "control," you will have a stiff, resistant, and definitely dull performance.

The best thing to do with the sort of horse who works himself up is to take him out again and again, each time doing only a small amount of work before returning to the stall (or trailer). Every time you take him back, you need to untack him completely and perhaps even give him a small bit of hay so that he thinks he has finished for the day. Let him relax and settle down and then an hour or so later take him out again. By about the second or third time, the horse will start to think that he has done a lot of work, and in this way you begin to wear him down mentally rather than tire him physically. He will start to think, "Oh, this again," and that will be the time his head drops a little and you can begin to put your legs on him and ask him to go forward. If you try to take him on while his mind is too keyed up, you will find that he rebels and uses his strength against you, and then you will wear each other out. Half the amount of energy used in the right direction would be enough to achieve the same result.

You may have to take him out three or four times to achieve the desired result, but if you succeed with this method at a couple of shows, the horse will learn to calm down and accept that there is nothing to be worried about. You will have shown him how to deal with his anxiety so that he can become more relaxed about the whole thing.

What if this is your horse's first show and you suddenly discover your horse is getting more and more nervous — what do you do? Very likely you are competing at Training Level at this point, so the simple thing to do is walk your horse a lot, try to keep him calm by being very calm yourself, and consider the tests as part of your warm-up.

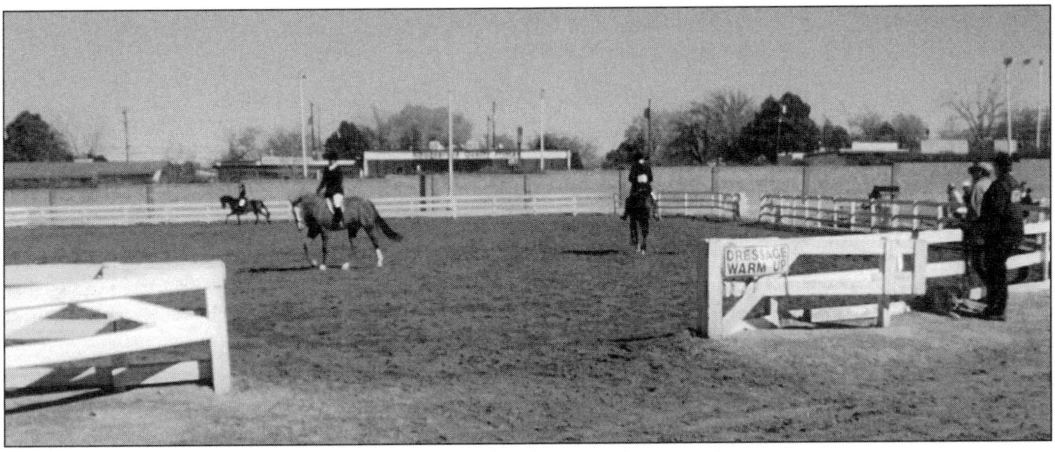

Figure 21.1 A comparatively uncrowded warm-up arena.

With the nervous or highly-strung horse, you need to be clear and consistent; don't pressure the horse or get too strong, just hold out quietly for what you want. A lot of riders become insecure in themselves when they feel that things are not working out; they begin to think that they must be doing something wrong and then change their tactics. If you change at the show, you may confuse the horse completely. If you keep your cool, you will usually achieve what you want.

Etiquette of the Warm-Up Arena

Schooling in a warm-up arena in a group can be chaotic and nerve-racking, even for veteran trainers. It can be downright scary when you're just venturing into the show world (figure 21.1).

The main rule is that all the while that you are warming up your horse, you must be aware of others in the warm-up ring. Be courteous to other exhibitors and do not disturb their horses by the actions of yourself or your horse. Usually they will be as courteous in return.

You may be used to working in a warm-up arena at a show that has mostly group classes, and most horses perform only at walk, trot, and canter. At these shows, the majority of riders will usually work in the same direction, either clockwise or counter-clockwise. Every so often, someone initiates a change of direction and most, if not all, the riders will reverse. Normal etiquette is that slower horses stay on the rail; if a horse must pass a slower horse, it is done toward the inside of the arena and the passing rider announces "inside." If a rider must pass next to the rail, they usually announce "outside," or simply "rail!" Riders should never pass very closely, especially head on.

At a dressage show, however, various horses are apt to be doing circles, figure eights, diagonals, and lateral work. It looks very chaotic, but if certain etiquette rules are observed, there are amazingly few close calls. The rules about passing when traveling in the same direction are the same as above. In addition, when traveling in opposite directions, you pass left shoulder to left shoulder (just like cars), and *look where you are going at all times.*

Horses doing extended gaits or lateral work have the "right-of-way," and slower horses should stay near the rail (when there is one). Plan halts for the center of the ring and be careful how you use your whip (don't "side-swipe" someone!).

Tune-Up

When your horse lets you know that he is "warmed up" by becoming relaxed and attentive, he is ready for a little "tune-up."

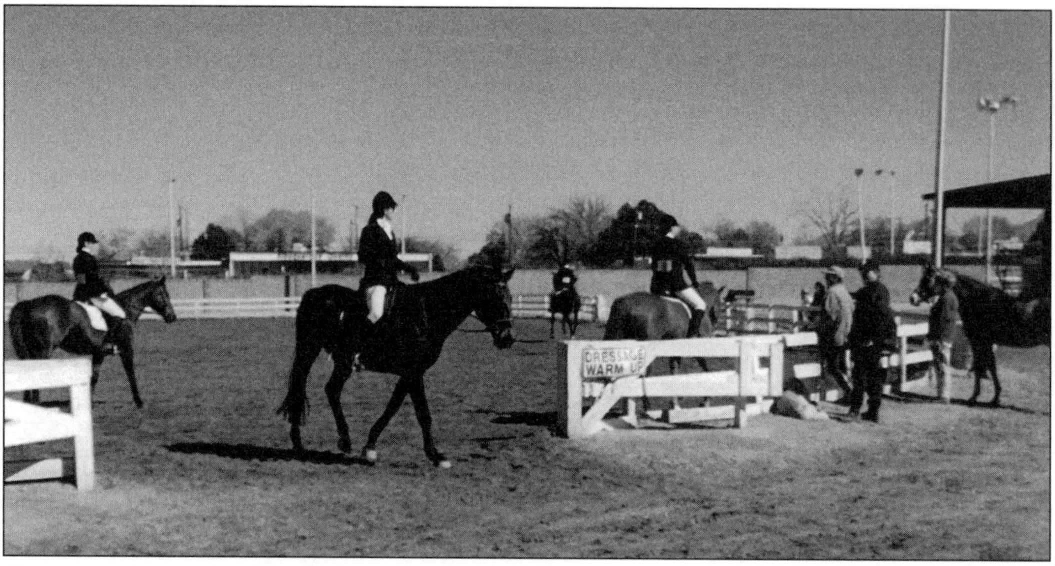

Figure 21.2 Time to head for the in-gate. Photo by the author.

Remember, do not try to do any last minute training at the show grounds. Your training was supposed to be done at home. At a show, your work session will be comprised of exercises designed to "tune the horse up" for the test that follows. They may be exercises to sharpen his responses or to focus his attention on the task at hand.

The riding of certain movements of the test in warm-up is to awaken the horse's memory, and, if need be, to sharpen his responses to a certain movement that he tends to be lazy about. For instance, the Training Level horse may need "sharpening up" for a prompt halt, or the First Level horse may need to be prepared for a lengthened trot as the first movement. If a horse has problems with a certain canter lead, a reminder may be necessary just before the test. Thus, the horse will not be surprised when asked to perform those movements in the test.

The rider will also have the opportunity to eliminate any unevenness, say between left and right leg yield and left and right circles. If the horse is having difficulties with movements during warm-up, the rider should always search for the cause, for only when the cause is known is a meaningful correction possible. However, after a movement is performed satisfactorily, one should not repeat it. Overly frequent repetition can only cause the movement to go bad during the test. **Do not leave your "best test" in the warm-up!** You need to know when to call it "ready."

Once you have done a few competitions, you will have quite a good idea about how your horse responds to changes of environment, and you will get to know what is the best time to take him to the in-gate for the test. You may need to vary your system the first few shows to find out what suits your particular horse best.

The Final Moments

At some point during your warm-up, you should have looked around the area to spot the horse that goes ahead of you. Keep an eye on this horse — when he goes to the in-gate for his ride you know you will be up soon.

Dressage competitions are scheduled to the minute. While they may get behind schedule, they can also catch up in a surprisingly short amount of time. It is your responsibility to present yourself at the in-gate on time. If you are late, you will probably be eliminated.

Should the show be running ahead of time, you cannot be required to ride ahead of your schedule, but management will appreciate it if you do. Your groom should occasionally check if the class is on time, or you can ride over to the gate person or ring steward and ask. About ten minutes before your ride time, you may want to pause on the outskirts of the warm-up area and have your groom wipe your horse's mouth and your boots and check his bridle and make sure all the keepers are fastened.

Your friend should have brought a towel, hoof pick, test book (if she is going to call your test), and your coat (if you're not wearing it). Be sure to remove all bandages or boots from the horse and have your test caller at the ready.

When the horse ahead of you enters for his test, you should make your way to the in-gate. (Gate persons get really nervous if you're not there.) Don't get so close to the arena that you distract the performing horse. Speak in low tones and don't make distracting movements (figure 21.2).

If you are late to the ring and the gate person says you're due in (the horse ahead of you has saluted), don't get flustered. You will have two to three minutes before the judge rings the bell and 60 seconds after that. You can pause for thirty seconds to take several deep breaths (they'll help you relax!) as your friend does her last-minute touch up.

You can enter the area around the outside of the dressage arena as soon as the rider ahead of you salutes. Take note of which way he or she will exit so you don't cross paths. You want to give your horse every possible opportunity to see the arena, the flowers, the judge's stand, the bleachers, and anything else he needs to look at. Be confident, your horse needs you to be calm and tell him what to do.

If you have a caller, be sure she knows her job and have her at ringside at the proper time. If your caller is late, but you know she is on the way, do not enter the perimeter of the arena until she gets there. If the judge whistles you in and your caller is not in place, you will have to continue without her. (It is considered "unauthorized assistance" for the caller to start after the test has begun to be judged.) Once you have entered the arena you may not speak to your caller, even if you get off course.

Chapter Twenty-Two

Ride Your Best Test

As your groom wipes your boots and checks that your coat collar and the horse's bridle are neat and straight (a crooked browband can make the horse's head look tilted), keep your eyes fixed on the arena. Imagine lines marking the arena in a perfect grid pattern, waiting for the test to be "drawn" in symmetrical circles and figures.

While you wait, ride the test in your mind's eye. To sharpen up before the moment of truth, "live the test" : the rhythm, the bends, and the authoritative half-halt at just the right moment. Visualize yourself as you watch another rider — you'll find yourself unconsciously applying the aids, going with the rhythms, and bracing your back.

Walk to the in-gate as the horse ahead of you nears the end of his test. Wait until the previous rider has completed her salute. As soon as you enter the perimeter of the arena, your caller should move into place, either at "E" or "B" (see Chapter 17).

You will need the full two or three minutes between tests to get your horse accustomed to the judge's box, flower decorations, or anything else near the arena that might unsettle him. You want him at his best for your entrance.

With some horses, you will slowly trot around the arena and let them look at the distractions; others you want to put on the aids and keep their mind on you and off any distractions that might alarm them. It is a good idea to check the "whoa" and "go" responses. You need to know at all times how much you need to do to stop and to start.

Trot up the side, then walk past the judge's box, turning and walking past it again so your horse can see it from both eyes. It is quite appropriate to greet the judge as you ride past (if he or she is not busy) with a "Good morning" (or afternoon). It demonstrates your confidence in being there. After showing your horse the judge's box, get in position for your final approach to "A". Of course, wait for the judge to ring the bell or blow a whistle.

Although you have a full minute after the bell to make your entrance — and if your horse needs the time, you should definitely take it — it's better to enter promptly. If you wait until the last seconds, the judge gets busy checking her watch to make sure you don't go over the time instead of looking positively at your horse.

The Test

The bell (or whistle) has sounded. You have your horse in his best working trot, he is listening to you, and you start running through your "checklist" of priorities:

1. Rhythm
2. Energy
3. Contact

You are ready. Map out your path so you can get lined up exactly on the centerline between "A" and "C". Do this by finding the exact center of the entrance and then making a loop that will take you very close to "A", so you only have to bend the horse a little to have him track right over your "spot." If your horse enters the gate at that exact spot, you know you have "A" directly behind you.

Now look up and make eye contact with the judge. Fixing your gaze on a specific point, in this case the judge, will keep you "aimed" straight on the centerline. It also communicates to the judge that you are confident.

Keep your head up and ride your horse in a "channel" between your hands and legs. The tops of his ears should frame the centerline. Feel his barrel to know if his body is straight. Use your legs evenly and enter boldly (figure 22.1).

If you enter with snap and zest, the horse is much less likely to drop behind the bit, or drift, or hollow to one side. Straightness and confidence are number one priorities.

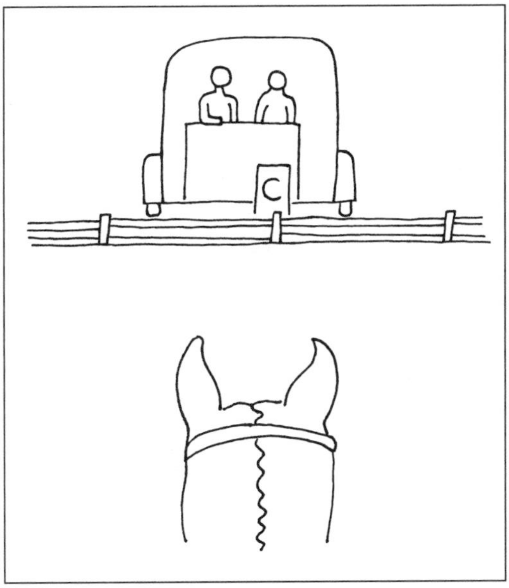

Figure 22.1 The view from "X".

You should know exactly how many strides it takes to get your horse to halt. Don't run up the centerline and suddenly lock the brakes! The judge will see your horse's head go up if the transition is too abrupt. You can glance very quickly to see where "E" or "B" is, but don't stare at the sidelines. Take a mental note of how far you have to go and start planning your halt. If you need two or three walk strides, think "walk" and put your body in walk mode. Keep it coming forward. Don't lose your straightness by meandering into the walk or pulling your horse to one side.

As you feel the walk materializing, keep asking with your hands and seat and you should have a smooth halt. If your horse is a bit resistant, keep asking a little stronger at each stride until you get it. Don't panic. Unless the arena floor is marked at "X," the judge will not know if you overshoot a stride or two. The importance of the movement is the quality of the transition. You will never get good scores producing a lousy halt even if it is exactly at "X" (figure 22.2).

If your horse has a habit of "dying" at the halt, or you feel the situation coming, keep your

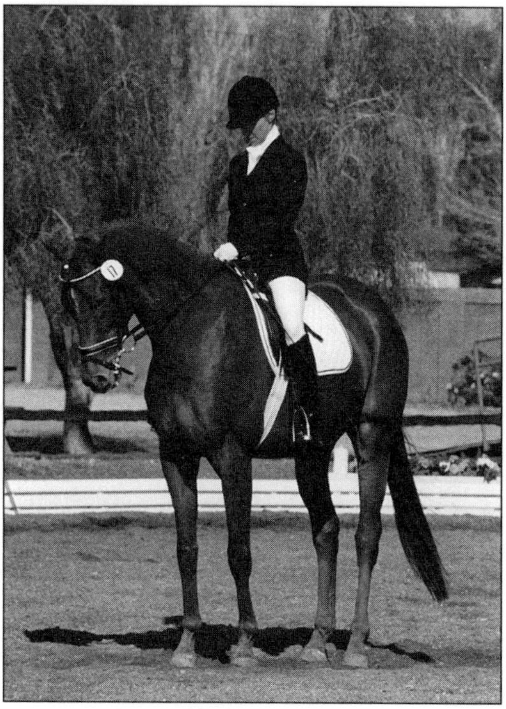

Photo 22.2 Scoring starts with the entrance and salute. Photo by Charlene Strickland.

legs on the horse and push him up to the halt (see Chapter 11 for more on the halt). Through all of this, clear through the halt, maintain eye contact with the judge.

Before your horse comes to a complete standstill and says to the judge, "This is my halt," check that he's halting square. If you feel a hind leg trailing, close your leg on that side, keeping the hand closed also.

Wait an instant to make sure you have a halt. If it feels crooked, don't try to adjust it. Immobility is the key requirement now. Never let the horse step backward. If the halt is not square, make a mental note that you need to practice it later.

Keep a feel on the reins to keep your horse steady, but sit heavy and think "halt." Don't make any moves that might communicate to your horse to move or shift his weight.

As you place your right rein into your left hand to prepare for the salute, try to keep the same feel in the horse's mouth. If he doesn't mind standing, pause for a second or two longer than you would on a fidgety horse. You don't want to drag out the halt, but showing that your horse stands obediently may earn you an extra point or two. As you pick up your right rein again, glance down briefly to make sure both reins are the correct length. If you felt your horse coming out of the halt, get going right away to make the departure look like your idea, and fix your reins at the trot.

The first forward step must be straight and energetic. Look ahead to convey that you're confident and feeling good about what you're going to do. Be careful not to drift to the opposite direction of the turn off centerline.

If you think your horse might spook at the judge's stand, firmly drive him up to the bit and then bend him a little early for the corner to keep him paying close attention to you. Don't leave your horse a choice of what he might do — tell him what to do. Look past what's worrying him. Ride toward a point, and if he hesitates, you can correct him before he shies.

Going down the long side, run through your checklist again:

1. Rhythm
2. Energy
3. Contact
4. The line of the test

Let's say the test calls for a 20-meter circle at "B". Begin to plan your circle as you approach "B". "Draw" the circle on the arena floor by finding the four outside points and riding a curved line between them. In the Standard arena, the letters are 12 meters apart (40 feet), so for a 20-meter (66-foot) diameter circle you must cross the centerline at a point approximately six feet inside the "odd" letters (R and S, V and P). For a 20-meter circle at "A" or "C," you would touch the track approximately 13 feet beyond the corner letter (M, K, H, or F) and cross the centerline six feet beyond the odd letters. You should know exactly where your figures should be "drawn" on the arena floor for any movements you need to do in your tests. This allows you to concentrate on keeping your horse "channeled" between your legs and hands and to keep reeling off your checklist.

The next movement may be a change of rein across the diagonal. This involves two corners and a straight line. Go as deeply into the corner as your horse can comfortably bend (and do aid him to bend), and then straighten and look up for your straight line. Again, go boldly on the straight lines to prevent your horse from drifting and wandering. From many practice turns, you should know exactly how much bend you need in the corner to come out "in line" with the diagonal.

On completion of the diagonal, drive your horse deeply into the corner — the rail should help to bend him, but you should still give the aids to bend. If you just let the horse follow the track around, he is likely to lean on his shoulder, or worse, counter-bend (look to the outside of the corner).

If this had been a lengthening of stride across the diagonal (First Level), you would shorten your horse, *then* bend him around the corner. Don't try to do two things at once — you will probably blow it.

Another word on lengthenings: if your horse is a little weak in the lengthening, build up to it gradually. If you come blasting out of the corner and then your horse "dies" by the time he gets to "X", it will be very disappointing to the judge. If you build to the lengthening, hold it for several strides in the middle of the arena before you fade, then still show a definite down transition. You will find that judges usually remember what they saw last. In addition, the transitions get a mark all their own, so you have got to show one in and one out.

If your horse has a good lengthening, definitely show it to the fullest. Prepare him in the corner, and go a stride or two past the letter if necessary before you straighten and lengthen. Maintain your rhythm and straightness and aim for the track a couple of strides before the letter. Don't forget to have good and definite transitions into and out of the lengthening — you need to show a difference in stride and frame. Don't throw a good lengthening away by never coming out of it.

Don't put your horse in a gait and then just sit there frozen — ride every stride according to your checklist:

1. Rhythm
2. Energy
3. Contact
4. Follow your game plan

Ride each movement to its fullest; prepare for the next movement at the proper time (not early, not late). The letter where a transition or movement is to happen is not where you *start* to ask for it. Prepare at the proper time, then it should happen at the letter.

When the test allows a transition or movement between two letters, use this space to your advantage. Where you will ask for it will depend on how responsive your horse is at that moment.

Halfway through one movement begin thinking what the next movement is. For instance, if you are finishing a diagonal of the arena and the next movement is "canter between A and K," plan for it so you can start preparing at the proper place. Don't get too far ahead of yourself, though. Don't be thinking about *all* the movements in the whole test. Think about the test one or two pieces at a time.

Pay special attention when striking off into the canter. Monitor the trot for a stride or two, look up, and try to appear confident, as though your horse never leads with the wrong leg, and if your aid is light but definite, he probably won't. Be sure he *is* on the correct lead. Should he not be, try not to lose your position or your composure, but quickly come back to trot again, organize the canter depart, and start again. Stay on the line of the movement, even if you have to go through a whole movement (say a circle) stopping and starting the canter. You will lose far fewer marks than if you continue on the wrong lead or have a lopsided circle.

Be confident at the walk. You have practiced the walk many times at home. Sit quietly, sit confidently, and ask for all the energy you can without exciting your horse — go for a 10!

If your horse breaks gait, quickly correct him and go on, perhaps being a little quieter with your aids (but don't stop riding)! It's crucial not to give up when something bad happens at the beginning of a movement. If your horse "breaks" at the beginning of the free walk, or the extended trot, or the canter, don't just figure that the movement is blown! Get him back and perform as much of the movement as you can. Some is better than none! The riders with polish and presence are the riders who never stop trying. Your best bet is to stay bold. A mistake on one movement won't change your final score that much. After a mistake, go for the big score on the next movement; you may be able to counterbalance the effect of the mistake. The test isn't over until the final salute. Each movement gets a score, so don't throw any of them away needlessly.

It is true that in very advanced classes, minor errors can mean the difference between a ribbon or none, but there are occasions when you may make some errors, and everyone else will make more of them!

Many novices ride the test instead of the horse. They appear to hurry from letter to letter, in an apparent attempt to "get it over with." The test becomes a series of disconnected movements done in robot fashion. Slow down! You have worked long and hard for these few minutes in front of the judge. Make the most of them. Your riding (position and aids) should be automatic by now, so keep reeling off your checklist in your mind. Each gait, each movement, each transition should contain the four elements. More than likely the judge is clicking off the same list. This gives your mind something to focus on — and you won't have time to be nervous or uncomfortable. Once your mind is engaged, your body automatically relaxes and frees your reflexes to act instinctively.

Ride each movement to the fullest. An example: your corners. The corner is your time to set up for the next movement. It is very important at all levels not to cut your corners or fall in on the corners. You can't coast through the short side of the ring — use this time to prepare your horse for the next movement.

- If your horse is getting a little strung out, do half-halts. If you feel he is not straight going down the rail, it is easier to bring his forehand in slightly rather than to try to push his quarters back into line.
- If the next movement is a lengthening, use the short side to get good collection. The quality of the lengthening is dependent on the quality of the collection.
- On a diagonal, go from letter to letter. Point the horse to a place on the opposite long side about half a horse length from the letter; that way, you will turn onto the side so that your body passes the letter. Many novices aim directly at the letter, and then "cram" their horses too deeply into the corner.
- If it is a posting diagonal, don't change your posting at "X" — continue on the same diagonal to the long side.
- It is better to have a transition or movement a bit early — seen as responsive — than late — seen as disobedient.
- Get a slight bend in the proper direction a stride or two *before* a circle.
- Continually check the tempo; especially if the horse is lazy.
- If your horse gets quick, take a deep breath and relax, and slow your seat aids.

Use the ends of the arena to re-establish roundness. Use the long sides to steady the rhythm and tempo, use the corners and short side to collect or rebalance or soften.

- Remember to breathe deeply and regularly.

Keep trying to improve your performance. Often horses go around the arena tensely or above the bit. Sometimes they are lacking impulsion, attention, or obedience. What is worse is that often the rider placidly accepts these shortcomings and goes through the motions of the test without ever having attempted the correction of their mounts. In many cases, it only takes a few seconds to re-establish your rapport, win your horse's attention, or relax and supple him. You should do it when at all possible.

The Unexpected

If you get "off course" — that is, deviate from the line of the prescribed movement (turn left instead of right for instance) — this will usually be caught by the judge, who will ring the bell, and you must stop. If you go off course, your caller *may not* correct you. The judge must signal you to stop and give you instructions on how or where to proceed. Your caller should take up reading the test at the point the judge designates.

You will lose two points on the first "off course," four for the second, and eight for the third. With the fourth error you are eliminated but are usually allowed (time permitting) to finish your test. If you make an "error of course" and the bell is sounded, you (usually) get to repeat that movement, and it gets a score for the second attempt.

Do not, no matter what, repeat a movement *unless the judge tells you to. "The judge must consider the first movement shown only and, at the same time, penalties for an error of course."* (AHSA, Art. 1922.4.3)

If you have a caller, she must read the test exactly as it is written. You may not speak to your caller (or anyone else) while riding your test. Only speak to the judge if spoken to.

If you can't hear your caller, a pre-arranged signal, for instance a look directly at the caller, is all you can do. In most instances, the judge will not object if the caller repeats a movement if it is clear that the rider did not hear.

If you know you are off course, and the judge does not realize it, stop, ride to the judge and explain you are off course, and ask the judge to direct you where to go.

If your mind goes blank during a test (and you have no caller), just continue whatever you are doing along the track and hope the pattern will come back to you. In many cases, you will remember in a second or two, and the judge may think you made a slightly delayed transition.

If a piece of equipment breaks during a test, you *may not* have someone come into the arena to fix it ("unauthorized assistance"). You may try to adjust it yourself, ride on as best you can, or ask for permission (from the judge at "C") to be excused.

If, during the test, the horse leaves the arena (all four feet outside the fence or line marking the arena perimeter), the competitor is eliminated. Pause for the judge to excuse you, then quietly exit the area. Never make a show of punishing the horse. It is not his fault he went wrong; it is yours.

Never blow your cool. Always appear to be in control, at least of your own composure. "Make like a duck" — cool and calm above the surface, while paddlin' like ... under the water!

Save Something for the Final Movements

Athletes know that the race is not over until the last lap has been run. When watching riders go through the movements of their tests, it often is obvious that, at a certain point, an

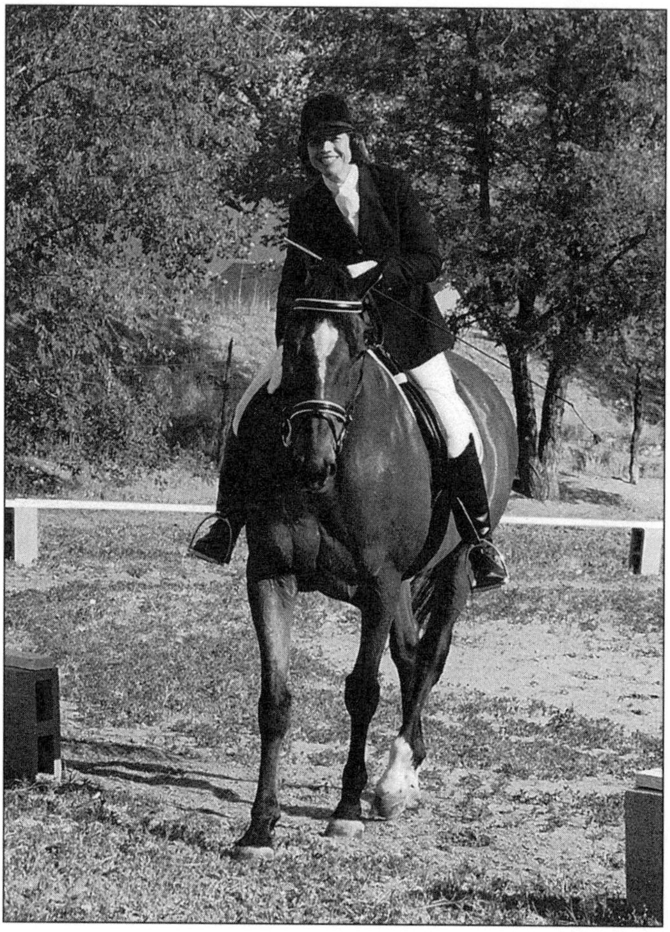

Photo 22.3 Let your horse know you appreciate his effort. Photo by Charlene Strickland.

emotional change takes place.

One can discern these rider's thoughts: "I have it made." "From here on it's a piece of cake." With these thoughts in mind, the scores usually go down until the rider's final halt is a spraddled out afterthought. If it has been a particularly difficult test, their expression clearly states, "Thank heavens. It is finally over."

Remember that your final impression is as important as your first. The last diagonal — regular, straight, well forward — a well-bent turn at "A"; an energetic advance, straight on the centerline; and a balanced halt will not only determine the score for the final movements, but will also influence the Collective Marks. Ride the entire test!

A word about the final turn up the centerline for the completion of the test. This turn is half of a 10-meter circle. This is a difficult move for the Training Level horse. To turn onto the centerline from the long side, think of a "U" turn, unless your horse is very good, don't go into the corner, but rather start the turn at the last letter. Try not to overshoot the centerline. To get your horse around, use rhythmic half-halts on the inside rein while supporting the horse with the outside rein and a strong inside leg.

Your pass up the final centerline should be as bold and confident as your entrance (rhythm

— energy — contact!). Be precise and positive with your final halt, and after the salute don't act as if it's a major miracle you completed the test! A judge who sees a rider explode with sighs of relief and apparent astonishment upon successfully completing a test, may drop that rider down a couple of marks in the Collective Marks, "Because she obviously didn't think she belonged there, if she is so surprised they got around."

You may pat your horse appreciatively after a good round, smile, and leave the ring as though you're the Queen of England! Let your face show a well-earned expression of satisfaction over a job well done. Thereafter, leave the ring with an active walk on a long rein. You may walk forward after the salute and walk around the track to "A", or you may make a generous turn at "X" and proceed directly toward "A". Do not make an additional circle before you exit. The judging is over and the show probably has a tight schedule to keep (figure 22.3).

So, there you have it. Dressage tests are really not that difficult once you "get your feet wet" and get over the "stage fright" of showing alone in the ring (dressage spectators are amazingly compassionate *they* have usually gone through the same insecurities as you).

These are only a few suggestions. It probably took longer to read this than it will take to ride it, but that is how it is. One more thing: When you finish a test, or a work session, and you are satisfied with it, pat yourself on the back or do a thumbs up or a "whoopee" (quietly if you're near the arena!) After all, you *did* make it through the test! At a competition, congratulate yourself before you check your scores. Ultimately, the ride may get a very good score, or it may not, but you are the only person who needs to be pleased with the performance.

Chapter Twenty-Three

Evaluating Your Test

You will get your test sheet back after the class is completed, and you should go over this carefully to see where you went wrong, what you did right, and where your weak points are. Read the comments carefully. Don't be disappointed if you have a lot of 5's. Fives mean you did what the test required, but "barely." "Fairly Good" performances receive 6's and 7's. 7's and 8's are really outstanding. Compare your performance as you remember riding it with the "Remarks" put down by the judge's secretary ("scribe"). These are meant to help you in your further training. Under the "Collective Marks" are four additional marks that reflect the judge's opinion of your "basics."

Don't get upset with the comments about "this wasn't right" and "that wasn't right" with your test. It is a whole lot easier for the judge to tell you what was less than desirable (less than perfect?) than to list all the things you probably did right! Often you must infer — especially with 6's and above; if no comment was made, it must have been at least "acceptable."

Don't take every comment as an insult or criticism. Very often the judge will give you a decent mark for a movement, and then comment on how it "could be better." This is not contradictory. For example, many judges talk about the shape of circles: "not round," "flat-sided," "egg-shaped," but discount it as "poor steering;" in other words, it was not the horse's fault, it was the rider's fault. It appeared that the horse went exactly where the rider told him to go!

Also, don't get hung up on the numbers. Each judge seems to have their own idea of what the numbers mean, but this is because some judges have higher expectations than others do. If the judging was fair, the horses will be placed in the order of their excellence on that particular day.

Judges are warned not to give a "riding lesson" (although many times they are tempted to!) on a test. The judge is supposed to tell you what is wrong (and right), but is cautioned not to tell you how to fix it — that is the realm of your trainer or instructor. In other words, judges are to state what they see and not what they think is the cause of the behavior. The fact that many judges offer hints and maybe even suggestions on how your performance can be improved is very much appreciated by all exhibitors. However, these comments are always sketchy and can even be misleading because no two horses are temperamentally alike or have the same background.

Another problem is that comments must be brief so the scribe (judge's secretary) has time and space to write them down. Refer to the Sidebar below for a listing of common scribe abbreviations.

Don't get hung up on placings. While other horses may *place* over you, remember: a dressage test score should reflect the true merit of the performance, while the placings categorize the horses that happen to be in that class that day. A good performance (score) remains a good score, whether it took first place or last! Just because someone rides better than you doesn't make you a bad rider. Conversely, just because you ride better than someone doesn't necessarily make you a good rider. It's all relative.

Fix the 4's

"The mark for each movement should first establish the fact of whether the movement is performed insufficiently ("4" or below) or sufficiently ("5" or above)." (AHSA, Art. 1922.6.1)

So, logically, focus on any 4's (or below) that you may have gotten. These should have sufficient comments to give you an idea of where to begin to fix them. Eliminating the cause of any 4's will raise the score to a

Glossary of Common Scribe's Abbreviations

Although scribes are not required to use these terms, they must be able to record comments swiftly and accurately. Thus, some form of easy-to-decipher "shorthand" is necessary.

abr	abrupt	f/hand	forehand	reg	regular
@	at	fwd	forward	res	resistance
attn	attentive	gd	good	rhy	rhythm
bk	back	ht	halt	rt	right
bal	balance	ha	haunches	sal	salute
bt	beat	h-in	haunches-in	satis	satisfactory
b/f	before	hd tilt	head tilted	serp	serpentine
b/hd	behind	h/legs	hindlegs	sh-in	shoulder-in
bend	bending	hur	hurried	sl, s/t	slight, slightly
bet	better	imp	impulsion	sm	small
b/t	between	inattn	inattentive	str	straight
cad	cadence	incomp	incomplete	□	square
ct/can	canter	inw	inward	thru	through
c-l	centerline	irreg	irregular	trans	transition
o	circle	lack imp	lack impulsion	tr	trot
col	collected	lat	lateral	tu ha	turn on haunches
cor	corner	ld	lead	tu for	turn on forehand
crkd	crooked	l	left	unstd hd	unsteady head
dpt	depart	ltr	letter	unus	unusual
dia	diagonal	not □	not square	us	usual, usually
dir	direction	obv	obvious	vert	vertical
disob	disobedient	ord	ordinary	v	very, volte
eng	engaged, engagement	outw	outward	~	weaving
ext	extended, extension	pos	position	w/	with
flex	flexed, flexion	prec	precise	wr	wrong

"sufficient" level. Next, concentrate on any 5's.

Elizabeth Searle, an "S" judge and an instructor in the USDF "L" Program, once said, "A '5' means the movement was *'barely' sufficient*, and a '6' is *'perfectly' satisfactory*." Look them up in the dictionary — "sufficient" and "satisfactory" have the same definition! So if you're getting a lot of 5's and possibly an occasional 4, work on getting those up to 6's, because every horse is capable of 6's.

Work on your problems one at a time — don't confuse your horse with half a dozen "cures" at once. Don't get in a hurry; nothing of lasting value comes fast.

Your major weakness may not be strictly a training error. If, for instance, you keep getting comments like "weaving on centerline," or "circle not round," or "loss of balance in corner," those are *rider* problems. *You* need to practice straight lines or "plan" your circles and corners. If your horse is anxious or inattentive, perhaps you need to work out a better warm-up for your horse. You want your horse paying attention to you but not tired or cranky from overwork.

Maybe you just need to ride more aggressively. A conservative, mistake-free ride will almost always get you 5's — you did the movement "sufficiently," but the judge would like to see *more*. Besides, if you ride too conservatively, that leaves no room for mistakes. If you get all 5's but maybe *one* 4, that will put you below 50%. Certainly not a disgrace, but discouraging to some people.

One last caution: you must not expect your horse to respond as well as he does at home or at lessons. Many trainers comment that on the average, a horse is 20 percent below potential when performing at a show. This varies from horse to horse, of course. If you tend to expect your horse to do the best of which he is capable on each movement, you will be disappointed. Naturally he is not going to be 100% when he does a series of movements, one after another, in a space of five or six minutes. In fact, you cannot expect him to even do his best on most movements when he is in unfamiliar surroundings and his rider is as nervous as he is. So, do not expect too much at first. Training Level is designed to be just that — training for horse and rider. If you and your horse do as well as you can reasonably expect, be satisfied, regardless of your score. Read the judge's comments thoroughly and discuss the score sheet with your trainer after the class is over if you do not understand something. Then resolve to work hard and ride a better test the next time.

Videos

"A picture is worth a thousand words," so have as many tests as possible videotaped. Many shows have a professional person there, and it is well worth the fee. Another appropriate phrase is "seeing is believing." Often, our instructors tell us over and over what we need to correct, but we either don't understand exactly what they are trying to tell us, or we don't realize the impact of the correction until we see it.

Some tips:

View your tests in private. We are tempted to give excuses ("the horse wasn't listening" or "the judge was blind" are always good ones), and get defensive in company.

View as if you are watching a complete stranger on a horse you never saw before. You must detach yourself to be completely honest.

Read through the test comments before you view the video. Maybe they will tell you what to look for, maybe they won't.

As you watch your tape, go through the following list, perhaps one item at each viewing, to discover your greatest problem.

1. **Energy level.** Is the horse stepping into or near his tracks? Is there a moment of suspension? Does the walk look "marching" or "determined"? Is the canter lively and balanced?

2. **Accuracy.** Are your straight lines (including diagonals) perfectly straight and your circles the right size and perfectly round? If you're weaving or crooked on the straight, your horse will not be exhibiting his best gaits. If your circles are not evenly bent, is it because your horse is not bending, or is it because you aren't steering correctly? Both will lose you points.

3. **Rhythm and tempo.** Some judges use rhythm and tempo interchangeably. Remember: "tempo" is the *speed* of the rhythm. Is the tempo even? Or does it speed up and slow down? It needs to be perfectly consistent.

Also, check that the tempo is correct for your horse. Find the tempo where he has maximum stride without looking "rushed." If the tempo is "too quick," the horse will go "on his forehand;" if too slow, he will look lazy.

4. **Is the horse in a good "frame"?** Is he consistently above or behind the bit? Is his neck shortened? Is he pulling on your hands? Do you get comments like "horse not enough 'through'" or "horse not connected"? If the answer is "yes" to any of these, you need to find a correction and be able to use it while riding a test.

5. **Are your transitions smooth?** "Abrupt" transitions usually mean the horse "fell" onto his forehand or almost stopped. "Above bit" in the canter depart usually means the horse was on his forehand *before* the transition and had to throw his head up to move into the canter.

6. **Entrance and halt.** This is only one movement, but it is a very important one. The score for this movement often "sets the mood" for the rest of the test. Although technically you are not "judged" until you enter at "A", in reality, the judge is watching you come around the last corner on your approach. She is noting the energy, the frame, the tempo, everything about your mount. Consider yourself being judged as soon as you ride around the outside of the arena.

7. Also, be critical of **your position on the horse.** Are you projecting a confident, comfortable, correct picture? If not, you need to work on this. If you get comments like "rider lacks confidence," but you feel confident and comfortable on that particular horse, remember that you must *look* confident on the horse. "Confident" riders sit tall and straight. If you correct your image, your scores could go up one point on almost every movement, a total of ten to twelve points!

Terminology, Misconceptions, and "Dressage Talk"

Some of the "dressage talk" one hears is incorrect, misleading, confusing, or occasionally amusing, especially if one understands how horses actually operate biomechanically.

Much of our terminology has perfectly normal, non-dressage definitions, but many terms having "normal" dictionary definitions are brought into use with a special meaning for dressage. This has led to misuse of some terms and therefore misunderstanding of the underlying concepts.

When in doubt as to what the judge means, use the *USDF Glossary of Dressage Judging Terms.* It was compiled by judges for judges and exhibitors to address the divergence of usage among judges and the confusion engendered by literal (but sometimes inaccurate) translations from other languages and other disciplines.

The Ten Most Common Judge's Comments

1. **"Not enough forward"; "not enough impulsion"; "not enough engagement"; "incorrect tempo":**

"Needs more forward" is not an accurate expression, yet many judges still use it (figure 23.1).

The "dressage" meaning of *"forward"* is: "to or toward the direction that is ahead of or in front of the horse, or moving or tending toward that direction." (USDF Glossary)

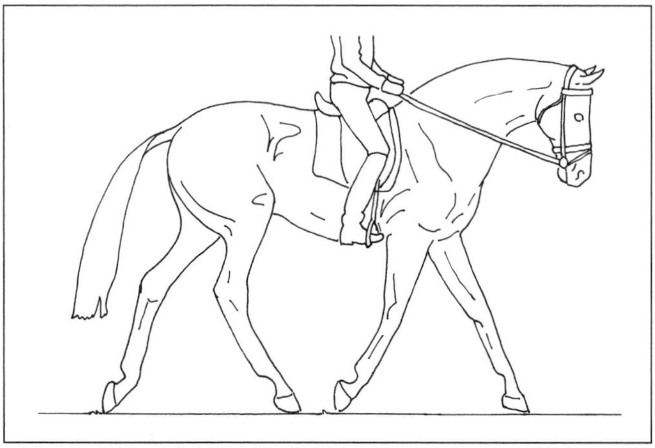

Figure 23.1 This horse has lowered his head, flexed at the poll, and is on the bit, but there is no impulsion. Note that all four feet are touching the ground. This would probably score a "5".

According to *Webster's Dictionary*, "Forward" should indicate *where* the horse goes, not how he gets there. That not withstanding, "needs more forward" is a common expression to indicate the need for more energy, tempo, or stride length.

In other words, the horse must give the impression of going in a forward direction with energy. This would be opposed to the horse who looks like it wants to "suck back" or stop.

If you get comments like "horse needs to go more forward" or something similar, it *usually* means not enough energy. The common reaction of the rider is to "put more leg on" the horse and hope that improves the scores, but often it doesn't. The horse just "runs onto his forehand."

The expression "working gaits" (see Chapter 12) doesn't mean you hurry your horse along; it means the horse's most attractive gaits for his level of fitness and balance. If you drive him beyond his ability to carry himself, you will only cause him to fall onto his forehand and "hurry." Each step will become not a thrust but a scramble to maintain his balance.

"Not enough forward" does not *always* mean "not enough energy." It is possible for the horse to have lots of energy and not be going forward! The most common case is when the horse is being held in by the rider, which is usually demonstrated by the horse going above or behind the bit (see Number 3 on this list).

Maybe he *is* lazy: be sure he is responding to your leg without rushing. Refer to Chapter 11, "All the Horse Needs to Know."

Sometimes judges will comment: "not tracking up." It was once a requirement of working trot that the horse "track up;" that is, at the trot the hind foot should step neatly into the track left by the front foot. Some horses cannot "track up" because of their conformation. If the horse "appears" to be capable of tracking up, but looks either lazy or stiff, the judge may make this simple comment to draw the attention of the rider to the fact that the horse should do better.

What you need to do is figure out the cause of "not enough." It could be that the horse cannot deliver full energy "forward" because he is going sideways. Likewise, he cannot get full lengthening (or mediums) if he is "crooked" (see Number 6).

Alternatively, maybe he's stiff through his back, neck, or poll. If he's "braced" in the bridle, the energy is being "blocked" in his spine. A horse must "swing" his back to achieve a "free" ground-covering stride (see Number 4, "Throughness").

The correction depends on whether the horse is lazy, stiff, or crooked. If a horse appears lazy and lacking impulsion and will not put itself out to take a good length of stride, this horse must be "woken up" with the use of the schooling whip so that he then has more energy to take him forward.

The stiff horse may be the complete opposite, but because he is tense and headstrong, the rider has to constantly restrain him.

Instead of taking long strides, the horse will take short hurried steps that cover little ground — with little "forward" progress.

This horse must first be brought down to a slower tempo by quiet slow work. Only when relaxed will he then begin to make longer steps, which may take quite a while to obtain. It does take a good deal of patience and constant correction. The horse should also be encouraged to lower his head and neck, which will come with the relaxation and will also help with this situation.

To develop more thrust from the hind legs, the rider must first put them in the right place. This means correcting the balance and straightness and developing muscle.

Many judges use the comment "transition not forward." An example of this is the horse that goes from the trot to the walk by way of an "almost" halt. The rider must ride the horse "forward" throughout the transition (see Chapter 11).

Many judges speak of "lack of engagement." Technically, engagement is not a requirement until Second Level, but it is necessary, at least in a small degree, from the very beginning.

"Engagement" is the support phase and shock absorption phase of the stride (approximately the first half of the ground time), in which the joints of the supporting hind leg are flexed and the leg is carrying proportionately more of the horse's weight; it is compression and support behind. It is the storing of energy. It is the prerequisite to "impulsion."

The USDF definition of "engagement" is: "increased flexion of the joints of the hind legs and the lumbosacral joint during the moment of support, causing a relative lowering of the croup/raising of the forehand, with the hind legs supporting a relatively greater proportion of the load. A prerequisite for thrust/impulsion." (USDF Glossary)

Energy is stored in the compressed hind leg(s) as in a compressed spring. The judge's visual indicator is the degree of flexion of the hind leg which is *grounded* and bearing weight, and the position of the trailing hind leg when it leaves the ground.

Articulating or bending of the hock of the raised hind leg is not engagement — it is "activity," articulation, bending of the hocks, or "hock action."

"Impulsion is the term used to describe the transmission of an eager and energetic, yet controlled, propulsive energy generated from the hindquarters into the athletic movement of the horse." (AHSA, Art. 1916) Technically, "impulsion" is not a requirement until Second Level. A prime ingredient of impulsion is the time the horse spends in the air rather than on the ground.

Impulsion should not be confused with mere speed, however, for it is largely a matter of how the horse responds to his rider's impulsive aids at all paces, particularly by engaging his hindquarters well under him.

"**Hurried**," "**hasty**," "**quick**," "**rushed**," "**rapid**" all refer to quickness of tempo and usually mean that the horse is rushing along without showing any real rhythm.

To correct this, first slow down, even if it feels as though you have no impulsion. If the "tempo is too fast," this means the horse is taking too many steps per minute. A freely moving horse will advance with a good tempo. A tense horse (see Number 10) will take short steps, and if urged to increase his speed, he will increase his tempo also. That is, he will take more quick, short steps per minute in order to go faster. Too quick a tempo is a symptom of being "on the forehand."

2. **"On the forehand"; "need better balance"; "not in self-carriage":**

"On the forehand" means "longitudinal poor balance; the horse places too much weight on the forelegs for the task at hand." (USDF)

Essentially, it means that the horse is

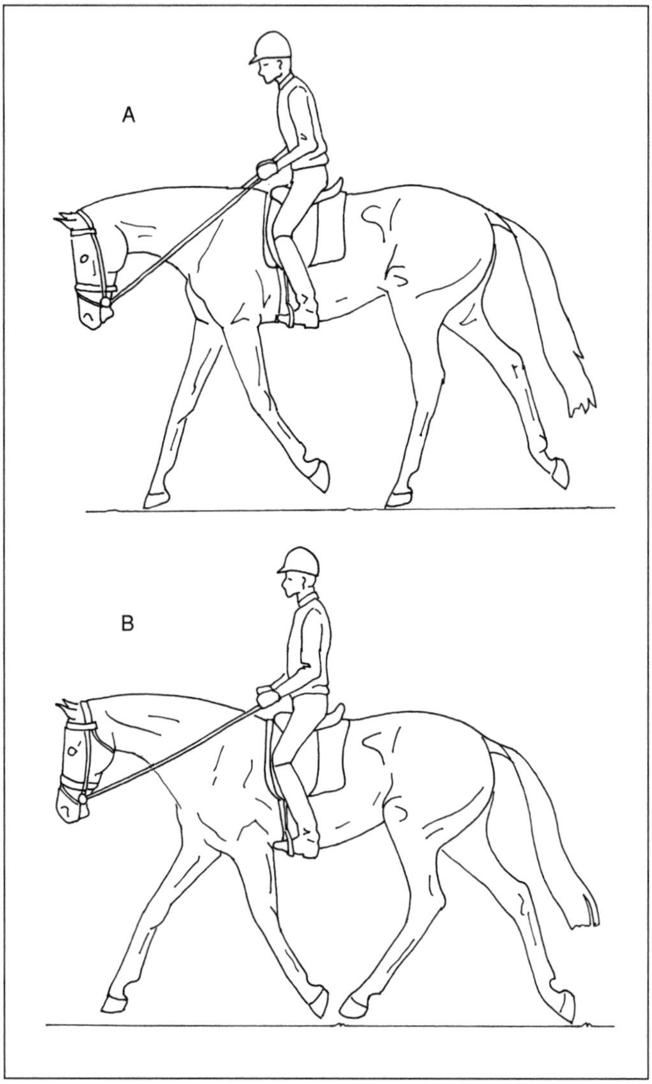

Figure 23.2 "On the forehand" is characterized by the horse "stabbing" his feet into the ground (A). It can be caused by the rider leaning forward. (B) is the same Training Level horse balanced by half-halts.

dilemma.

The visual clue to being on the forehand is that the forelegs are grounded too long, thus making it difficult, if not impossible, for the hind legs to step into the proper spot (still occupied by the forefeet). This results in no place for the hind legs to step, so:

a. They step short ("stabbing hind legs")

b. The haunches go to one side ("crooked")

c. They go wide ("wide behind")

d. The gait becomes impure ("uneven")

On the forehand is a lack of "self-carriage." "Self-carriage" is: "state in which the horse carries itself without taking support or balancing on the rider's hand." (USDF)

We do not expect the same kind of balance that would indicate "collection" in the Training or First Level horse. The Training Level horse should be in "horizontal balance," however, carrying an approximate amount of weight on the fore- and hind legs (figure 23.2).

If the comments are "on the forehand," the usual tendency is to try to "hold the horse up" with the reins, which doesn't work. You need to get to the root cause of the problem.

If your horse is leaning on your hands, or what some riders call "pulling" on your hands, the horse is probably on his forehand. *Do not fiddle with the reins* (unless one good tap will get him "off" your hands). Instead, tune him in to your *legs*. Use changes in direction and bend, with sharp taps of the leg to get him back

operating under the effect of momentum or gravity. Usually the horse's head is too low, but a horse can have a high poll (with a vertical face — "high head set") and *still* be very much "on the forehand" because of sagged withers.

Actually, *all* horses are built heavier on the forehand, simply because that is the heaviest part of their anatomy. When left to their natural state, this is not a problem, but when a rider is added to the picture, it becomes a balancing in self-carriage. At all times, the horse must accept the bit with an elastic contact. See Chapter 6, "The Horse", for additional corrections.

Another cause for being on the forehand can be the rider perching forward. This puts more weight on the horse's forehand, as well as not letting the rider use her seat and legs to best effect (see Chapter 9, "The Rider").

Sometimes the saddle is too far forward over the horse's shoulders (see Chapter 7, "Equipment"). By moving the saddle and rider back a couple of inches you can sometimes improve the look of the whole picture, and more importantly, give the rider a chance to influence the haunches more and lighten the forehand, making the horse more comfortable in the process.

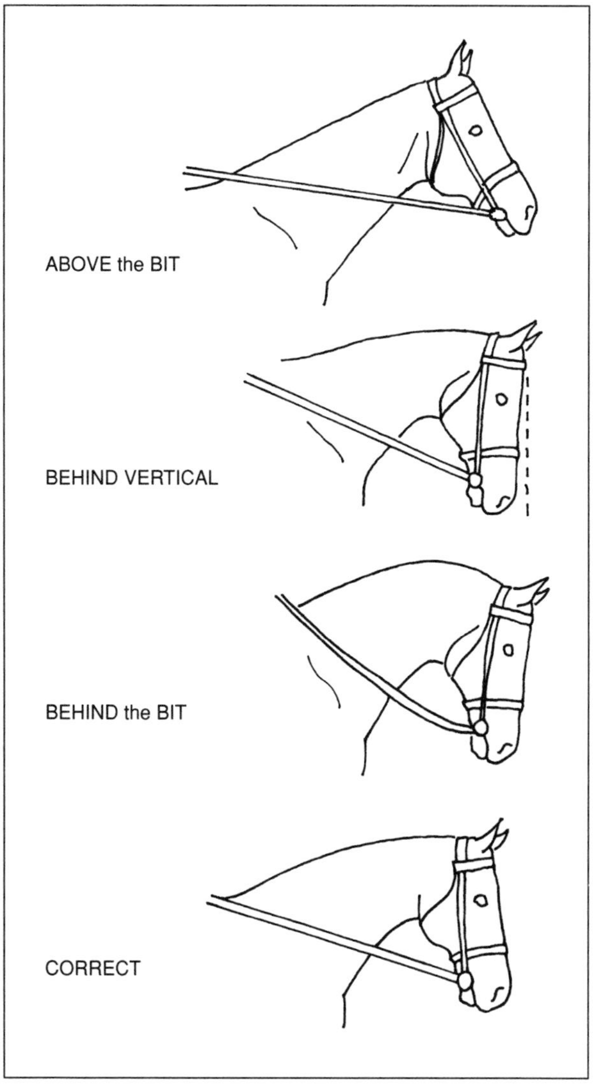

Figure 23.3 Above, behind, and correct on the bit.

"Balance" is: "the relative distribution of the weight of horse and rider upon the fore and hind legs (longitudinal balance), and the left and right legs (lateral balance). The horse is in good balance when the weight is distributed evenly left and right, and sufficiently toward the rear legs that it can easily manage the task at hand. (No matter what the level.) Loss of balance means the sudden increase of weight onto the forehand and/or to one side." (USDF Glossary)

If the horse is "well balanced," he does the various movements and figures smoothly and easily without stumbling or lurching or leaning on the bit. Some horses are naturally athletic and agile; others seem clumsy and awkward and lose their rhythm at the slightest difficulty.

Momentary loss of balance is not necessarily a great crime, so long as the horse was balanced (most of the time) in the first place, but if the balance is lost for any length of time, many things can go wrong. The horse will probably alter rhythm, be irregular in the stride, come off the bit, fall on the forehand, and the like. All these problems will lose the rider many points.

Corrections for these problems are keeping the horse straight (see Chapter 11), keeping the tempo correct and even, and bending the horse on circles and curves.

3. **"Above the bit"; "behind the bit (vertically);" "unsteady head":**

The horse must first of all *accept the bit.* That is, he must go willingly forward against a lightly stretched rein and must not in any way fight or avoid the contact of the bit on the bars of his mouth. He must not fight it by tossing or shaking his head, or avoid it by raising his head (above the bit), poking his nose, opening his mouth, or tucking his chin into his chest. Of course, he must not go to the other extreme and pull, or lean on the bit and expect the rider to hold his head up for him. His head must be steady. He should have a wet mouth, and if he chews the bit and drips foam, so much the better (figure 23.3).

With older horses that are just being started in dressage, a hard mouth is a common problem, and the horse must be taught to loosen his jaw before he can have a good contact (see Chapter 11).

On the other hand, the position — the angle of the face plus the height, bending (arching) and angle of the neck — should never be "fixed" or "set," that is, stiff and static.

Where the head is carried is dependent on the stage of training (or lack of it) and conformation. A steady head carriage is only achieved by good balance and the correct acceptance of the bit.

Balace must be maintained by the rider if

Terms and Phrases Applying to Head Carriage

Position — The direction in which the horse looks, especially on curved lines.

Nodding Head — This non-lameness issue gives the appearance that the horse nods (as though lame), but at *every beat* of the trot. It can be caused by the use of draw reins or other gadgets. The horse learns to "nod" to compensate for the lack of freedom to the head and neck. It can be caused by weakness in the back and loin, appearing to "throw" himself forward rather than lifting with the hind legs. The rider needs to develop the horse's muscles in the back so the horse can transfer more weight to his hindquarters.

Circling Nose in Canter — Another manifestation of the above.

Unsteady Head — Horse usually alternates between above and behind the bit. The horse is seeking evasion of the influence of the bit.

Above the bit — The horse's face usually goes in front of the perpendicular, the rein is taut and the neck goes stiff or inverted, the back hollows, and the hind legs make short stiff strides.

Behind the Bit, Behind the Vertical — Usually the horse drops contact on the bit, the face goes behind the vertical. The horse is holding back, both physically and mentally. Usual correction is to push the horse forward to a sympathetic hand.

Leaning on the Bit — same as leaning on the forehand.

Bracing the Neck or Shortened Neck — similar to Above the Bit. It is more a stiffness or tension than a resistance.

Over Bent — Horse bends at the third vertebra instead of at the poll — same as "Behind the Vertical."

Chewing the Bit — In a relaxed movement, the horse works the bit around with his tongue, usually creating saliva. Not the same as "Open Mouth," which is a resistance.

Wagging — This is usually seen when the rider purposely seesaws the head side to side in an attempt to "lighten" the contact. It may work initially, but the rider should not do it in the competition arena.

Unsteady Head — Describes the lack of steadiness of the head carriage, not to be confused with a *still* head carriage. Some horses may be unsteady in their head carriage throughout the test. Some may be unsteady due to a loss of balance in the difficulty of a movement.

Tilting Head — Means the head is slanted to the right or to the left. This is not just faulty head position but an evasion in which the horse avoids contact on one side of the mouth, thus avoiding stretching the musculature on one side of the body (figure 23.4).

the horse is to be able to control his neck and head, which he will use naturally to balance himself. By being at the correct speed and in rhythm, any movement the horse will need to make will be minimal, so the rider is able to ask him to keep his head comparatively still (according to the gait and movement).

4. **"Not coming through," "not connected," "lacks suppleness"**: "Throughness" is "the supple, elastic, unblocked, connected state of the horse's musculature that permits an unrestricted flow of energy from back to front and front to back, which allows the aids/influences to freely affect all parts of the horse (e.g., the rein aids go through and reach and influence the hind legs). Synonymous with the German term 'Durchlaessigkeit,' or 'throughletting-ness'." (USDF Glossary)

The judge can discern horses that are not coming "through" because their backs appear rigid. They are not moving with suppleness

Figure 23.4
Tilting head.

and the hocks don't "connect" up to the bit; half-halts aren't going "through." In other words, nothing really runs back from the bridle to the hocks, because nothing connects from the hocks to the bridle. The rider cannot affect the horse unless she is somewhat harsh and must supplement the seat aids with her hands.

The horse's spine, between withers and hindquarters, has very little flexibility (see Number 7, "Bend"). The horse may move, and many do move, by use of the legs alone, in which case the back is like a rigid girder, connecting forehand and quarters, whereon the rider must sit in comparative discomfort. A horse can move, and when well-trained and well-ridden should move, so that the muscles of the back bend and flex in unison with those of the legs.

A "swinging" back is "the alternating rhythmic contraction and stretching of the long back muscles, first on one side, then the other, which give springiness and elasticity to the horse's movements, and allows the thrust from the hind legs to 'come through the back'." (USDF Glossary)

If the horse is swinging his back, it will be seen that as the horse picks up each hind foot in energetic steps, his hip will drop on that side. If the horse is holding his back rigid (stiff), as he will tend to do when first ridden, this swing is apt to be absent, making for a stiff, bouncy gait on which the rider "bounces" in discomfort, encouraging the horse to stiffen even more. In dressage, we must teach the horse to use his whole body, not just his legs.

When the horse "uses" his back muscles, his gaits will be springier; he will land lighter, providing less jar and concussion. The back and loins will aid the hind legs in the "push off," thus providing action that is more efficient. Also, it stands to reason that, the rider being seated on the horse's back as she is, it will be a lot more comfortable if the horse has a degree of "swing" to his back rather than stiffness.

"Connection" (in the dressage sense) is a "state in which there is no blockage, break or slack in the circuit that joins horse and rider into a single harmonious unit. The unrestricted flow of energy and influence from the rider to (and throughout) the horse, and back to the rider." (USDF Glossary)

"Blocked" is "impaired in the connection due to sustained muscular contraction." (USDF Glossary) In other words, the rider "blocks" or restrains the efforts of the horse.

Usually, a horse becomes blocked or restricted because he is pulling or trying to go too fast and the rider tries to keep him under control with the hands only. This will cause the horse to become slower but without engaging the hindquarters. He may become overbent (see Number 3) and shorten his strides so that he hardly puts one foot in front of the other.

The rider must endeavor to gain control over the speed by using half-halts rather than a sustained "pull." Corrections to virtually all these problems ("blocked," "not through," "not connected") will be found in Chapter 11.

5. **Transitions: "too abrupt," "on forehand," "above bit":**

A "transition" is the movement from one gait to another gait or to a variant within a gait.

The AHSA tells us: *"The changes of pace and speed should be clearly shown at the prescribed marker; they should be quickly made yet smooth and not abrupt. The cadence of a pace should be maintained up to the moment when the pace is changed or the horse halts. The horse should remain light in hand, calm and maintain a correct position."* (AHSA, Art 1907)

In other words, the horse must show clear rhythm before, during, and after the transition. The transition should be clear, with no intermediate steps of any other gait or pace not asked for in the transition. The horse should be well-balanced and engaged (relative to the level).

Some of the most common reasons for these poor transitions are: The horse goes against the rider's hands, loses connection, or comes above the bit (usually from loss of balance onto the forehand). The transition is not straight — the hindquarters deviate to one side. The transition is not prompt (too many steps, as when changing canter leads through the walk or trot) or has intermediate steps (such as trot steps when asked to canter from walk, or vice versa). If the horse changes rhythm before or after the transition, it means it was not in good balance or impulsion was lacking or not coming "through."

At the lower levels, it is better to be early than late with a transition; otherwise you might run into the next movement (and lose points on *two* movements).

Throughout the training, the rider should aim to make all transitions as smooth as possible. To achieve this, there are several factors the rider must take into consideration. First, the rider must allow for the time lapse, however small, which occurs when her thoughts have to be transferred to her muscle system, and in turn, to the horse's brain and muscle system.

Secondly, the rider must prepare the horse and warn him that something is going to happen. These "warning" aids are called half-halts (see Chapter 11 for more on half-halts).

If the horse is correctly prepared for the transitions by the use of the half-halts to maintain balance, and if there is no resistance to the hand, the rider should be able to take the horse smoothly from one pace to the other (while keeping the horse straight). If the horse is allowed to "drift" from one pace to the other, the transition will hardly be seen and may be described as "not defined" or "not clear."

6. **"Crooked"** (not straight), **"haunches falling in" or "out," "leaning on shoulder," "popping shoulder":**

"Crooked" is: "1. Lack of parallelism to required line of travel (e.g. haunches left or right of centerline). 2. Misalignment of the horse's

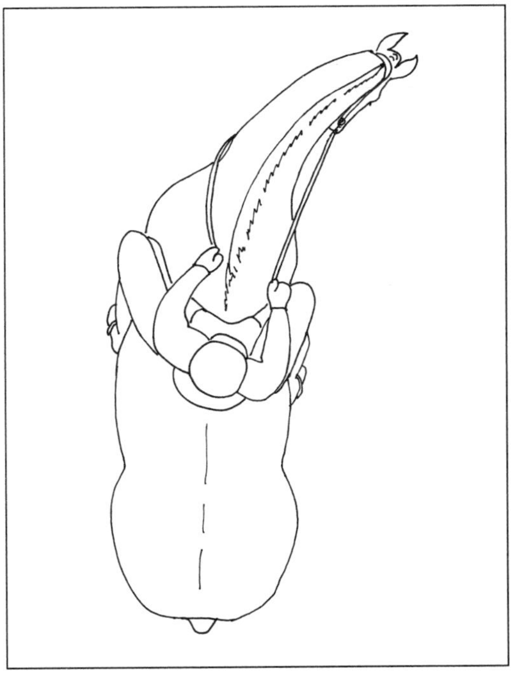

Figure 23.5 "Falling over outside shoulder." Many riders tend to overuse the inside rein in an attempt to bend the horse. When the rider "forgets" her outside rein, the horse bulges his outside shoulder outward.

To correct: ride the horse straight forward, regain equal contact on both reins and try the bend again.

body parts from tail to poll (e.g. popped shoulder or twisted neck). 3. Lack of directness of line of travel (e.g. weaving)." (USDF Glossary)

Crookedness is not merely a steering error. The horse goes crooked because he is weak or lazy with one hind leg, or his forefeet are on the ground too long, so that he can't get them out of the way soon enough for the corresponding hind feet to be put down in their place. Crookedness in the canter is a twisting of the spine to one side.

"Haunches in" or "out" is caused either by this natural crookedness or the horse failing to bend on a circular movement (see Number 7). "On inside shoulder" means the horse is twisting his neck to maintain balance and "leaning" on his inside shoulder. "Falling over outside shoulder" is a common evasion to either turning or leg yield where the horse turns his neck to the inside and "counterbalances" — protruding his opposite shoulder outward (figure 23.5). See Chapter 11 for corrections.

"Wandering," "weaving," "meandering," "drifting," is "not moving forward on a straight line from one point to another." (USDF Glossary)

If the horse "wanders," it is usually the fault of the rider who has failed to keep him between the hand and leg and has allowed him to come off the aids. You need to ride aggressively enough that your horse quits "wandering around." If the horse is being made to go forward from the rider's leg aids and is kept at a steady tempo, he should have enough energy going into the bridle to prevent sloppiness. If this is so, the rider will be able to keep a good contact with a steady rein to keep the horse straight. The horse should then be purposeful in his strides. In other words, if the rider is decisive in his directions, the horse will be less likely to wander about.

Another thing that is really important for maintaining straightness, but so basic that a lot of people forget to even mention it, is looking up when you ride. Do not look at the horse's neck. If you do look down, you'll be slower to feel any crookedness, loss of pace, or loss of pattern.

7. **"Needs more bend," "quarters in,"** or **"out," "wrong bend," "counter bent":**

The unridden horse does not need to bend around circles — he just leans against the centrifugal force, and, since he only has to worry about his own balance, there is no problem; he just "leans" on the corner (figure 23.6).

This changes, however, when we put a rider on the horse and ask him to negotiate tight, precise turns. Only if the horse bends his body on the curved line will he be able to remain upright with his weight balanced over his four legs.

Nor can a horse move evenly through a curve without bending to its arc. If the horse

Figure 23.6 Leaning on inside shoulder (no bend on circle).

Figure 23.7 The illusion of bending.

keeps his body stiff, he will move in a series of jerky pivots rather than a continuous forward gait. In such a case, there will be a visible "break" in his stride as he props himself up to avoid "falling" in. He'll lose forward momentum, and he can't sustain the balanced rhythmic gaits the judges expect to see.

"Bend" is "the lateral arced position in which the horse's body appears to form an even curve from poll to tail. Examples of faulty bend are: bending only in the neck, only at the base of the neck, or bent toward the wrong direction." (USDF Glossary)

Actually, horses have almost no "bending ability" in their spine. The neck is of course quite flexible, but there is only limited lateral bending from the withers to the 13th thoracic (rib) vertebra (approximately under the rider's seat). There is almost no lateral flexibility available in the lumbar span (behind the saddle).

Many authors point out that the horse "appears" to bend by positioning the shoulders, which are attached to the trunk by muscle rather than a bony connection. The rib cage then "rolls" in its cradle (suspended between the shoulder blades), thus allowing the hind feet to step under the mass and follow in the same track as the front foot and providing an optical illusion of a greater bend then there actually is (figure 23.7).

This is not a strictly sideways bend or bow, however. As the inside hind leg reaches under, the horse must arch his spine upward, thus the bending is actually a subtle spiraling of the spine upward and sideways, a powerful aid to a "swinging" back.

"Shoulders fall in," or "out." The rider must be well aware of the use of her inside rein and leg when riding a curve. She must avoid too much bend of the neck, which will give a false curve and allow the shoulder to fall in or out. She should ask for the bend with the inside rein and leg, but then control the amount of bend with the outside rein and leg. She should aim at being able to ride a curve with a very light inside rein contact.

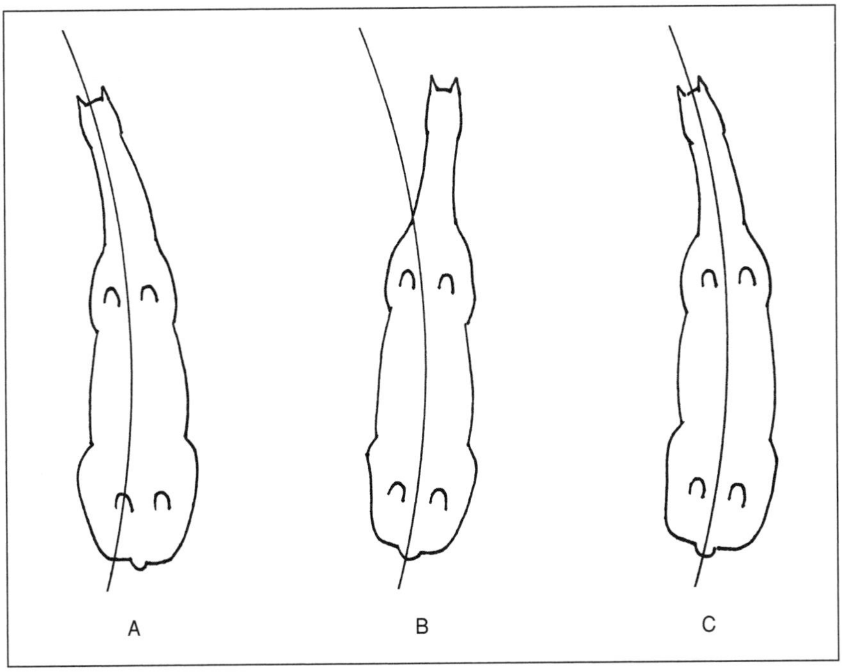

Figure 23.8 Right and wrong bends: (A) Quarters out; (B) Stiff horse (no bend); (C) Correct bend.

"Quarters out," means that instead of the hind legs following the forelegs as they should, they are on a track to the outside of the forelegs. The horse is stiff (not bending) through his body. If the rider uses too much inside rein or allows more bend in the neck than the rest of the horse, she will be encouraging the quarters to fall out, so this must be avoided (figure 23.8).

"Quarters in," less common, means the hind legs are on an inner track to the forelegs. This can be found in the horse that is physically "crooked" (see Chapter 6, "The Horse") and usually only occurs in one direction. Leg yielding (or shoulder-in if the horse is advanced enough) is the logical correction to "even-out" the musculature.

"Wrong bend" or "counter bend" is a very serious fault. It results in loss of balance, and rhythm, among other things. It is the horse's "natural" way of negotiating a turn, but since we have "unbalanced" the horse by sitting on his back, it is our duty to show him how to balance on a turn by bending and staying upright.

To correct this fault, the rider should first make sure she can ride straight with even acceptance of the bit and leg aids. Then she should try to make the horse flex to one hand and then the other. This should be very slight and is only done to check on the "give" of each side of the mouth.

The horse must then also yield to the leg when it is applied. The schooling whip can be used to achieve this (see Chapter 7, "Equipment").

Once the horse will "give" to the hand and leg, a bend can be arrived at. The horse must be bent uniformly (or appear to be) from nose to tail, with no more bend in the neck than the rest of the horse. Consideration must also be given to the outside leg of the rider, which has to control the quarters and keep the bend around the inside leg.

8. **"Four-beat canter," "labored canter,"** or **"rocking horse canter"**:

Causes and corrections for four-beat canter were discussed in Chapter 12. Many novice riders imagine the horse is too fast and try to hold him back. They end up with a stiff, straight, or counter bent, going nowhere "leg mover." The key is to bend the horse toward the inside (toward the leading leg). This gives the canter the three beat sequence and encourages "over stride," which is necessary for a fluid, well-engaged canter.

If the judge says, "canter labored," she usually means the horse is lacking sufficient energy to produce a fluid, graceful gait. Inspiring more energy and/or collection will usually correct this problem.

"Rocking horse canter" is a canter in which the neck and forehand go up and down too much, due to lack of sufficient ground coverage, lack of sufficient engagement, or to interference by the rider.

9. **"Broke gait," "cross canter"** or **"disunited canter," "wrong leads,"** and **"jigging"** (at the walk):

"Broke gait" is used when the horse changes, of his own will, the pace he is in to another. For example, if the horse is in a canter and falls for a moment to the trot and then back to the canter, that is a "break" in the gait.

Breaks in the gait are usually caused by a loss of balance, possibly a mistaken aid, or loss of impulsion (or "forward urge"). The rider must make sure the tempo at which she is riding is not unbalancing the horse. Very often, less experienced riders allow their horses to go too fast, so that the horse tips onto his forehand and cannot control his own balance, and he breaks gait to compensate; or they canter too slowly and the horse loses his balance and must trot.

When the horse is properly balanced, he can "carry himself" at any gait without falling out of it, with only light contact from the rider's hands and legs.

Half-halts play a big part in balancing the horse. The rider should also make sure that her aids are always clear so that the horse will not misunderstand and break the gait for this reason.

"Cross canter" or "disunited canter" is almost always a balance problem. The canter is an asymmetrical gait toward one side. If the horse is unbalanced, he may canter one lead in front and the opposite lead behind to keep from falling. The rider should be able to recognize this fault by an uncomfortable feeling through the horse's back. Cross cantering is not uncomfortable to the horse, so the rider must correct it immediately, even if (especially if) in a test.

Competitors sometimes wonder if they should correct a wrong lead in a test. Of course you should — immediately! If a horse in a test takes the wrong lead and continues along for two, three, or even four movements, he will score at best a "2" *for each movement involved.* If the rider had corrected it immediately, the first movement might be a "3" or "4", but the other following movements may have had a potential for 6, 7, 8 or higher.

Young horses are, of course, easily distracted and will sometimes "miss a lead." Older horses may be somewhat "one-sided" (see Chapter 11) and need a lot of work to "even them out." Some horses have been taught to take leads by having their head pulled toward a fence or rail. In dressage, the arena is seldom enough of a barrier. Besides, it will lose points because the horse will be "counter bent" (see Number 7) and will probably have a stiff or awkward canter as a result of the wrong bend.

The bottom line is, teach your horse the proper way (bent toward the lead) to take his leads, and always check your leads. If you can't feel the lead — go ahead and look over his shoulder!

Correcting the "jig." If a horse is tense or if he is pushed beyond his physical ability to take long walk strides, he may "break gait" or "jig." Jigging is the behavioral by-product of discomfort, anticipation, or insecurity. Some horses only jig in a competition test, but not at home.

Horses that are tense often need to be reassured. They try too hard or they don't understand what is expected of them. You can calm the horse by sitting relaxed and conveying confidence to him. At home, press the horse on to see where his "breaking point" is, then at a show, still use your leg aids, but lighter.

Make every effort to remain relaxed and fluid in response to "hyper" behavior. By loosening the grip of the reins, relaxing your knee, hip and ankle joints, and breathing rhythmically and deeply, you'll send the calming "vibes" to counter the nerves behind the horse's jigging. Additional suggestions for keeping yourself and your horse calm are in Chapter 16 ("Warm-Up") and Chapter 20 ("Nerves").

10. **"Disobedience," "resistance," "tense," "shying":**

"Disobedient" is a short remark frequently used by judges when the horse is evading the rider's aids and/or not performing the movement required. Sometimes the horse has shied, bucked, kicked at the rider's leg, or taken a wrong canter lead.

Sometimes the horse is openly resistant, sometimes overly nervous. It is up to the rider to discern the cause, so the incident can be avoided in the future. Some horses are genuinely frightened by distractions and need to be calmed, whereas others are just naughty.

Disobedience, if shown once only, affects the score in the movement only. For instance, judges tend to count off for shying only as it affects the particular movement. If a horse shows the same disobedience several times, scores will plummet.

"Obedience" is "willingness to perform the movement, transition, or figure asked by the rider." (USDF Glossary)

As obedience is required, the horse must be taught to answer the aids when given and not be allowed to have his own ideas. Most corrections will be found in obtaining obedience to the aids (see Chapter 11).

The rider should be careful never to allow the horse to find out his own strength. It is a mistake to think that one cannot be firm with a young horse. He must know that when the rider wishes to go forward, he must go, and when asked to accept the bit, he must do so. This should be the rider's first job. It should not be left, as it so often is, with the horse being ridden on a loose rein at his own pace. He then learns to go that way and when the rider takes a contact, he usually objects.

Some riders find difficulty in being firm enough with their own "pet" horse, but it is to the horse's own advantage to know exactly what he is meant to be doing. It is sometimes necessary to discipline a horse to be kind, and this discipline should start at home.

At a show, it is permissible to discipline a horse, but discreetly. The rider should never make a show of punishing the horse, especially in a test.

If the horse is scared, punishment will only do harm; the best option in this case is for the rider to "finesse" the horse through the test and be a good sport.

"Resistance" is "physical opposition by the horse against the rider. Not synonymous with disobedience nor with evasion. Can be momentary or pervasive."

The horse "may demonstrate resistance or evasion yet still be 'obedient' (e.g. perform a series of flying changes without mistakes and in the right place, but is behind the bit, tilted in the head with mouth open and tail swishing, reluctant to cover enough ground, etc. thus he obediently performs the task, but not necessarily submissively, supplely, etc.)" (USDF Glossary)

The judge has a difficult task here. Most "resistance" displayed by a young horse is due to nervousness in strange surroundings and not "willful resistance."

While inexperience may be the cause of inattention or resistance, it should not be skipped over lightly. The rider must understand that her horse's acceptance of the show atmosphere must be obtained before the horse can be expected to receive good scores. Lack of attention and confidence result in nervousness, looking around, whinnying, and shying.

Putting out the tongue, grinding the teeth, and swishing the tail are mostly signs of nervousness, tenseness, or resistance on the part of the horse and must be taken into account by the judge in marks for the movement concerned, as well as in the Collective Mark for "Submission."

Other occurrences that might be classed as "resistances" are: **Mouth open.** If the mouth is ajar part of the time, it is probably okay, but an open mouth with a tight jaw or tongue out for a length of time will usually get marked down. **Grinding teeth.** Some horses grind their teeth when they are concentrating. If the horse is tense, tight, *and* grinding the teeth, it is penalized severely. **Wringing tail.** The horse may be tense, may have lost balance, or the rider may be over-using spurs.

If a horse is not submissive, the trouble may be that his rider's aids are inconsistent and confusing, with the result that he does not know what to do. Or the aids may be clear enough, but the horse may be unable to do what is required. He may not have been trained long enough or gradually enough. Some item of tack may be wrongly adjusted and causing pain. It is also possible that he has a nervous and fretful disposition and may never become confident and dependable. Dressage training can correct many faults when carried out intelligently and tactfully, but it cannot correct all faults.

The rider must bear in mind that if a horse has been ridden incorrectly for years, all his muscles and his physique may be developed incorrectly. It will take great patience and much riding of the school exercises to soften the hard muscles so that the horse is able to change his way of going. He may not be resisting because he is a "pig," but simply because he has been badly ridden. The rider will have to use all her intelligence and knowledge of the correct basic training to enable the changes to take place.

When an older horse is spoiled, it is much more complicated to overcome bad habits and resistance. Expert help may be needed. The best advice is to go back to basics and start again! Treat the horse as a youngster and go through the basic program, making the corrections as and when required.

Also, don't confuse resistance with physical inability. For instance, a horse built heavy on the forehand is going to have difficulty performing any collected movement, including a really good working canter.

"Tense" describes the state of the horse mentally and physically when he is "worked up," either by outside distractions or because he has not been taught to be relaxed. Whether it comes from resistance, inattention, or just lack of relaxation, tension is evidenced by tightness in the neck and back and can result in impurities in the horse's rhythm.

"Relaxation" is not sloppiness; it is an "unruffled mental state. Calmness, without anxiety or nervousness. Absence of muscular tension (contraction) other than that needed for optimal carriage, strength, and range and fluency of movement." (USDF Glossary)

It is necessary for the horse to be calm mentally if he is to be able to perform optimally. He will be receptive only when he is unbothered in the mind and physically relaxed. Stiff, tense muscles cannot easily comply with the rider's aids.

How does one achieve this, especially when some horses are much more nervous than others? If the horse is tense and headstrong, the rider has to constantly restrain him. Instead of taking long strides, the horse will take short, hurried steps that cover little ground. This horse must first be slowed down and brought into a slower tempo by quiet slow work.

Speed is a bugbear in the case of the tense horse. Usually he is too impulsive, so it is necessary to go very slowly until the horse realizes there is nothing to be excited about. Warm up with large circles, in a steady trot, and possibly at a slower tempo than ideal, encouraging a comparatively loose, swinging trot. Only the quiet, slightly "lazy" horse will allow the rider to carefully coax the hindquarters into carrying more weight without trying to "hurry."

This is a stage some horses must go through in order to relax mentally and accept that the rider is not going to get him in a situation that he cannot handle.

Only when relaxed will the horse begin to take longer steps, which may take quite a while to obtain. It will take a good deal of patience, and constant attention. The horse should also be encouraged to lower his head and neck ("stretching into the rein;" see Chapter 13), which will come with the relaxation and will also help with this situation.

Relaxation can be induced in a horse by inspiring confidence. Working in a small part of the warm-up area and then venturing closer and closer to the competition arena may work. A steady rhythm will create relaxation through repetition. For the highly nervous horse, it may be necessary to achieve relaxation by sheer boredom (see Chapter 16, "Warm-Up").

"Shying" is a special problem with dressage horses. Every dressage horse must learn to keep his attention on the rider. If his mind is elsewhere, his attention will be on finding the spooky things.

Horses "spook" or "shy" because of fear of an object or situation, being surprised or frightened, because they are "fresh" or playful, and sometimes because they have learned from past experience they can "scare" their riders into putting them away or riding them at a slower pace.

From the beginning, the horse should pay attention to what he is being asked to do and be obedient to the aids. Young horses must learn to concentrate on what they are being taught and not on what is going on around them. Some are better at this than others (see Chapter 17, "More Practice").

Be the Best You Can Be

If you happen to be one of the lucky winners, and the show has announced an awards ceremony (more common at recognized shows), be prepared to be suitably dressed and have your horse tacked up as well to accept a trophy or ribbon in person. Always congratulate others in your class.

If, on the other hand, it did not go well, don't get mad or punish your horse — he doesn't understand what you are striving for. He only knows if he did a good or a poor job by *your* emotional reaction.

Also remember, you can't control everything. Was the weather bad? The footing deep? Was your horse tired? Anxious? If your whole test was a disaster, don't give up! Maybe you need to back up a test or a level and concentrate on the bare basics.

Today is important, but you also have to be aware of the progressive plan that you have for yourself and your horse. However large your goals as a competitor may be, make sure you have some small successes to celebrate in the meantime. Ask yourself if your performance today was an improvement over last time. Riding is more fun if you can see progress. You'll have more confidence in your ability, you'll score better, and you and your horse will enjoy the day more.

As long as you learn something about your riding or your horse every time out, you're a winner. Maybe you'll discover you need to be more of a technician so that you pick up extra

COMMENTS – FIRST L

TEST/DATE SCORE → MOVEMENT↓	1-4 3/28/95 56.33%	1-4 6/12/95 57.33%	1-3 7/3/95 57.67%	1-4 7/3/95 60.333%
Halts from Trot	*6 str line slight crooked halt 5 not sq*	*7 str CL □ halt 7 □ halt 6 (No Comment)*	*6 nice str CL off bit 5 not sq 7 (No Comment)*	*6 fell left into halt slight weaving 5 ↑ sit not still 7 (No Comment)*
10 m Trot Circle Right	*7 consist pace*	*6 avoid bit very good vigor*	*6 nice roundness*	*6 needs more supple bend*
10 m Trot Circle Left	*6 lost imp*	*6 tilt head above bit*	*7 nice round circle*	*7 better*
Leg Y Right	*5 neck tense*	*5 haunches trailing on last half*	*5 stiff & neck tense lost pace*	*6 losing fwd*
Leg Y Left	*5 resist, lost pace*	*5 need more imp*	*5 neck too tense lost pace*	*7 needs str neck*
Lengthen Trot	*5 no leng shown 5 (No Comment)*	*5 avoid bit, hurried, no leng 5 (No Comment)*	*5 has no lengthening 5 no leng*	*6 needs to cover more ground 5 (No Comment)*
Lengthen Canter	*5 resist in down trans*	*6 tilt head to right (can leng more)*	*5 has no lengthening 6 some leng*	*6 needs to cover more ground 5 (No Comment)*
10 m Canter Circle Right	*5 lose bal resist of neck*	*4 irr circle & break to trot*	*6 neck tense*	*6 needs more supple bend*
10 m Canter Circle Left	*5 lose balance*	*7 round circle*	*7 nice roundness*	*7 needs more supple bend*
Free Walk	*6 needs steadier neck*	*6 good stretch, regular*	*6 needs to stretch out*	*6 needs longer neck & stride*
Canter from Trot Transition	*6 ↑ bit, needs steadier neck*	*5 avoid bit in trot*	*5 above bit*	*5 ↑ bit in depart counterflexed in corner*
Change lead through Trot	*7 nice roundness 6 resisting in trans*	*6 abrupt trans 7 (No Comment)*	*6 above bit 5 above bit, tense neck*	*6 needs fwd & stretch through frame 5 (No Comment)*
COL. MARKS: Gaits	6	6	6	7
Impulsion	5	5	6	5
Submission	5	5	6	6
Rider Position/ Aids	6	6	6	6
REMARKS:	*Needs to work on freedom & reg of gaits, also develop impulsion fwd by stretching his pace w/o increasing tempo*	*Use legs more. Keep horse more underneath. Stay round on the bit. Showed great moments.*	*Needs to work on lengthening, smooth trans & also to improve his movement by swinging his back from back fwd*	*Needs more energy throughout.*

Chart 23.9 Log of Comments

points for accuracy. Perhaps you'll learn your horse needs a shorter (or longer) warm-up for the second ride, or maybe you'll find out that you shouldn't watch other riders before you compete because you psych yourself out. All of this is good information to store and put to use the next time.

Chart for the Future

After several shows, you may want to compile a log of test comments. This may assist you in creating a more complete view of your goals and will help keep you focused on the facts and in touch with specific tasks, as well as let you know when you have achieved a specific goal (figure 23.9).

If, for example, your horse is a bit weak in one area of his tests, congratulate yourself on what you *have* accomplished. If you get a "6" on a lengthened trot when before you were always getting 4's or 5's, pat yourself on the back and give your horse a pat, also.

If you see a trend or a problem area, you may want to look over the requirements of these tests again. Was your horse "forward" enough? Was he accepting the bit? Was he "attentive," or off in his own world? Were the two of you working with each other, or fighting each other? These are the basic principles of dressage. If any one of these were lacking, it will be more and more obvious as you go up the levels. You cannot "fake" the basics. They are either there or they are not.

If you need help, don't be afraid to ask someone for it. If you do not understand the comments on your test, or have difficulty reading them (have some compassion for the scribe), ask the show secretary if you may speak with the judge after the show, or find someone who may be able to interpret for you. Surely someone on the sidelines saw your test and could make some constructive comments on it.

Always remember that you're not judged on any one class or show. The picture you create as a rider is bigger than that. It is very important for riders to place the emphasis on their own level of performance, rather than basing their happiness on what the judge says. You might have the best ride of your life and get a low score. Or you might have a ride that was not very good in your estimation, but it scores high. If you concentrate on improving your own level of performance each time you compete, you will feel, and be, successful.

The bottom line: Don't blame the judges, don't blame your horse, don't make excuses. 10's are a rare thing indeed; go for the best you can be!

Chapter Twenty-Four
Musical Freestyle

The musical freestyle is becoming more and more popular. There is no doubt it is a crowd pleaser, but it also gives the rider a chance to be creative and can be a pleasant break from riding endless tests.

The equivalent of figure skating's long program, where required movements are interwoven with individual choreography set to music, the freestyle is a welcome addition to any competition. The World Cup and the individual medals of the Olympics are decided by a musical freestyle. The dressage musical freestyle is an exciting combination of the technical and artistic aspects of classical dressage.

At the lower levels, riders can design their own freestyles, but at the FEI levels, it is very competitive and very complicated. Most upper-level riders contract someone who has an understanding of music (perhaps a background in dance) and an understanding of the horse (how they move, requirements of the test, and so forth).

The rules for FEI level (Intermediare I and Grand Prix) are in the *AHSA Rule Book*, while the rules and score sheets for First through Fourth Level freestyles are published by the USDF.

Much of the following is taken from the *USDF Freestyle Rules and Guidelines* (1996 edition).

USDF Freestyle Rules

1. Time limit: maximum time for First through Fourth Levels is five minutes. There is no minimum time requirement. Movements performed after the time allowed will not be scored. Two points will be deducted from the total points for exceeding the time limit. The ride is timed and judged from the horse's

move-off after the initial halt and salute. Timing will cease at the final halt. Judging will cease at the final salute.

2. Music is mandatory.

3. The rider does not submit a written copy of the choreography pattern to the judges or management.

4. The rider may carry a whip in regular freestyle classes. In the case of championships, management may opt to follow the AHSA championship rules, which do not allow whips in championship classes. In such cases, check the prize list.

5. Only conventional attire and turnout is appropriate for riding in judged freestyle classes. Demonstrations or exhibitions are not covered by USDF or AHSA rules.

6. Each level has specific movements, gaits, and figures that are compulsory. Score sheets can be obtained from the USDF office.

7. Compulsory movements may be performed in any order. If a compulsory movement is not shown, a score of "0" will be given for that movement.

8. Certain compulsory movements must be shown on both reins, but not necessarily symmetrically. Compulsory movements shown in only one direction will be scored, but a "0" will be given (and averaged into the final score) for compulsory movements not shown in the other direction.

9. Two sets of marks, one for Technical Execution and one for Artistic Impression, are given by the judge. Each set of marks is totaled separately, then added together and converted to the final percentage score (figure 24.1).

10. At the USDF levels (First, Second, Third, and Fourth Levels), any point spread is possible between the technical and artistic scores.

11. In case of a tie, the higher total for Technical Execution will break the tie. (This is the same as the FEI rules; their freestyle ties are broken by the higher technical score also.)

12. If the music source fails, the competitor may (time permitting and at the discretion of management): 1. restart immediately; or 2. ask to be rescheduled to perform the freestyle in its entirety at some later time during the competition.

13. Both the technical and artistic portions of USDF freestyles at USDF/AHSA recognized competitions must be judged by AHSA licensed dressage judges. If there are two judges, one will judge the technical and one will judge the artistic.

14. USDF Freestyle Score Sheets (First, Second, Third, and Fourth Levels) that are current at the time of the competition must be used at AHSA/USDF recognized competitions.

15. The arena shall be 20 meters by 60 meters.

Terminology

The **elements** of a dressage test or freestyle include: dressage movements, test movements, figures, patterns, combinations, transitions, and gaits.

Dressage movements: Leg-yield, rein back, shoulder-in, travers, renvers, half-pass at trot and canter, flying change, pirouette, turn on the haunches, piaffe, and passage.

Test movements: All of the elements to be scored in one box on a test sheet.

Figures: Circles, half-circles, changes of rein, and serpentine. Figures may be of any size in freestyle, regardless of level.

Patterns: The design by which the other elements are linked together. (There are some patterns, at some gaits, that are not allowed at the lowest level).

Combinations: Sequences of movements or transitions (simple change, zigzag in canter with flying changes, change of lead through trot).

Transitions: Changes between two different gaits or from one pace to another within the same gait.

TECHNICAL EXECUTION

NOTE: *Movement must be shown in both directions. Half points allowed for judge's final marks.

TIME MAXIMUM: **5 minutes**

FIRST LEVEL

COMPULSORY MOVEMENTS	POSSIBLE POINTS	PRELIMINARY MARKS	CO-EFFICIENT	FINAL MARKS	REMARKS
* 1. Walk (minimum 20M)	10				
2. 10-meter circle in trot*	10	* ⁞ *			
3. Leg-yield in trot*	10				
4. Lengthen stride in trot	10				
5. 15-meter circle in canter*	10				
6. Change of lead through trot*	10				
7. Lengthen stride in canter	10				
8. Quality of gaits	10				
9. Impulsion	10		2		
10. Submission	10		2		
11. General impression of overall technical quality: transitions; execution (including non-required movements and figures)	10		2		

Further Remarks:

SUBTOTAL	
DEDUCTIONS	
TOTAL TECHNICAL EXECUTION (140 total possible)	

ARTISTIC IMPRESSION

NOTE: Tenth points allowed

NO.

	POSSIBLE POINTS	JUDGE'S MARKS	CO-EFFICIENT	FINAL MARKS	REMARKS
1. Rhythm, energy and elasticity	10		2		
2. Harmony between horse and rider	10		2		
3. Choreography, use of arena, inventiveness, design cohesiveness, balance, ingenuity and creativity	10		4		
4. Degree of difficulty	10		1		
5. Choice of music & interpretation of music	10		5		

Further Remarks:

SUBTOTAL	
DEDUCTIONS	
TOTAL ARTISTIC IMPRESSION (140 total possible)	
TOTAL TECHNICAL EXECUTION (140 total possible)	
FINAL SCORE (280 total possible)	
PERCENTAGE (Final Score divided by 280)	

Figure 24.1 (freestyle score sheet)
** This is the 1996 edition; be sure to use the current requirements.*
** * The dotted line indicates that the movement must be shown on both reins.*
Reprinted by permission of the United States Dressage Federation.

Gaits: walk, trot, and canter and variants within these gaits.

There is obviously some overlap between these categories, for instance:

- A simple change is a combination of three gaits and two transitions.
- A half-pass is a dressage movement, but a zigzag is a combination.
- Change rein in lengthened canter is a pattern and a pace.
- A three-loop serpentine in a large arena is a dressage movement, pattern, and a combination (three 20-meter half-circles).

Requirements of Each Level

Following is a sample of the compulsory movements for First Level. Always consult the current guidelines for the list of required, allowed, and clearly forbidden movements.

Technique Execution: First Level

Compulsory movements:

1. Walk (minimum 20 meters)
2. 10-meter circle in trot, both reins
3. Leg-yield in trot, both reins
4. Lengthen stride in trot
5. 15-meter circle in canter, both reins
6. Change of lead through trot, both reins
7. Lengthen stride in canter.

Clearly allowed:

- Counter-canter (any configuration)
- Zigzag leg yield
- Leg yield along wall (like shoulder-in)
- Lengthen trot or canter on 20-meter circle
- Canter serpentine
- Simple change
- Change of lead through trot
- Canter-walk transition
- Canter-halt transition

Clearly Forbidden:

- Rein back
- Shoulder-in
- Travers
- Half-pass
- Flying changes
- Turn-on-haunches or pirouette at walk or canter
- Piaffe
- Passage

Movements exceeding the difficulty of the level (clearly forbidden) will be penalized by a deduction of four points, from the total points, for each occurrence.

In order to make some logical sense out of the contentious areas, a list of what is forbidden and what is allowed at each level is provided by USDF (see latest edition of *Guidelines for Freestyles*). And it is imperative to keep in mind that only *movements* above the level (not transitions, combinations, or figures) are forbidden in the USDF rules.

Any combination or transition composed of elements (gaits, movements, or transitions) permitted in the current tests of the level entered are permitted in the same level freestyle, even if the resulting specific transition or combination is found in higher level tests. There are no limitations on size, shape, or combination of figures, even if the resulting configuration is found in higher level tests.

Movements not listed on the score sheets and not found in any higher level test can be rewarded or penalized in the "General impression of overall technical quality" box on the Technical Execution side of the score sheet (see Number 11 on the sample score sheet, Fig. 24.1) and/or "Degree of difficulty" on the Artistic Impression side of the score sheet (Number 4).

Scoring

In addition to the Compulsory Movements, each test is scored on:

Technical Execution

Quality of gaits

- *Impulsion* x 2
- *Submission* x 2
- *General impression of overall technical quality: transitions, execution (including non-required movements and figures)x 2*

The criteria for freestyle correspond to the AHSA tests at the same level.

Tenths of points (0.1, 0.2, 0.5, etc.) are permitted.

Artistic Impression

- *Rhythm, energy and elasticity* x 2
- *Harmony between horse and rider* x 2
- *Choreography. Use of arena. Inventiveness, design cohesiveness, balance, ingenuity and creativity* x 4
- *Degree of difficulty.* x 1*
- *Choice of music & interpretation of the music.* x 5

(* For Fourth Level Freestyle, degree of difficulty has a coefficient of 2.)

Degree of Difficulty and Creativity

A common complaint of judges at the lower-level freestyles is that the horse just goes around and around in testlike patterns. A good freestyle shows a horse that can do a lot of technically difficult (for the level) exercises in rapid succession and can tolerate relatively loud music and the excitement of a crowd. "Degree of difficulty" is a measure of the sufficiency and suitability of the degree of difficulty (enough or too much for the present competence level).

"Creativity" is the non-test-like nature and the ingenuity or originality of the patterns and combinations.

Choice of Music and Interpretation of the Music

While this will always be subjective, the choreographic expression of the phrasing, highlights, and "messages" in the music are the characteristics being judged.

Create Your Own

At the FEI levels, you would probably want to have your music professionally recorded, but at the national levels (First through Fourth), you can probably adequately edit and record your tape yourself.

While it can cost from $500 to $800 to have your music and/or choreography done by a professional, you may well get more satisfaction out of the process if you do it yourself.

All you need is:

1. A "boom box" with "high speed synchronized dubbing" that will record from one audiocassette tape to another or from a compact disc to a tape. At present, competition management wants tapes, although the discs are better to record from.
2. Three 30-minute high-quality tapes
3. A watch or clock with a second hand
4. Your music
5. A little time (a couple of hours for three or four days, after you have found your music), a little patience, and a willingness to experiment.

Choosing Your Music

Unless you compose and create your own music (or pay a composer to do it), you must get permission from the publisher or record company to use prerecorded music. Contact the USDF on how to go about this. "Buying" permission to use a piece of music can cost anywhere from a few cents to a few thousand dollars.

Although personal taste in music should not enter into the judge's mind, it may. The music should contain parts that can be interpreted — not just background music. The use of vocal selection should not be penalized *per se,* although such music is controversial. A cohesive musical theme will be scored higher than a disjointed mish-mash of musical selections.

It is strongly recommended that the music for a freestyle ride be of one genre, and have one style, or a theme; mixing musical genres within one program rarely works well.

The music need not match the horse's stride exactly, but should not be markedly faster or slower than the horse. It is more important that the music fit the horse. That is, powerful music should not be used for a light, floaty mover, nor should light, floaty music be used for a big powerful mover — it just doesn't look right.

The music may begin before, while, or after horse and rider enter the arena. It is advisable to have entrance music so you know immediately that the tape is working.

Since the first concern is that the music fit the horse from an aesthetic point of view, the "beats" should match his walk, trot, and canter. This means that you will probably need at least three pieces of music. Movie themes and TV theme music or music done by a single performer often have tones and theme that will be consistent from piece to piece.

Time Your Horse's Gaits

Either have someone time your horse as you ride (keep a good, consistent rhythm), or time your horse while you longe him. Do not do this initial timing from a video, because sometimes VCRs speed up or slow the actual tempo.

Count the beats — the footfall as one leg strides or hits the ground, except at the walk, where you count right *and* left front feet — for 10 seconds. Do this three or four times, so you get a good average. If you want, you can multiply by six and get the timing for a minute, but the 10-second timing — both watching the horse and listening to the music — is easier to work with.

The critical timing is for the trot — it should match exactly. You can "fudge" a little at the canter and walk. Your canter music should have some "roll" to it and the walk music should have some "interest" — so it keeps the judge awake!

Listening to the timing of the music is your next step (and usually the most time consuming). Just listen for the prominent beat and again count it for 10 seconds. Jot down some notes about each tune and its timing, whether it's suitable for walk, trot, or canter, whether it's lively, swingy — whatever you notice.

Pick your trot music first. Try to find several selections with the proper timing. When it comes to matching the right tune to the horse, you may be surprised. Something that you didn't think would work might be just the one.

There are three ways you can do your final selection of music for your horse.

1. Record about a minute of each of several pieces of music that you think might work. If you have walk and canter music, record this too. This will give you practice in recording and splicing music, but most important, you can ride or longe the horse while your music plays and check the effect.

2. You can play a video of your horse (preferably while he is performing a test at a competition) and play your music simultaneously.

The music should complement the horse. He should look better with the music than he does without it.

Splicing the Music

Unless you are extremely talented (or have very sophisticated equipment), you will have to let the music dictate where your splices are. Listen to your pieces (you should have one for canter, one for walk, and one or two for trot) and decide where the natural "breaks" are.

These are called "phrases" — they are natural lulls in the music. You might also want to have "entrance" music that sets the mood and has a climax for your entrance halt.

"At the beginning of a Free Style Test a halt for the salute is compulsory. Time begins when the horse moves forward after the competitor's halt and ends with the final halt and salute." (AHSA, Art. 1928.2)

"A rider must enter the arena within 20 seconds of the music starting. The music must cease at the final salute." (AHSA, Art. 1928.6)

Your entrance music does not necessarily have to match the horse's "beat." You might also use a short piece of the same music for your end salute.

Now get out your pencil, paper, and watch and time all the natural breaks in your various pieces of music. Many pieces have a break every 20 seconds. You need to have a five-minute tape (check the latest rules to be sure) from first salute to final salute. It can be shorter but it can't be longer.

A good average is: approximately two to two and a half minutes trot; approximately two minutes canter; minimum 20 seconds, maximum 50 seconds for walk.

Now put your mathematician's hat on (or get out your calculator!) and start figuring out exactly where you are going to put your splices so the tape is five minutes or less and your gaits come in a logical order.

Editing should be fluid and smooth. Choppy or disruptive editing on the music tape will detract from the overall artistic impression.

To splice, you need to be very familiar with your music, and you should use high-grade tapes. You don't want to spend all this time getting it perfect, only to have the tape lose quality (if you record from a recorded tape, that is from a recorded tape, that is from a recorded tape, it will lose quality). In other words, record from a recording no more than twice. If you don't like your first attempt, start over, recording from your original music again.

The easiest way to record is to memorize the three or four notes before the place you want to start the music (with the help of a clock with a second hand). For example, if your first break is 23 seconds into the music, hit the "record" button one beat before that point. If the music should then play for one minute, 50 seconds, watch the clock, then let the music record about five seconds after the next splice spot. Play back the recorded tape and stop it on the last note that you want. Play the next piece, pressing "record" button one note before, and so on.

Your first attempt may not be perfect, so record about 10 seconds of "dead" time and try again. If you get a 30 minute tape to record on, you can just keep trying until you get it right.

Once you get it just right, record your finished piece onto two other tapes: One for competition, one for practice, and one backup.

Your competition tape should have only the freestyle ride on it. The cassette should be clearly labeled on the music side of the tape with competitor's name, horse's name, level of ride, and written instructions of when to push the "play" button at the start of the ride.

Always take an extra copy of the music tape to the competition. Mark it the same way as the original plus some additional notation indicating that it is a backup copy.

Consult the competition prize list for information about sound checks and to whom to give the tape and instructions. Before giving the music tape to the person who will run the sound equipment during the competition, cue it up so that the music is ready to play when the "play" button is pushed. (If help is needed, ask the advice of the sound technician.)

Each competitor should be permitted one representative in the sound system booth to supervise the handling of the tape. This person should not interfere with the show announcer or management in any way.

Choreography

You have your music; now fit your ride to it. Let's say you have 30 seconds of introductory music, a three second pause for the salute, two minutes of trot, 35 seconds of walk, one minute and 40 seconds of canter, and 40 seconds of trot, climaxing for the salute (total ride is four minutes 55 seconds).

Consult the USDF Freestyle Rules and Guidelines for what movements are required for your level and what movements are prohibited.

Competitors should be careful not to use movements that are clearly above the level being shown. Permitted and compulsory movements may be shown in any pattern, placement, or order.

Give some thought to your horse's strong points and how best to show them off, while "playing down" his weak points. A composition that is creative will be scored higher than one that looks like a reworked dressage test set to music.

The beginning and end of the freestyle should be executed facing "C" with a halt and salute. This should be on the centerline.

The freestyle choreography should utilize the entire arena, not just the rails and diagonals. Creativity in the use of figures and space is encouraged. Movements should be presented clearly enough to be easily identifiable by the judge (or you risk getting a "0" if it's a required movement).

While riders are encouraged to take chances and increase the degree of difficulty, care should be taken to present movements (in terms of choice and placement) that show off the horse's best technical ability.

The "degree of difficulty" will only get you extra points if it works. If the ride looks too busy — if it makes you tired just to watch it, or if the movements are very difficult but the basics are missing and almost none of the movements are performed correctly, then the difficulty cannot be scored higher, either.

Begin by drawing some movements on paper, but be prepared to rearrange or reposition them later. Pay particular attention to how the movements will appear from the judge's point of view (at "C"), because that is where the technical judging takes place.

Max Gahwyler's book, *The Competitive Edge*, has some very good comments on what works and doesn't work in a test ride. As far as ease of judging (you want the judge to *recognize* what you are doing), it's important that your ride not be difficult to judge because of placement in the arena.

For instance:

Shoulder-in should always be performed toward the judge. Going away, the judge can see the footwork but may get the illusion that the horse has too much bend in the neck. Shoulder-in on the centerline will impress the judge if you are accurate with your three tracks.

Weak lengthened or medium trot may look more impressive on the diagonal going away from the judge. If the horse has impressive front-end action but is a little weak behind, come toward the judge — either on the long side or diagonal, preferably a *short* diagonal, so the judge will have less time to evaluate (or the horse to "fade").

If the horse has good up and down transitions, be sure to place them where the judge can easily see them. If they are sometimes lacking, do them with your back to the judge (if possible).

Draw your patterns on paper, then go out and try them on the horse while your music plays. If you have a helper, the helper can stand by with watch and note pad, write down which sections are too long or too short, make suggestions, and draw the finished patterns. This is important, because if you are trying a lot of different patterns, you may forget which worked best!

Work out the timing for one section at a

time. Your helper can start and stop the music if need be. If you find you have five or ten seconds left over in a section, or you run out of time in a section, or you would like to "time" your transition to a certain place in the arena, look at your pattern and see where you can either stretch or shrink it. Sometimes you want your first canter to be on a certain lead. You can simply reverse your trot work (for instance, the first time you turn off the centerline) to get you going in the right direction. You don't have to have transitions or figures at letters in freestyle, although many judges think it adds polish if they are.

After you have all the sections choreographed, you should check for "balance" (use of the whole arena). Get out another piece of paper, draw a dressage arena, and draw your whole test (one movement on top of another). If the whole arena is marked on, with no blank spots, you're okay.

To find where to start your ride (the place you will stand until the music starts), ride to the place on the centerline where you will salute, face toward "A", and start your music. Ride out of the ring and around the outside of the arena until the music gets to your halt. This is your starting point.

In a competition, you will ride around the outside of the arena until the judge rings the bell, then go to your starting position, raise your hand, and the music should be started. You have 60 seconds after the bell to signal for your music, and 20 seconds after the music starts to enter at "A".

Practice

Now you need to practice your freestyle so you know what beats precede transitions or figures, how long to stand for the salute, how many seconds (or beats) it takes for smooth transitions, and so forth. If you find yourself getting ahead of your music, go deeper into corners; if you're getting behind the music, round your corners (note that the footing will affect your horse's speed). On at least one of these rehearsals, have someone watch you from "C" to get the judge's view (a video from there would be even better).

Also, practice smiling! Showmanship plays a big part of a successful freestyle. This is your chance to "show off," so good luck and **enjoy**!

Chapter Twenty-Five

Quadrille

Quadrille, a group riding in formation, is another way to enjoy the sport of dressage. Although it has been popular for a long time in Europe, the quadrille is fairly new in the United States.

Many of the suggestions here can also be used to develop a *Pas de Deux*, which is a "ride of two" (figure 25.1).

Riding in a group or pair gives the rider a sense of camaraderie and a team spirit and heightens the sense of timing and precision. It also is very enjoyable to the horse, a herd animal, and teaches him to pay attention to his rider while interacting with other horses — a valuable asset for working in a crowded warm-up arena!

Essentially, a quadrille is a four horse performance test, usually executed to music (music is optional). The official quadrille tests have set patterns. You can, however, develop your own patterns and ride in groups of four, six, eight, or more.

When ridden properly, the quadrille demonstrates the same good qualities that judges look for in a straight dressage test. Quadrille riders, however, have an additional challenge because they must maintain their position and correct spacing within the group.

The public loves these performances and they are a splendid promotion of the equestrian sport. It is an avenue where horses that are not especially talented can excel in dressage.

There are several other reasons why quadrille is becoming increasingly popular: First, for years the only organized outlet for dressage riders in this country has been riding in tests. Additionally, some people simply do not *like* to compete. Third, quadrille riding is inherently social, both for the riders and for the horses. Most horses love it — which makes it more fun for their riders! Finally, quadrille is a tremendous learning experience, requiring far greater riding skills than one can easily learn in several years' worth of private lessons.

Quadrille riding promotes control — of oneself as well as one's horse. The rider must learn to harmonize with several other horse-and-rider pairs; she must adjust the horse's stride length and tempo to stay with the group, which might consist of horses much larger or smaller than her own. Further, accuracy in riding figures is essential, because each rider depends on all the others to be at predetermined places at certain times to avoid collisions.

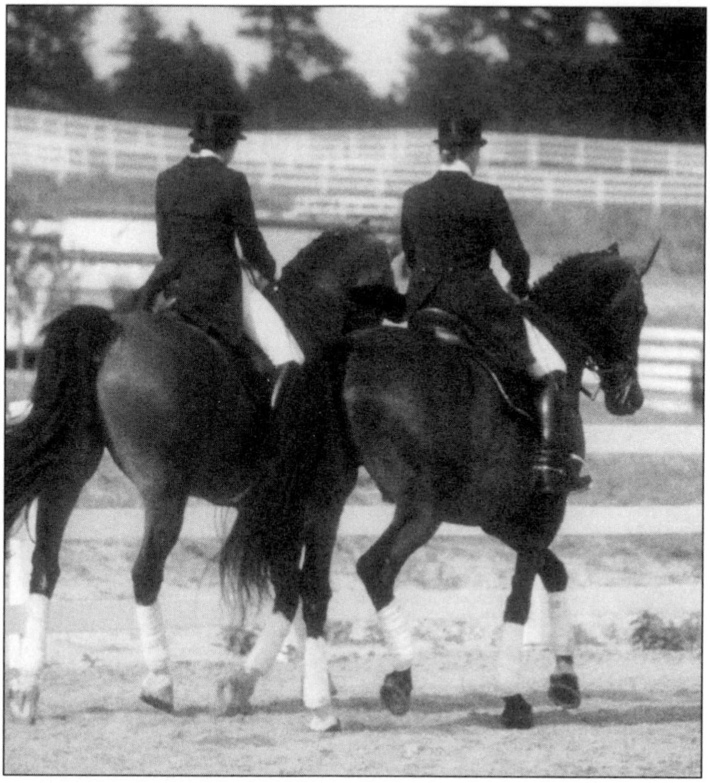
Photo 25.1 Pas de Deux is a real crowd pleaser. Photo by Charlene Strickland.

While one can learn all these things riding alone, one tends to learn them faster in formation riding because the consequences are more immediate. The consequence of a sloppy circle in formation riding is a "train wreck"!

Quadrille riding also tends to promote teamwork and a certain selflessness. Since the goal is always an artistic performance (whether public or private), it is to everyone's benefit to help one another. Good riders automatically begin to help the less skillful riders, and everyone gives up the "blaming game" in a search for solutions to problems. When it all comes together, riders feel the sheer pleasure of artistic expression.

Getting Started

Getting a quadrille started is easier than you might think. To start, it is the USDF, not the AHSA, that is the regulating organization for quadrilles. Therefore, your first step is to contact the USDF to invest in a *Quadrille Handbook*. It contains the compulsory and freestyle tests, the Rules and Guidelines (which can be purchased separately), and the different aspects of quadrilles.

In organizing a quadrille, there are two general caveats to consider. The first is commitment. Without this, the coach has to keep teaching the same things over and over again because each week a new group of riders show up. The result is that regular attendees got bored or frustrated, and the occasional attendees are confused because they don't know what is going on. You need to tell prospective quadrille members that if they want to ride, they have to come to practice sessions (at least twice a month) unless the absence is clearly a once-in-a-while event.

You need at least four riders for competition — preferably five who are ready to make a commitment to the effort.

The USDF decided on the number four because when getting started it is so difficult to get more than four people together consistently to practice. Having a back-up rider will improve your chances for success when a team rider or horse cannot compete.

The quadrille competition tests are performed in a Small arena (20 x 40 meters) because four riders are lost in a Standard arena. You may not believe this at first but after riding with the group in the Small arena, it will feel quite comfortable. If you are developing a quadrille of more than four, you may want to use the Standard arena, but with four riders, it is much easier to judge and maintain close spacing between horses (such as half a horse length) than wider spacing (such as two or three horse lengths).

The second caveat is that there must be someone to coach and direct the quadrille. The director's role is to provide encouragement, instruction, and correction.

Designate either the last rider or the ground person to give the signals for each turn and practice with a whistle or voice command. A whistle is easier to hear. It requires that each member of the team know the test, however.

In the very beginning, someone needs to stay on the ground and tell riders what they are doing wrong and right, to design the figures, and initially to serve as a traffic cop. This could be the team member with the most tactful, but direct, manner. It could be your fifth rider, who can not only observe the practice sessions from the judge's point of view, but can also fill in for a team member when needed. Because the director needs to be someone everyone respects, it often helps to appoint the team's trainer to this position. Regardless of who it is, however, everyone must agree to listen to the director's suggestions.

In setting up beginning quadrilles, riders should be grouped by skill level, although a novice in a group of more advanced riders can work quite well, as the novice receives a great deal of help from the others, and so improves quickly. Skill level or quality of the horses is not as important in the beginning, because the figures needn't involve advanced movements to be challenging. Work in the quadrille will bring even young horses up to a decent standard of performance rather quickly. In fact, it is a wonderful experience for the young horse to bring them to the quadrille (after they are reliable under saddle, of course). They learn to go in company with good manners and they learn to go forward and straight without much rider interference. Just remember to put the young horse behind an experienced, calm horse.

Unless public performance is the group's immediate goal, the appearance or size of the horses is irrelevant. However, the horses you use must be well-mannered and compatible temperamentally.

Remember, horses are herd animals. Working in groups is natural for them, although sometimes they need to be reminded of this. Horses also have "pecking orders" — you must be the "leader" of your herd of two, so your horse will listen to you and not another equine who wants to be dominant.

Horses that kick are not acceptable. It is too much of a risk to allow a quarrelsome horse on the team. If you have a horse that might be a potential kicker, put a red ribbon in his tail to remind everyone to be aware.

While it is nice to have horses similar in size and color, do not sacrifice rideability and manners for appearance. Nor is it particularly important to have good movers. More emphasis is put on the performance as a group than on gaits. A horse who's consistent, well-mannered, and shows energy might find a great niche in a quadrille.

The next step is to meet as a mounted group and arrange horses in order. Choose a calm horse with a very steady rhythm and a competent rider as your lead horse. If horses and riders are pretty equal in ability, you could arrange by size — largest to smallest — or by color — dark to light — or whatever characteristic you want. You'll still need to experiment with the placings of the horses. Horses that hate each other shouldn't be adjacent, and those that are nervous about other horses being close should be at the end of the line, at least initially. Believe it or not, most horses learn pretty quickly to behave, so long as their riders remain calm and keep them in the line.

If a rider can't keep her horse on the bit, putting side-reins on should help, but be sure the horse will longe in side-reins without a rider first. This is a particularly valuable strategy for children riding experienced horses, since it's not unusual for some horses to get a little bullish while riding in formation. It's hard to stop or slow a horse that gets above the bit, and the side-reins help the rider keep control.

Keep Your Place

Before the group can begin to put patterns together and actually ride as a quadrille, they must learn several skills. The director can teach these skills in the first several sessions, then begin to arrange the patterns, and finally design a complete ride on paper, which can be copied and distributed to the group.

The group should discuss at the outset the rules of formation riding.

1. Get the horses used to each other. Watch their ears to see how they feel about each other. Some really don't like working together, so be ready to reprimand instantly if they even think of threatening each other: *you* must be the "boss" of your own horse.

2. Get them used to riding toward each other. For example, ride a 20-meter circle in opposite directions so they pass each other.

3. Always pass left hand to left hand. This is a permanent convention and is reflected in the tests.

4. Decide as a group on a following distance and practice it. In most cases, a close distance is easier to control.

Most groups space horses about one horse length apart to start. Gradually move up to half a horse length, then no closer than two feet apart. Any closer and the horse in the rear can inadvertently step on the heels of the horse in front.

The riders need to learn to keep the specified distance from the horses in front of them in walk, trot, and later — perhaps much later, depending on riders' skill levels — in canter.

It is easier for the ground person or director to line all the horses up, space them, and instruct everyone to memorize the distance from the next horses. Then all move off at the walk, and walk around the arena keeping this distance. This will require much prompting from the director to start with, especially after the corners.

5. Match tempo. The rides may be performed to music (although it is not considered in the judging). Music helps everyone keep the tempo. Still, it is the front rider (leader) that is responsible for setting the tempo and leading the patterns. The rider in the back will find it easier to see the spacing, synchrony, and alignment. She will also be responsible for communicating what she sees to the rest of the team — everyone else must keep quiet!

When the group can keep their distances single file around the rail at a walk, move on to the trot and practice on the rail again until the tempo is "set." If one horse is always lagging behind or one horse is always crowding and the rider cannot adjust, then talk to each other and see if the tempo needs to be adjusted or compromised for the benefit of the team's performance and safety.

When the group can keep their distances around the rail at the trot, the pattern can be varied — across the short diagonal, the lead rider must learn to ride a *straight* line so that others can follow more easily. If the leader rides a crooked line, everyone tends to follow — a wavy line looks very sloppy! Down the centerline the director should tell riders to keep their horse's poll in line with the tail of the horse in front of them. It will take a little while for the horses to learn to adjust their stride lengths. Some are very clever about this and learn immediately to shorten or lengthen to keep up, but others definitely have problems. The spacing at the canter can be deferred until other skills are mastered and the group is riding some patterns. (The Introductory Quadrille tests are walk and trot; the Novice and Preliminary tests are walk, trot, and canter.) Until the members can ride collection, the canter doesn't look very good in formation anyway — it's a little wild and woolly, reminiscent of the charge of the Light Brigade!

6. No one in line should stop, unless the group is told to stop by the leader or director. No one should pass another rider unless instructed to do so. No rider should pull out of the line unless she absolutely must to avoid a collision. If a rider turns the wrong way or starts to perform the wrong figure, no one needs to stop, unless *everyone* is in chaos — which does occasionally happen! Just catch up to the rest of the group, and proceed.

Next, riders have to learn to move off in walk and trot as one and to halt as one. Mainly this is an attention issue and an obedience (on the part of the horses) issue.

Like other dressage tests, you may have a caller for the quadrille ride. This caller can substitute their own commands, and unlike other tests, a rider can call time or blow a whistle.

This is a good time to decide on how to time your execution after the whistle cue. You can count aloud together: "one, two, and turn" (or whatever). This helps you develop the same reaction time and stay more in "sync" through the turns.

So, for example, a rider blows the whistle,

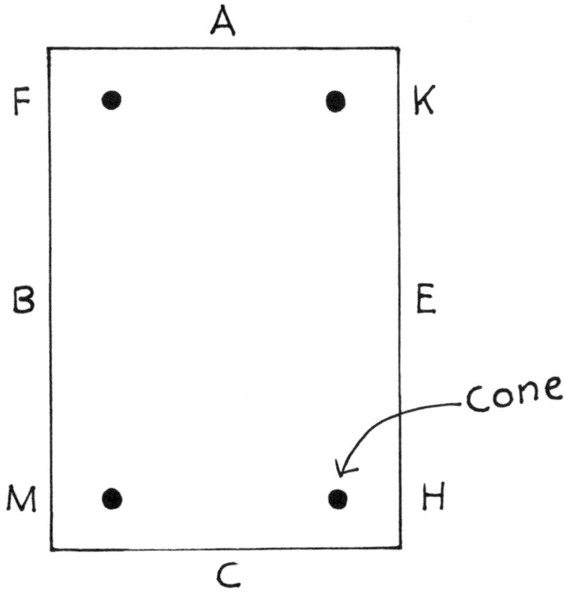

Figure 25.2 Use traffic cones to mark strategic points of the arena.

and everyone mentally counts "one, two, turn," or "one, two, halt." The "one, two" gives the riders time to get organized to ask for the transition in unison with each other. Opinion varies as to whether it should be the first or last rider giving the commands.

Some time should be spent teaching riders to ride correct turns and corners, because if everyone rides these precisely, it's much easier to maintain proper spacing.

Cones and ground poles help define the geometry of your test. You can use these props to learn how to make your lines straighter and your circles correct in size. They also help riders learn where in the ring they need to be in movements. Another trick is to videotape the team from the judge's point of view; a picture will make things clear (figure 25.2).

Next comes riding side by side. A quadrille pattern often calls for riders to pair up, or to ride across the arena simultaneously side by side. The audience tends to look at the riders, rather than the horses, so the riders must be lined up, regardless of the length of the horses in each pair. Instruct each pair to ride with their knees right next to each other. For riders to do this well, they simply *must* look at each other. The riders will not believe the director on this point, insisting they cannot guide their horses, or insist that they are looking at each other, when they definitely are not.

If you have a coach, you should hear a constant "check in front, check beside," or if you are all crossing the width of the arena, a "check left, check right." It may even be good to check left and right in unison until the habit is formed.

After forming pairs, the riders begin to ride around the rail, not only keeping together, but also maintaining their distance from the horses in front. On the corners, the outside horses must extend a bit, while the inside horse must collect. When the walk looks acceptable, try the trot. When the riders can ride around the rail, the leader can introduce some changes in pattern.

When performing moves like turning across the arena, remember that not only must you all turn at the same time, you must also arrive at the same time. Thus, you must constantly rate your horse to the others.

Try Some Basic Patterns

As members of the quadrille begin to develop the necessary control, the group can learn other maneuvers that will form components of a performance.

1. One very simple pattern is to ride down the centerline in pairs; at "C", the pairs split and proceed up the long sides of the arena toward "A". Each rider must stay even across the arena with her partner from the original pairs, so that when the lines pass left hand to left hand at "A", each pair should meet exactly at "A", not a few feet before or after. The director should instruct the riders to check their positions by comparing their locations relative to certain letters. For example, when a rider's partner reaches "E", that rider needs to be at "B" — to be precise, the two riders' shoulders should pass the letters at the same time. The same applies at "F" and "K" (figure 25.3).

2. Threading the needle is fun and sometimes a bit challenging, especially at the extended trot. Practice first at the walk (or working trot). After riders have split into two lines and crossed left hand to left hand at "A" or "C", each line rides a short diagonal from, say "M" and "H" to "E" and "B". Horses should cross alternately, so corners must be ridden precisely, and the spacing must be increased and carefully maintained to allow the horses to pass. If the riders get too close to each other, some horses might throw their heads or shy away from the approaching horse, especially initially. Just keep calm and keep practicing (figure 25.4).

3. Left turn/right turn begins in a single line, with riders proceeding along the long side. At the command, "Left turn...hup!" all riders make a 90-degree angle turn to the left and proceed across the arena, keeping exactly even with each other. To do this, the lead rider looks at the rider next to her, while all other riders look at the rider who was immediately in front of her in the line. Once again, to do this successfully, all of the riders must look at each other all the way across the arena. This is much more difficult than it sounds, because the riders have to make fine adjustments to their horses' stride lengths, especially in the beginning when the turns aren't exactly the same. Remember, the turn is not a 10-meter circle. It is a quarter volte (six meters). As always, practice first in the walk, then at the trot. This maneuver can also be performed from the short side (figure 25.5).

4. Crossovers consist of two lines of riders riding simultaneously across the arena from one long side to the other, crossing left hand to left hand as they pass each other on the centerline. Of course, this is complicated by the requirement to stay exactly even with the other riders in one's own line (figure 25.6).

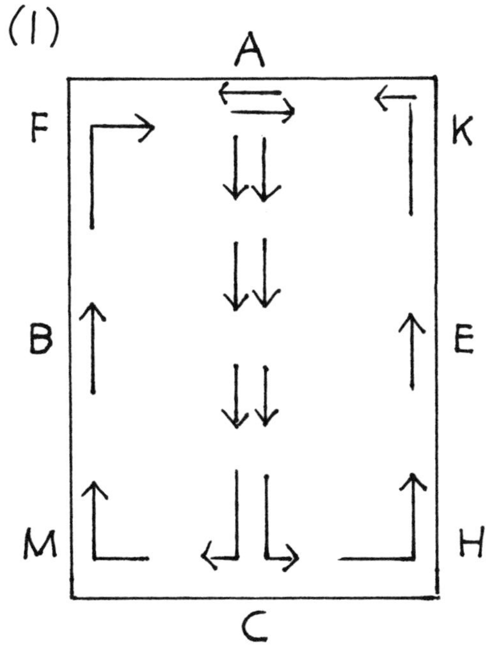

Figure 25.3 Pairs up the centerline, split at "C", "crossover" at "A".

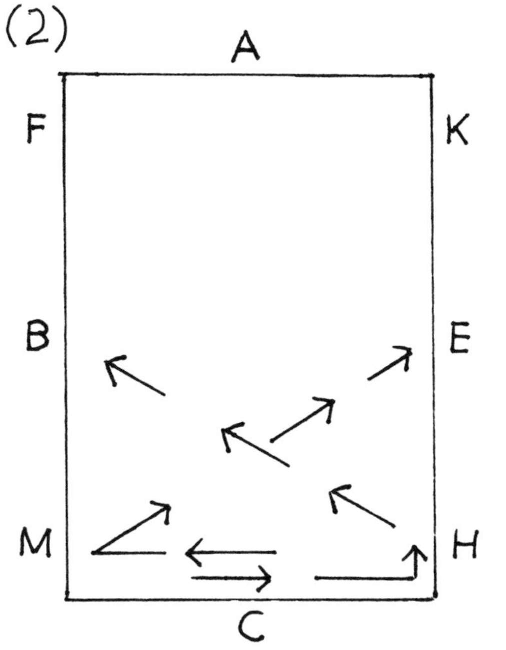

Figure 25.4 Thread the needle.

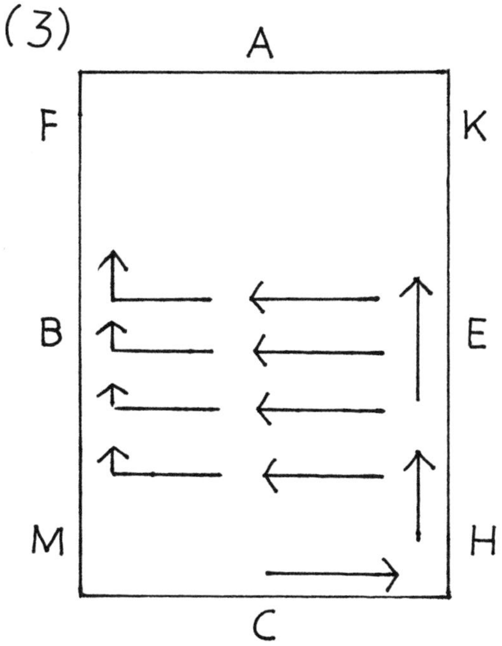

Figure 25.5 Turning left, then right, individually.

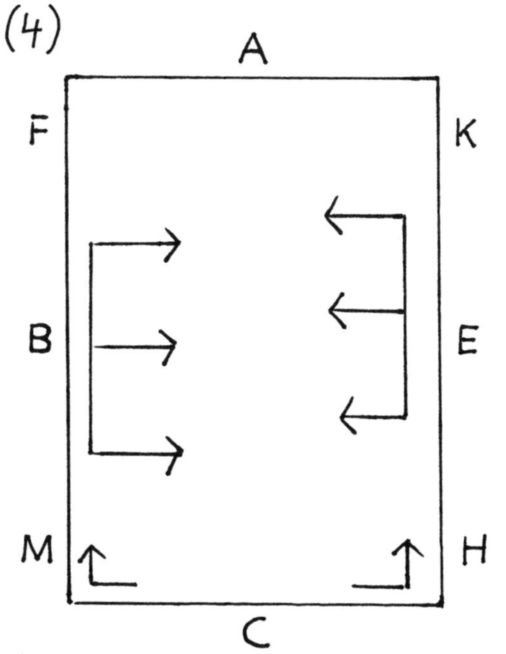

Figure 25.6 Individual right/left turns and pass through on centerline.

5. Simultaneous 10-meter circles is a maneuver that seems to separate the wheat from the chaff, because many riders discover (to their amazement) that they don't know how to ride a circle! With riders in single file, at the command, "10-meter circle, one, two, now!" all riders immediately perform a 10-meter circle. There is nothing complicated about this, except that all riders must ride a 10-meter circle and nothing else — no "eggs," no ovals, no 10½-meter circles, and all must start and finish together.

In close formation, a rider who loses her horse's shoulder for one or two strides will collide with the rider to the left or right of her. If all the circles are not precise, then a "train wreck" of massive proportions occurs. The leader then needs to teach the riders individually how to ride the 10-meter circle — a figure occurring in the First Level tests.

Terms for Patterns

These are some of the terms used in the compulsory tests. They also make communication easier.

Fan formation — Side-by-side lines all four abreast

Crossover — Passing single file, head on

Columns — single file

Oblique — at an angle to the long sides, as a diagonal

Snake line —a loop or curved pattern that does not follow the track

Threading the needle — Alternating riders cross each other's path

These are the basic maneuvers. As your quadrille group becomes proficient in performing them, you will think of ways to vary them and combine them to create a kaleidoscopic effect with the horses.

Polish

As the riders become more proficient, the director needs to spend time encouraging them to make their horses more beautiful as they do all the other things they need to do to ride in the group.

Quadrille gaits are collected gaits — to the extent possible with the horses available. This means, of course, pushing the horse up to the bit so the neck becomes arched and the quarters are rounded in engagement. The horses need to be active and energetic, but not fast — rather somewhat stately.

Practicing Tests

To learn the tests, whether a compulsory or your own freestyle, begin by outlining it on paper. Start with a paper on which you have drawn several dressage arenas, complete with letters. These are the frames on which you will draw each successive pattern the riders are to perform. Indicate direction of travel with arrows, and annotate with comments as necessary.

Once you have your test on paper, then practice by walking the test *on foot.* Set up a miniature dressage ring with cones or buckets, whatever you can find to define the rails and letters. Then practice going through all the patterns that you will be working with in your test. This is not only a great way to learn the test, but also to learn the terminology without boring the horses.

You will also be amazed at how easy it is to get out of place and mixed up even when you are just walking through the movements. Therefore, you save a lot of frustration by practicing on foot, because if it is hard on foot, imagine what it will be like in the saddle. Then, when everyone is feeling confident, it is time to work with the horses.

The entrance, halt, and salute are performed in the compulsory tests by entering in pairs. The first pair enters as close to each other as possible. The second pair watches each other and split to come up on either side of the first pair (called a "fan"). Keep the group as close as possible. For the halt, one rider whistles and says "One, two, halt!" then whistles again and says "One, two, salute."

To move off, the designated rider says "One, two, trot," and so forth through the test.

Some Pertinent Rules

Whether showing compulsories or freestyles, team members choose their own music (usually background music), as well as their dress and color scheme, to characterize their "style." The overall look can reflect the team's music, but should be relatively conservative. The horses may be shown in matching leg wraps and their normal equestrian attire (such as matching saddle pads and brow bands) may be colored. However, they may not be decorated with items such as pompoms, tassels, or ribbons. Bits must be regulation bits and bridles. The riders may wear dressage attire or any matching uniforms (anything from T-shirts to dresses). The uniforms may even be different if they follow a theme: like Dorothy, Tin Man, Lion, and Scarecrow, as an example.

Spurs and whips are not only optional for teams, but for individuals as well. All the members of the team do not have to wear spurs or carry whips.

The AHSA "level rule" does not apply to quadrilles. A rider who is showing Grand Prix is allowed to ride in an Intermediate (Second Level) quadrille.

Please do not forget that in championship classes (regular dressage tests), another rider at the show cannot ride your horse, even if the other rider is in a quadrille. This rule stands.

A fall of a rider, or fall of a horse in which the rider is separated from the horse, will also incur elimination of the team. A horse leaving the arena will also result in elimination, provided the fence is standard (an actual low fence, not just a line on the ground).

If the team enters the ring with a lame horse, the team will be eliminated. However, if a horse appears to become lame during the ride, it will result in a lowered score, but the team is not eliminated, provided they can continue. If one horse goes off course, it will lower the score. It is only an error of test if the whole team goes off course.

The Levels

There are four levels:

- Introductory — (Walk/Trot)
- Novice — (Training Level)
- Preliminary — (First Level)
- Intermediate — (Second Level)

The names of the levels are intentionally different from the corresponding dressage tests because it is too tempting for the judges to expect the frame of the horse to match the dressage level. These are not dressage tests and do not have the same performance requirements.

Basically, the levels have the same movements as their corresponding dressage test, but not the same performance measures. The trot work in the tests may be either sitting or posting as long as the team is consistent.

The Introductory Level is designed for the beginning team. This level starts with the basic movements, such as full and half-circles and obliques (diagonals ridden singly) at the walk and trot. Canter work is introduced at the Novice Level, which is similar in difficulty to Training Level in regular dressage. The Preliminary Level is close to First Level, incorporating leg yields and intricate patterns. The quadrille Intermediate Level parallels Second Level, with shoulder-ins and medium trot.

There are also freestyle classes so riders can create their own tests on their levels if there is enough interest. These are offered at all levels, including at higher levels than those available in the compulsories.

Scoring

During competition, quadrille teams work toward performing the movements precisely, just as in regular dressage. Gaits and rider position have minimal bearing on the scoring, but spacing, alignment, and synchrony are paramount. The team is also judged on a different set of Collective Marks: spacing, synchrony and alignment, impulsion, submission, and performance as a group.

Spacing refers to the distance between horses. It includes the distance from nose to tail when riders are following each other and the distance from side to side when riders are riding in a line or pair.

There is no set spacing that teams must use, and it can change from movement to movement. Whatever it is, it must be maintained by all.

Alignment refers to the fact that when the team travels down the centerline, the judge should only be able to see the first horse or pair of horses. Each horse should travel directly behind or beside the other. When the team splits, they should arrive at their parallel letters for the next transition at the same time.

Synchrony refers to alignment in motion. When one horse turns, they all turn. When one horse transitions down, they all do.

In the same fashion as regular dressage, **impulsion** is key. Teams that ride forward to the markers score higher than those that are sluggish.

To score **submission**, the judge looks for an acceptance of the aids of the team as a whole. If equine members are missing leads or tossing heads, this will affect the score.

Performance as a group is based on the overall feeling that the team projects, which includes tack and attire. The judge considers whether the group shows the ability to perform with uniform quality and in a harmonious, cooperative manner.

Create Your Own

If you do not have any shows that are holding quadrille classes, ask a show manager if your team could ride a demonstration test during a break in the program. It will be a real crowd pleaser.

Quadrille is ridden in a Small arena (20 x 40 meters), so if the show is only using a large arena, offer to cordon off the appropriate size with cones or ground poles. The show organizers may also be willing to comply if you suggest bringing your own boom box to play the music. In these ways, you can make it simple for show organizers to include quadrille classes.

If it is a quadrille competition, consider that many technical delegates have not had an opportunity to obtain experience with the quadrille rules. Show management should document on the class sheet that the level rule does not apply to the quadrille classes, and that horse and rider attire for the quadrille rides will follow USDF rules. It may also be helpful to document that horses and riders may be substituted in the quadrille teams.

The Freestyle

Remember, the quadrille is presented to a judge seated at "C", so dramatic patterns should face the judge as much as possible. Generally, more acute angles (as in changing rein across the diagonal) are more attractive than more open ones — so it is best to use the short diagonal, even when "threading the needle." Keep in mind that you can use the quarter lines as well for added interest. Just remember that you're trying to paint pictures with the horses, using the borders of the dressage arena as a frame. Be creative — try not to repeat patterns used in the dressage tests.

In addition, you will have to experiment to a degree. Some patterns that look good on paper appear perfectly awful when they're ridden. Moreover, some that seem "do-able" just won't work in practice. When you have the quadrille designed, copy it, and distribute it to the group. They should memorize it, or at least be familiar with it, before they try to ride it. You can have a "caller" just as in a standard test. After the first rehearsal, revise as necessary. Your group will very likely have some excellent suggestions for improving the flow of the ride.

Finally, remember above all else to have a good time. Quadrille is a fun sport, and everyone will enjoy the laughs that go along with the mistakes that are inevitable as the riders learn the patterns. When the riders are experienced, and the quadrille patterns really flow, you'll be amazed at how beautiful the ride can be. It is aesthetically appealing, and somehow does the heart good to see pride in team association.

Chapter Twenty-Six

Onward and Upward

Eventually, you will develop a rhythm in your training and your horse will learn to expect something new every so often. If you continue to supply new experiences that are safe and successful, unexpected occurrences will bother your horse much less.

Whenever a horse appears to have reached a plateau, that's your cue to experiment with moving up a test or a level. You may not be able to master all the movements of the new test, but it gives you and your horse something to think about.

Keep in mind there are not drastic separations between levels; one test blends into the next. Perhaps your horse is not ready to go to the next *level*, but is ready to move up a test or two. Remember that you usually can enter as many tests as you wish in two consecutive levels at any show.

Knowing when to pause and regroup, when to move on, or when to back up in training and developing a competition horse can only be learned by experience. Sometimes you need to move on, to go to a higher level or test, and incorporate some new movements. Then your horse will "figure out" the ones that don't seem to be going smoothly.

In other words, don't bore your horse (or yourself) trying to get perfection in every movement of a test before you move on. Striving for "perfection" is too far out of reach. You must learn to accept the best you can do. Dressage will never be boring for you or your horse if you keep advancing and growing.

Some riders, because they are getting high scores in Training Level, for instance — or maybe because they are not getting expected high scores — hesitate to move up, fearing their scores will get worse. If you stay in the "easy" levels too long, your horse may decide he doesn't want to expend the extra effort

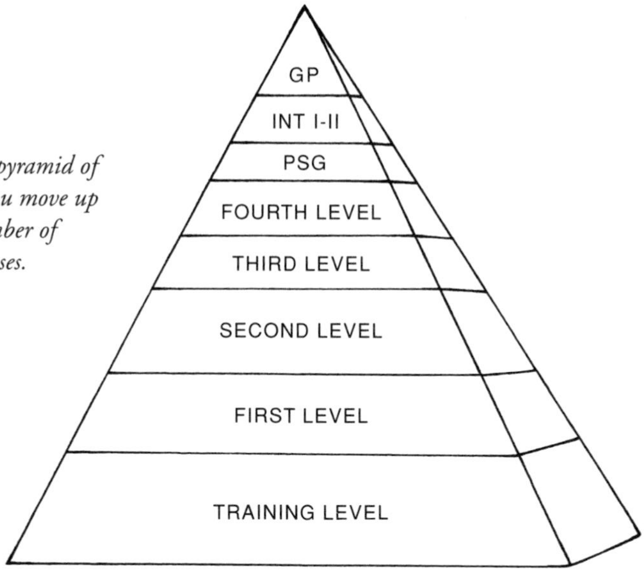

Figure 26.1 The pyramid of competition: As you move up the levels, the number of competitors decreases.

to move on, or worse, he may "tune you out" and get sulky.

Drilling will dull even a young horse and you may lose that spark of interest — the horse must want to do this thing called "dressage." You must have his cooperation and his enthusiasm. Bored horses either "shut down" (become dull and sulky) or demonstrate irritability. If you don't give them enough variety, they may invent their own! Never expect perfection from your horse, but demand perfection from yourself!

Unless a horse is hopelessly unsuitable, you should be able to get "passing" scores and work up from level to level. It is perfectly respectable in dressage to advance if you get scores in the range of 50 to 60 percent, even if your horse never wins a blue ribbon.

Most horses can score reasonably well up into First Level. Somewhere at Second or Third Level each horse and rider team comes to a moment of truth. Is the horse "good enough" to go on? Is the rider good enough? How important are scores and awards to you or do you just want to learn all you can learn?

Depending on the section of the country, your horse may not be "competitive" (place in the ribbons) unless he is in the 6-7-8 score range, but this should not prevent you from *schooling* at that level. Once a horse's performance at a particular level or test is consistently in the 6 and 7 range ("satisfactory" to "fairly good"), he is probably ready to move up.

Then again, if your horse is getting increasingly irritated with the routine, perhaps you have reached the limit of his potential. As you progress up the levels, you may reach a point where the horse can "do" the movements, but they are not up to competition standard because of conformation restrictions. Here the rider must make a decision to accept low scores or move on to another horse.

Any horse can do any and all of the dressage "movements," but it takes special conformation to do them with enough style and flair to receive really good scores. (More on suitable/unsuitable conformation for upper-level horses later in this chapter.) At Second Level, the horse must be able to show a little collection, which is a lightening of the forehand. At Third Level, the emphasis is on extended, medium, *and* collected gaits. At Fourth Level, flying changes must be perfected. The competition starts thinning out as you go up the levels. If you are wondering if your horse measures up, take it to a reputable trainer who competes at the upper levels and ask for an honest evaluation (figure 26.1).

If you believe your horse is good enough to compete at the upper levels, you should try it. There is little to lose and much to gain if you experiment — who knows you may have a diamond in the rough! If you give it an honest try at Third or Fourth Level, you will learn *so* much.

If you believe you have a horse that is conformationally and temperamentally suitable, but you've never competed or trained for the higher levels, you need to make a decision:

1. Hand the horse to a trainer and watch with pride as the team reaches into the upper levels, or;

2. Commit to doing it all yourself. If you hit a training snag, understand you must find help. Or;

3. Sell the horse and start the next one, solidifying your Training Level skills.

Time to Upgrade?

The newcomer to dressage is seldom planning on taking their present horse all the way to Grand Prix level. Usually it will take two or three (or more) horses to learn on and perhaps to progress up the levels, if that is your goal.

You may eventually get to a point that your present horse simply cannot progress. If conformation is the cause of deficiencies and the horse can't meet the "standard" of the level, he is doomed to low scores. After the rider has advanced to the stage at which she has good balance and can get all that this particular horse has to offer, then she may want to move up to a horse that has a bigger stride, a more beautiful way of movement, and more "suitable" conformation. Her "school horse" can then move on to another novice rider. There is always a market for reliable, happy, "schoolmasters."

A rider who is lucky enough to have ridden various horses can draw comparisons and improve her techniques, which is an important part of learning to ride dressage. Furthermore, the diversity of horses likely to be encountered should add to the rider's experience and enlarge her "vocabulary" of communication skills to a greater extent than might be the case if she always rode the same horse in the same conditions year after year.

Dressage riders who have to give up the sport, or whose horses have reached their peak in performance, are often anxious to sell their mounts to suitable owners who will continue dressage riding. These horses may be suitable and often quite competitive at the medium levels. You may be able to purchase a Third or Fourth Level horse that can further your education and still be salable in a couple of years.

If you are in the market for a competition horse, you will want to select the best horse you can afford and then upgrade from time to time. Study what temperament and conformation traits make it easier or harder for the horse to perform the movements.

The following is meant to help you decide if you can realistically go on with your present horse, or if you should embark on the selection of a more suitable competition prospect. Remember, no horse is perfect — it is a matter of whether you can deal with, or sometimes live with, whatever faults your horse may possess.

A Suitable Temperament

The art of training is to recognize the potential of the horse and to develop it to the utmost. We must know how and to what extent we can eliminate or cope with faults in temperament and conformation. This requires considerable experience, which can only be gained by handling different horses over the years.

While suitable conformation may improve the scores, the horse's mental attitude and temperament have just as much, if not more to do with the outcome. **The most perfect specimen in the world is of no use if the human cannot command him to perform.**

As a trainer, you should be able to deal with almost any horse's particular temperament or personality. There are, however, cases where the trainer's personality clashes with that of the horse. In these cases, the horse would obviously be better off with a different trainer! In some cases, the horse's temperament makes him difficult to deal with in a competition setting. The competition horse must have a mind that will put up with the stress of travel and performing under difficult circumstances. Whether or not the rider wants to deal with these shortcomings is a personal matter.

It can be very difficult to assess a horse's personality in a short period of time, as when examining a horse for purchase. It can take thirty days to a year to really figure out the true personality of an equine. Nonetheless, with careful observation you can come to a pretty good conclusion as to a horse's true "inner self." This in turn can help you decide if the horse is suitable to go on with.

Every horse is a unique blend of personality, intelligence, sensitivity, and attitude. Of the four, only sensitivity and attitude can be altered by the environment or human intervention. While poor feed or stressful conditions may temporarily mask a horse's inborn personality, once these are corrected, the horse's true personality or temperament will resurface.

As with humans, some personalities are better suited to a competition setting than others. Horses can be divided into three broad temperament or personality types: aggressive, submissive, and timid. Individuals can, of course, be inbetween two types, such as "submissive but a little timid," or "slightly aggressive but mainly submissive," and so forth.

The Aggressive Horse

The aggressive horse will show initiative and will be sure of its own strength. If well-schooled, the aggressive or dominant horse steps out boldly, yet may show a hint of resentment if "made" to work. He will try to exert his own desires on the unheeding rider or handler.

With a confident and skillful rider, the aggressive horse will seemingly go through fire, but a similar horse that has had a bad upbringing (or has learned that you are a timid rider) will only willingly do those things it enjoys or does not mind doing. That horse will fight you every step of the way to avoid what it doesn't want to do of its own accord.

The aggressive type is full of confidence. Proper training can bring this confidence under control, but no amount of training can instill this confidence in a horse if it is not present in the first place.

The top dressage horses are often of the aggressive personality. They have the desire to "show off." The down side of this personality type is that it often takes a very knowledgeable and talented rider to keep this exuberance under control without stifling it.

You can recognize the aggressive horse by observing him in his stall or paddock. The aggressive horse will probably come right up to meet you as you approach his stall or pasture gate. He will show curiosity for new places and objects. He tends to be alert, but not fidgety, and he stands proud with chest out and neck up.

The aggressive horse is more likely to put his nose on you, sniffing and investigating your clothes. If you shove him away, he is likely to come right back. An aggressive animal is more likely to treat his handlers as another horse — shoving, rubbing and attempting to "walk over" the less dominant handler.

Under saddle, the aggressive horse gives the impression of knowing where he is going and how he is going to get there. He either marches out boldly, or you feel him purposely "holding back." He knows his power and you better hope he has been trained to use it *for you* and not *against you.*

It should be apparent that the aggressive horse requires a fair but fearless rider. When you ask him to do something in the early stages of training, he is more likely to refuse you than the submissive horse. He's a little bit of a smart aleck until you have demonstrated that you're even more dominant then he is.

You establish your dominance not by overdisciplining the horse, which is likely to cause resentment and a "fight," but rather by "out-smarting" him. With the aggressive animal, you must know all the pressure points or control points. For instance, when you longe him, *always* use a strong longeing cavesson or bridle. When you lead him, put a chain on the halter. Make sure he is taught obedience to the leg and the hand (see Chapter 11, "All the Horse Needs to Know"). He must never find out your weaknesses.

Once you have established your authority, his natural boldness extends to his trust in you. He accepts that you, the dominant figure, know even more than he does. So you bring him into a strange looking arena or past a scary looking judge's box, and he says, "okay boss," and he struts his stuff.

If the aggressive horse has been badly treated in the past, he may be either overly bold or overly shy. To differentiate between the aggressive horse that has been turned shy and the naturally timid horse, observe how the horse "defends" itself. The aggressive horse may run to the back of his stall and hunker his back to you, but he is out to get the first lick in — he'll try to get you before you get him. Conversely, if the timid horse cowers in the corner, he will try every way possible to get away from the handler. If the timid horse kicks, it does so while retreating.

In general, you will have to assert your dominance often with the aggressive horse, once in a while with the submissive, and rarely with the timid. The aggressive temperament or personality will be an asset to some riders, but a liability to others.

The Submissive or Passive Horse

The vast majority of horses fall somewhere in the submissive group, and this is an advantage for the vast majority of horse owners!

The passive horse will have the look of docility — calmer eyes, ears at rest — and will show less interest in things surrounding him, especially if they are familiar. The submissive horse may turn his rump to you when you enter the stall, or simply stand his ground, allowing you to walk up to him but not offering to advance. If he retreats, it may be that he has not been handled much, or that he anticipates work.

The submissive horse adjusts his behavior to maintain the "status quo." He is a tolerant horse that takes his handler's inconsistencies, mistakes, mood swings, and harmless threats in stride and bears no grudges. The submissive horse usually stays cooperative under conditions that may even conflict with his own desires. This does not mean he is doltish or that he will not react when suddenly frightened or subjected to unfair or painful demands. The submissive horse is not above exerting his influence if he thinks he can, but will be quick to back down at the least show of authority. He has little strength of will and can be made to do almost anything. Such a horse will be comparatively easily managed and not so apt to get excited over things that would throw the timid type into a fretting lather or cause the aggressive type to rebel. These horses make the best amateur horses — mounts for people who do not have the time, energy, or maybe the desire to compete in the "big time."

It also takes a submissive horse to be a "schoolmaster." A horse that will have the patience to submit to a less-than-expert rider who may be trying to figure out how to get the complicated movements. Granted, he won't be very brilliant in his movement, but at least he will make the effort when the rider "finds the right buttons." The aggressive type is likely to argue with an inexperienced handler and a timid horse is just downright unpredictable.

The submissive horse will put in a performance that is calm and consistent, since he is not so easily distracted, but the rider may have to really work in order to get any semblance of brilliance.

The Timid Horse

The timid type will be lacking in courage or self-confidence. He will be nervous and tense even when there is little reason to be, and he will often act before he thinks. He may be difficult to handle when something unusual is expected of him. He will be very cautious or hesitant about entering unknown territory. It may be difficult to get the horse to stand still and his attention always seems to be elsewhere.

The timid horse will be erratic under saddle, being distracted by every little thing. He often shows moments of incredible brilliance, but can't seem to sustain it for any length of time or appear to be doing so in response to the handler's cues.

You will be able to "feel" the lack of self-confidence of the timid horse under saddle. The movements will be quick and often short, the muscles tight. His attention shifts quickly with each little distraction. The timid horse's goal in life is to stay away from dangers. With timid riders, these are the horses that spook, shy, and "run away." With an overbearing or impatient rider, they turn into stupid blunderers.

The timid horse will tend to overreact to punishment. Any show of rough treatment will cause him to break out in a nervous sweat, liable to explode at the slightest provocation, impervious to his surroundings and capable of blundering into or over anything or anybody in his attempt to escape. He actually tries to please his human handlers (because he is afraid to misbehave) and he's friendly as a puppy when he's in a settled state.

He will never be lazy, and will seldom tire. He is the kind that runs his heart out on the track and dies standing on his feet.

A timid horse is not a good choice for a competition horse. For one thing, being required to go into the arena with only two or three minutes to become acquainted with the surroundings is an almost impossible task with the really timid horse.

In addition, an excessively nervous horse may not hold up well under the stress of training or travel, and may be prone to gastrointestinal disorders such as diarrhea or colic when under stress. Though he may mellow with age and good experience, though he may come to rely on your good judgment most of the time, that quivering creature is never going to solidify into unflappable steadfastness. A timid horse is suitable only for a calm, experienced rider in a non-stressful environment.

What's the Best Temperament?

Is there a best temperament or personality for a horse to have? If you call yourself a trainer, you must be able to adapt to the horse's temperament. Only if you learn to work with the individual horse's personality will you be successful. If you are purchasing a horse, however, with the idea of it being your personal competition mount, look for a horse of the temperament with which you will be most comfortable working. Try him out thoroughly and be sure you feel at ease when riding, handling, and doing what you plan to do with him. You should also genuinely like the horse and enjoy riding and working with him.

"Suitable" Conformation

Dressage is good for every horse, but not every horse is good for (competition) dressage.

Figure 26.2
At about Second Level you may have to consider whether your horse is capable of moving "up". This horse does look "capable." Photo by Charlene Strickland.

Probably any horse, no matter what its "type" or conformation, can reasonably be asked to perform the dressage movements required in the dressage tests through at least Second Level — and will probably be a better athlete for it. It *does,* however, require a certain "type" or build of horse to execute the movements up through Fourth Level and certainly for the Grand Prix level (figure 26.2).

In horses, as in humans, build or "body type" determines movement. A horse built for one profession is likely to be very "misshapen" (for lack of a better term) for another.

There are football players who take ballet lessons to improve their suppleness and maneuverability. Likewise, the agility of horses of "inappropriate" conformation can be improved by dressage methods, but the judge is not going to give high marks to the football hero dancing "Swan Lake," any more than the typical retrained racehorse will get high marks on his collected trot or canter. Neither is "built" to perform the movements as defined in competition rules. Both will be scored behind an individual who moves better — all other things being equal.

What Does an Upper Level Dressage Horse Look Like?

Prior to 1912, dressage exhibition horses — which is what the dressage-trained horses of the officer's schools, as well as institutions like the Spanish Riding School of Vienna, were called — in reality were *specialists.* Each horse had one or two movements that they performed to perfection, and only these movements were shown in public.

As dressage competition evolved (being separate from exhibition performances), the extended and strong gaits of the officer's mounts (mostly Thoroughbreds) were added to the collected movements of the Classical School. Thereafter, the dressage horse had to possess multiple talents.

Not surprisingly, the sport horse breeds evolved simultaneously with the competition,

Photo 26.3
A "good mover" will land hind foot first, as this horse is about to do. Photo by Charlene Strickland.

and the European warmbloods have come to dominate high level dressage. The FEI rules and guidelines for competition dressage were written by the Europeans for the European sport horse.

Individuals from other than warmblood breeds can be successful in competition, but you need to take a close look at the conformation of the individual (even if it is a warmblood) before you decide if this horse is capable of doing what you want.

Movement is Everything

Three absolutely pure gaits are required. The walk should be elastic (loose and unconstrained), with four distinct beats. The trot must have two beats; elastic, powerful, and "scopey", with reach and roundness (the flight of each foot describes an arch rather than a flattened arc). Each hind foot should give the impression of touching the ground in front of the stifle, and of lifting off while the cannon is still fairly close to the vertical and fairly soon after the point of the buttock has passed over it. There must be a powerful thrust from the hindquarters producing suspension and overtrack with a naturally slow rhythm. The action should be balanced front and rear (same amount of lift and stretch), with lots of freedom to the shoulders and hips. The canter must be three beats with a clear phase of suspension, "scopey" and round. The outside hind should seem to pass the inside hind generously; the outside fore should lift off the ground when the cannon bone is fairly close to vertical. If the forefoot leaves the ground much past vertical, the horse will be "on his forehand." It is often mentioned that high level dressage horses typically possess a greater range of motion, combining both strength and extension, than what is desired in a pleasure riding animal.

While it is comparatively easy to ruin good gaits, it is very difficult to improve upon nature. You can improve the trot somewhat, the canter slightly, and the walk the least.

The Ideal Conformation for Dressage

The conformation that is most likely to produce the desired kind of movement is depicted in figure 26.4.

A brief list of the desired features:

1. Body shape: The body is slightly longer than it is tall. The measurement from the point of shoulder to the point of buttock should be three to five inches longer than the height at the withers. The horse should divide into three nearly equal parts of: (1) well laid-back shoulder, (2) strong, broad, well-coupled back, and (3) long powerful hip. This facilitates sufficient power in the hindquarters to lift and lighten the forehand.

2. Body balance: The withers should be at least level or preferably slightly higher than the peak of the croup. The elbow and stifle should be at approximately the same level. A body build "up hill" makes collection easier. The withers should be of medium height and extending well back for a good saddle fit.

3. Body width and depth: These need to fit the rider. Medium width is probably best, to provide a solid frame for strength and balance. The body should be nearly as deep as it is long in the leg. Short legs (the measurement from ground to elbow is less than elbow to withers) would lower the center of mass and make it difficult for the horse to lighten the forehand, especially in canter. The horse should be deep in the groin area. Strong belly muscles lift and round (arch) the back. Each side of the horse must be equally developed in order for the horse to be straight and even in all his movements.

4. Neck set: The neck must be easily carried at 45 degrees or higher. It should be broad at the base, tapering to a flexible joining at the poll. The wing of the atlas must be near horizontal so the jaws can accommodate the windpipe when the horse draws the face to vertical. The neck is the major balancing factor for the horse. A high set and properly flexed neck allows the horse to move his weight rearward. A large mouth makes it easier to take the bits.

5. Shoulder and arm: The shoulder blade can be fairly short to medium length, well "laid back" (sloping 45 to 50 degrees). The arm should be comparatively long and upright and should form an angle of 90 degrees at the point of the shoulder. This allows free forward, upward, and sideways motion.

6. Hip: The hip (measured from the point of hip to the point of buttock) must be quite long (at least 33% of body length) and at approximately 18 to 23 degrees for an equal mix of upward and forward thrust, with deep muscling on top (between the pelvis and croup). The dressage horse can get by with a more level hip angle than a jumper, but should not be less than 15 degrees.

7. Sacro-lumbar joint: This joint should be no more than an inch or two back from an imaginary line connecting the points of the hips. This has been called the most important joint in the body of a dressage horse. If well forward, as described above, it allows the horse to compress and extend the back, the major prerequisite of collection.

8. Hind leg: You want average angulation at the hock, but a long, forwardly sloped femur and well bent stifle to provide strong forward thrust and power. The thigh and gaskin should be of equal length, which facilitates a comparatively show rhythm. Ideal angles are 90 degrees at the hip joint and 130 degrees in the stifle and hock.

9. Muscle mass: Medium muscling is preferable. Short, bulky muscles restrict the strides, while too long and lean structure may not provide enough strength.

10. Sound legs and feet are important — as they are for any high performance horse. If the horse won't hold up to reasonable work, all the training will be for naught.

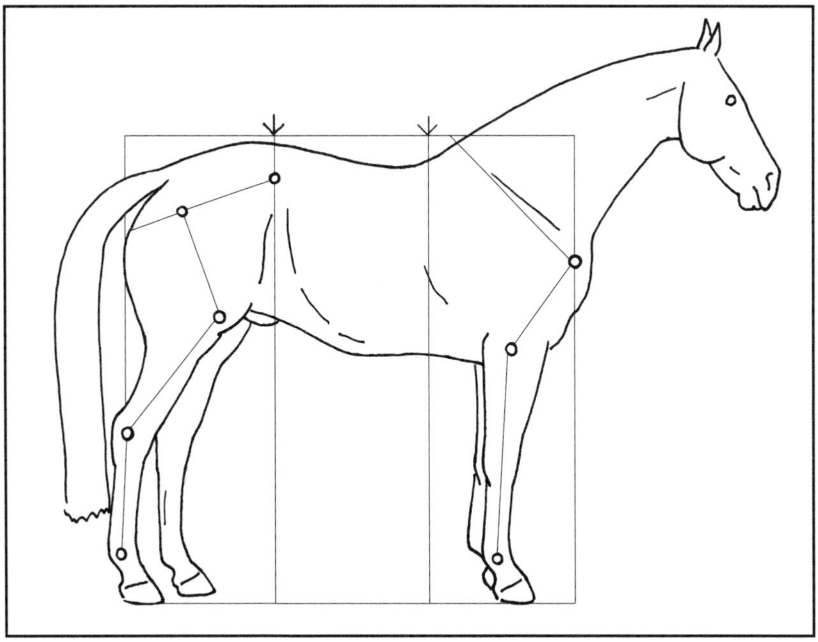

Figure 26.4
Ideal dressage horse conformation.

Flaws to avoid in the walk are a lateral walk, and irregularity behind. Both can be caused by conformation when the angles of front and hind legs don't match.

The trot must be absolutely parallel in all phases. Actually, it has been proven by slow motion photography of elite Grand Prix horses that the diagonal pairs of legs do not strike the ground at the same time. In a desirable horse, the hind leg of the diagonal pair actually will land before its partner, called "positive diagonal advance placement" (PDAP). This means the hind foot lands first. The trait seems to be linked to conformation; it can seldom be "trained" into the horse if he does not possess it naturally (figure 26.3).

Even more important than PDAP is that the front and hind legs are matched in movement. That is, the cannons of front and hind follow the same arc. If a horse is high and round in front, but short and low in back, he will never be balanced in action.

Avoid trots that are either inactive behind or the horse appears to be "running" (quick rhythm). Also, don't get too impressed with a big floaty trot that leaves the horse's hocks way out behind. That kind of horse gets "passagey" (a hesitation in the rhythm) when you try to get him truly forward and connected, and the collected trot won't be correct. It may always be hard to make him go forward.

Watch out for lateral canters and four-beat canters. If the canter is too "earth bound," the horse will have difficulty with flying changes. The horse that goes like a rocking horse, kind of nodding along on his forehand, is flawed. Judges like to see a horse that canters "uphill," that doesn't leave his legs out behind him or appear to pull himself along with his front legs.

Less than Ideal Conformation

If you intend to take a horse above Second Level, there are certain conformation features to avoid.

LOW-SET NECK

This is where the neck is "set on," or comes out of the shoulders low down. Usually, if the point of the shoulder is low, the neck will be set low (figure 26.5B).

The height of the neck affects the height of the stride of the front legs. A horse with a

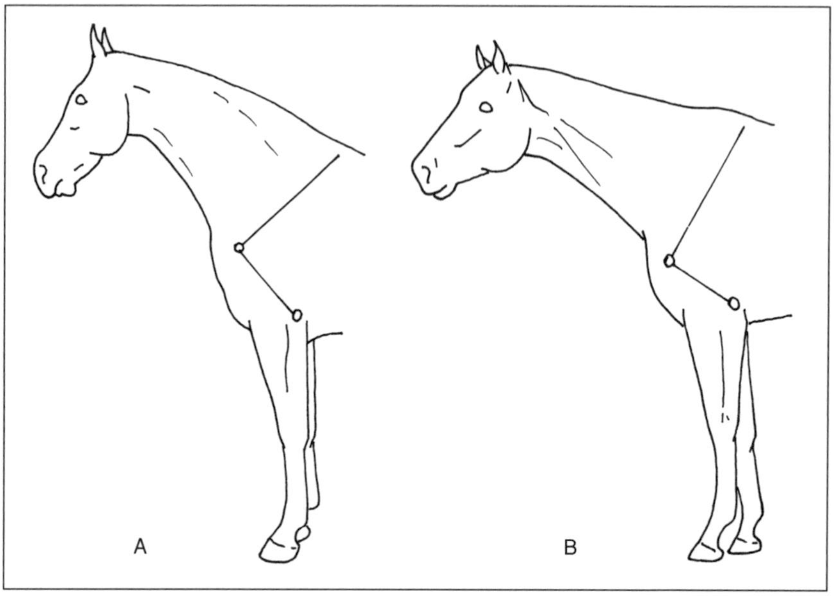

Figure 26.5 Correct versus low neck.

naturally low-set neck will have to "ewe" his neck to raise it. This will place him in an "above the bit" position and the muscles on the lower side of the neck will become noticeably developed. This makes it difficult for the horse to change his balance point. (This is seldom a problem in the lower levels.)

THICK THROATLATCH

If the horse has a heavy, thick lower jaw, the chances are slim for a true collection. A thick lower jaw makes it physically impossible for the horse to give easily in the neck, as the lower jawbone presses against the windpipe and therefore obstructs it. Again, this is not a handicap at the lower levels.

SWAN NECK

A long, thin neck that has a prominent bend at the top and joins the chest at a high point (has a narrow base) is called a "swan neck." Horses with a swan neck usually have difficulties in establishing a steady contact. They go above or behind the bit or "break" at the third vertebra very easily (see Chapter 23).

If horses with swan necks are asked too early for a high head carriage, they will often become "wobbly" at the withers. The neck is not stable and it can be pulled in or moved sideways, which can create "rubber necking" and allow the outside shoulder to fall out. It is especially important to ride horses with swan necks actively forward. Should the horse not take the bit, try a thicker snaffle or a rubber bit. When riding through turns, use stronger outside aids. The fault can sometimes be lessened by strengthening the lower neck muscles through riding forward with the neck long and low (see Chapter 13).

HIGH HINDQUARTERS

Young horses are often higher in the hindquarters than their withers. As a result of this, more weight is put on the forehand. If the young horse does not grow out of this, it is unsuitable for upper-level dressage. If the horse is only slightly different in height between withers and croup, work him on hills (at slow gaits), and over cavaletti. This may help the horse bend his hind joints more and lower the quarters slightly. Also proper work "on the bit" will strengthen the muscles of the barrel and raise the withers somewhat. A horse with higher hindquarters should not be ridden "long and

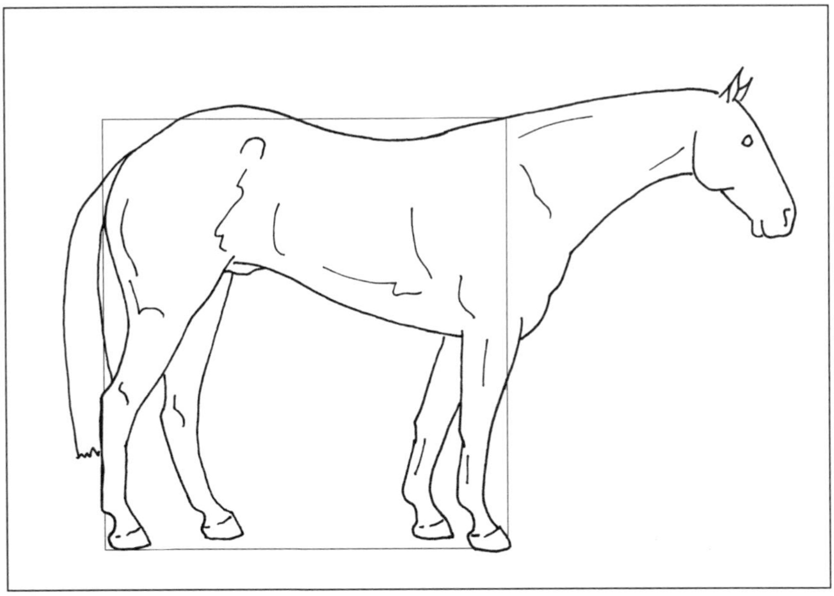

Figure 26.6
This horse is not only higher at the croup than the withers, he is also longer than he is tall. This is typical conformation for a sprinting racehorse.

low" for any length of time. Even during the loosening up period, he should be asked to carry his head without "leaning" on the rider's hands (figure 26.6).

LONG BACK

Horses with this conformation do not always have a problem. If the back is well-muscled between withers and loin and the hindquarters are not higher than the withers, the back cannot be called faulty. On the contrary, a long, supple, and *strong* back allows the horse to show good lateral work. However, if the back is so long that the hind legs cannot reach the center of gravity, then this makes canter work difficult. The back can be strengthened with hill work, repeated transitions, and half-halts.

SHORT BACK

Horses with short backs would appear to be easier to collect, as their hind legs come under more easily. To the contrary, they can tighten the back very easily, blocking true collection and making lateral work and piaffe difficult. If the back is tense and tight, the horse will also have a tendency to four-beat at the canter. Yet another problem is the horse may forge (hit the front heels with the back feet).

Short-backed horses are often very athletic and (depending on other conformation points) often make excellent jumpers or event horses. For dressage work, the short back is usually rather tight and needs a comparatively long neck to relax it. If this relaxation does not occur, it is practically impossible to obtain ground-covering strides. Short-backed horses can be uncomfortable to ride. Even if relaxed, they have difficulty bending and may receive low scores in lateral and circle work. They can only be brought to their full potential when the rider pays special attention to loosening exercises and works with exceptionally light hands.

FAULTY COUPLING

The sacro-lumbar (S-L) joint is a conformation feature that will either limit or enhance your horse's chances in dressage competition in the higher levels. While any horse can extend and collect his frame to some extent, in higher competition he must be able to show a big difference between extension and collection. This is where conformation comes in.

The medium, collected, and extended gaits are distinguished by being "bigger" (having

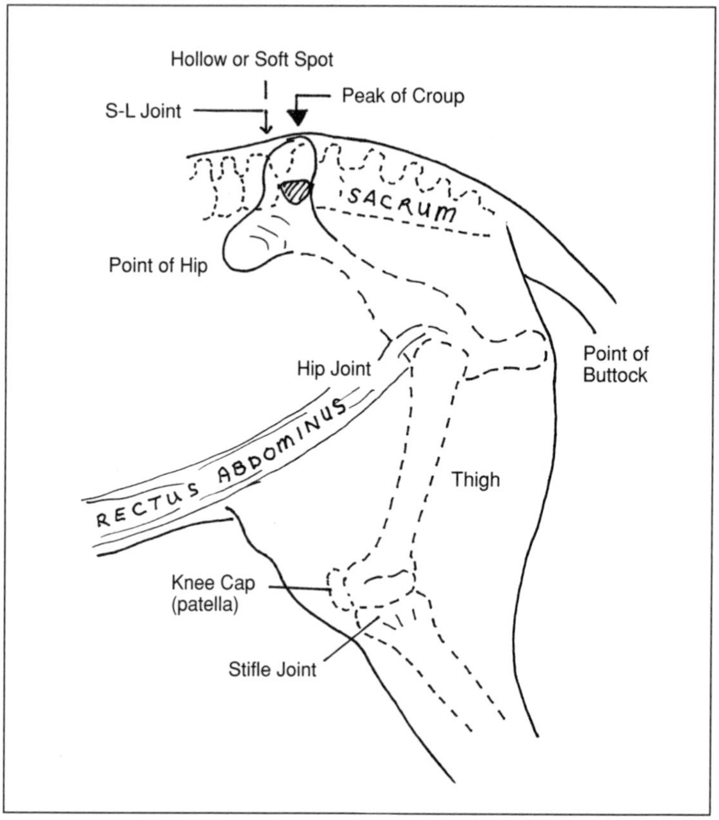

Figure 26.7 Anatomy of the S-L joint.

greater range of motion) than the working gaits. While every horse is capable of showing some difference in the gaits, some are endowed with physical characteristics that make it easier for them.

Collection and extension are accomplished by engaging the hindquarters. The ability to engage (bend the joints of the hindquarters) is partly training but largely conformation. The act of collection is initiated by encouraging the horse to shorten his base by "tucking" his hindquarters under (accompanied by arching the neck and raising the root of the neck). This ability to coil the body "like a spring" adds to the ability to extend the gaits as well. The dressage horse that can show the greatest difference between his collected and extended (and medium) gaits will — all other factors being equal — get the higher scores for those movements.

The conformation feature that allows the greatest degree of engagement is the ability to rotate the sacrolumbar (S-L) joint. To locate the S-L joint, find the peak of the croup — the peak of the croup is the upper most point of the pelvis. Immediately in front of this peak is a slight hollow or soft spot along the spinal column. You may have to palpate your horse's top line to locate this spot. This is the S-L joint. It is the joint between the last lumbar vertebra and the sacrum (the fused vertebrae of the croup). The first vertebra of the sacrum is bonded to the inner wings of the pelvis; thus, the S-L joint must flex to allow the pelvis to "tuck" under (figure 26.7).

An ideally placed sacro-lumbar joint lies as far forward as is anatomically possible on an imaginary line connecting the left and right points of the hip, as seen with Horse A (see figure 26.8). This not only shortens the functional back; it provides the greatest possible arc of rotation for the pelvis. The further the pelvis can rotate downward, the greater the resulting bascule or ability to collect or engage, and the greater the range of collection and extension the horse will be capable of at all gaits.

The further back this joint is placed (from a line connecting the points of the hip), the less range of motion between collection and extension. If it is too far back (four inches or more), the horse will find it very difficult, if not impossible, to engage ("tuck") the hindquarters to show a difference in collection and extension. A horse with ideal placement of the SL joint will be able to lengthen and lower his

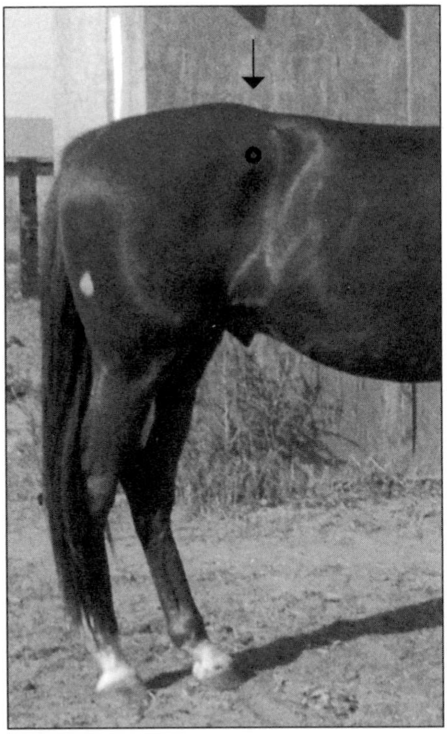

Photo 26.8 Horse A: excellent S-L placement.

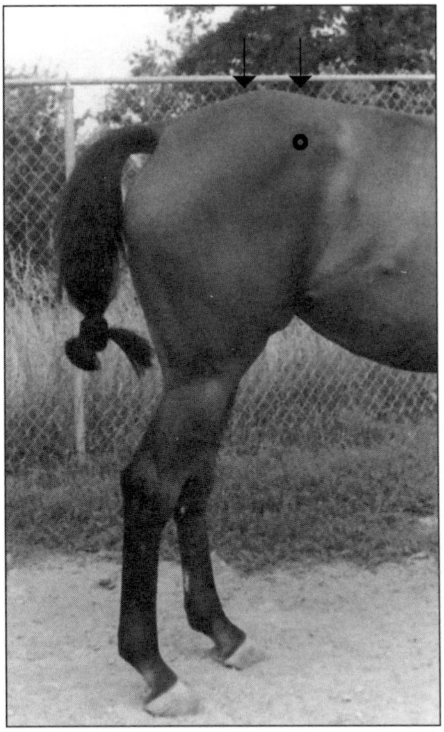

Photo 26.9 Horse B: poor S-L placement (too far back).

stride and then shorten and raise the arc of his stride. Because Horse B (see figure 26.9) has a poor S-L placement, the angle of push off is fairly fixed in place. This horse has two speeds within each gait — fast and slow.

S-L placement also affects the quality of the canter. The further forward this joint, the more "uphill" (engaged) the canter can be (see Chapter 12). The further back, the more the canter will lack flexibility and engagement. Cantering (or galloping) is in fact impossible without some flexion of the S-L joint. Too much trotting will stiffen a horse's loin and decrease the flexibility he might normally have. This is why some Standardbreds (harness racehorses) "lose" their ability to canter. It is also why saddle horses need to be cantered enough to keep them flexible (figure 26.10).

SICKLE HOCKS

Horses with hind cannons that perpetually angle forward are said to have "sickle hocks". Because the hock joints can not fully straighten, they will have difficulty developing strong and active action behind (engagement). This fault also makes them prone to "curbs" (strain of the ligament at the back of the hock), so one has to be careful as to their use for dressage. It is true that such a horse can bring his hind legs well under his body, but this puts additional strain on the back, which can also cause trouble. They should be ridden actively to build muscle strength but collection should be used judiciously (figure 26.11).

STRAIGHT STIFLES

If a horse has very open angles in his hind legs, he is termed "straight-legged" or "post-legged."

The straighter a hind limb, the more directly it can deliver thrust to the ground. This is because the horse can easily and quickly straighten his hock fully. By lining up the bones in the hock (as opposed to pushing against the

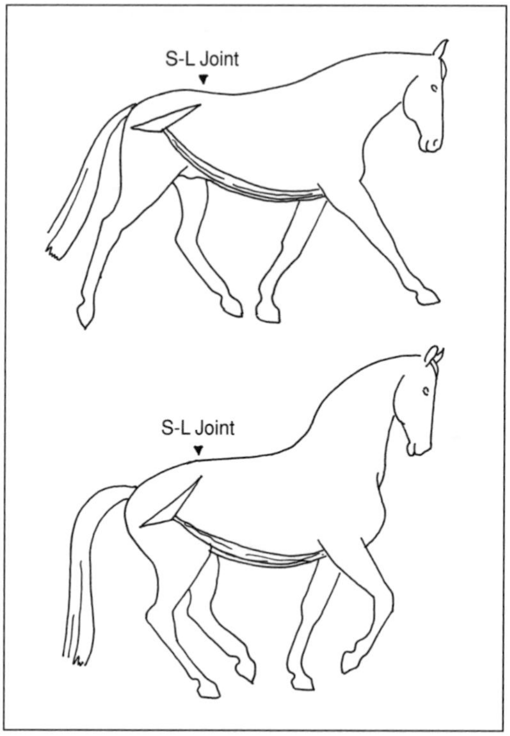

Figure 26.10 "Tucking" (flexion) of the S-L joint is what produces "engagement."

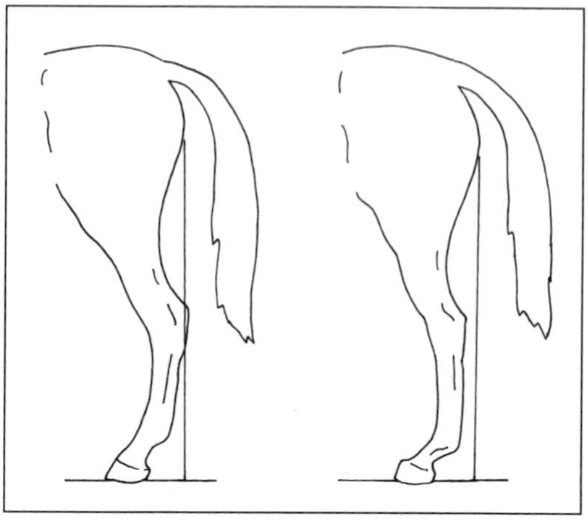

Figure 26.11 The sickle-hocked horse prefers to stand with the hind cannons slanted forward (left). Line up the cannon vertically and the unnatural pastern angle gives the horse away (right).

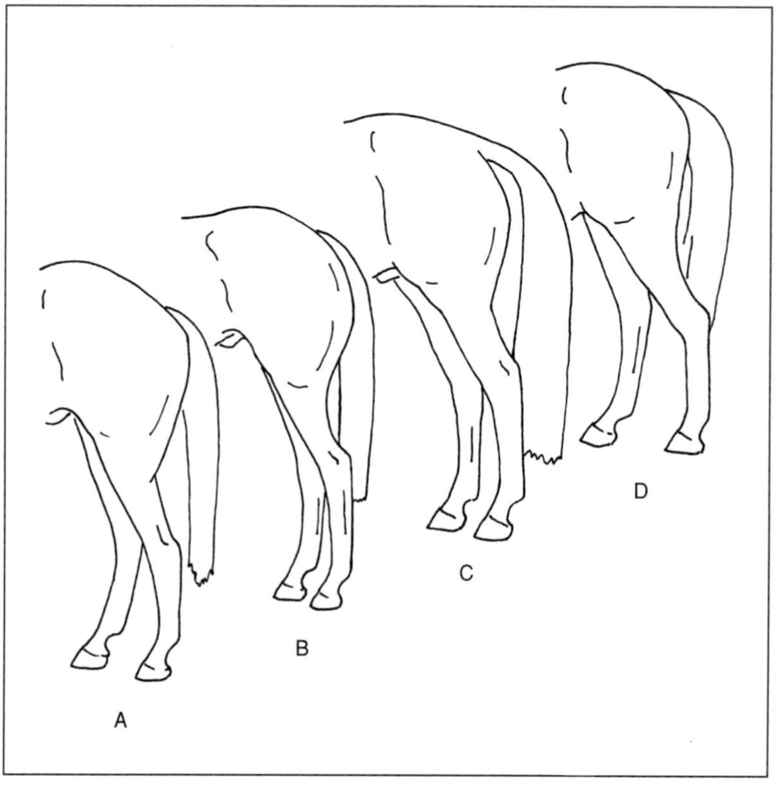

Figure 26.12
The easiest way to assess a horse's hind leg conformation is to drop a vertical line from the point of the buttock. (A) is termed a "straight" hind leg: it is ideal for racehorses, show hunters, and drafts; (B) is "average" angulation: suitable for most uses; (C) is the "ideal" for dressage. It delivers an equal amount of forward and upward thrust; (D) is termed "over bent" (the vertical line falls within the cannon bone); it is not a fault in pacers and gaited horses, unless extreme.

ground with a partially bent hock), the horse can deliver more "push." For this reason, "straight-legged" horses are favored for racing and jumping.

A straight-legged horse does not bend his hocks very much; instead, he moves forward by swinging his hind leg under his body from the hip — the type of motion you might want in a pleasure horse or a show hunter. This type of movement not only keeps the horse's hind foot close to the ground; it also provides a comparatively smooth ride.

A straight leg is also a "short leg." The more post-legged a horse is, the more he will tend to be short-strided and fail to lift his hocks, which will affect his scores.

Another problem of this construction is that if the hind limb is too straight at the stifle joint, it is prone to "loose stifles", which is a painless but very inefficient slippage of the stifle joint in movement. Loose stifles can be improved with exercise, such as trotting the horse over cavaletti, which tightens the tendons involved. "Locked stifle" is when the stifle joint dislocates (subluxation), usually only momentarily. Repeated dislocations can damage the joint by wearing the bone surfaces and stretching tendons.

An underdeveloped gaskin muscle is a characteristic of a horse who fails to sufficiently flex his stifles and hocks at each stride. A "straight-legged" horse can often be seen dragging or dipping his hind toes through the dirt at a normal trot. Yet another down side of this trait is that a horse who is too straight tends to develop concussion-related problems affecting the joints and ligaments (figure 26.12).

OTHER FAULTS IN THE HIND LEGS

The hocks of the dressage horse take more strain than any other joints, therefore correctness here will help keep a horse sound for many years. Avoid "bowed" hind legs (hocks too far apart), or "cow hocks" (hocks angle in excessively) — both put too much strain on the joints. Elite dressage horses were found to have hind toes that point out slightly, which aids in flexibility in both forward and sideways movements.

What It's All About

Dressage competition is not just a horse performing a test; it's an expression of the finest qualities of life. All your feelings: elegance, persistence, power, precision, grace, charm, and understanding — can be learned and expressed through dressage riding. The horse adds his own personality, presence, and strength. Dressage suggests a method of solving problems and making what's good better. Those who have what it takes to pursue dressage for years also tend to have depth of character, not only because of what it takes out of you, but what it puts into you. Dressage, if pursued long enough, eventually becomes a philosophy — not just of training horses but also a way of living — an approach to life. You soon realize that with dressage, the only person you need to please is yourself. If you like the way your horse goes, even if the scores aren't world beating, be proud of your accomplishments. We compete for reasons other than prizes.

Appendix

American Horse Shows Association, Inc.
4047 Iron Works Pike
Lexington, KY 40511
phone: 606-258-2472; fax: 606-231-6662
web site: www.ahsa.org

United States Combined Training Association, Inc.
525 Old Waterford Road, NW
Leesburg, VA 20176
phone: 703-779-0440; fax: 703-779-0550
e-mail: uscta4u@aol.com

United States Dressage Federation, Inc.
P. O. Box 6669
Lincoln, NE 68506-0669
phone: 402-434-8550; fax: 402-434-8570
e-mail: usdressage@navix.net

United States Equestrian Team, Inc.
Pottersville Road
Gladstone, NJ 07934
phone: 908-234-1251; fax: 908-234-9417
web site: www.uset.com

United States Pony Clubs, Inc.
4071 Iron Works Pike
Lexington, KY 40511-8462
phone: 606-254-PONY; fax: 606-233-4652
e-mail: uspc@uspc.org

Bibliography

TRAINING, GENERAL:

Crossley, Anthony. *Training the Young Horse, The First Two Years.* London: Stanley Paul & Co. Ltd., 1978, 1980, 1983, 1984, 1986, 1987, distributed by Trafalgar Square Publishing, North Pomfret, VT.

Dickerson, Jan. *Training Your own Young Horse.* Garden City, NY: Doubleday & Co., Inc., 1978.

Froissard, Jean. *An Expert's Guide to Basic Dressage.* London: Thomas Nelson and Sons, Ltd., Beverly Hills: Hal Leighton Printing Co., 1971.

Klimke, Reiner. *Basic Training of the Young Horse.* Translated by Sigrid Young, Edited by Jane Kidd. London: J.A. Allen & Co., Ltd., 1985.

Littauer, Vladimir S. *Commonsense Horsemanship, Second Edition.* New York: ARCO Publishing Co., Inc., 1972.

Seunig, Waldemar. *Horsemanship, Third (American) Edition.* Translated by Leonard Mins. New York: Doubleday & Co., Inc., 1956.

Wynmalen, Henry. *Dressage, A Study of the Finer Points of Riding.* No. Hollywood, CA: Wilshire Book Co., 1972.

EQUINE PSYCHOLOGY:

Blake, Henry. *Horse Sense.* N. Pomfret, VT: Trafalgar Square Publishing, 1979.

Williams, Moyra. *Horse Psychology.* South Brunswick, NY: A. S. Barnes and Co., 1969.

TRAINING FOR COMPETITION:

Davison, Richard. *Dressage Priority Points, Training for Competition.* New York: Howell Book House, Macmillan, 1995.

Disston, Harry. *Elementary Dressage.* Cranbury, NJ: A. S. Barnes and Co., Inc., 1970.

Eilberg, Ferdi & Gillian Newsum. *Dressage for the Event Horse.* Addington, Buckingham, UK: The Kenilworth Press Ltd., 1993, distributed by Half Halt Press, Boonsboro, MD.

German National Equestrian Federation. *Advanced Techniques of Riding, The Official Instruction Handbook of the German National Equestrian Federation.* English language edition. London: Threshold Books Ltd., 1986, distributed by Half Halt Press, Boonsboro, MD.

German National Equestrian Federation. *The Principles of Riding, Official Instruction Handbook of the German National Equestrian Federation.* Translated by Gisela Holstein. New York: ARCO Publishing Inc., 1985, distributed by Half Halt Press, Boonsboro, MD.

Klimke, Reiner. *Ahlerich, The Making of a Dressage World Champion.* Edited by Felicitos von Neumann-Cosel. Translated by Courtney Searls Ridge, Adtech Translations. Gaithersburg, MD, distributed by Half Halt Press, 1986.

Podhajsky, Alois. *The Complete Training of Horse and Rider.* Translated by Eva Podhajsky & Col. V.D.S. Williams. Garden City, NY: Doubleday & Co., 1967.

COMPETITION RULES AND GUIDELINES:

Albrecht, Brig. General Kurt. *A Dressage Judge's Handbook.* (First published 1760). London: J.A. Allen & Co., Ltd., 1988.

American Horse Shows Association. *American Horse Shows Association Rulebook, 1998-99.* New York, NY, 1997.

Blake, Neil ffrench. *The World of Dressage.* Garden City, NY: Doubleday & Co., Inc., 1969.

Gahwyler, Max. *The Competitive Edge, Improving Your Dressage Scores at the Lower Levels, Revised Edition.* Boonsboro, MD: Half Halt Press, 1989.

United States Dressage Federation. *Glossary of Dressage Judging Terms.* Lincoln, NE: The United States Dressage Federation, 1992, 1996.

United States Dressage Federation. *Musical Freestyle Rules, Guidelines & Definitions.* Lincoln, NE: The United States Dressage Federation, Inc., 1996.

United States Dressage Federation. *Pas de Deux Rules, Guidelines & Definitions.* Lincoln, NE: The United States Dressage Federation, Inc., 1996.

United States Dressage Federation. *Quadrille Rules and Guidelines.* Lincoln, NE: The United States Dressage Federation, Inc., April 1996.

EQUITATION:

Schusdziarra, Heinrich M.D. and M.D. Volker. *An Anatomy of Riding.* Translated from the German by Sandra L. Newkirk. Ossining, NY: Breakthrough, 1978.

Swift, Sally. *Centered Riding.* North Pomfret, VT: Trafalgar Square Publishing, 1985.

Wanless, Mary. *The Natural Rider.* North Pomfret, VT: Trafalgar Square Publishing, 1996.

RIDER MENTAL AND PHYSICAL HEALTH:

Bailey, Covert. *The Fit or Fat Target Diet.* Boston, MA: Houghton Mifflin Co., 1984.

Bailey, Covert. *The New Fit or Fat.* Boston, MA: Houghton Mifflin Co., 1977, 1978, 1991.

Holmes, Tom. *The Total Rider, Health & Fitness for the Equestrian.* Boonsboro, MD: Half Halt Press, 1995.

Savoie, Jane. *That Winning Feeling! Program Your Mind for Peak Performance.* North Pomfret, Vermont: Trafalgar Square Publishing, 1992.

MISCELLANEOUS:

Bennett, Deb, PhD. *Principles of Conformation Analysis, Vol. I, II, III.* Gaithersburg, MD: Fleet Street Publishing Corp., 1988.

Campbell, Mary. *Dancing With Your Horse.* Boonsboro, MD: Half Halt Press, 1989.

Harris, Susan E. *Grooming to Win.* New York: Howell Book House, 1977.

Harris, Susan E. *Horse Gaits, Balance and Movement.* New York: Howell Book House, 1993.

Strickland, Charlene. *Show Grooming, The Look of a Winner.* Ossining, NY: Breakthrough, 1986.

Strickland, Charlene. *The Warmblood Guidebook.* Boonsboro, MD: Half Halt Press Inc., 1992.

Turke, Diana R. *Bit by Bit.* London: J. A. Allen & Co., Ltd. First printed 1965. Reprinted 1969 & 1972.

Index

Above the bit, 237-238, *238,* 240
Acceptance of the bit, 26, 131
Accuracy of tests, 20, 150-152, *151,* 233
Adult Division, 194
Aggressive horses, 273-274
AHSA (American Horse Shows Association, Inc.), 2, *5,* 287
Aids
  behind the rider's aids, 128
  driving, reinforcing, 71-74, *72-73*
  half-halts, 118, *118,* 152
  horse's response time to, 152
  scoring of, 26
  timing of, 110, 113, 117
Amateur Division, 194-195
American Horse Shows Association, Inc. (AHSA), 2, *5,* 287
Anxiety. *See* Nerves, dealing with
Arenas, 7, *7,* 147-150, *149-150,* 169, 171-172
Attire. *See* Dress code

Balance (horse's), 133-134, 237
Balance (rider's), 92-94, *93*
Bandages for exercise, 69-71, *70*
Behind the bit (behind vertical), 237-238, *238*
Behind the rider's aids, 128
Bending, 241-243, *242-243*
Bits, 63-66, *64,* 69, 111-112, 215
Blocked, 240
Bowed hind legs, 285
Bracing the neck (shortened neck), 238
Breathing and nerves, 206
Bridle lame, 53
Bridles, 66-68, *67-68,* 69
Broke gait, 244-245
Budget and starting tips, 43-46

Callers, 7, 41, *41,* 140, 169, 170, 263
Canter
  circling nose in canter, 238
  cross/disunited canter, 244
  downhill canter, *124,* 125
  evaluation, 243-244
  gallop versus, *125,* 125-126
  leads, 54, 128, 171, 244
  lengthened canter, 134-135
  level canter, *124,* 125
  overview, 54, *55,* 56, 279
  rocking horse canter, 244
  to trot transitions, 117
  uphill canter, *124,* 125, 126, 279
  warm-ups using, 164-167, 217, 218
  working canter, *124-127,* 125-128
Cavesson (nosebands), 66-68, *67-68*
Centered Riding (Swift), 206
Centerline, 170, 171
Certificate of veterinary inspection (CVI), 46
Championship classes, 195, 197
Change the rein, 74, 156-157
Cheat sheets, *141,* 141-142
Chewing the bit, 111, 238
Chewing the reins, *132,* 133, 217
Circles, how to draw, 153, *153*
Circling nose in canter, 238
"C," judge's position at, 9, 11, *12,* 172
Clipping horses, 182-183, *183,* 184-185
Clothing. *See* Dress code
Coggins Test, 46, 198
Collection (engagement), 24, *25,* 26, 135-136, 235
Collective Marks
  judging, 15
  levels (tests), 133, 134, 137
  for quadrille, 268
  scoring, 18, *19,* 22-26, *23, 25,* 27
Combined training, 31-35, *33-34*
Comments on tests, 230-231, *248,* 249
Competitive dressage, 1-11
  competition pyramid, *271*
  mechanics of competition, 4-9, *5-8*
  moving to upper levels, 270-272
  overview, xi-xiii, 1-11
  and spectators, *9,* 9-10
  terminology, 233
  See also Dress code; Horses; Judging; Levels (tests); Memorization and visualization; Musical freestyle; Nerves, dealing with; Practicing tests; Quadrille; Rider; Scoring; Show, first; Starting tips; Tack and equipment; Test evaluation; Test, riding best; Warm-ups
Competitive Edge, The (Gahwyler), 257
Conformation of horses, 56-59, *57-58,* 275-285, *276-277, 279-284*
Connection, 111, 164, 240
Contact with the bit, 111
Cool downs, 177-178
Corners, 148, 150, *150,* 154, *154*
Coupling (faulty), 281-283, *282-284*
Cow hocks, 285
Crookedness (horse's), *53,* 54, 115-116, *116,* 240-241, *241*
Curb (leverage) bits, 63, *64,* 65
CVI (certificate of veterinary inspection), 46

Directive ideas for movements, 50, *50*
Disobedient, 245
Distractions, 172-175, *173-174*
Divisions, 194-195
Double bridles (snaffle and curb), 63, 66, 71
Dover, Robert, 101
Downhill horses, *57,* 58-59, *124,* 125
Dressage, xi-xiii, 2.
  See also Competitive dressage
Dressage equitation class, 195, *196-197*
Dressage sport horse breeding class, 198, *199*
Dress code, 75-83
  basics, 2
  boots, 79, 81, *81*
  breeches, 78-79
  on a budget, 43
  chokers, 79
  coats or jackets, 76-78
  derbies, 82
  field boots, 79, 81
  gloves, 82
  for hair, 82
  hats, 82
  helmets, 82
  hunt caps, 82
  hunt coats, 76, 77
  jodhpurs, 78-79

riding pants, 78-79
rules for, 75-76, *76*
shadbellies (tailcoats), 77
shirts, 79
spurs, 82-83
stock ties, 79, *80*
top hats, 82
Drifting, 114-115, *115*
Drilling and training, 39
Drop nosebands, 66, *67*, 68, *68*
Drug rules, 193-194
Dual-judged tests, 17-18
Durchlaessigkeit (throughness), 111, 134, 164, 239-240

Earth bound, 52, 279
EIA (Equine Infectious Anemia), 46
Elasticity of steps, 24
Eliminations, 12, 22, 227
Energy level, 232
Engagement, 24, *25*, 26, 135-136, 235
Entrance and salute, *157-158*, 157-159, 222-223, *223-224*, 233
Entry forms, filling out, 200
Equine Infectious Anemia (EIA), 46
Equipment. *See* Tack and equipment
Equitation, 37-38
Errors. *See* Penalty points

Falling over outside shoulder, 241, *241*
Falling over the left shoulder, 114-115, *115*
Fall of horse or rider, 21
Faults, 20
Fédération Equestre Internationale (FEI), 4, *5*
Figure of eight, 154, *155*
Figure "S," 155, *155*
Final impressions, 228
First impressions, 157, 171
First Level, 130, 133-135, *135*
Fitness. *See* Rider fitness and diet
Flash nosebands, 66, *67*, 68, *68*
Flexibility of riders, 98, 99-100, *102*
Floor exercises for riders, *102-103*
Forward movement, 109, 131, 233-234, *234*, 235
Freedom of gaits, 9, 22-24

Gadgets, avoiding, 43
Gahwyler, Max, 257
Gaits. *See also* Canter; Trot; Walk; Working gaits
broke gait, 244-245
freedom and regularity of, 9, 22-24
longeing to assess, 54-55, *55*
for musical freestyle, 253, 255
overview, 49-56, *50-53*, *55*
shoeing and, 71, 181
transitions, 7, 116-118, 152, 233, 235, 240, 251
uneven/unlevel gaits, 23, 53-54
Gate person, 192
Geometric memorization, *141*, 141-142
GMOs (Group Member Organizations), 4, *5*
Grand Prix, 5
Green Horses classes, 29
Grinding teeth, 246
Gripping knees or thighs, 87-88, *88*
Grooming, 179-189
basket-weave braid for manes, 186, *186*
bathing, 184-185
clipping, 182-183, *183*, 184-185
daily routine, *180*, 180-181
French braid for manes, 186, *186*
hunter style mane braid, 186-187, *186-187*
mane braiding, 181-182, 184, 185-187, *186-187*
at shows, 187-189, *189*
before shows, 182-185, *183-185*
tails, 182, *183-185*, 184, 185
tips, 188
and warm-ups, 162
Ground jury, 191
Ground person, 40
Group Member Organizations (GMOs), 4, *5*

Half-circles, 155, *155*
Half-halts, 118, *118*, 152
Halt and rein back, 138, 159
Halting square, *113*, 113-114, *157-158*, 157-159, 171, 233
Hands, obedience to, 109, 111-114, *112-113*
Haunches in/out, 241
Head carriage, 237-239, *238-239*
Head set training, 23-24
Hind leg assessment, 278, 283, *284*, 285
Hindquarters
engagement, 24, *25*, 26, 135-136, 235
high, avoiding, 280-281, *281*
Hollow
back (horse's), *122*, 122-123
side of horses, 54, 115-116, *116*, 159
Horses for dressage, 47-59
bridle lame, 53
conformation of, 56-59, *57-58*, 275-285, *276-277*, *279-284*
crookedness, *53*, 54, 115-116, *116*, 240-241, *241*
directive ideas for movements, 50, *50*
downhill horses, *57*, 58-59, *124*, 125
earth bound, 52, 279
eligibility rules, 192-193
on the forehand, 52, 235-237, *236-237*, 240
hollow or stiff sides, 54, 115-116, *116*, 159
leg protection, 69-71, *70*
mental attitude, importance of, *58*, 59
older horses, care and feeding of, 48
over striding, 52
qualities for, 2, 3, 47, 49
rein lame, 53
rhythm, 23, 117-118, 131, 233, 235
riders and, 47, 49, 56, 83, 110
school masters, 48, 274-275
stifle problems, 53, 283, *284*, 285
suitability, *58*, 59, 198
tracking up, 52
transitions, 7, 116-118, 152, 233, 235, 240, 251
See also Canter; Gaits; Grooming; Horses, training; Horses, upgrading; Practicing tests; Show, first; Trot; Walk; Warm-ups; Working gaits
Horses, training, 108-118
on the aids, 111, 137
aids, timing of, 110, 113, 117, 152
on the bit, 111
calm requirement for, 108-109
chewing the bit, 111, 238
connection, 111, 164, 240
contact with the bit, 111
crookedness, *53*, 54, 115-116, *116*, 240-241, *241*
drifting, 114-115, *115*
falling over the left shoulder, 114-115, *115*
forward movement requirement, 109, 131, 233-234, *234*, 235
half-halts, 118, *118*, 152
halting square, *113*, 113-114, *157-158*, 157-159, 171, 233
hands, obedience to, 109, 111-114, *112-113*
hollow or stiff sides, 54, 115-116, *116*, 159
leaning on the wall, 115, *115*
legs, obedience to, *109*, 109-110
leg yields, *109*, 109-110
lengthening strides, 117, 120, 134-135
positioning, 112, *113*
pressure points, 110
reins, obedience to, 109, 111-114, *112-113*
rhythm, 23, 117-118, 131, 233, 235
riders and, 47, 49, 56, 83, 110
shortening strides, 117
and snaffle bits, 63-66, *64*, 69, 111-112, 215
staying on the bit, 112
straightness requirement, 109, 114-116, *114-116*
stretching the frame, 111, *132*, 133, 217
take the reins, 111
throatlatch (thick), avoiding, 280
throughness, 111, 164
transitions, 7, 116-118, 152, 233, 235, 240, 251
Uberstreichen (release of the reins), 111
whips, introducing to, 71-73, *72-73*
yes and no joints, 111-112, *112*
See also Canter; Gaits; Grooming; Practicing tests; Show, first; Trot; Walk; Warm-ups; Working gaits
Horses, upgrading, 270-285
aggressive horses, 273-274
body balance and shape of, 278
competition pyramid, *271*
conformation of, 56-59, *57-58*, 275-285, *276-277*, *279-284*
coupling (faulty), avoiding, 281-283, *282-284*

crookedness, *53,* 54, 115-116, *116,* 240-241, *241*
decision making, 272-275
earth bound, 52, 279
hind leg assessment, 278, 283, *284,* 285
hindquarters (high), avoiding, 280-281, *281*
hip of, 278
legs and feet of, 278
long back, avoiding, 281
low-set neck, avoiding, 279-280, *280*
movement of, 277, *277,* 279
muscle mass of, 278
neck set of, 278
perfection, striving for, 14-15, 270-271
positive diagonal advance placement (PDAP), 279
sacro-lumbar (S-L) joint, 278, 281-283, *282-284*
school masters, 48, 274-275
short back, avoiding, 281
shoulder and arm of, 278
sickle hocks, avoiding, 283, *284*
stifle problems, 53, 283, *284,* 285
submissive (passive) horses, 274-275
swan neck, avoiding, 280
temperament of, 272-275
throatlatch (thick), avoiding, 280
timid horses, 275
See also Horses, training

Hot horse warm-up, 218-219

Impulsion, 9, 24
In-gate, ready for, *220,* 220-221
Intermediare I and II, 5
International "I" judges, 13

Jigging, 122, 244-245
Judging, 11-16
average horses, 15
brilliant horses, 15
classifications of, 13
Collective Marks, 15
combined training, 32, 35
excusing horses, 12
expectations of, 14-15
horse eligibility rules, 192-193
horses' suitability, *58,* 59, 198
and luck, 15-16
movements, 15-16
musical freestyle, 257
over-performance, 130
perfection, 14-15
Pony Club, 36, 287
position at "C," 9, 11, *12,* 172
qualities of judges, 11-13
requirements for, 14
and rule enforcement, 12-13
schooling shows, 31
talking to judges, 16
See also Scoring; Test evaluation

Junior Rider Division, 194

Lameness, 21
League competitions, 30
Leaning on inside shoulder, 241, *242*
Leaning on the bit, 238
Leaning on the wall, 115, *115*
Learner Judge Program "L," 13, 14
Legs, obedience to, *109,* 109-110
Leg yields, *109,* 109-110, 135, *135*
Lengthening strides, 117, 120, 134-135
Levels (tests), 129-139
acceptance of the bit, 26, 131
on the aids, 111, 137
balance, 133-134, 237
chewing the reins, *132,* 133, 217
collection (engagement), 24, *25,* 26, 135-136, 235
Collective Marks, 133, 134, 137
competitive dressage, 2, 4-7, *6*
First Level, 130, 133-135, *135*
forward movement, 109, 131, 233-234, *234,* 235
leg yields, 135, *135*
lengthening strides, 117, 120, 134-135
medium gaits, 136-137
over-performance, 130
purpose of, 130-131
rein back, 138, 159
rhythm, 23, 117-118, 131, 233, 235
Second Level, 130, 135-138, *136-137*
self-carriage, 137
shortening strides, 134
shoulder-in, 137, *137*
stretching the frame, 111, *132,* 133, 217
suppleness/looseness, 24, 131
tests as training gauges, 129-130
test selection guide, 138-139
throughness, 134, 137
thrust (pushing power), 133
Training Level, 4-5, *6,* 130-133, *132*
See also Memorization and visualization; Practicing tests; Test, riding best

Leverage (curb) bits, 63, *64,* 65
Lightness of the forehand, 26
Line of sight, *151,* 151-152
Lodging, 44-45
Long back, avoiding, 281
Longeing and warm-ups, 39, 162, 215
Longeing to assess gaits, 54-55, *55*
Low-set neck, 279-280, *280*

Mane braiding, 181-182, 184, 185-187, *186-187*
Meaning of the Marks, 18
Memorization and visualization, 140-146
acting it out, 142
callers, 140
cheat sheets, *141,* 141-142
geometric memorization, *141,* 141-142
multiple tests, 143-144
narrative memorization, 142
photographic memory, 143
and self-talk, 144
sequence memorization, 142-143
tips, 143
visualizations, 144-146, 207-208, 222
See also Practicing tests; Test, riding best

Meters, 148, *149*
Modifiers of movements, 20
Mouth open, 246
Movement of horses, 277, *277,* 279
Movements
accuracy of, 20, 150-152, *151,* 233
directive ideas for, 50, *50*
judging, 15-16
for musical freestyle, 251
scoring, 7, 8, 18-20, *19,* 26

Muscles used in riding, *97,* 97-98
Musical freestyle, 250-258, *252*
choreography, 257-258
combinations, 251
creativity, 254
degree of difficulty, 254
dressage movements, 251
elements, 251, 253
entrance music, 256
figures, 251
First Level compulsory movements, 253
gaits, 253, 255
judging, 257
music for, 254-256
patterns, 251
phrases or lulls in music, 256
practicing, 258
rules for, 250-251
scoring, *252,* 253, 254
splicing the music, 255-256
test movements, 251
transitions, 251

Musical Freestyle Ride, 195

Narrative memorization, 142
Nerves, dealing with, 201-209
anxiety triggers, 201-202
by being kind to yourself, 203-204
by breathing, 206
causes and cures, 204-206
emotions, taking control of, 207-209
by goal setting, 207
by negativism elimination, 208-209
by relaxing, 208
self-analysis for, 202
by soft eyes, 206
by stress management, 204
symptoms of, 201-202, 202-203
by visualization, 207-208
See also Memorization and visualization; Practicing tests; Rider fitness and diet

New Rider classes, 29
Nodding head, 238
Nosebands (cavesson), 66-68, *67-68*
Nutrition. *See* Rider fitness and diet

Off course, 20, 21, 227
Olympic judges "O," 13
On the aids, 111, 137
On the bit, 111
On the forehand, 52, 235-237, *236-237,* 240
Open Division, 195
Over bent, 238
Over-performance, 130
Over striding, 52

Pace. *See* Gaits
Pas de Deux (ride of two), 195, 259, *260*
Passagey horses, 279
PDAP (positive diagonal advance placement), 279
Pelvis, rider's, *90-91,* 90-92, 93
Penalty points, 18, *19,* 20-21, 26
Perfection, striving for, 14-15, 270-271
Photographic memory, 143
Pony Club, 35-36, 287
Position (of head), 238
Positioning, 112, *113*
Positive diagonal advance placement (PDAP), 279
Post entries, 199
Practicing tests, 147-159, 168-178
 accuracy, 20, 150-152, *151,* 233
 anticipation, 171-172
 arenas for, 7, *7,* 147-150, *149-150,* 169, 171-172
 callers, 169, 170
 canter leads, 171
 centerline, 170, 171
 change the rein, 74, 156-157
 checklist of priorities for, 170
 circles, how to draw, 153, *153*
 cool downs, 177-178
 corners, 148, 150, *150,* 154, *154*
 distractions, 172-175, *173-174*
 entrance, *157-158,* 157-159, 222-223, *223-224,* 233
 figure of eight, 154, *155*
 figure "S," 155, *155*
 first impressions, 157, 171
 free walk, 171
 half-circles, 155, *155*
 halt and rein back, 138, 159
 halting square, *113,* 113-114, *157-158,* 157-159, 171, 233
 judge's stand, 172
 line of sight, *151,* 151-152
 meters, 148, *149*
 musical freestyle, 258
 pieces of tests, 169-170
 planning for, 170-171
 preparation, 176
 Pythagorean Theorem for square corners, 148, 150, *150*
 quadrille, 266-267
 rein in opposition to the haunches, *173-174,* 174
 salute, *157-158,* 157-159, 222-223, *223-224,* 233
 serpentines, 156, *156*
 shying or spooking, 172-175, *173-174,* 247
 for stress management, 204
 tips for, 168-171
 trailering, 44, 176
 transitions, 7, 116-118, 152, 233, 235, 240, 251
 tying the horse, 176-177, *177*
 voice, use of, 21, 175
 See also Levels (tests); Memorization and visualization; Test, riding best
Premium (prize list), 198-200
Pressure points of horses, 110
Prix St. Georges, 5
Program, 199, 213
Protocol, 18
Pythagorean Theorem, 148, 150, *150*

Quadrille, 259-269
 alignment, 268
 benefits of, 259-260
 callers, 263
 Collective Marks, 268
 columns, 266
 crossover, 266
 demonstration tests, 268
 fan formation, 266
 horses for, 261-262
 levels, 267
 oblique, 266
 Pas de Deux (ride of two), 195, 259, *260*
 patterns, basic, 264-266, *265*
 performance as a group, 268
 practicing, 266-267
 riding rules for, 262-264, *263*
 rules, 267
 scoring, 268
 snake line, 266
 spacing, 268
 starting, 260-266, *263, 265*
 submission, 268
 synchrony, 268
 threading the needle, 266
 tips, 268-269
Quadrille Handbook, 260
Qualified Rider Awards (USDF), 30
Quarters in/out, 243, *243*

Recorded "r" judges, 13, 14
Regional Dressage Championship, 197-198
Registered "R" judges, 13, 14
Regularity of gaits, 9, 22-24
Rein back, 138, 159
Rein in opposition to the haunches, *173-174,* 174
Rein lame, 53
Reins, obedience to, 109, 111-114, *112-113*
Relaxation evaluation in tests, 246-247
Relaxation, warm-ups for, 161
Release of the reins (Uberstreichen), 111
Remarks section for errors, 21
Resistance, 166, 245-246
Rhythm, 23, 117-118, 131, 233, 235
Ride of two *(Pas de Deux),* 195, 259, *260*
Rider fitness and diet, 96-107
 caffeine, avoiding, 106
 carbohydrates, 105, 107
 cardiovascular exercise, 98-99
 cautions, 100
 diet and nutrition, 104-107, *107*
 endurance, 98-99
 fats, 105
 flexibility, 98, 99-100, *102*
 floor exercises, *102-103*
 food pyramid, 104
 foods, eating a variety of, 45, 106
 muscles used in riding, *97,* 97-98
 need for, 96-97
 proteins, 105
 snack foods, 45, 107
 sodium, avoiding, 106
 and stable work, 97
 strategy for competition, 106-107
 strength, 98, 100-101, *102-103*
 for stress management, 204
 stretching, 98, 99-100, *102*
 sugar, avoiding, 106
 time, finding, for, 101, 104
 vitamins and minerals, 106
 water, 105-106
Rider position and posture, 84-95
 ankle stiffness, standing in stirrups, 88-89
 back hollow or collapsed, *90-91,* 91-92
 balance, poor, 92-94, *93*
 chair seat, *90-91,* 91-92
 crookedness, 92, *92*
 driving seat, 94
 fetal crouch, 86-87, *87*
 gripping knees or thighs, 87-88, *88*
 head down, 94-95
 hip collapsed, 92, *92*
 leaning back, 94
 leaning forward, 92-94, *93*
 muscle tone, 93
 pelvis, *90-91,* 90-92, 93
 position for dressage, 84-86, *85*
 posture tips, 95
 scoring, 26, 233
 seat bones, *90,* 90-91
 seat comparison, *3,* 3-4
 shortening the reins, *94,* 95
 shoulders hunched, 94-95
 for stress management, 206
 tension and posture, 86-87, *87*
 toes pointing out, *89,* 89-90
 warm-ups for, 164
Riders, 1, *3,* 3-4. *See also* Aids; Dress code; Levels (tests); Memorization and visualization; Musical freestyle; Nerves, dealing with; Practicing tests; Quadrille; Rider fitness and diet; Rider position and posture; Show, first; Starting tips; Tack and equipment; Test evaluation; Test, riding best; Warm-ups
Riding-in period. *See* Warm-ups
Ring steward, 192
Rounded back, *122,* 122-123
Rule Book, 4, 9, 13

Sacro-lumbar (S-L) joint, 278, 281-283, *282-284*
Saddles, 60-63, *61-63,* 69, 215
Salute, *157-158,* 157-159, 222-223, *223-224,* 233
Savoie, Jane, 144
Schooling horses, 38-39
Schooling shows, 28-31, 31, *33-34*
School master horses, 48, 274-275
Scorer, 192

Scoring, 17-27
acceptance of the bridle, 26, 131
accuracy of movements, 20, 150-152, *151,* 233
basic faults, 20
Collective Marks, 18, *19,* 22-26, *23, 25,* 27
dual-judged tests, 17-18
elasticity of steps, 24
elimination, 12, 22, 227
engagement (collection), 24, *25,* 26, 135-136, 235
fall of horse or rider, 21
freedom of gaits, 22-23
gaits (freedom and regularity), 22-24
impulsion, 9, 24
lameness, 21
lightness of movements, 26
main faults, 20
Meaning of the Marks, 18
minor faults, 20
modifiers of movements, 20
movements, 7, 8, 18-20, *19*
musical freestyle, *252,* 253, 254
overview, 7-9, *8*
penalty points, 18, *19,* 20-21, 26
protocol, 18
quadrille, 268
regularity of gaits, 23
Remarks section for errors, 21
rhythm versus tempo, 23, 233, 235
rider's position, seat, correctness, effect of aids, 26, 233
submission, 9, 25-26, 268
suppleness of the back, 24, 131
uneven/unlevel gaits, 23, 53-54
voice penalties, 21, 175
winner, the, 26-27
See also Judging; Test evaluation
Scribe, 192, 231
Searle, Elizabeth, 23, 232
Seats of riders, *3,* 3-4, *90-91,* 91-92, 94
Second Level, 130, 135-138, *136-137*
Self-carriage, 137
Self-talk, 144
Senior "S" judges, 13, 14
Sequence memorization, 142-143
Serpentines, 156, *156*
Shoeing, 71, 181
Short back, avoiding, 281
Shortening strides, 117, 120, 134
Shortening the reins, *94,* 95
Shoulder-in, 137, *137*
Shoulders fall in/out, 242
Show fees, 45-46
Show, first (horse's), 210-221
arriving at the competition, 213-214
chewing the reins, *132,* 133, 217
hot horse warm-up, 218-219
in-gate, ready for, *220,* 220-221
longeing, 39, 162, 215
packing list for, *211-212*
planning for, 210-213, *211-212*
tacking up, 215
time table for, 213
tune-ups, 219-220
warm-ups, 214-219, *219*
See also Show, first (rider's); Warm-ups
Show, first (rider's), 190-200
Championship classes, 195, 197
competition rules, 192-193
divisions, 194-195
dressage equitation class, 195, *196-197*
dressage sport horse breeding class, 198, *199*
drug rules, 193-194
entry forms, filling out, 200
first come-first served, 198-199
gate person, 192
ground jury, 191
horse eligibility rules, 192-193
mandatory work time, 200
Musical Freestyle Ride, 195
opening date, 199
Pas de Deux (ride of two), 195, 259, *260*
planning for, 191
post entries, 199
premium (prize list), 198-200
program, 199, 213
Regional Dressage Championship, 197-198
ring steward, 192
scorer, 192
scribe, 192, 231
show manager, 191
show secretary, 191
suitable to become a dressage horse class, *58,* 59, 198
technical delegate (T.D.), 191-192
tests, entering, 190
See also Show, first (horse's); Warm-ups
Show manager, 191
Show secretary, 191
Shying, 172-175, *173-174,* 247
Sickle hocks, 283, *284*
S-L (sacro-lumbar) joint, 278, 281-283, *282-284*
Snaffle bits, 63-66, *64,* 111-112, 215
Soft eyes, 206
Spectators, *9,* 9-10
Spooking, 172-175, *173-174,* 247
Spurs, 82-83
Stabling, 45
Stage fright. *See* Nerves, dealing with
Starting tips, 37-46
and blame, 43
for a budget, 43-46
callers, 41, *41*
coaches for, 40
competitions, finding, 40
concentration, importance of, 38
drilling and training, 39
equitation, 37-38
food, 45
gadgets, avoiding, 43
ground person for, 40
and homework, 42
lodging, 44-45
and longeing, 39, 162, 215
mistakes, making, 43
organization at shows, 40-41, *41*
outside the ring riding, 39
and problem-solving, 42
and schooling horses, 38-39
show fees, 45-46
stabling, 45
and tests, 42
time involved, 39
trainers for, 40
transportation, 44, 176
videos, using, 43
warm-up strategy, *42,* 42-43
Stiff side of horses, 54, 115-116, *116,* 159
Stifle problems, 53, 283, *284,* 285
Straightness, 109, 114-116, *114-116*
Strength of riders, 98, 100-101, *102-103*
Stress management, 204, 205, 206
Stretching
for horses, 111, *132,* 133, 217
for riders, 98, 99-100, *102*
Submission, 9, 25-26, 268
Submissive (passive) horses, 274-275
Suitability judging, *58,* 59
Suitable to become a dressage horse class, 198
Suppleness/looseness, 24, 131
Suppling exercises, 163-164, 166, 217
Swan neck, 280
Swift, Sally, 206
Swinging back, 239, 242

Tack and equipment, 2, 60-74
bandages for exercise, 69-71, *70*
bits, 63-66, *64,* 69, 111-112, 215
boots for exercise, 69-71, *70*
bridles, 66-68, *67-68,* 69
on a budget, 44
care of, 69
curb (leverage) bits, 63, *64,* 65
double bridles (snaffle and curb), 63, 66, 71
drop nosebands, 66, *67,* 68, *68*
equipment breakage, 227
flash nosebands, 66, *67,* 68, *68*
leg protection, 69-71, *70*
nosebands (cavesson), 66-68, *67-68*
other equipment, 71
pads, 60, 63, 69
restrictions, 69, 71, 215
riser pads, 60, 63
saddles, 60-63, *61-63,* 69, 215
shoeing, 71, 181
snaffle bits, 63-66, *64,* 111-112, 215
in warm-up area, 69, 71, 215
whips, 71-74, *72-73*
Tails, grooming, 182, *183-185,* 184, 185
Take the reins, 111
Talking to judges, 16
Technical delegate (T.D.), 191-192
Temperament of horses, 272-275
Tempo, 23, 233, 235
Tense horse, 246-247
Test evaluation, 230-249
4's, fixing, 231-232
5'-8's, 230, 231, 232
above the bit, 237-238, *238,* 240

accuracy, 20, 150-152, *151,* 233
behind the bit (behind vertical), 237-238, *238*
bending, 241-243, *242-243*
blocked, 240
broke gait, 244-245
canter, 243-244
comments, 230-231, *248,* 249
crookedness, *53,* 54, 115-116, *116,* 240-241, *241*
cross/disunited canter, 244
disobedient, 245
dressage talk (terminology), 233
energy level, 232
engagement (collection), 24, *25,* 26, 135-136, 235
entrance, *157-158,* 157-159, 222-223, *223-224,* 233
falling over outside shoulder, 241, *241*
on the forehand, 52, 235-237, *236-237,* 240
forward movement, 109, 131, 233-234, *234,* 235
grinding teeth, 246
halting square, *113,* 113-114, *157-158,* 157-159, 171, 233
haunches in/out, 241
head carriage, 237-239, *238-239*
horse's frame, 233
jigging, 122, 244-245
leads, canter, 244
leaning on inside shoulder, 241, *242*
learning from, 247-249, *248*
mouth open, 246
performance at home versus show, 232
quarters in/out, 243, *243*
relaxation, 246-247
resistance, 166, 245-246
rhythm and tempo, 23, 233, 235
rider's position and posture, 26, 233
rocking horse canter, 244
scribe abbreviations, 192, 231
shoulders fall in/out, 242
shying or spooking, 172-175, *173-174,* 247
swinging back, 239, 242
tempo, 233, 235
tense, 246-247
throughness, 239-240
tracking up, 234-235
as training gauges, 129-130
transition not forward, 235
transitions, 7, 116-118, 152, 233, 235, 240, 251
videos for, 43, 232-233
wanders, 241
See also Judging; Levels (test); Riders; Scoring
Test, riding best, 222-229
checklist of priorities, 223, 224, 225
eliminations, 12, 22, 227
entrance and salute, *157-158,* 157-159, 222-223, *223-224,* 233
equipment breakage, 227
final impressions, 228
final turn up centerline, 228
off course, 227
tips for, *223-224,* 223-229, *228*
visualizing, 144-146, 207-208, 222
See also Levels (tests); Memorization and visualization; Practicing tests; Show, first; Test evaluation
That Winning Feeling! (Savoie), 144
Three-day events, 31
Throatlatch (thick), avoiding, 280
Throughness, 111, 134, 137, 164, 239-240
Thrust (pushing power), 133
Tilting head, 238, *239*
Timid horses, 275
Tracking up, 52, 123, 234-235
Trailering, 44, 176
Training Level, 4-5, *6,* 130-133, *132*
Transitions, 7, 116-118, 152, 233, 235, 240, 251
Triangle for dressage sport horse breeding classes, 198, *199*
Trot
canter to trot transitions, 117
irregular trot, 53
lengthened trot, 134
overview, *52-53,* 52-54, 55, 279
posting trot, 125
sitting trot, 124-125
uneven/unlevel, 23, 53-54
walk to trot transitions, 117
to walk transitions, 117
warm-ups using, 163, 164, 166, 217
working trot, *122-123,* 122-125
Tune-ups, 219-220
Tying the horse, 176-177, *177*

Uberstreichen (release of the reins), 111
Uneven/unlevel gaits, 23, 53-54
United States Combined Training Association (USCTA), 31, 32, 287
United States Dressage Federation, Inc. (USDF), 4, *5,* 287
United States Pony Club, 35-36, 287
Unsteady head, 238
USDF Dressage Sport Horse Breeding Guidelines, 198
USDF Freestyle Rules and Guidelines, 250
USDF Glossary of Dressage Judging and Terms, 233

Videos of classes and tests, 43, 232-233
Visualizations, 144-146, 207-208, 222
Voice, use of, 21, 175

Wagging, 238
Walk
free walk, 121-122, 171
lateral walk, 51-52, 279
lateral walk, correcting, 121
medium walk, *51,* 52, 119-121
overview, *51,* 51-52, 54-55, 279
trot to walk transitions, 117
to trot transitions, 117
warm-ups using, 162-163, 166, 167, 217, 218
Wanders, 241
Warm-ups, 160-167, 214-219
area, tack restrictions, 69, 71, 215
arena etiquette, 219, *219*
and cantering, 164-165, 166-167, 217, 218
by grooming, 162
and horses' mood, 165-166, 216
hot horse warm-up, 218-219
by longeing, 39, 162, 215
for physical readiness, 160-161
problems and solutions, 165-166, 216-217
rehearsal for, 167
for relaxation, 161
resistance as input, 166, 245-246
for rider's position and posture, 164
samples, 166-167, 214-219
strategy, *42,* 42-43
for stress management, 205
by suppling exercises, 163-164, 166, 217
by trotting, 163, 164, 166, 217
by turn outs, 162
by walking, 162-163, 166, 167, 217, 218
Warning aids. *See* Half-halts
Whips, use of, 71-74, *72-73*
Working gaits, 119-128
behind the rider's aids, 128
downhill canter, *124,* 125
free walk, 121-122
gallop versus canter, *125,* 125-126
hollow back, *122,* 122-123
jigging, 122, 244-245
lateral walk, correcting, 121
leads, canter, 128
lengthening strides, 117, 120, 134-135
level canter, *124,* 125
medium gaits, 136-137
medium walk, *51,* 119-121
posting diagonals, 125
posting trot, 125
rounded back, *122,* 122-123
shortening strides, 120
side reins, hands as, 120
sitting trot, 124-125
tracking up, 123
uphill canter, *124,* 125, 126, 279
working canter, *124-127,* 125-128
working trot, *122-123,* 122-125

Yes and no joints, 111-112, *112*
Young Rider Division, 194

About the Author

Having taught equitation in saddle seat, stock seat, and dressage for more than 35 years, Barbara Burkhardt produced several state equitation champions during the 1960s and 1970s. She competed as an amateur on three-and five-gaited American Saddlebreds and professionally showed Arabians in halter, English and Western pleasure, park, and dressage, and Quarter Horses in Western pleasure and dressage. She has also participated in competitive trail riding. Beginning in 1975, she began to seriously study dressage, working with various breeds and cross-breeds, expanding her well-rounded background of practical experience.

She now specializes in dressage training, teaching, competing, and judging. She especially enjoys introducing newcomers to the theories and practices of dressage and has coached many beginning riders to numerous local and national awards. Of the twelve horses she has introduced to dressage competition, two achieved Fourth Level. She is currently taking a third horse "all the way," and is presently competing at Fourth Level and Prix St. Georges.

Barbara is a founder, past president, and current board member of the Southwestern Dressage Association, a Group Member Organization (GMO) of the United States Dressage Federation Region 5. Barbara graduated the USDF "L" Judges Education Program with honors and plans to enroll as an American Horse Shows Association dressage learner judge. She has managed several dressage competitions and has judged numerous dressage schooling shows.

She has authored dozens of articles for such equine magazines as *Western Horseman*, *The Quarter Horse Journal*, *The USDF Bulletin*, and *Dressage & CT*, on subjects ranging from the history of breed registries to equine biomechanics and psychology. In addition, she has been the sole writer, editor, and artist for a large club newsletter for several years.

Even with all of her other involvement with horses and riding, she admits her greatest pleasure remains teaching others the joys of dressage.